THE ARCHAEOLOGY OF THE HOLY LAND

This book provides an introduction to the archaeology and history of ancient Palestine – modern Israel, Jordan, and the Palestinian territories – from the destruction of Solomon's temple in 586 B.C.E. to the Muslim conquest in 640 C.E. Special attention is paid to the archaeology of Jerusalem and to the late the Second Temple period, that is, the time of Herod the Great and Jesus. For each period, the book offers historical background for the Mediterranean world, the ancient Near East and Palestine. Major sites such as Masada, Caesarea Maritima, and Petra are examined in archaeological and historical detail, along with the material culture – coins, pottery, glass, and stone vessels – typical of each period. This book provides a thorough overview of the archaeology of this historically rich part of the world.

Jodi Magness is the Kenan Distinguished Professor for Teaching Excellence in Early Judaism in the Department of Religious Studies at the University of North Carolina at Chapel Hill. She is the author and editor of several books, including *Stone and Dung, Oil and Spit: Jewish Daily Life in the Time of Jesus* (2011); *The Archaeology of the Early Islamic Settlement in Palestine* (2003); and *The Archaeology of Qumran and the Dead Sea Scrolls* (2002).

THE ARCHAEOLOGY OF THE HOLY LAND

From the Destruction of Solomon's Temple to the Muslim Conquest

Jodi Magness

University of North Carolina, Chapel Hill

CAMBRIDGE
UNIVERSITY PRESS

CAMBRIDGE
UNIVERSITY PRESS

University Printing House, Cambridge CB2 8BS, United Kingdom

One Liberty Plaza, 20th Floor, New York, NY 10006, USA

477 Williamstown Road, Port Melbourne, VIC 3207, Australia

4843/24, 2nd Floor, Ansari Road, Daryaganj, Delhi - 110002, India

79 Anson Road, #06-04/06, Singapore 079906

Cambridge University Press is part of the University of Cambridge.

It furthers the University's mission by disseminating knowledge in the pursuit of education, learning and research at the highest international levels of excellence.

www.cambridge.org
Information on this title: www.cambridge.org/9780521124133

First published 2012
3rd printing 2015

A catalogue record for this publication is available from the British Library

Library of Congress Cataloging in Publication data
Magness, Jodi.
The archaeology of the Holy Land : from the destruction of Solomon's Temple to the Muslim conquest / Jodi Magness.
p.   cm.
Includes index.
ISBN 978-0-521-19535-5 (hardback)
1. Palestine – Antiquities.   2. Bible – Antiquities.   3. Excavations (Archaeology) – Palestine.   I. Title.
DS111.M324   2012
933–dc23   2011050688

ISBN   978-0-521-19535-5   Hardback
ISBN   978-0-521-12413-3   Paperback

⊙⊘ ⊙⊘ ⊙⊘ ⊙⊘

To Jim, with love

CONTENTS

CONTENTS

꒰꒱ ꒰꒱ ꒰꒱ ꒰꒱

LIST OF ILLUSTRATIONS

@@ @@ @@ @@

PREFACE

For more than twenty years I have wanted to write this book. That's how long I have been teaching the material covered here as an introductory-level course to undergraduate students. Over the years, repeated proposals that I submitted to various presses were rejected on the grounds that there was not enough demand to make such a textbook profitable. Therefore, I am grateful to Beatrice Rehl at Cambridge University Press for offering me a contract. I also thank Mary Robinson-Mohr and Jason Staples for their helpful comments on an earlier draft of this manuscript.

I got the time I needed to write this book thanks to a Chapman Family Faculty Fellowship at the Institute for the Arts and Humanities (IAH) at the University of North Carolina at Chapel Hill. The research fund awarded with the fellowship paid for the reproduction rights and preparation of many of the images. My work on the book was enriched by weekly meetings with the other Fellows at the IAH during the fall of 2010. I also wish to thank the faculty and staff of the Department of Religious Studies and Dean William Andrews at UNC-Chapel Hill for their support, including granting me a leave of absence for the 2010–2011 academic year.

I am grateful to the many friends and colleagues who generously granted reproduction permission or provided the images that are a key component of this book, including Todd Bolen (BiblePlaces.com), Felicity Cobbings (Palestine Exploration Fund), Gwyn Davies, Hillel Geva (Israel Exploration Society), Gabi Laron (Hebrew University Institute of Archaeology), Leen Ritmeyer, Ronny Reich, Zev Radovan, Hershel Shanks (Biblical Archaeology Society), Zeev Weiss, and Jane Cahill West. I owe special thanks to Jeffrey Becker and Richard Talbert at the Ancient World Mapping Center at UNC-Chapel Hill, who prepared an original series of maps for this book.

This book is informed by decades of learning from teachers, students, colleagues, friends, and family. Although it is impossible to acknowledge them all, I wish to remember some of those who are no longer with us: James A. Sauer and Keith de Vries, who were my teachers and dissertation advisers at the University of Pennsylvania; my close friend and colleague Hanan Eshel; and my dear friends Tsvi (Harvey) Schneider and Ora Sinai. They had a lasting impact on my life and are deeply missed.

I am fortunate to have a loving and supportive family, including my parents, Herbert and Marlene Magness; my husband, Jim Haberman; and my nephew Mike Miller. This book is dedicated to Jim, for whose unconditional love and companionship I am grateful. Jim works as the photographer on my excavations, and he gets the credit for preparing many of the illustrations in this book as well.

⊚⊚ ⊚⊚ ⊚⊚ ⊚⊚

ONE

INTRODUCTION

In the heart of the ancient Near East (modern Middle East), at a crossroads between once-mighty powers such as **Assyria** to the east and Egypt to the south, is a tiny piece of land – roughly the size of New Jersey – that is as contested as it is sacred. One cannot even name this territory without sparking controversy. Originally called **Canaan** after its early inhabitants (the **Canaanites**), it has since been known by various names. To Jews this is *Eretz Israel* (the Land of Israel), the Promised Land described by the Hebrew Bible as flowing with milk and honey. To Christians it is the Holy Land where Jesus Christ – the messiah, or anointed one – was born, preached, and offered himself as the ultimate sacrifice. Under the Greeks and Romans, it was the province of **Judea**, a name that hearkened back to the biblical kingdom of **Judah**. After the **Bar-Kokhba Revolt** ended in 135 C.E., Hadrian renamed the province Syria-Palestina, reviving the memory of the long-vanished kingdom of Philistia. Under early Islamic rule the military district (*jund*) of Filastin was part of the province of Greater Syria (Arabic *Bilad al-Sham*). In this book, the term *Palestine* is used to denote the area encompassing the modern state of Israel, the Hashemite kingdom of Jordan, and the Palestinian territories.

This book introduces readers to this complex and fascinating land, the birthplace of Judaism and Christianity, drawing on archaeological evidence and literary (historical) information, including the Bible. Archaeological remains give voice to the narratives of forgotten peoples who contributed to its rich cultural tapestry: Phoenicians, **Edomites** and **Idumaeans**, **Moabites**, **Ammonites**, **Ituraeans**, **Nabataeans**, **Samaritans**, **Philistines**. Today, scholars generally use the term "biblical archaeology" to refer to the archaeology of Palestine in the Bronze Age (ca. 3000–1200 B.C.E.) and Iron Age (ca. 1200–586 B.C.E.) – that is, the Old Testament period, when the land was inhabited by Canaanites and

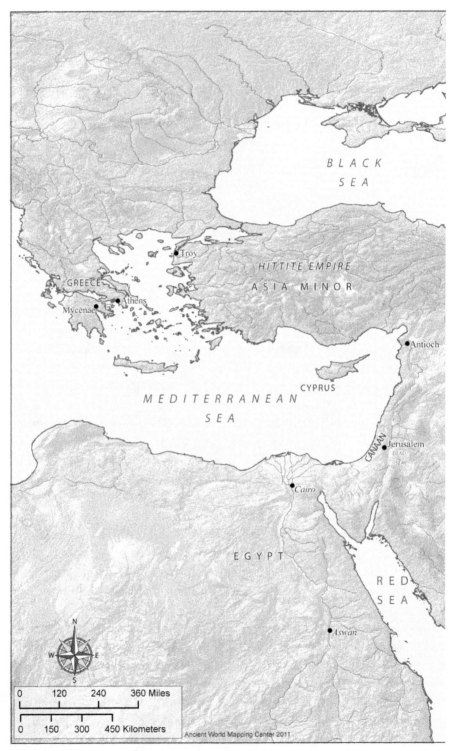

1.1 Map of the ancient Near East. Ancient World Mapping Center, University of North Carolina at Chapel Hill (www.unc.edu/awmc).

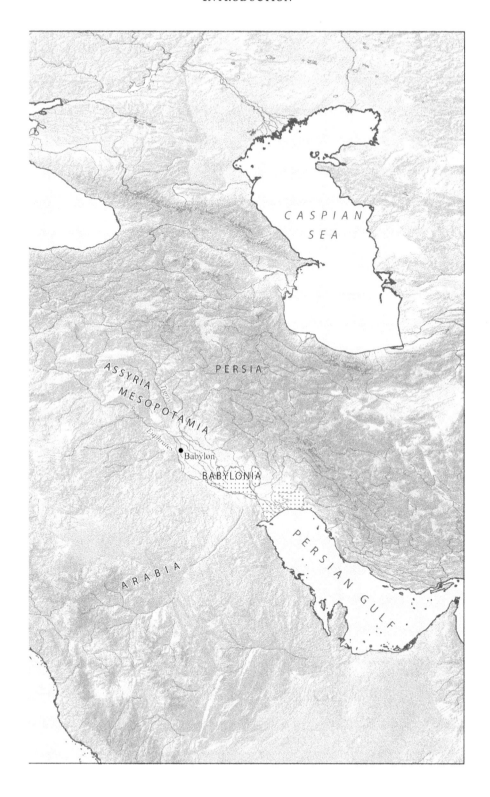

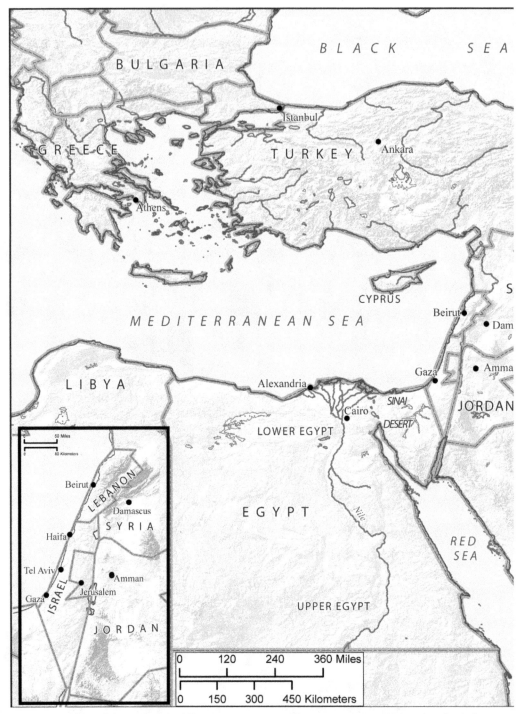

1.2 Map of the modern Middle East. Ancient World Mapping Center, University of North Carolina at Chapel Hill (www.unc.edu/awmc).

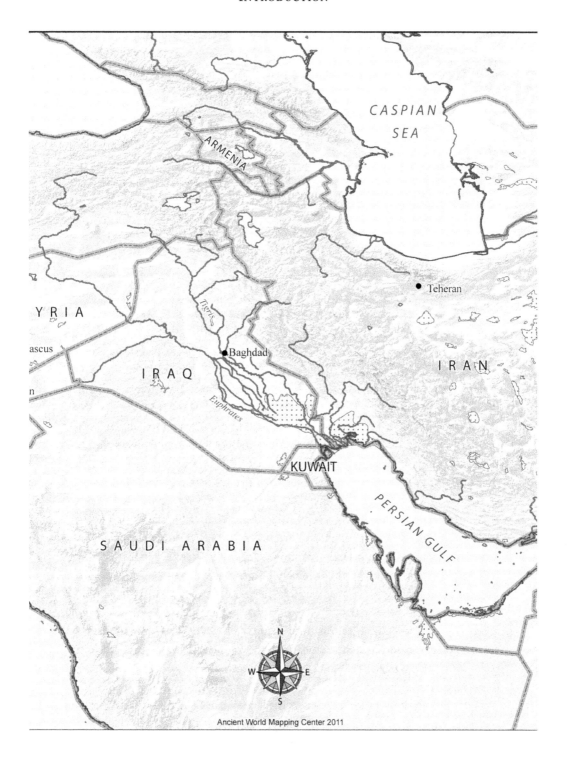

Ancient World Mapping Center 2011

Israelites. In contrast, our focus is on the period from 586 B.C.E. to 640 C.E. – that is, from the fall of the kingdom of Judah and the destruction of **Solomon**'s temple (the end of the First Temple period) to the Muslim conquest of Palestine. In other words, this book covers the "post-biblical" periods (from a Jewish perspective) or the New Testament period (from a Christian perspective), including the Second Temple period (516 B.C.E.–70 C.E.).

Because this book is intended as an introductory text it is not footnoted, but a glossary of terms and timelines are included for reference purposes. For additional information, readers are encouraged to consult the recommended readings at the end of each chapter.

CHRONOLOGICAL FRAMEWORK

In the Mediterranean world and ancient Near East (the "Old World"), historical periods begin around 500 B.C.E. because this is when history writing began in the modern sense of the word, with Greek authors such as **Herodotus**. The prehistoric periods in the Old World are defined according to the most advanced material used at the time to manufacture tools: Stone Age, Bronze Age, Iron Age. Each of these periods is further subdivided – for example, Old Stone Age (Paleolithic), Middle Stone Age (Mesolithic), New Stone Age (Neolithic); Early Bronze Age (EB), Middle Bronze Age (MB), Late Bronze Age (LB).

This system of periodization was developed in the nineteenth century, when scholars sought to impose order on the thousands of ancient artifacts that had been amassed in museums and private collections. It is not a coincidence that in the nineteenth century – at the height of the Industrial Revolution – scholars devised a chronological framework defined by the materials used to make tools. This reflects the view current at that time that civilizations using stone tools were less advanced (or more "primitive") than those using metal tools, especially iron tools. Of course, we now recognize the inherent bias of a system of periodization that ranks human progress according to materials used for tool making. Furthermore, there existed highly developed civilizations in Mesoamerica and other parts of the world that never emerged from the "Stone Age." Nevertheless, because this terminology is entrenched, it is still used by scholars working in the Mediterranean world and the ancient Near East. In other parts of the world, such as the Americas, where scholarly interest in archaeology developed later, other systems of periodization are employed.

Historical periods (after ca. 500 B.C.E.) are dated on the basis of events recorded in written sources. For example, in Palestine the early Hellenistic period begins with **Alexander the Great**'s conquest in 332 B.C.E. and ends with the Maccabean revolt in 167 B.C.E. In contrast, although the Stone Age–Bronze Age–Iron Age system of periodization helps organize artifacts in a relative sequence (meaning that, relatively speaking, the Stone Age is earliest and Iron

Age is the latest), it does not provide absolute dates for these periods. For the Iron Age (beginning ca. 1200 B.C.E.), some dates can be gleaned from written sources, such as the Hebrew Bible and Assyrian records. However, before the invention of radiocarbon dating in 1950 (discussed later), Egypt was the main chronological peg for prehistoric periods in the Mediterranean and ancient Near East, as it is the only country with a continuously dated calendar going back approximately 5,000 years (although scholars disagree about the precise dates of many events). Egyptian artifacts found at sites around the Mediterranean and ancient Near East provided absolute dates for associated remains and levels. The reliance on Egyptian chronology underlies the tripartite division of the Bronze Age around the Mediterranean, with the Early Bronze Age corresponding roughly with the Old Kingdom in Egypt, the Middle Bronze Age with the Middle Kingdom, and the Late Bronze Age with the New Kingdom.

What Is Archaeology?

Before embarking on our journey through the Holy Land, we must first understand the fundamental principles of archaeology. Archaeology is the study of the past as evidenced by human material culture – that is, built features and **artifacts** such as architecture, works of art, tools, and vessels that were manufactured and used by people. Only a small portion of human material culture has survived the ravages of time, most of it having been irretrievably destroyed by natural disasters or human agency, or – in the case of perishable materials – simply having disintegrated. Archaeology does not include the study of remains that predate humans (such as dinosaurs), the physical remains of humans (skeletons), or floral and faunal remains (animals and plants). These types of remains are studied by specialists in allied disciplines such as paleontology, physical or biological anthropology, zooarchaeology, paleobotany, and so on. Of course, archaeologists often include information from these disciplines when studying the remains of human material culture.

History is also the study of the past, but it is based on information provided by written documents or texts rather than material culture. In other words, although both archaeologists and historians study the past, they use different methods and sources to obtain the information. These sources of information often provide different (although not necessarily mutually exclusive or conflicting) pictures of the past. For example, because many texts were written by or for the ruling classes (elites) of ancient societies, they tend to reflect the concerns, interests, and viewpoints of those classes. In comparison, although archaeologists often uncover the palaces and citadels of the ruling classes, they also dig up houses and workshops that belonged to the poorer classes of ancient societies. Archaeological evidence can be used to complement or supplement the information provided by written records, and in cases in which there are

1.3 A tel (Beth Shean).

no written records (such as prehistoric societies), it may be our only source of information.

PRINCIPLES OF ARCHAEOLOGY

Whereas some ancient sites were inhabited for only one brief period or phase, many sites in Palestine were occupied over longer periods. At such multiperiod sites, the buildings and debris from the successive phases of occupation accumulated, forming a series of levels one above the other, like a layer cake. At many biblical (Bronze Age and Iron Age) sites in Israel, there are twenty or more different occupation levels, forming an artificial mound called in Hebrew a *tel* (Arabic **tell**). The famous tels of **Megiddo** and Hazor provided the models for James A. Michener's 1965 novel, *The Source*. Although many people think that successive layers of occupation at a site will always take the shape of a tel, this is not the case. In fact, tels derive their distinctive shape from a specific type of fortification system that was widespread in Middle Bronze Age Palestine and elsewhere in the ancient Near East. This type of system, called a **glacis** or **rampart**, was created by digging a deep ditch or dry moat around the outside of a town, piling up the dirt from the ditch in a huge embankment encircling the town, and plastering the embankment (the glacis or rampart) to make a steep, smooth slope. Fortification walls were erected at the top of the slope. This type of defensive system must have developed in response to the introduction of a new type of offensive warfare – perhaps chariots or battering rams – or, perhaps, it was intended to prevent the mining of the fortification walls from below. By the post-biblical periods, new types of weapons and warfare had rendered the glacis and rampart system ineffective and obsolete. Therefore, sites established in these periods are not tels, even if they were occupied continuously for centuries, as, for example, Caesarea Maritima.

Archaeologists refer to occupation levels at sites as **strata** (singular, **stratum**), and to the sequence of levels as **stratigraphy**. Although it is helpful to visualize the strata of ancient sites as a layer cake, the reality is never that neat and simple. This is because the inhabitants frequently disturbed earlier levels when constructing the foundations of buildings or digging pits. In the course of such activities, they cut into or through earlier strata, churning up earlier material (potsherds, coins, etc.) with the dirt and stones. This means that at multiperiod sites, we always find earlier artifacts mixed in with later material. For this reason, we use the latest artifacts to date the stratum we are excavating and disregard the earlier material (at least for dating purposes).

Imagine that we are standing in a modern school building in Los Angeles that was built in 1972. When the school was built, a deep pit (trench) was dug into the ground for the foundations. At the time the floor was laid, it sealed the foundation trench and everything in it. If the floor is intact and we dig under it today, we should find nothing later dating than 1972 in the fill. However, we will almost certainly find objects that were manufactured before 1972, such as old Coke bottles, coins dating to the 1950s and 1960s, and so on, which were mixed with the dirt and deposited when the foundation trench was filled in. Now, let us suppose that the latest datable object we find under that floor is a penny minted in 1968. This coin will provide what archaeologists call a *terminus post quem* (Latin for "date after which") for the construction of the school. In other words, the coin will tell us that the school was constructed no earlier than 1968. Further, let us suppose that the school was destroyed by an earthquake in 1985, which caused the building to collapse, burying everything inside. The objects found on top of the floors will represent the items in use at the moment when the building collapsed. They will also provide us with a *terminus ante quem* (Latin for "date before which") for the construction of the school. In other words, if the latest datable objects found buried in the collapse were books printed in 1985, the school building must have been constructed on or before that date. One of the most famous ancient examples of such a catastrophic destruction is the eruption of Mount Vesuvius in 79 C.E., which buried Pompeii and Herculaneum in volcanic ash and mud. Walking through the excavated streets of these towns today gives us a glimpse into what they looked like at the moment of their destruction.

1.4 Excavated square at an archaeological site (Huqoq). Photo by Jim Haberman.

METHODS OF ARCHAEOLOGY

During the course of excavation, archaeologists destroy the remains that are dug up. This is because once a shovel of dirt or a stone is removed from the ground it can never be put back the same way. For this reason, archaeologists record the excavation process using every means possible. If you have ever visited an excavation, you might have noticed that archaeologists dig in squares measuring 5 × 5 or 10 × 10 meters. The squares in the grid are separated from each other by banks of earth about 1 meter wide called **baulks** (or **balks**). This system enables archaeologists to measure and record the exact location of every excavated object and feature (by "feature," I mean something that is constructed, as opposed to an artifact, which is a portable, manufactured object). The recording is done by measuring levels (absolute heights or elevations within the excavated squares), keeping daily diaries, making drawings and taking photographs, and increasingly using computers and other technologies. Ideally, once a final excavation report is published, it should be possible for the reader to reconstruct the site as it looked before everything was dug up.

Archaeologists use various devices to keep track of the point of origin (**provenance** or **provenience**) of every excavated artifact and feature. One way to do this is to subdivide each square horizontally and vertically. One of the most common subdivisions used in excavations is a **locus** (plural **loci**). Locus means "spot" or "place" in Latin; archaeologists use this word to designate any excavated feature. For example, a locus can designate an oven, a pit, a room, or any part of a room. It is simply a device to help subdivide the area being excavated, to enable us later to pinpoint the exact spot where an artifact or feature was found. For example, let's say that we begin excavating a square on top of the present ground surface. We would give the entire square one locus number (L1 [L = Locus]). About 10 centimeters below the surface, we notice that the soil is changing in color and composition from reddish brown to dark brown mixed with lots of stones. At this point, we would measure the absolute height or elevation (with the same kind of equipment used by surveyors), and change the locus number from L1 to L2. Five centimeters below this, we begin to come upon a line of stones cutting diagonally across the square, which looks like the top of a wall. We would again measure the absolute height and change the locus number, giving the areas on either side of the wall different locus numbers (L3 on one side and L4 on the other). The pottery and other artifacts discovered during the course of excavation are saved and labeled according to their context.

This system of excavating and recording is the standard one used by archaeologists working in Israel and neighboring countries today (with minor variations from excavation to excavation). This system developed gradually, with the growing realization that ancient sites are composed of successive layers of occupation, with the earliest layers at the bottom and the most recent at the top (stratigraphy). Thomas Jefferson, the third president of the United States, was among the first to recognize this fundamental principle of archaeology, which he applied to his excavation of a Native American burial mound. The importance of stratigraphy to understanding and excavating multilayer sites began to have an impact on archaeologists in the Mediterranean world in the 1880s, with Heinrich Schliemann's excavations at the mound of Hissarlik (Troy). The principle was first applied to an excavation in Palestine by the British archaeologist Sir William Flinders Petrie, who excavated at Tell el-Hesi in 1890. Because the system of stratigraphic excavation has developed over time, not all the elements of this system were used by earlier generations of archaeologists, just as this methodology undoubtedly will continue to be refined by future archaeologists.

METHODS OF DATING

When we excavate an ancient house, what types of artifacts tell us when it was built, occupied, and destroyed or abandoned? The answer is artifacts that are very common finds on archaeological excavations, or artifacts that carry their own date. The main methods of dating used by archaeologists working in historical periods in Palestine include (1) **radiocarbon dating** (sometimes called carbon 14 or C14 dating), (2) coins, (3) inscriptions or other written materials found in excavations, (4) ancient historical or literary sources, and (5) pottery (ceramic) typology.

Before we discuss each of these dating methods, note that this list does not include human or animal bones, tools, or architectural styles. Although human and animal bones can provide much useful information (for example, animal bones can tell us about the ancient environment and diet, and human skeletons can provide information about ancient populations), they cannot be dated unless enough collagen is preserved for the purposes of radiocarbon dating.

Tools are another matter. Stone tools used by prehistoric populations can be dated according to their type in a manner analogous to the way pottery is dated (discussed later). But once pottery appears in Palestine (ca. 5000 B.C.E.), it replaces stone tools as a more precise method of dating. Remember the criterion that the object must be a very common find on archaeological excavations? Tools made of bronze or iron are not common finds, because all metals were valuable in antiquity and therefore usually were recycled rather than discarded. For example, nearly all the Classical Greek statues of the fifth and fourth centuries B.C.E. were made of cast bronze. Most disappeared long ago because they were melted down and made into something else. What survive today are later Roman copies in stone of lost Greek masterpieces and rare examples of bronze originals, most of which have been recovered from ancient shipwrecks. In addition, because metal tools tend to be utilitarian, they did not change much in shape over the centuries. For these reasons, metal tools are not useful for dating even when they are found in excavations.

What about architectural styles? Although archaeologists sometimes use distinctive architectural styles (or tomb types) as a means of dating, this can be done accurately only in rare instances. This is because once an architectural style was invented it could be copied or imitated by later generations. If you have ever seen the 30th Street Station in Philadelphia or any other modern building constructed in a Classical Greek style, you know what I mean. However, most of the remains archaeologists dig up are not that distinctive. For example, much of the ancient construction in Palestine is very simple, consisting of rough (uncut) field stones and mud brick.

Now let's discuss the dating methods we have just listed. Each method has its own advantages and disadvantages.

Radiocarbon (Carbon 14) Dating

The Oxford Companion to Archaeology defines radiocarbon dating as "an isotopic or nuclear decay method of inferring age for organic materials." This method works roughly as follows. Carbon 14 is a radioactive isotope of carbon 12. All plants and living creatures contain carbon 14 while they are alive. When a living thing dies, it begins to lose the carbon 14 at a steady rate: approximately half the carbon 14 is lost every 5730 years (the "half-life" of radiocarbon). Therefore, if archaeologists find a piece of charcoal in an excavation, by measuring the amount of carbon 14, a lab can determine roughly when the tree from which the charcoal came was chopped down. A type of radiocarbon dating called *accelerator mass spectrometry* (AMS) can be used for dating smaller samples of organic matter. Because wood was valuable in Palestine's arid environment and therefore sometimes was in use for long periods or recycled, it yields less precise dates than grain and seeds (in other words, a piece of wood could have been used or reused as a ceiling beam for decades and even centuries before it was burnt).

Radiocarbon dating has the advantage of being the only "scientific" method listed here (meaning that the date is supplied by a laboratory). However, it has the disadvantage that every date returned by the lab has a plus/minus range, representing a margin of statistical error. There is a 67 percent chance that the date provided by the lab falls within the plus/minus range. A date of 4000 plus/minus 100 would mean that our tree was chopped down 4000 years ago, with a 67 percent chance that it was chopped down within a range of 100 years either way (the accuracy goes up if the range is doubled). Radiocarbon dates conventionally are published in the form of uncalibrated radiocarbon years before present (BP), with "present" measured from 1950 C.E., when the method was invented. Conversion of these dates to calendar years requires calibration because of past fluctuations in the level of carbon 14 in the atmosphere. Calibration can increase the range of a radiocarbon date.

For these reasons, radiocarbon dating is most useful in cases in which there are no other closely datable types of artifacts, such as prehistoric sites in Europe or Native American sites in the United States. It is less useful for historical period sites in Palestine, where other, more accurate methods of dating are available. Nevertheless, radiocarbon dating is valuable even in Palestine, as indicated by its centrality in the ongoing debate about the kingdom of **David** and Solomon (the key question being whether certain archaeological remains are associated with these kings or are later in date). Another disadvantage of radiocarbon dating is that it can be used only on organic materials, which are exactly the kinds of remains that are rarely preserved at ancient sites. Organic materials such as wooden furniture, rugs, woven mats and baskets, clothing, leather, and scrolls may survive in extremely arid conditions such as the area around the Dead Sea, but for the most part have disintegrated in other parts of Palestine as a result of humidity.

There are other scientific methods of dating such as **dendrochonology** (tree-ring dating), but they are rarely employed for the historical periods in Palestine.

Coins

Coins have the advantage of carrying their own date. However, there are also disadvantages associated with coins. First, coinage was not invented in the

Mediterranean world until about 600 B.C.E. Therefore, coins are not found at Mediterranean sites or levels that antedate the sixth century (or in other parts of the world, such as North America, until much later). Second, in antiquity coins often remained in circulation for long periods – up to hundreds of years – after they were minted. Although this is especially true of gold and silver coins, it can also be true of lower-value bronze coins. For this reason, finding a coin that was minted in 100 C.E. on the floor of a house can be misleading if it fell onto the floor 100 or 200 years later. It is best to use more than one coin when possible, or coins along with other methods of dating, to obtain an accurate date. Third, because coins were valuable, ancient peoples were careful not to lose them. This means that it is possible to excavate a level at a site and not find any coins. Fourth, because most ancient coins are tiny pieces of bronze (much smaller than our modern pennies), they have often corroded to the point at which the date can no longer be read. Excavation reports typically include lists of illegible coins.

Inscriptions or Other Written Materials Found in Excavations

Although this type of object is an archaeological find because it comes from an excavation, it falls into the category of historical materials (written texts). Sometimes inscriptions or written materials include a date. For example, a monumental inscription from **Justinian**'s **Nea Church** in Jerusalem provides the dedication date (see Chapter 15). However, most inscriptions do not record a date but instead consist of very brief texts – sometimes just a name or even a single letter. Often these texts are written in ink on broken pieces of pottery (**ostraca**; singular **ostracon**), the "post-it notes" of antiquity. Nevertheless, even brief, undated texts can yield valuable information. For example, the language of the inscription may reflect the ethnicity of the writer: Latin was used mostly by Romans, Hebrew by Israelites and Jews, and so on. Even undated texts can be given an approximate date by specialists who study the development of handwriting styles and letter forms over time (**paleographer**s or **epigrapher**s).

Relevant Ancient Literary Sources

Ancient literary sources can be helpful for dating purposes but must be used carefully and critically. The Hebrew Bible is often used as a source of information by archaeologists excavating Iron Age sites in Israel. However, because the biblical writers had certain biases and agendas (and were not motivated by a desire to write history in the modern sense of the word) their accounts cannot always be taken at face value. Furthermore, many of the events described occurred long before the Hebrew Bible was written down, which calls into question the accuracy of these accounts. This problem is most acute for the period prior to the arrival of the Israelites in Canaan (ca. 1200 B.C.E.), because the composition of the earliest books of the Hebrew Bible probably did not begin before the eighth and seventh centuries B.C.E., although scholars now debate the historicity of the biblical account for the Iron Age as well. For the Second Temple period in Palestine, **Flavius Josephus**, the Jewish author of the first century C.E., is our most valuable historical source. Other historical or literary sources for the periods covered in this book include the **Dead Sea Scrolls**, **apocrypha** and **pseudepigrapha** (deutero-canonical and noncanonical books), the New Testament, **Philo Judaeus**, **rabbinic** literature (the **Mishnah** and **Talmud**), and the church fathers.

Pottery

This is the only type of artifact in this list that does not carry its own date. Have you ever wondered how an archaeologist can pick up a seemingly nondescript potsherd (sherds are pieces of broken pottery, as opposed to shards, which are glass) and tell you the date? Here is how the process of dating pottery works. Imagine that we are excavating a multiperiod site with three main occupation levels (strata), one above the other. In the lowest (earliest) stratum, we find a certain type of bowl with red-painted decoration. In the next stratum above (the middle level), we find a different type of bowl with rounded walls and a flat base. In the uppermost (latest) stratum, we find another type of bowl covered with a black glaze. We can now establish the following relative typology (that is, a relative sequence of types): the bowl with the red-painted decoration is the earliest type; the bowl with rounded walls and a flat base is the middle type (in date); and the bowl with the black glaze is the latest type. In other words, we can construct a relative sequence of types in which one type is the earliest (relatively speaking), another is in the middle, and another is the latest. We determine the absolute dates of these pottery types based on their association with dated objects. For example, if we find coins minted by the Roman emperor Tiberius together with (in the same stratum as) the bowl with the red-painted decoration, we can assume that this type of bowl dates to the first century C.E. If, in the future, we find that same type at the next site down the road, we will know its date.

Dating pottery in this way is a complex process that is done by specialists. Not only do pottery types change over time, but they also vary among geographical regions. For example, when I was working on my dissertation, I found that the pottery types characteristic of Jerusalem and Judea in the fourth to seventh centuries C.E. are completely different from those found in **Galilee**. In addition, certain pottery types are better chronological indicators than others (that is, certain types can be dated more precisely). The best types for dating purposes are fine wares and oil lamps, as they tend to change in form and decoration fairly quickly. Fine wares are the dishes that were used for dining – that is, they are table wares such as cups, plates, and bowls. Fine wares and oil lamps are often decorated, whereas utilitarian vessels such as storage jars and cooking pots tend to be plain and are more difficult to date precisely. We refer to plain, undecorated vessels as *coarse wares*. Because of their utilitarian nature, storage jars and cooking pots usually display only minor changes in shape over long periods. For these reasons, pottery typologies must be constructed for different sites in different geographical regions and for every period and every vessel type. This has to be done on the basis of carefully excavated, multiperiod sites that provide sequences of levels and associated pottery types. There are still huge spans of time and space for which we lack ceramic typologies. Ironically, the biggest gaps in Palestine are the most recent periods (Islamic to Ottoman), which have received less attention from archaeologists than earlier periods.

Sometimes people wonder how ceramics specialists can tell different types apart. After all, couldn't the same types have been imitated in later periods, as were architectural styles? In fact, this is not true of pottery. The combination of shapes, clays, firing processes, and decorative techniques yielded a unique product. This means that even if a shape was duplicated in a later period (and this rarely happened), the combination of different clays, firing processes, and decorative techniques yielded a visibly different product. For example, even a nonspecialist can distinguish between modern imitations of Greek black-figured vases, such as those offered for sale to tourists in shops in **Athens'** Plaka, and the original masterpieces displayed in museums.

Why do archaeologists go to so much trouble to date pottery? Why not rely on other methods of dating? The reason is simple: pottery is ubiquitous at archaeological sites in the Mediterranean and Near East. In antiquity, everyone owned and used pottery. Wealthy people might have owned fine imported wares, whereas poorer people had only the cheap knockoffs from the local potter. However, every household was equipped with pottery vessels. Furthermore, once that pot was fired in the kiln, it might break into pieces but it would not disintegrate. This means that an archaeologist might excavate a structure that yielded no organic materials (for radiocarbon dating), no coins, no inscriptions or written materials, and about which no historical sources provide information. But if archaeologists find nothing else, we know that we will find potsherds – and lots of them – at ancient sites in Palestine. If we can date the pottery, we can date the levels and remains we are excavating.

Pottery can be dated using scientific techniques such as thermoluminesence (which can give the approximate date of the last firing), although these have not been widely employed because of their cost and difficulty. A new technique for dating pottery, called **rehydroxylation**, is more promising, as it is less expensive and yields relatively precise dates. Rehydroxylation works by measuring the hydroxyl groups (OH) in pottery, which are molecules in clay that react with environmental moisture (H_2O). The process of firing a ceramic pot in a kiln dehydrates the clay. From that point on, the pot reacts with water vapor in the atmosphere and begins to form hydroxyl groups. Rehydroxylation dates pottery by measuring the hydroxyl groups, taking into account environmental factors such as changes in temperature over time. This technique has not yet been employed on pottery from Palestine, but presumably this will change in the future.

ARCHAEOLOGY AND INDIANA JONES

Although films such as the *Indiana Jones* series have succeeded in thrusting archaeology into the public spotlight, they have also created a highly romanticized and grossly inaccurate image of the discipline. Often, when I tell people that I am an archaeologist, they ask, "What is the best thing you've ever found?" I am always at a loss to answer this question (which is asked in innocence), because it stems from the popular misconception of archaeologists as treasure hunters. Archaeologists are scientists; whatever we find is not our personal property but belongs to (and usually must remain in) the host country. Archaeologists seek to understand the past by studying human material remains through the process of excavation and publication, as described earlier. For this reason, professional archaeologists do not search for objects or treasures such as Noah's Ark, the Ark of the Covenant, or the Holy Grail. Usually these sorts of expeditions are led by amateurs (nonspecialists) or academics who are not archaeologists. Therefore, I have no good answer to the question, "What is the best thing you've ever found?" – because there is no single "thing." Archaeology is a process, a journey of discovery.

The archaeological endeavor involves piecing together all available information, not just one artifact taken out of context. Context is the reason that archaeologists go to so much trouble to document the provenance of every feature and artifact dug up on an excavation. Archaeologists oppose the sale of undocumented artifacts on the antiquities market because they come from illegal excavations, meaning these artifacts were removed without scientific excavation and documentation. Without context, most of the information about an artifact is irretrievably lost. Take, for example, a Roman statue, displayed in a museum, that was purchased on the antiquities market but lacks documentation of its origin (provenance). Based on its style, art historians might be able to estimate the rough date of the statue. Had the statue been properly excavated and documented, the context would have provided a secure and more accurate date for the statue. Scientific excavation could provide other information, such as the statue's original use – was it set up as decoration in a private house or garden, or was it a cultic object in a sanctuary? Not only was all this information lost when the statue was ripped from its context by looters, but the illegal excavations also destroyed the area around the statue and other parts of the site.

Illegal excavations and looting destroy evidence of a world heritage that belongs to all of us. Archaeologists seek to illuminate the past through scientific excavation and publication, thereby preserving and making this heritage accessible to everyone.

SETTING THE STAGE

To set the stage for the rest of this book, the next chapter presents a brief overview of the Bronze Age and Iron Age – that is, the Canaanite and Israelite periods. We focus especially on Jerusalem, to which much attention is devoted throughout the book. The remaining chapters cover the period from 586 B.C.E. to 640 C.E. In 586 B.C.E. the kingdom of Judah fell to the Babylonians, Jerusalem and Solomon's temple (the first temple) were destroyed, and the Judahite elite were exiled to **Babylonia**. Sixty years later the Persian king Cyrus allowed the exiles to return to Judea and rebuild the Jerusalem temple, ushering in the beginning of the Second Temple period. By the late Second Temple period (first century B.C.E.–first century C.E.), ancient Palestine (= modern Israel, Jordan, and the Palestinian territories) had come under Roman rule and its population was divided along religious, ethnic, economic, class, and sectarian lines. Seventy years after the death of King **Herod the Great** and about forty years after Jesus' death, a Jewish revolt against Rome erupted, culminating in 70 C.E. with the destruction of Jerusalem and the second temple. A second Jewish revolt against Rome led by a messianic figure known as Bar-Kokhba ended disastrously in 135 C.E. The centuries that followed witnessed the rise of Christianity and the transformation of Judaism from a religion centered on a temple with a sacrificial cult led by priests to the rabbinic Judaism of today, characterized by congregational prayer and worship in synagogues. Our story ends in 640 C.E., when Caesarea Maritima – the last major city in Palestine still under Byzantine control – fell to the Muslims after a seven-month-long siege. A brief epilogue examines the transition to early Islamic rule.

The material in this book is presented in chronological order, divided into successive periods. Each period begins with a historical summary, followed by a presentation of the major archaeological sites and monuments, and descriptions of various categories of artifacts (mainly pottery, oil lamps, and coins). Some chapters are thematic, focusing on topics such as the site of Qumran and the Dead Sea Scrolls, ancient Jewish tombs and burial customs, and ancient synagogues.

Sidebar: What do the terms B.C.E. and C.E. mean, and why are they used in this book?

Today, many people use the terms B.C. and A.D. when referring to calendar dates. B.C. is an abbreviation for "Before Christ," and A.D. stands for "Anno Domini" – Latin for "in the year of the/our Lord" (that is, the year of Jesus Christ's birth). Because these terms presuppose the acceptance of Jesus as the messiah, some people (especially, but not only, those who are not of the Christian faith) prefer a more neutral terminology: B.C.E. ("Before the Common Era" or "Before the Christian Era") instead of B.C., and C.E. ("Common Era" or "Christian Era") instead of A.D. The more neutral terminology has been adopted for this book.

Recommended Reading

*For the material covered throughout this book, readers are also referred to the popular journals or magazines *Biblical Archaeology Review* and *Biblical Archaeologist/Near Eastern Archaeology*.

Eric H. Cline, *From Eden to Exile: Unraveling Mysteries of the Bible* (Washington, DC: National Geographic, 2007).

Martha Joukowsky, *A Complete Manual of Field Archaeology: Tools and Techniques of Field Work for Archaeologists* (Englewood Cliffs, NJ: Prentice-Hall, 1980).

Jerome Murphy O'Connor, *The Holy Land: An Oxford Archaeological Guide* (New York: Oxford University, 2008).

Ephraim Stern (ed.), *The New Encyclopedia of the Archaeology of the Holy Land, Vols. 1–5* (New York: Simon and Schuster, 1993 [vol. 5 published in 2008]).

Bruce G. Trigger, *A History of Archaeological Thought* (New York: Cambridge University, 2006).

TWO

THE TOPOGRAPHY AND EARLY HISTORY OF JERUSALEM (TO 586 B.C.E.)

TOPOGRAPHY OF JERUSALEM

Jerusalem sits atop the watershed between the wooded Judean hills and fertile lowlands (Shefelah) to the west, and the barren wilderness of Judea (Judean desert) to the east, at an elevation of 800 meters above sea level, compared with the Dead Sea at 400 meters below sea level. The landscape provides a dramatic setting for this holy city, which is powerful and inspiring because of its starkness rather than its natural beauty. The first people who settled Jerusalem some 5,000 years ago were attracted to this spot for more prosaic reasons – specifically, by water. Jerusalem's earliest settlement was located on a small hill that forms a spur to the south of the **Temple Mount** (in Hebrew, *har ha-bayit*; in Arabic, **al-haram al-sharif**, which means the Noble Enclosure or Sacred Enclosure), the great esplanade (open platform) in the southeast corner of the modern Old City. This small hill came to be known by several names: the **City of David**; the **eastern hill**; and the **lower city**. Despite its size (only about 11 acres) and relatively low elevation, Jerusalem's first inhabitants settled on this hill because of its proximity to the only perennial source of fresh water in the area: the **Gihon spring**, which gushes forth at the foot of the eastern slope of the City of David. The City of David offered early inhabitants the additional advantage of natural protection, consisting of the **Kidron Valley** to the east and, to the west, the **Tyropoeon** [pronounced tie-rho-PEE-un] **Valley** (an ancient Greek name meaning the "Valley of the Cheesemakers"; it is sometimes also called the Central Valley because it begins at the modern Damascus Gate and runs south through the center of the Old City today). The Kidron and Tyropoeon valleys meet at the southern tip of the City of David. The **Mount of Olives**, which is the highest mountain ridge in Jerusalem, rises to the east of the Kidron Valley

2.1   Aerial view of Jerusalem from the south. Courtesy of Zev Radovan/BibleLandPictures
.com.

before dropping steeply down toward the Dead Sea further to the east. The
configuration of bedrock in the City of David is such that the bedrock is lowest
at the southern tip and rises steadily toward the north, culminating in a rocky
outcrop that eventually became the Temple Mount.

Archaeological remains – consisting mostly of pottery vessels from tombs
and fragmentary walls belonging to houses – indicate that Jerusalem was first
settled in the Early Bronze Age (ca. 3000 B.C.E.). By the Middle Bronze Age
(ca. 1800 B.C.E.), the settlement was fortified and equipped with a sophisticated
water system (discussed later). Bronze Age documents from Egypt called the
Execration Texts (ca. 1900 B.C.E.) and the el-Amarna letters (ca. 1400 B.C.E.)
confirm the existence of a settlement in Jerusalem at this time. These documents
refer to Jerusalem as "Rushalimum," similar to the name "Urusalim" which is
mentioned in later Akkadian texts. The original Hebrew name was probably
Yerushalem. Although by the late Second Temple period Yerushalayim had come
to be understood as deriving from the Hebrew word *shalom* (peace), the original
name probably referred to Shalem, apparently the patron god of the city. In
antiquity, many towns and cities were named in honor of the patron deity. For
example, Athens was named after Athena, and **Jericho** (Hebrew *yericho*) was
probably named in honor of the moon god (*yare'ach*). Genesis 14:18 mentions
Melchizedek, the king of Shalem, likely a reference to Jerusalem: "And King

Melchizedek of Salem (Hebrew: *Shalem*) brought out bread and wine; he was priest of God Most High" (New Revised Standard Version [NRSV]).

During the Bronze Age the rest of the country was inhabited by the Canaanites, who established an urban civilization centered on fortified cities such as Hazor, Megiddo, Shechem, Gezer, and Lachish. In contrast to other parts of the ancient Near East, such as Egypt and **Mesopotamia** (the area of modern Iraq), the Canaanite city-states were never united under the rule of a single monarch. According to the Hebrew Bible, by the time the Israelites arrived in Canaan (ca. 1200 B.C.E.), Jerusalem was inhabited by the **Jebusites**. We do not know whether the Jebusites were Canaanites or an ethnically unrelated population. The original settlement in Jerusalem was confined to the small hill south of the later Temple Mount, which became known as the City of David after King David conquered the Jebusite city (ca. 1000 B.C.E.).

David reportedly brought the Ark of the Covenant to Jerusalem and made it the capital of his kingdom. Jerusalem was a logical choice as capital city both because of its central location and because it was conquered by David, and therefore did not belong to any one of the twelve tribes. David's son and successor, Solomon, expanded the city to the north, building the first temple (Solomon's temple) and a new palace on the Temple Mount. The temple apparently stood on a natural outcrop of bedrock (today enshrined in the Muslim **Dome of the Rock**), which physically dominated the City of David and transformed the Temple Mount into the city's acropolis. Although today many people associate an "acropolis" with Athens, most ancient towns and cities had an acropolis – that is, a fortified citadel that contained key political and religious buildings.

By the latter part of the eighth century, Jerusalem's population could no longer be accommodated on the small hill of the City of David alone. The city did not expand to the east – the Mount of Olives always lay outside the walls and was used from the earliest periods as Jerusalem's **necropolis** (cemetery/burial ground) – but instead grew to the west, across the Tyropoeon Valley. This area, called the **western hill**, is larger and higher in elevation than the City of David, and therefore is also known as the **upper city** (in contrast to the City of David, which is the lower city). The western hill had the advantage of natural protection on three of four sides. On the east, the western hill is bounded by the Tyropoeon Valley, which separates it from the Temple Mount and City of David. On the west and south, the western hill is encircled by the **Ben-Hinnom Valley**, which begins by the modern Jaffa Gate (the main gate in the middle of the western side of the Old City today), and joins the Kidron and Tyropoeon valleys at the southern tip of the City of David. The Ben-Hinnom Valley is notorious as the place where some Israelites offered child sacrifices, a Canaanite and Phoenician practice that was condemned by the prophet Jeremiah: "'For the people of Judah have done evil in my sight,' says the Lord; they have set their abominations in the house that is called by my name, defiling it. And they

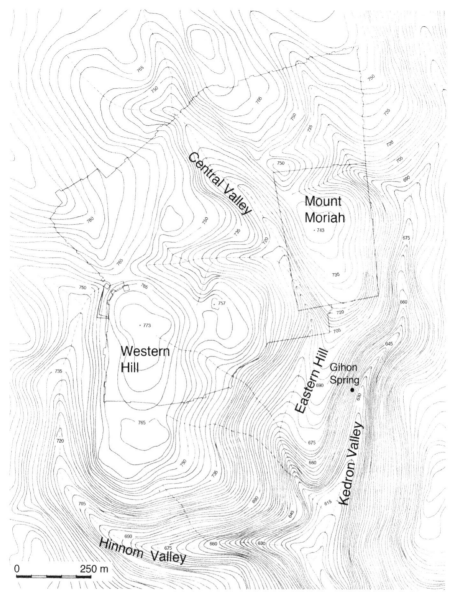

2.2 Topographic map of Jerusalem. A reconstruction by Leen Ritmeyer ©.

go on building the high place of Topheth, which is in the valley of the son of Hinnom (Ben-Hinnom), to burn their sons and their daughters in the fire" (Jeremiah 7:30–31; NRSV).

Only the north side of Jerusalem was not protected by deep natural valleys. Instead, a shallow ravine called the **Transverse Valley** marks the northern end of the western hill, running east from the modern Jaffa Gate to the Temple Mount, where it joins the Tyropoeon Valley. In antiquity, Jerusalem usually was attacked from the north because of the lack of natural defenses. For example, when the Romans besieged Jerusalem in 70 C.E., they attacked from the north, even though this side of the city was protected by three successive lines of walls.

The area we have just described – the City of David, Temple Mount, and western hill – constituted the city of Jerusalem until its destruction by the Romans in 70 C.E. (although by then settlement had expanded farther to the north). Nowadays many visitors to Jerusalem have the mistaken impression that the Old City is the ancient city. In fact, the current walls of the Old City date to the Ottoman Turkish period (sixteenth century C.E.), and they enclose only part of the original ancient city but leave outside the City of David and the southern part of the western hill (now known as **Mount Zion**). In other words, the walled city has shifted to the north since antiquity. This shift occurred when the Roman emperor **Hadrian** rebuilt Jerusalem in the second century C.E. as a pagan Roman city called **Aelia Capitolina** (see Chapter 13). The line of the current Ottoman walls reflects this later shift to the north.

Today the area inside the walls of the Old City is divided into four quarters. The Jewish Quarter occupies the southern part of the city – that is, the area around and opposite the Western Wall ("Wailing Wall") and the Temple Mount. The Christian Quarter is in the northwest part of the city, surrounding the **Church of the Holy Sepulcher**. The Armenian Quarter is in the southwest corner of the Old City, and the Muslim Quarter occupies the northeast part. The huge esplanade of the Temple Mount takes up the southeast corner of the Old City.

HISTORICAL BACKGROUND: THE IRON AGE (1200–586 B.C.E.)

By the end of the Late Bronze Age (thirteenth century B.C.E.), the eastern Mediterranean was ringed by mighty powers, including the New Kingdom in Egypt, the **Mycenean kingdoms** in Greece, and the **Hittites** in **Anatolia** (**Asia Minor** or modern Turkey). Documents such as the el-Amarna letters indicate that the rulers of these empires and kingdoms corresponded with one another, and imported artifacts found in archaeological excavations attest to lively international trade and contacts. Around 1200 B.C.E., these powers collapsed. The reasons for the collapse are debated, although it must have been caused by a complex and interrelated series of events. Certainly the collapse involved large-scale movements of peoples, some of whom may have been hostile invaders responsible for the waves of destruction, whereas others were refugees uprooted from their homes as a result of the upheavals. The year 1200 B.C.E. marks the great watershed between the Bronze Age and the Iron Age around the eastern Mediterranean. According to later tradition, the **Trojan War** was fought around this time, followed by the Dorian invasion of Greece (the arrival of tribes speaking the Doric Greek dialect).

It was against the backdrop of these events that the Israelite tribes arrived in Canaan and settled the interior hill country from Galilee to the northern **Negev**. Many scholars now believe that at least some of the early Israelites were actually Canaanites, who joined with new arrivals (including perhaps a small group from Egypt – hence the story of the Exodus) to form a new group unified by their worship of a patron deity known as YHWH (Yahweh). The interior hill country is a harsh, rocky, and relatively arid region compared with the fertile lowlands and coastal plain to the west. The Israelite settlement, at least initially, consisted of small villages whose inhabitants survived by raising crops such as grain, olives, and grapes, and herding animals, mainly sheep and goats. The coastal plain was settled around the same time by groups of refugees from the Aegean (the **Sea Peoples**). One of these groups, the Philistines, established a kingdom (Philistia) on the southern coastal plain centered on five cities: **Gaza**, Ashdod, **Ashkelon**, Gath (Tell es-Safi), and Ekron (Tel Miqne). The Hebrew Bible describes ongoing hostilities between the Israelites and their Philistine neighbors, including episodes involving Samson and Delilah, David and Goliath, and the death of Saul (the first Israelite king) and his three sons in a battle against the Philistines at the foot of Mount Gilboa.

The Iron Age in Palestine is characterized by a process of state formation that gave rise to the emergence of different – albeit sometimes related – peoples and kingdoms. In addition to the Israelites and Philistines, the Hebrew Bible mentions Ammonites (in the area around modern Amman in Jordan), Moabites (in the territory to the south of Amman, east of the Jordan river and northeast of the Dead Sea), and Edomites (in the territory to the south of Moab, southeast of the Dead Sea). The area to the north, corresponding with modern Lebanon, was occupied by the **Phoenicians**, who were the Iron Age descendants of the Canaanites. The designation *Phoenician* originated with ancient Greek writers, who grouped under this rubric the inhabitants of independent cities such as **Tyre**, **Sidon**, Byblos (Gebal), and Beirut (Berytus). With access to the interior blocked by the anti-Lebanon mountain range, the Phoenician coastal cities turned to the sea, controlling much of the trade around the Mediterranean basin during the Iron Age. The Phoenicians established a series of trading posts and colonies around the Mediterranean littoral, and traded with the Greeks, who adopted the Phoenician alphabet in the eighth century. **Carthage** (in modern Tunisia), which was founded as a Phoenician colony, later became a great power that threatened Rome.

The Hebrew Bible describes contacts – sometimes hostile and sometimes friendly – between the Israelites and the surrounding peoples. For example, King Solomon formed political alliances with neighboring kingdoms by marrying their princesses: "King Solomon loved many foreign women along with the daughter of Pharaoh: Moabite, Ammonite, Edomite, Sidonian [Phoenician], and Hittite women" (1 Kings 11:1; NRSV). Solomon also signed a commercial treaty

Sidebar: What Is a Temple?

In antiquity a temple was the house of a god or goddess – a concept expressed in the Hebrew Bible by the use of the term "house" (*bayit*) for Solomon's temple (and hence *har ha-bayit* – the mountain of the house – for Jerusalem's Temple Mount). The earliest Greek temples resembled modest houses, but eventually the Greeks began to build larger and more elaborate houses for their gods, which led to the development of the Doric and Ionic orders of architecture. Because a temple was conceived of literally as the house in which the deity dwelled, most people in the ancient world never entered the building. Instead they stayed outside the temple, congregating around an open-air altar where sacrifices were offered. Usually only priests entered the temple, to service the needs of the deity (feed, clothe, and bathe the god). The temples of the God of Israel (the first and second temples in Jerusalem) functioned in this manner, with the main differences from other ancient temples being that (1) there was no cult statue or depiction of the God of Israel; and (2) whereas other gods could be worshiped at more than one temple, the Temple Mount came to be the only acceptable spot for the house of the God of Israel (even this principle was not observed universally, though, as ancient temples with sacrificial cults to the God of Israel existed at **Elephantine** and **Leontopolis** in Egypt).

Synagogues, churches, and mosques are congregational halls that accommodate groups of people for the purposes of worship and prayer. In contrast to temples, people assemble inside these buildings, rather than standing outside and watching sacrifices offered by priests. Despite the modern custom of referring to synagogues as "temples," they are not the same at all.

with King **Hiram** of Tyre, trading wheat and oil for cedars of Lebanon (used to build the Jerusalem temple and Solomon's new palace). Together Solomon and Hiram opened a new port on the Red Sea, through which they imported valuable luxury items such as gold, silver, and ivory.

The kingdom of David and Solomon is known as the **United Monarchy** or **United Kingdom**. One of the hottest debates among biblical scholars and archaeologists in recent years is whether the biblical description of the United Kingdom is relatively accurate, highly exaggerated, or completely fabricated. Scholars who believe it is exaggerated claim that David existed but was a minor tribal chief, and that Jerusalem of the United Monarchy was a modest settlement lacking monumental structures. Other scholars claim that the Hebrew Bible was composed so long after the time of David and Solomon that the description of the United Monarchy is completely tendentious and lacks any historical basis. Archaeological remains in Jerusalem seem to support a position midway between

2.3 Map of Iron Age Palestine. Ancient World Mapping Center, University of North Carolina at Chapel Hill (www.unc.edu/awmc).

the first two views – that is, the biblical account may be somewhat exaggerated, but not to the degree claimed by some scholars.

When Solomon died (ca. 930 B.C.E.), the United Kingdom split into two: the northern kingdom of Israel and the southern kingdom of Judah, reflecting pre-existing tensions between the northern and southern tribes. Eventually the northern kings established a capital city at **Samaria**, whereas Jerusalem remained the capital of the southern kingdom. The biblical writers generally present the kings of Judah in a positive light while condemning the kings of Israel. Their negative presentation of the northern kings stems partly from a preference for exclusive Yahwism (the worship of the God of Israel alone) over the inclusive Yahwism of the northern elite (who worshiped other gods alongside the God of Israel). The biblical writers also promoted the centralization of the cult of the God of Israel in Jerusalem, condemning the establishment of rural sanctuaries around the country. These views privileged Judah, which controlled the Jerusalem temple, over Israel. The biases of the biblical writers are evident in their negative portrayal of northern kings such as **Ahab**, whom they condemned for marrying **Jezebel**, the daughter of the king of Tyre. Jezebel is accused by the biblical writers of having induced Ahab to build a temple ("house") to **Baal** in Samaria. Indeed, the name Bel/Baal, the national deity of the Canaanites and Phoenicians, is embedded within Jezebel's own name (in other words, Jezebel's name is **theophoric**, meaning that it contains the name of a deity). The Hebrew Bible describes repeated confrontations between Ahab and Jezebel on the one hand and the staunchly Yahwist prophet **Elijah** on the other hand. Jezebel's gory death at the hands of a military officer named Yehu – who had Jezebel thrown out of a second-story palace window and left her remains to be devoured by dogs – is portrayed by the biblical writers as a fulfillment of Elijah's prophecies.

During the ninth and eighth centuries B.C.E., the [neo-] Assyrian empire became the dominant power in the ancient Near East, extending its control westward and launching a series of invasions into the kingdoms of Israel and Judah. Israel finally fell in 722 B.C.E., when the Assyrians took Samaria and exiled the northern elite (an event that is the source of the legend of the Ten Lost Tribes, referring to the members of the northern tribes who were dispersed). Twenty years later, the Assyrians invaded Judah (701 B.C.E.). They destroyed a number of towns, including the important southern town of **Lachish** (between Jerusalem and **Beersheba**); ravaged the countryside; and besieged Jerusalem. In advance of the Assyrian siege **Hezekiah**, the king of Judah, fortified Jerusalem and built a new water supply system. The Assyrians ended up withdrawing without taking Jerusalem (according to the biblical account, a plague sent by God broke out in the Assyrian camp, but Assyrian sources suggest that the king withdrew because of unrest elsewhere in the empire). The kingdom of Judah survived the invasion but became a vassal state of Assyria.

Eventually the Assyrian empire weakened, and in 612 B.C.E. it collapsed and was replaced by the [neo-] Babylonian empire as the dominant power in the ancient Near East. Whereas the Assyrian empire was based in the northern part of Mesopotamia (northern Iraq), the Babylonian empire was centered in the south (southern Iraq). It was against the backdrop of power struggles among Assyria, Babylonia, and Egypt that **Josiah**, the king of Judah, was killed by the pharaoh Necho (II) in 609 B.C.E. at the foot of Megiddo, the Book of Revelation's Armageddon (Greek for *Har* [Mount] *Megiddo*). Josiah is a favorite of the biblical writers because he eliminated sanctuaries and cultic practices associated with other gods, and insisted on the worship of the God of Israel in the Jerusalem temple alone. According to the biblical account, Josiah's reforms were implemented after a fifth book of Moses, **Deuteronomy** (Greek for "second law"), was discovered during repair work on the temple.

The Babylonians soon launched a series of invasions into Judah, which culminated with the destruction of Jerusalem and Solomon's temple in 586 B.C.E. The Judahite elite were exiled to Babylonia. The year 586 B.C.E. is the watershed marking the end of the Iron Age and the First Temple period in Palestine, and the beginning of the Babylonian exile.

THE ARCHAEOLOGY OF BIBLICAL JERUSALEM (TO 586 B.C.E.)

Nothing survives of Solomon's temple (the first temple), although the remains of scattered and fragmentary walls between the Temple Mount and City of David (the **Ophel**) might be associated with Solomon's palace complex. More substantial remains of the Bronze Age and Iron Age have been discovered around the City of David, especially on the eastern slope above the Gihon spring. The first excavations in this area were conducted from 1923 to 1925 by Robert Alexander Stewart Macalister and J. Garrow Duncan on behalf of the Palestine Exploration Fund, a British organization. Macalister and Duncan opened a trench at the crest of the hill above the spring, which is a natural high point because of the manner in which the bedrock rises toward the north. Macalister and Duncan's excavations brought to light a fortification wall with towers, which they attributed to the Jebusites because the biblical account describes Jerusalem as so strongly fortified that the Israelites were unable to take it until the time of David.

In the 1960s this area was re-excavated by the British archaeologist Kathleen M. Kenyon, who dug on the slope below the fortification wall uncovered by Macalister and Duncan. Kenyon demonstrated that the fortification wall and towers date not to the time of the Jebusites (Bronze Age) but to the Second Temple period (after 586 B.C.E.). Furthermore, Kenyon's excavations revealed that the fortification wall sits atop a massive stepped stone structure (glacis), which she assumed was intended to buttress the fortification wall. Kenyon therefore dated the glacis to the Second Temple period as well. In the 1970s this area was re-excavated by the Israeli archaeologist Yigal Shiloh (Area G in his excavations). Shiloh uncovered more of the glacis, revealing that Israelite houses of the eighth and seventh centuries B.C.E. (or perhaps earlier) had been built on

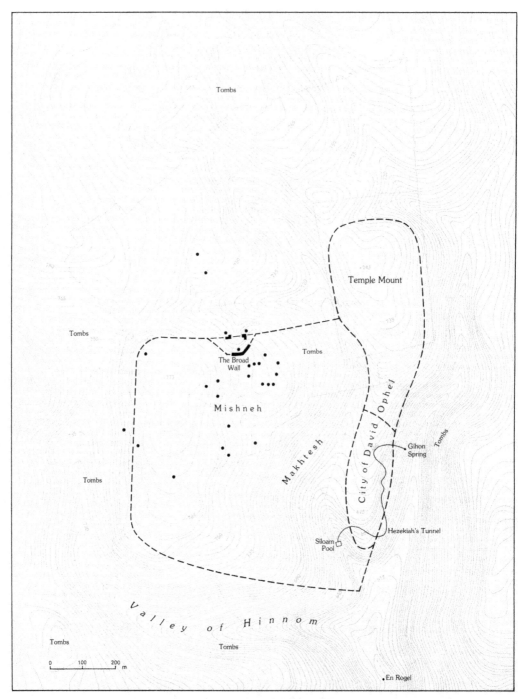

2.4 Plan of Jerusalem at the end of the First Temple period. From E. Stern (ed.), *The New Encyclopedia of Archaeological Excavations in the Holy Land* (New York: Simon and Schuster, 1993), vol. 2, p. 707. By permission of Hillel Geva and the Israel Exploration Society.

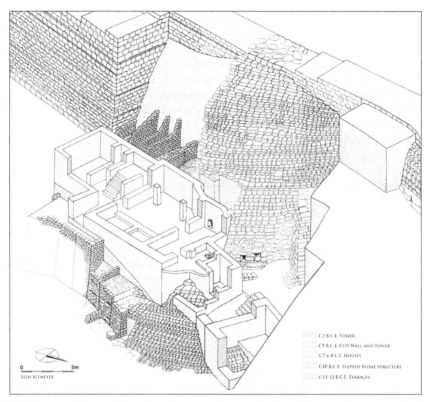

C2 B.C.E. TOWER
C5 B.C.E. CITY WALL AND TOWER
C7-6 B.C.E. HOUSES
C10 B.C.E. STEPPED STONE STRUCTURE
C13-12 B.C.E. TERRACES

LEEN RITMEYER

0   5m

2.5 Diagram of Area G showing the stepped stone glacis and houses. Reconstruction by
     Leen Ritmeyer ©.

top of the lower part of the glacis. Shiloh's discovery provides an eighth-century
terminus ante quem for the glacis, meaning that the glacis must have been built
before the eighth century. Therefore, the glacis does not date to the Second
Temple period and could not have been intended to buttress the fortification
wall above, as Kenyon thought. To summarize, various excavations at the crest
of the hill above the Gihon spring have brought to light the following remains:
(1) a fortification wall with towers; (2) a massive stepped stone structure (glacis)
on the slope below the wall; and (3) Israelite houses of the eighth and seventh
centuries B.C.E. on top of the lower part of the glacis.

Shiloh's excavations indicate that the glacis was built first. By the eighth and
seventh centuries B.C.E., houses were built on top of the glacis. In 586 B.C.E. the
houses and other structures in this area were destroyed by the Babylonians. In
the Second Temple period the fortification wall and tower were built at the crest
of the hill, with no direct relationship to the glacis. But if the glacis was not built
to buttress the fortification wall and towers that Macalister and Duncan found,
what was its purpose? Presumably it buttressed some monumental structure
that stood in the area above prior to the eighth century. This area would have
been the acropolis – that is, the natural high point – of the City of David before

---

Solomon built a new palace and the temple on the Temple Mount farther to the north. In other words, the area above the glacis must have been the citadel of the city in the time of the Jebusites and David. In fact, potsherds found among the stones of the glacis and in the fills inside it suggest that it was built at the end of the Late Bronze Age or in the Early Iron Age.

Recent excavations by the Israeli archaeologist Eilat Mazar in the area above the glacis have brought to light the remains of a large stone building that she identifies as the palace of David. If Mazar is correct, her discovery would support the traditional understanding of the biblical account by demonstrating that monumental architecture existed in Davidic Jerusalem, suggesting that David was more than merely a tribal leader of a minor chiefdom. Mazar's discovery has generated controversy not only because of its implications but also because some scholars point to a lack of secure evidence for dating the structure to the time of David (ca. 1000 B.C.E.), as in many cases the connections between the walls and the excavated floors (with associated pottery) were not preserved. Furthermore, some archaeologists, such as Israel Finkelstein, argue that Iron Age pottery types have been dated too early by as much as 50 to 100 years, not only in Jerusalem but elsewhere around the country. For this reason, Finkelstein and others claim that buildings and other remains at sites around the country that have been attributed to David and Solomon should instead be dated to the ninth century. Radiocarbon dating of organic remains found with pottery in Iron Age levels has yet to resolve this debate to the satisfaction of either side. Perhaps the eventual employment of other techniques, such as rehydroxylation (see Chapter 1), will provide more definitive answers.

The eighth- and seventh-century B.C.E. houses that Shiloh discovered on top of the glacis represent a common Israelite type called a **four-room house**. This type is so called because the ground floor plan typically is divided into three long (parallel) spaces, with a short space running along the width at the back. The three long spaces consisted of a central open courtyard with pillared porches on either side. Animals could be stabled in the porches, and the courtyard was used for cooking, spinning and weaving, and other work. The room at the rear of the house was used for storage. The sleeping quarters were upstairs, away from the noise, dirt, and animals on the ground floor, accessed by a staircase abutting the outside of the house.

One of the four-room houses that Shiloh excavated yielded fragments of wooden furniture that was burned in the Babylonian destruction of 586 B.C.E. Another house – the most complete one – was dubbed by Shiloh "the **house of Ahiel**" because this name is mentioned in an inscription on an ostracon (inscribed potsherd). Nevertheless, we do not know whether anyone named Ahiel owned or lived in this house. Large numbers of Judean pillar figurines, consisting of simple clay cylinders depicting women cradling their breasts, were also discovered in the City of David. These figurines, which are found at Israelite

2.6   Bulla of Gemaryahu, son of Shaphan. Courtesy of Zev Radovan/BibleLandPictures.com.

sites around the country, resemble the fertility goddesses worshipped by other ancient Near Eastern peoples. Their discovery at Israelite sites might illustrate the adoption of the type of foreign cultic practice that was condemned by the prophets.

Another four-room house excavated by Shiloh – the "house of the **bullae**" – is so called because it yielded a cache of 51 bullae (singular: bulla), which are small clay lumps used to seal documents and containers. As there were no envelopes in antiquity, documents were rolled up and tied with string (or similar material). Documents and containers were sealed by placing a lump of raw clay over the string and making an impression with a ring or pendant that bore the owner's name or personal symbol. To open the document, the seal had to be broken by removing the lump of clay. Bullae are rare finds because unfired clay turns back into mud. The bullae found by Shiloh were preserved thanks to the Babylonian destruction of 586 B.C.E., which burned the archive of documents originally stored in this house but fired the clay sealings. These bullae are important because they have a documented and securely dated archaeological context, whereas many of the ancient bullae in museums and private collections were purchased on the antiquities market and come from illegal excavations.

The bullae that Shiloh found are impressed with personal names, presumably of the owners of the seals. As is still common in many parts of the Middle East today, ancient Jerusalemites did not have a first name and last name but instead were identified as someone's son or daughter. This is reflected in the formula that appears on the bullae found by Shiloh: "belonging to X son of Y." One typical example reads "belonging to ʿAzaryahu son of Hilkiyahu," which, like many of the names on the bullae, contains the theophoric suffix *–yahu* (from YHWH). Although most of the names are known from the Hebrew Bible, in most cases it is impossible to determine whether they are the same individuals who made the impressions on the bullae, because these were common names in seventh-century Judah. However, at least one bulla bears a name that is so unusual, it almost certainly is the same person mentioned in the Hebrew Bible: "belonging to **Gemaryahu son of Shaphan.**" Gemaryah[u] son of Shaphan is mentioned in Jeremiah 36:10 as a scribe in the court of Jehoiakim the king of Judah (the son of Josiah), who reigned from ca. 609 to 598. A scribe is just the sort of person we would expect to seal documents, and the timing corresponds well with the archaeological evidence, because the "house of the bullae" was destroyed in 586 B.C.E.

THE WATER SYSTEMS OF BIBLICAL JERUSALEM

Access to the Gihon spring was closely connected with the fortification system. If the wall that Macalister and Duncan uncovered on the crest of the City of David dates to the Second Temple period, where were the fortifications of the Bronze Age and Iron Age city? The excavations of Kenyon and Shiloh brought to light the remains of walls dating to the Middle Bronze Age and the Iron Age II about midway down the eastern slope. The placement of fortifications at this spot seems to make good topographic sense, as it leaves space for building inside the city wall while raising the defenses above the floor of the Kidron Valley. Because this arrangement left the Gihon spring outside the wall, however, it meant that in times of war or siege Jerusalem's inhabitants had to risk their lives to obtain water. Because of this problem, over the course of the Bronze Age and Iron Age, Jerusalem was equipped with three different water systems, which are now called **Warren's Shaft**, the **Siloam Channel**, and **Hezekiah's Tunnel**.

Warren's Shaft

Warren's Shaft is named after Captain Charles Warren, the British explorer who discovered it in 1867. The system provided access to water from the Gihon spring through an underground tunnel, which was entered from within the fortification wall. From the entrance a stepped diagonal passage led to a horizontal tunnel, all below the surface of the ground. For a long time scholars thought that the horizontal tunnel terminated at the top of a deep vertical shaft, at the base of which was a channel that brought water from the spring. According to this understanding, water would have been obtained by dropping a bucket from a wooden platform at the top of the vertical shaft. However, recent excavations by the Israeli archaeologists Ronny Reich and Eli Shukron indicate that the horizontal tunnel originally bypassed the vertical shaft (which is a natural karstic formation), and instead terminated at an enormous, rock-cut pool (ca. 10 × 15 meters) that collected water from the spring. Water was drawn by dropping a bucket from a platform overlooking the pool. A later recutting of the tunnel lowered the floor level and exposed the top of the vertical shaft. The excavations by Reich and Shukron also have brought to light an associated fortification system consisting of massive towers built of cyclopean stones that abut the pool and enclose the spring (the "pool tower" and "spring tower"). The spring tower measures ca. 16 × 16 meters and its walls are up to 7 meters thick! After the pool went out of use it was filled with dumped debris, including hundreds of bullae and unstamped lumps of clay of the Iron Age II (eighth–seventh centuries). Their fragmentary condition is due to the fact that the bullae were broken when the documents and containers that they sealed were opened. The impressions on the bullae include Egyptian hieroglyphs and pseudo-hieroglyphs as well as other designs, indicating that the documents and containers they sealed had been imported to Judah.

Shiloh, who cleared Warren's Shaft, dated it to the time of David and Solomon on the basis of comparisons with Israelite water systems at sites such as Megiddo and **Hazor**. However, the Middle Bronze Age II date (ca. 1800 B.C.E.) favored by most scholars has been confirmed by Reich and Shukron's excavations. Reich and Shukron also question whether Jerusalem was fortified by a wall in the Middle Bronze Age, as the only wall discovered by Shiloh on the eastern slope to the south of the spring dates to the Iron Age II. Therefore, they suggest that the Middle Bronze Age wall discovered by Kenyon on the slope above the spring might be a "local" feature, perhaps belonging to a fortification system around the spring rather than a city wall. At the same time, Reich and Shukron are careful to point out that we still do not fully understand ancient Jerusalem's fortification system. Presumably we will learn more as their ongoing excavations and future projects bring to light new remains.

The Hebrew Bible describes as follows David's conquest of Jerusalem:

> The king and his men marched to Jerusalem against the Jebusites, the inhabitants of the land, who said to David, "You will not come in here, even the blind and the lame will turn you back" – thinking, "David cannot come in here." Nevertheless, David took the stronghold of Zion, which is now the City of David. David had said on that day, "Whoever would strike down the Jebusites, let him get up the *tsinnor* to attack the lame and the blind, those whom David hates." . . . David occupied the stronghold, and named it the city of David. (2 Samuel 5:6–9, NRSV; also see 1 Chronicles 11:4–7, which adds that Joab son of Zeruiah was the first to go up the *tsinnor* and became David's commander)

This passage raises many questions. What does it mean when the Jebusites tell David that even blind and lame men can keep him out? One possibility is that the Jebusites were taunting David, saying that their city was so strongly fortified that even the blind and lame could defend it. Another question concerns the

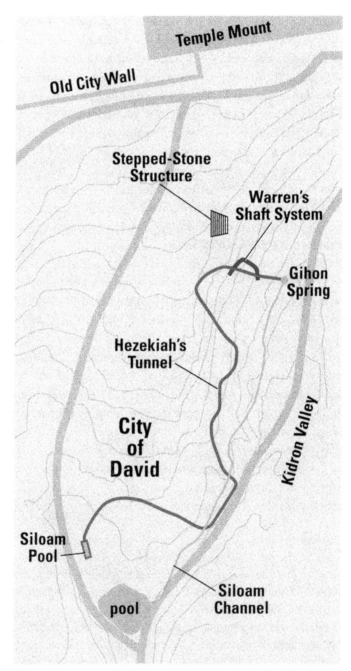

2.7 Plan of the water systems of biblical Jerusalem. From R. Reich and E. Shukron, "Light at the End of the Tunnel, Warren's Shaft Theory of David's Conquest Shattered," *Biblical Archaeology Review* 25.1 (1999), p. 25. By permission of Hershel Shanks and the Biblical Archaeology Society.

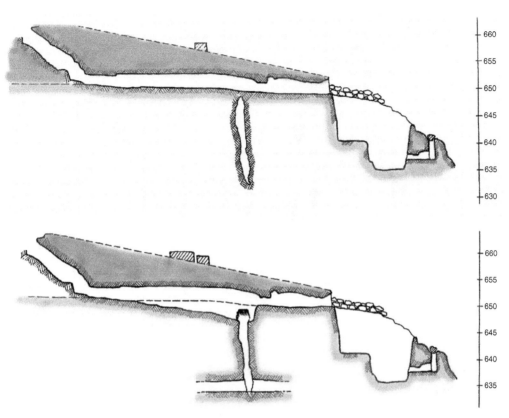

2.8 Section through Warren's Shaft, showing the original system (above), and the later cutting of the floor into the vertical shaft (below). From R. Reich, *Excavating the City of David, Where Jerusalem's History Began* (Jerusalem: Israel Exploration Society, 2011), Fig. 107. Courtesy of Ronny Reich.

meaning of *tsinnor*. This word is a **hapax legomenon**, which means that it occurs nowhere else in the Hebrew Bible. In modern Hebrew *tsinnor* means pipe (the kind used in plumbing). Many scholars think that *tsinnor* in the biblical account refers to a water system, which would mean that Joab managed to penetrate Jerusalem's defenses by climbing up through the water system. If this is correct, the logical candidate is Warren's Shaft, which apparently was in use at the time David conquered Jerusalem.

The Siloam Channel (Channel II)

The second water system, called the Siloam Channel or Channel II, consists of a rock-cut channel that was covered by large stone slabs, which runs along the lower eastern slope of the City of David. The channel carried water from the Gihon spring to a large pool at the southern tip of the hill (the original pool of Siloam). This system might be "the waters of Siloam [Shiloah] that flow gently" mentioned in Isaiah 8:6. Unlike Warren's Shaft, the Siloam Channel was not a

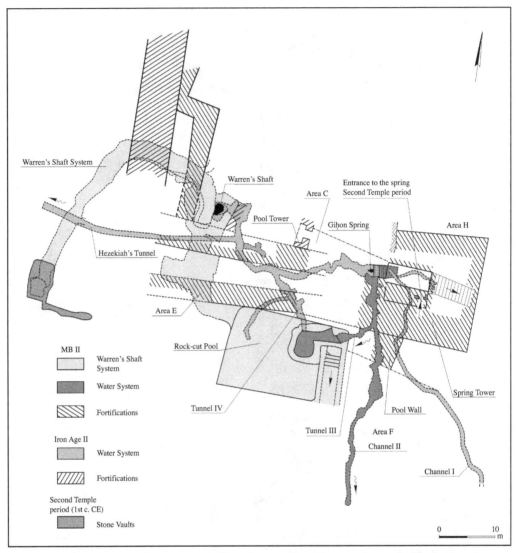

2.9 Plan of the fortifications around the Gihon spring. From R. Reich, *Excavating the City of David, Where Jerusalem's History Began* (Jerusalem: Israel Exploration Society, 2011), Fig. 168. Courtesy of Ronny Reich.

defensive system. Its main purpose was to provide an outlet for excess water from the Gihon spring and channel the water to a storage pool. There is evidence that openings on the sides of the channel allowed water to flow into agricultural terraces or fields below.

Hezekiah's Tunnel

In 701 B.C.E., in preparation for the Assyrian siege, King Hezekiah equipped Jerusalem with a third water system. Unlike Warren's Shaft and the Siloam

2.10 The inscription from Hezekiah's Tunnel. Courtesy of Zev Radovan/BibleLandPictures
.com.

Channel, water still flows through Hezekiah's Tunnel today. The tunnel begins
at the Gihon spring and ends at a storage pool (the current **pool of Siloam**)
on the southwest side of the City of David. Hezekiah's Tunnel is a marvel of
ancient engineering. It is entirely underground and was hewn through bedrock
by two teams of men who started at either end (that is, one team at the Gihon
spring and the other team at the outlet end with the pool), as indicated by the
cutting marks left by iron tools. The difference in the level of the floor from
beginning to end is 30 centimeters – a gradient of just 0.6 percent! Although
the tunnel winds back and forth for a distance of more than 500 meters – about
twice the distance from the spring to the pool, as the crow flies – the two teams
met roughly in the middle. How they managed to do this is still a mystery.
According to one theory, the teams followed a natural crack in the bedrock
through which water was already flowing. But if this is true, why is the ceiling
of the tunnel so much higher at the outlet end than at the spring end (where
it drops to under five feet in height)? Why would the workers have expended
so much unnecessary effort? Furthermore, false starts are clearly visible in the
tunnel – that is, places where the teams began to cut through the bedrock in one
direction, but then stopped and continued in another direction – which makes
no sense if they were following an existing stream of water.

Why did Hezekiah find it necessary to provide Jerusalem with a new water
system when the other two systems were still functioning? According to 2
Chronicles 32:2–4: "When Hezekiah saw that [the Assyrian king] **Sennacherib**
had come and intended to fight against Jerusalem, he planned with his officers
and his warriors to stop the flow the springs that were outside the city; and
they helped him. A great many people were gathered, and they stopped all the

2.11 The pool of Siloam of the late Second Temple period. Courtesy of Zev Radovan/
BibleLandPictures.com.

springs and the wadi (or stream) that flowed through the land, saying, 'Why
should the Assyrian kings come and find water in abundance?'" (NRSV) This
passage indicates that Hezekiah made a new water system because the Siloam
Channel lay outside the city's fortifications. Hezekiah wanted to prevent the
Assyrians from having access to the water in the Siloam Channel ("the **wadi**
or stream that flowed through the land"). Therefore, he blocked off the Siloam
Channel and redirected the water into this new underground tunnel, which
carried the excess water from the Gihon spring to a new storage pool on the
southwest side of the City of David, an area that was inside a new city wall.

After capturing the Old City in the 1967 Six-Day War, the state of Israel
decided to rebuild the ruined Jewish Quarter. In advance of the renewal project,
the Israeli archaeologist Nahman Avigad conducted excavations in the Jewish
Quarter that brought to light remains of various periods. Because the Old City
is a densely built-up, living city, archaeologists rarely have an opportunity to
conduct excavations on such a large scale. The remains discovered by Avigad
included part of a new city wall built by Hezekiah on the eve of the Assyrian
invasion in 701 B.C.E. Avigad was able to date the wall to Hezekiah's time
because it was built on top of – and therefore put out of use – houses that were
occupied until the late eighth century B.C.E. The wall is so thick (more than
20 feet!) that Avigad called it "the **Broad Wall**." This wall encircled the western
hill and terminated at the southern tip of the City of David. By the late eighth
century the settlement in Jerusalem had spread onto the western hill, swelled

by refugees who poured into the city after the kingdom of Israel fell to the Assyrians. Hezekiah built the wall because the new suburb on the western hill was unfortified and therefore vulnerable to attack by the Assyrians.

Sidebar: The Alphabet

Script and language are different things. Script is what we might call an alphabet – the letters used to write a language. Different and even unrelated languages can be written in the same script, as is the case with English, French, Spanish, German, and Italian, for example. Conversely, the same language can be written in different scripts, as occurred, for example, when Mustafa Kemal Atatürk changed the alphabet used to write the Turkish language from Persian-Arabic to Latin (in 1928).

The earliest systems of writing (which were not technically alphabets) developed in the ancient Near East around 5000 years ago: **cuneiform** script in Mesopotamia and hieroglyphic script (**hieroglyphs**) in Egypt. The term *cuneiform* comes from the Latin word for wedge (*cuneus*), because wedge-shaped symbols were formed by making impressions in a raw (unbaked) clay tablet with the sharpened tip of a reed. Although cuneiform and hieroglyphic inscriptions have been discovered in Palestine, a native system of writing did not develop until the Late Bronze Age. This system of writing is called **proto-Canaanite** or **proto-Sinaitic** (because some of the first inscriptions were discovered in the Sinai desert). Proto-Canaanite is the earliest true alphabet. Unlike hieroglyphs (from which it adopted some symbols), in which each pictograph could represent up to three consonants, in Proto-Canaanite each symbol represents a single syllable. This reduced the number of symbols from hundreds to about two dozen, which could be combined as needed to form words. This innovation revolutionized reading and writing because it opened literacy to the masses, as a small number of symbols could be learned much more easily than hundreds of symbols (for which specially trained scribes who devoted a lifetime to learning were needed). Although literacy did not immediately become widespread as a result, it was the Canaanite invention of a true alphabet that eventually made mass literacy possible.

When the Israelites (and some of their neighbors, such as the Moabites) made the transition from a tribal society to monarchy, which is a type of government requiring record-keeping and official correspondence, they adopted a slightly modified version of the Canaanite-Phoenician alphabet. The early Hebrew alphabet is called **paleo-Hebrew**. The bullae from the "house of the bullae" in the City of David and the inscription from Hezekiah's Tunnel are written in paleo-Hebrew script. After 586 B.C.E. the Jews stopped using the paleo-Hebrew alphabet and adopted the Aramaic alphabet, which was used in the Persian Empire. Modern Hebrew is still written in **Aramaic script**.

Our alphabet is derived from the Phoenician alphabet by way of the Greeks. In the Late Bronze Age a script called **Linear B** was used in Mycenean Greece (Linear B is unrelated to the later Greek alphabet, although the language is Greek). After the collapse of the Mycenean kingdoms ca. 1200 B.C.E., writing disappeared from Greece for several centuries. In the eighth century B.C.E., when the Greeks began to write again, they adopted the Phoenician alphabet, with which they had become familiar through trade with the Phoenicians. The Greeks modified and adapted the Phoenician alphabet to suit their needs. For example, the first letter of the Phoenician (and Hebrew) alphabet is *aleph*, a silent letter. The Greeks did not need a silent letter so they converted it into the vowel "A" or *alpha* (Phoenician, Hebrew, and other **Semitic** languages are written without vowels). The second letter of the Phoenician alphabet – the letter *bet* (or *beth*) – became the Greek *beta* (hence the word "alphabet"). Later the Greek alphabet was adopted by the Romans to write Latin, which is the source of our alphabet.

In 1880 a boy from the nearby village discovered an inscription high up on the wall of Hezekiah's tunnel, close to the pool. After the inscription was removed from the tunnel it was taken to Istanbul (because Palestine was under Ottoman rule at the time), and it is now displayed in the Istanbul Archaeological Museum. The inscription is in biblical Hebrew and is written in paleo-Hebrew script (see the Sidebar). This remarkable document commemorates the completion of the tunnel – the moment when the two teams of men were so close they could hear each others' voices through the bedrock, and finally met:

> [A]nd this was the matter of the tunnel: While [the hewers wielded] the axe(s), each man towards his fellow, and while there were still three cubits to be he[wn, there was hear]d a man's voice calling to his fellow; for there was a fissure (?) in the rock on the right and [on the left]. And on the day it was tunneled through, the hewers struck [the rock], each man towards his fellow, axe against axe. And the water flowed from the spring towards the pool for one thousand and two hundred cubits. And a hundred cubits was the height of the rock above the head(s) of the hewers. (from Amihai Mazar, *Archaeology of the Land of the Bible*, p. 484)

The pool of Siloam at the outlet of Hezekiah's Tunnel has acquired its current appearance since the Byzantine period (fifth century C.E.), when a church was erected there. Recent excavations by Reich and Shukron have brought to light an enormous pool below it (to the south), at the southern tip of the Tyropoeon Valley and City of David. This pool dates to the late Second Temple period (first century B.C.E.–first century C.E.), roughly on the spot where the original pool of Siloam (at the outlet of the Siloam Channel) must have been located. Not

Sidebar: Charles Warren's Exploration of Hezekiah's Tunnel

In 1867, the British explorer Captain Charles Warren surveyed Hezekiah's Tunnel using a measuring tape, compass, notebook, and pencil. Nowadays a walk through the tunnel is a pleasant way to spend a half hour on a hot summer day, with the water usually rising no higher than hip level. However, conditions were different in the nineteenth century. First, because there were no flashlights, Warren and his companions (Sergeant Birtles and a local villager) had to use candles. Second, the floor of the tunnel was covered with a thick layer of crusty mud silt that reduced the height of the tunnel. Warren and his companions entered from the outlet end (the pool of Siloam), because the ceiling is higher there, which made access easier. Warren's visit was complicated by the fact that the water began rising soon after they entered the tunnel. The Gihon spring is a karstic spring, which means that the water gushes and abates intermittently (like a geyser). Finally, Warren and his companions conducted the survey in the month of December, when the water and air temperature are quite cold. They ended up spending four hours in the tunnel. The following is Warren's account of his visit, in his own words:

> In the month of December 1867, I made a thorough examination and survey of the passage leading from the Virgin's Fount [Gihon spring] to Siloam. We entered from the Siloam end, so as to have as much clean work as possible.
>
> For the first 350 feet it was plain sailing . . . At 450 feet the height of the passage was reduced to 3 feet 9 inches. . . . At 600 feet it is only 2 feet 6 inches high. . . .
>
> Our difficulties now commenced. Sergeant Birtles, with a Fellah (villager), went ahead, measuring with tape, while I followed with compass and field book. The bottom is a soft silt, with a calcerous crust at the top, strong enough to bear human weight, except in a few places, where it let us down with a flop. . . . The mud silt is from 15 inches to 18 inches deep.
>
> We were now crawling on all fours, and thought we were getting on very pleasantly, the water being only 4 inches deep, and we were not wet higher than our hips. Presently bits of cabbage-stalks came floating by, and we suddenly awoke to the fact that the waters were rising. The Virgin's Fount is used as a sort of scullery to the Silwan Village, the refuse thrown there being carried off down the passage each time the water rises. The rising of the waters had not been anticipated, as they had risen only two hours previous to our entrance.
>
> At 850 feet the height of the channel was reduced to 1 foot 10 inches, and here our troubles began. The water was running with great

violence, 1 foot in height, and we, crawling full length, were up to our necks in it.

I was particularly embarrassed: one hand necessarily wet and dirty, the other holding a pencil, compass, and field-book; the candle for the most part in my mouth. Another 50 feet brought us to a place where we had regularly to run the gauntlet of the waters. The passage being only 1 foot 4 inches high, we had just 4 inches breathing space, and had some difficulty in twisting our necks round properly. When observing, my mouth was under water.

At 900 feet we came upon two false cuttings, one on each side of the aqueduct. They go in for about 2 feet each. . . . Just here I involuntarily swallowed a portion of my lead pencil for a minute or two.

We were now going in a zigzag direction towards the northwest, and the height increased to 4 feet 6 inches, and at 1100 feet we were again crawling with a height of only 1 foot 10 inches.

We should probably have suffered more from the cold than we did, had not our risible faculties been excited by the sight of our Fellah in front plunging and puffing through the water like a young grampus. At 1150 feet the passage again averaged in height 2 feet to 2 feet 6 inches; at 1400 feet we heard the sound of water dripping. . . .

At 1450 feet we commenced turning to the east, and the passage attained a height of 6 feet; at 1658 feet we came upon our old friend, the passage leading to the Ophel Shaft [Warren's Shaft], and, after a further advance of 50 feet, to the Virgin's Fount. . . .

When we came out it was dark and we had to stand shivering for some minutes before our clothes were brought us; we were nearly 4 hours in the water.

only did this pool store excess water from the Gihon spring, but the distinctive arrangement of the steps surrounding it on all sides – with alternating deep and narrow treads – indicates that it was used as a ritual bath (*miqveh*) (see Chapter 6). The pool's size suggests that it served the masses of Jewish pilgrims who made their way up the Tyropoean Valley to the Temple Mount, by way of a paved street that Reich and Shukron have also uncovered. Reich and Shukron identify this as the pool of Siloam in the late Second Temple period, where the **Gospel** of John (9) says that Jesus healed a blind man.

Recommended Reading

Gösta W. Ahlström, *The History of Ancient Palestine* (Minneapolis: Fortress, 1994).
Dan Bahat, *The Illustrated Atlas of Jerusalem* (Jerusalem: Carta, 1990).
William G. Dever, *Who Were the Early Israelites and Where Did They Come From?* (Grand Rapids, MI: Eerdmans, 2003).

Avraham Faust, *Israel's Ethnogenesis, Settlement, Interaction, Expansion and Resistance* (London: Equinox, 2006).

Israel Finkelstein and Neil Asher Silberman, *The Bible Unearthed: Archaeology's New Vision of Ancient Israel and the Origin of Its Sacred Texts* (New York: Free Press, 2001).

Philip J. King and Lawrence E. Stager, *Life in Biblical Israel* (Louisville: Westminster John Knox, 2001).

Amihai Mazar, *Archaeology of the Land of the Bible, 10,000–586 B.C.E.* (New York: Doubleday, 1990).

Ronny Reich, *Excavating the City of David, Where Jerusalem's History Began* (Jerusalem: Israel Exploration Society, 2011).

⊚⊚ ⊚⊚ ⊚⊚ ⊚⊚

THREE

THE BABYLONIAN (586–539 B.C.E.) AND PERSIAN (539–332 B.C.E.) PERIODS

HISTORICAL BACKGROUND: GENERAL

By the waters of Babylon – there we sat down and there we wept when we remembered Zion. . . . How could we sing the Lord's song in a foreign land? If I forget you, O Jerusalem, let my right hand wither! Let my tongue cleave to the roof of my mouth, if I do not remember you, if I do not set Jerusalem above my highest joy. (Psalm 137:1, 4–6; NRSV)

Despite the despair expressed by the author of Psalm 137, the Judeans who were exiled to Babylonia in 586 B.C.E. not only adjusted to their new setting but also managed to preserve their religious identity under community leaders called elders. Some scholars believe that the institution of the synagogue originated during the Babylonian exile, providing a framework for the dissemination and study of God's laws. These laws are contained in the **Torah (Pentateuch** = the Five Books of Moses), which may have been edited in Babylonia together with the books of the Former Prophets (Joshua, Judges, Samuel, and Kings).

By the second half of the sixth century, Babylonia and the rest of the ancient Near East had come under the rule of the **Persian (Achaemenid)** Empire, which was based in the area of modern Iran. Persian rule extended as far as the western coast of Asia Minor (modern Turkey), which was inhabited by Greeks. In 499 B.C.E., with the encouragement and backing of Athens, the East Greeks rebelled against Persian rule (the Ionian revolt). After subduing the uprising, the Persians retaliated by invading mainland Greece, first in 490 B.C.E. and again in 480 B.C.E. Despite sustaining heavy losses, including 300 heroic Spartan troops at the pass of Thermopylae, and despite being hugely outnumbered, the Greeks managed to defeat the Persians and preserve their independence. Thanks to its leadership role during the Persian wars, Athens emerged as a political force at the head of an alliance of Greek city-states, which eventually became a de facto empire (the **Delian League**). The Athenian acropolis, which had been ravaged by the Persians, was rebuilt, its ruined temples replaced by iconic Classical monuments such as the **Parthenon** and the **Erectheum**. Athens witnessed a flourishing of the arts with rapid advances in architecture, sculpture, wall painting, vase painting, literature and drama, and philosophy.

A second major power bloc in Greece formed around Athens' rival, **Sparta**. In 431 B.C.E. a war erupted between these two city-states – the **Peloponnesian War** (after the Peloponnese, the southern part of mainland Greece). Although Sparta emerged nominally victorious thirty years later (404 B.C.E.), the war drained both city-states and their allies of their finest young men and valuable resources.

Winston Churchill once remarked, "History is written by the victors." Not only did the Greeks defeat the Persians (twice), but we also have only their side of the story, as reported by our main surviving source, the Greek historian **Thucydides**. Therefore, the Persians often are presented as villains – aggressors led by a despotic king who wrought havoc and sought to subjugate the freedom-loving Greeks. This point of view may be understandable from a Greek perspective, but it is biased and inaccurate. In fact, the Persian Empire was one of the most enlightened and tolerant powers of its time. Ancient powers often dispersed native elites to break up local power bases, replacing them with non-native populations brought from elsewhere, as the Assyrians and Babylonians did when they conquered Israel and Judah. Persian policy was just the opposite: the Persians repatriated displaced peoples, allowing them to return to their homelands and worship their native gods. Thus, in 539 B.C.E., the Persian king **Cyrus II** issued an edict granting the exiled Judeans permission to return to their homeland and rebuild the Jerusalem temple:

> In the first year of King Cyrus of Persia, in order that the word of the Lord by the mouth of Jeremiah might be accomplished, the Lord stirred up the spirit of King Cyrus of Persia so that he sent heralds throughout all his kingdom, and also in a written edict, declared: "Thus says King Cyrus of Persia: The Lord, the God of heaven, has given me all the kingdoms of the earth, and he has charged me to build him a house at Jerusalem in Judah. Any of those among you who are of his people – may their God be with them! – are now permitted to go up to Jerusalem in Judah, and rebuild the house of the Lord, the God of Israel – he is the God who is in Jerusalem." (**Ezra** 1:1–4; NRSV)

The author of the book of Ezra makes it appear as though the God of Israel was the agent responsible for Cyrus' actions. However, a Persian cuneiform

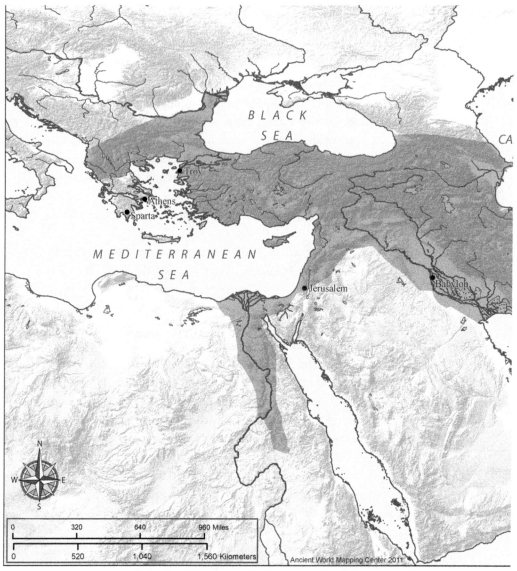

3.1 Map of the Persian Empire. Ancient World Mapping Center, University of North Carolina at Chapel Hill (www.unc.edu/awmc).

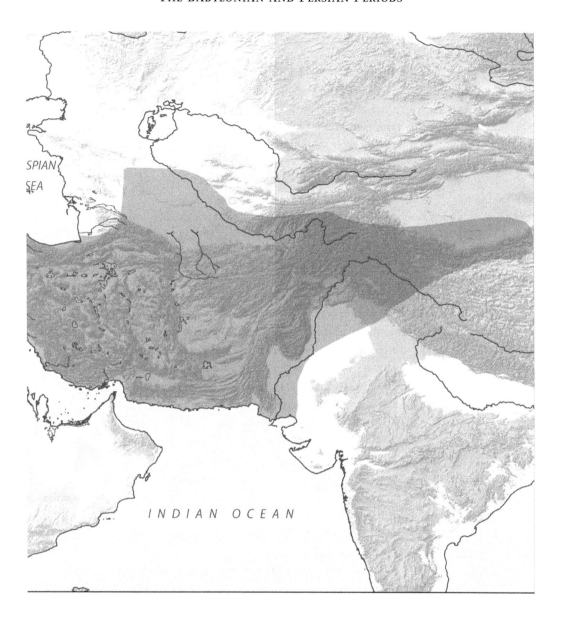

CASPIAN
SEA

INDIAN OCEAN

text called the Cyrus cylinder reveals the king's motives for rebuilding (other) temples:

> I am Cyrus, king of the world . . . from as far as the settlements on the other side of the Tigris, where their temples have long lain in ruin, I returned the gods who lived therein to their places and provided them with permanent temples. I gathered all their inhabitants and returned them to their homes. Daily, may all the gods whom I have brought back to their holy sites speak on my behalf for long life and plead my favor before Bel and Nebo.

As a result of this policy of toleration and repatriation, many of the peoples of the Persian Empire lived in peaceful coexistence for hundreds of years.

HISTORICAL BACKGROUND: PALESTINE

The Persian Empire was the largest ancient empire of its time. For the purposes of government and administration, the empire was divided into units, similar to the way the United States is divided into states, each of which is further subdivided into counties and townships. The largest administrative units of the Persian Empire were called satrapies, which were vast territories governed by **satraps**. Palestine belonged to a **satrapy** called *eber hanahar* (Aramaic *abar nahara*), Hebrew for "[the land] beyond the river," as this territory lay to the west of the Euphrates River – that is, beyond the river from the point of view of the Persians, to the east. Each satrapy was divided into smaller administrative units called *medinot* (singular **medinah**). Palestine included several *medinot*:

- Judea (Persian **Yahud**) was the core of the former kingdom of Judah, comprising the territory around Jerusalem.
- **Idumaea** was the southern part of the former kingdom of Judah. After 586 B.C.E., Edomites (the inhabitants of the kingdom of Edom to the southeast of the Dead Sea) settled in this region. Their descendants became known as Idumaeans, and the territory became known as Idumaea.
- Samaria was the core of the former kingdom of Israel, centered on the city of Samaria, its ancient capital.
- The area of the former kingdom of Ammon (centered on the ancient capital of **Rabbath-Ammon**, which is modern Amman in Jordan) was under the governorship of a Jewish (Judean) family called the **Tobiads**.
- The coastal plain of Palestine was placed under the rule of the Phoenician cities of Tyre and Sidon, which were granted autonomy by the Persian kings in exchange for their naval support against the Greeks. To prevent the Phoenicians from becoming too powerful, the Persians divided the coastal plain into strips, which were assigned alternately to Tyre and Sidon.

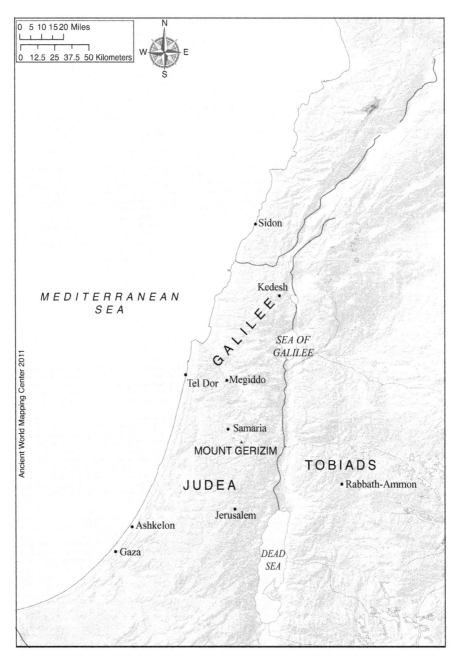

3.2   Map of Persian Palestine. Ancient World Mapping Center, University of North Carolina at Chapel Hill (www.unc.edu/awmc).

In the wake of Cyrus' edict, waves of Judean exiles returned from Babylonia to Judea and rebuilt the Jerusalem temple, which was consecrated in 516 B.C.E., marking the beginning of the Second Temple period. The Persian policy of religious freedom meant that Jewish law was the law of Judea. In other words, the inhabitants of Judea were not only free to worship the God of Israel as their national deity, but were also obligated to follow his laws (the Torah). Therefore, in 458 B.C.E., a priest and scribe named Ezra arrived in Jerusalem on behalf of the Persian king. His mission was to instruct the Judeans in the law and its proper observance. The Judean exiles returned from Babylonia in clans, as the Assyrian and Babylonian conquests had destroyed the tribal structure and bonds that had characterized Israelite and Judahite society. Whereas we refer to the religion of the twelve tribes before 586 B.C.E. as Israelite religion, Judaism is the religion of the returning Judean exiles, implemented under the guidance of Ezra.

As members of the elite, Ezra and the returning Judeans were concerned with the purity of bloodlines, as reflected in the genealogical lists in Ezra 8:1–14. This concern accounts for Ezra's prohibition against intermarriage, an innovation that became a lasting hallmark of Judaism (remember that even Solomon had numerous foreign wives). Many of the poorer people who remained in Judea after 586 B.C.E. had intermarried in the meantime. The impact of Ezra's implementation of this new prohibition is described vividly in the Hebrew Bible:

> Then all the people of Judah and Benjamin assembled at Jerusalem within the three days; it was the ninth month, on the twentieth day of the month. All the people sat in the open square before the house of God, trembling because of this matter and because of the heavy rain. Then Ezra the priest stood up and said to them, "You have trespassed and married foreign women, and so increased the guilt of Israel. Now make confession to the Lord the God of your ancestors, and do his will; separate yourselves from the peoples of the land and from the foreign wives." (Ezra 10:9–11; NRSV)

The new prohibition against intermarriage also affected the inhabitants of the *medinah* of Samaria, to the north of Judea, whose inhabitants claimed descent from the old Joseph tribes (Ephraim and Manasseh). Ezra's decree excluded this population, which had intermarried with peoples brought in by the Assyrians in the centuries following the fall of Israel in 722 B.C.E. Nonetheless, the inhabitants of Samaria viewed themselves as the true Israel and worshiped the God of Israel as their national deity. Excluded by the Judeans from the Jerusalem temple, the Samarians (later known as the Samaritans) eventually erected a temple to the God of Israel on their own sacred mountain, **Mount Gerizim** (discussed later). The Judeans considered the Samaritans schismatics, and despite (or perhaps because of) being closely related, they were bitter enemies.

Nehemiah served as governor of Yahud (Judea) from 445 to 424 B.C.E. He was a Judean who had attained high office in the Persian administration (as the cupbearer of the Persian king). Under Nehemiah's supervision Jerusalem's fortifications were rebuilt, a project that was opposed by the governors of the surrounding *medinot*:

> So we rebuilt the wall, and all the wall was joined together to half its height; for the people had a mind to work. But when Sanballat and Tobiah and the Arabs and the Ammonites and the Ashdodites heard that the repairing of the walls of Jerusalem was going forward and that the gaps were beginning to be closed, they were very angry, and all plotted together to come and fight against Jerusalem and to cause confusion in it. (Nehemiah 4:6–8; NRSV)

Nehemiah's foes included **Tobiah**, the governor of Ammon, and **Sanballat** I, the governor of Samaria. The latter's grandson, Sanballat III, was the governor of Samaria at the time of Alexander the Great's conquest (332 B.C.E.). Josephus reports that in exchange for his support against the Persian king, Alexander granted Sanballat III permission to build a temple to the God of Israel on Mount Gerizim, the sacred mountain of the Samaritans overlooking the biblical city of Shechem. Manasseh, the brother of the Jewish high priest Jaddua in Jerusalem, married Sanballat III's daughter Nikaso and became the high priest of the new Samaritan temple.

ARCHAEOLOGY

> Then I said to the king, "If it pleases the king, and if your servant has found favor with you, I ask that you send me to Judah, to the city of my ancestors' graves, so that I may rebuild it." (Nehemiah 2:5)

No identifiable remains of the second temple survive, which was much less impressive than Solomon's temple because of the limited resources of the returning exiles, some of whom wept when they compared it with its predecessor: "But many of the priests and Levites and heads of families, old people who has seen the first house [Solomon's temple] on its foundations, wept with a loud voice when they saw this house" (Ezra 3:12; NRSV). The book of Nehemiah indicates that the returning exiles rebuilt Jerusalem's fortifications by filling in the breaches that had been made in the walls at the time of the Babylonian conquest. However, along the eastern crest of the City of David they erected a new wall, higher up the slope than the Bronze Age and Iron Age walls. This is the wall that Macalister and Duncan uncovered and erroneously attributed to the Jebusites (with the addition of a Hasmonean period tower; see Chapter 2). During the Persian period, Jerusalem's settlement was limited to the City of David, including the temple on the Temple Mount but no occupation on the

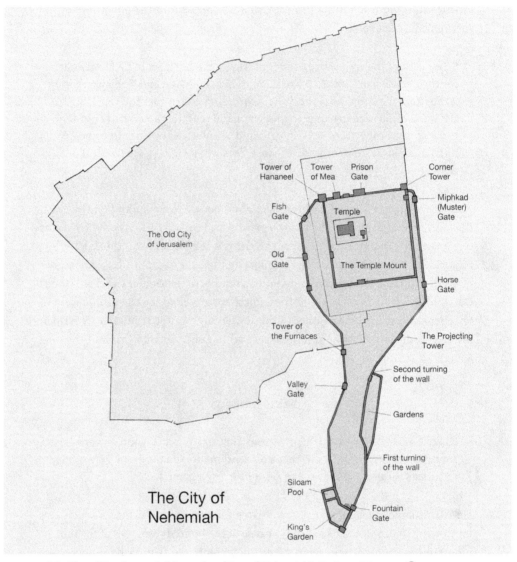

Tower of Hananeel

Tower of Mea

Prison Gate

Corner Tower

Miphkad (Muster) Gate

Fish Gate

Temple

The Old City of Jerusalem

Old Gate

The Temple Mount

Horse Gate

Tower of the Furnaces

The Projecting Tower

Second turning of the wall

Valley Gate

Gardens

First turning of the wall

Siloam Pool

The City of Nehemiah

Fountain Gate

King's Garden

3.3 Plan of Persian period Jerusalem (time of Nehemiah). By Leen Ritmeyer ©.

western hill, which lay outside the walls. The city's size suggests a small population, which is not surprising, as many Judean exiles chose to remain in Babylonia, forming a large and prosperous **Diaspora** community that flourished for centuries.

Excavations on Mount Gerizim have brought to light a fortified village and sacred enclosure that were established in the fifth century B.C.E. (a couple of centuries earlier than Josephus reports) and rebuilt in the early second century B.C.E. The top of the mountain was surrounded by a *temenos* wall (*temenos* is a Greek word denoting a sacred precinct). Finds from this enclosure include hundreds of inscriptions, many of which mention YHWH and sacrifices, and

3.4 Monumental staircase of the Samaritan temple on Mount Gerizim. Courtesy of Todd Bolen/BiblePlaces.com.

thousands of charred bones belonging to sacrificial sheep, goats, cows, and pigeons. Unfortunately, nothing survives of the temple building that originally stood inside the enclosure, which was destroyed by the Hasmonean king **John Hyrcanus I** in the late second century B.C.E. and obliterated when a church was constructed on that spot centuries later. A monumental staircase connected a fortified village on the mountain's west slope with the sacred enclosure at the top. The houses in the village were large and sturdily built of stone, with two stories of rooms arranged around a central courtyard. Pressing installations and storage facilities indicate that the village's main economic base was the cultivation of grapes and olives and the production of wine and oil.

Although Persian-period remains have been found at sites around Palestine, archaeologically this is one of the least-known periods in the country's long history. In part this is because many sites that had been occupied for centuries were abandoned after the Persian period. Because the Persian period occupation is the last (uppermost) stratum, it tends to be eroded, damaged, and less well preserved than earlier levels. For this reason, Persian pottery types are less well known than those of other periods. Persian pottery has also been difficult to identify because the types generally developed out of the local Iron Age tradition.

At many Persian period sites, a palace, fortress, and/or central administrative building were erected on the summit of the earlier tel. These buildings typically consisted of a room surrounding a central open courtyard, a layout

3.5 Houses at Tel Dor with pier and rubble construction.

that was introduced to Palestine during the Assyrian period. For example, the last phase of occupation at **Tell Jemmeh** in the northwest Negev dates to the Persian period, when a fortress and then a large building with storehouses were constructed in succession. Recent excavations at **Kedesh** in Upper Galilee have brought to light a monumental building with columned halls that was established on top of the south tel. The building was constructed in the Persian period and continued to function until the site's abandonment in the mid-second century B.C.E. Kedesh appears to have served as a regional administrative center under Persian rule. Although it is not clear whether this administrative center was independent or operated under the hegemony of Tyre (one of the autonomous Phoenician cities), Phoenician influence on the local material culture suggests a Phoenician presence at Kedesh.

At the Phoenician site of **Tel Dor** on the northern Palestinian coast, a residential quarter dating to the Persian period has been uncovered. On one hand, the quarter has a Greek type of layout called a **Hippodamian** town plan (see Chapter 4), reflecting Greek influence on this Phoenician coastal town. On the other hand, the walls of the houses are constructed in a typical Phoenician style, with **ashlar piers** alternating with stretches of rubble fill (perhaps a device intended to limit earthquake damage to sections of wall). This construction style, called a *telaio*, is known from Phoenician colonies in the west including Carthage, but so far has been found in the eastern Mediterranean only at Tel Dor.

There is extensive evidence of Persian period occupation at Ashkelon, one of the cities of the former Philistine pentapolis, including monumental ashlar buildings and warehouses. Among the Persian period remains is a huge dog cemetery, out of which more than 800 canine burials have been excavated. The dogs are male and female, of medium height and build, and include adults and puppies, with a high percentage of puppies (62 percent) that statistically resembles modern urban populations. Each dog was laid on its side in a shallow pit, with the tail around the hind legs. The dogs seem to have died of natural causes and there is no evidence of butchering. Although a number of ancient Mediterranean peoples venerated canines, the excavator believes that the dogs buried in the cemetery most likely were connected with a Phoenician healing cult.

Important evidence of everyday life at the end of the Persian period was discovered in a cave in **Wadi ed-Daliyeh**, north of Jericho. In 331 B.C.E., the population of Samaria revolted against the governor appointed by Alexander the Great. Approximately 300 men, women, and children from the city of Samaria took refuge in this cave, bringing their most valuable possessions. The refugees were discovered by Alexander's troops and suffocated to death when the soldiers lit a large fire at the cave's entrance. **Bedouins** found the victims' skeletons lying on mats inside the cave. The most important finds from the cave are fragments of papyri from personal documents that belonged to the refugees, along with clay bullae bearing names or motifs in various styles, including local, Persian, and Greek.

MATERIAL CULTURE

Pottery

During the Persian period, fine table wares were produced in Greece and exported around the Mediterranean. Athenian (Attic) table wares dominated the markets in the fifth century, characterized especially by red-figure ware, so called because figures were reserved in the natural red color of the clay and set against a shiny black "glazed" background. The fine table wares were widely exported because of their value and were used for dining, similarly to expensive modern china dishes. Many of these table wares are wine sets that include drinking cups and bowls, **kraters** (large bowls) for mixing wine and water (following the Greek custom), and jugs for pouring wine. In addition, large numbers of Greek **amphoras** have been discovered at Persian sites in Palestine. Amphoras are large jars for transporting wine and other liquids. They were equipped with two handles and a pointed base so they could be loaded easily onto ships, using one hand to grasp the handle and the other hand to lift the base. Not surprisingly, the largest quantities of Greek pottery – both fine wares and amphoras – have been found at coastal sites such as Tel Dor and Ashkelon.

3.6 Greek black-glazed and red- and black-figured pottery found in Israel, including a krater (rear center) and an early closed oil lamp (front left). Courtesy of Zev Radovan/BibleLandPictures.com.

The concentrations of Greek pottery at these sites suggest that small numbers of Greeks might have settled among the native population, and at the very least it indicates that some locals hosted Greek-style symposia (drinking parties).

The local pottery continues the Iron Age tradition and tends to be plain (undecorated). For example, open oil lamps with a thick stump base and wide ledge rim are similar to the characteristic Iron Age type. On the other hand, some new types and features were introduced, including local (undecorated) imitations of Greek imports. One hallmark of the Persian period is mortaria (singular: **mortarium**) – large, shallow, thick-walled bowls with a ring base made of coarse, light yellow ware. Scientific analyses and signs of abrasion indicate that the mortaria were used for grinding. Also common in Persian period assemblages is a distinctive type of amphora of light brown or light red clay, with two high, vertical ("basket") handles and an elongated, pointed base. An inscription on a basket-handled amphora from Kadesh Barnea (in the northern Sinai) suggests that oil was one of the products transported in these jars.

Coins

Coins first appeared at sites in Palestine in this period. Coinage was invented in western Asia Minor, either by the East Greeks or by indigenous peoples such

3.7 Amphoras. Courtesy of Zev Radovan/BibleLandPictures.com.

as the Lydians. Scholars disagree about exactly when coinage was invented in the seventh century, but there is no doubt that it existed by ca. 600 B.C.E. Whoever was responsible for inventing coinage drew on two existing traditions: (1) small lumps of precious metals called "dumps" had long circulated in trade and commerce; and (2) seals carved with inscriptions or designs had been used for millennia to make impressions in raw lumps of clay, sealing documents or the contents of containers. Coins differ from dumps in being stamped with the seal of a minting authority, which guaranteed the purity and weight of the lump of precious metal.

The earliest coins are often made of **electrum**, a natural alloy of gold and silver common in western Asia Minor. They are stamped on the obverse with the symbol of the minting authority, and they have cuttings on the reverse to show

3.8   Electrum coin. Courtesy of Zev Radovan/BibleLandPictures.com.

that the metal was pure all the way through, not just used as a coating. Soon after the invention of coins, it became common practice to stamp the reverse with a design rather than cuttings. Eventually ridges were added around the edges of some coins to track wear and loss of metal content (weight).

Originally the value of a coin was equal to the value of its weight in precious metal. This is reflected in the names given to some coin denominations, such as the ancient Jewish sheqel or (more recently) the British pound. The right to mint coins has always been a prerogative of the central governing authority, although in antiquity rulers sometimes allowed individuals, cities, or provinces to mint their own coins – usually small, inexpensive denominations made of bronze or copper rather than precious metals. Even today, only the federal government, not individual states, can mint coins within the United States.

Using coins in trade and commerce eliminated the need to weigh metals for the purposes of payment, as coins were minted in standard weights that were guaranteed by the governing authority. Nevertheless, coin circulation remained limited for a long time, and even the most advanced ancient civilizations were never fully monetized.

The earliest coin found in Palestine so far is a Greek coin ca. 570 B.C.E. from the Aegean island of Kos, which was found in a late Iron Age tomb at **Ketef Hinnom** (see Chapter 11). By the fifth century B.C.E., various kingdoms and city-states around the eastern Mediterranean minted their own coinage. The coins of Athens circulated widely because they were made of high-quality silver from the mines at Laurion in **Attica**. Athenian coins are stamped on the obverse with the head of Athena in profile, and on the reverse with an owl and olive branch (both attributes of Athena) and the inscription "Athe[nae]." The coins

3.9 Coin of Yahud. Courtesy of Zev Radovan/
BibleLandPictures.com.

of Athens were so popular that other cities, including the coastal Phoenician
cities and the former Philistine cities of Gaza, Ashkelon, and Ashdod, minted
imitations.

In the fourth century numerous cities and districts around Palestine minted
their own low-denomination silver coins, which bear a wide variety of motifs,
including heads of deities, figures of animals and mythological creatures, ships,
and buildings. These apparently are seals reflecting the authority of different
officials responsible for minting. The coins of Yahud have the same diversity
of motifs but typically include an eagle and a lily flower (a symbol that the
state of Israel adopted for its modern sheqel coins). The inscriptions on some of
the Yahud coins – which name individuals bearing the title "priest" (Hebrew
kohen) – suggest that there was an active mint associated with the Jerusalem
temple and its priests. One silver coin connected with Yahud is exceptional
because of its large size and weight and the motifs on it. The obverse shows
a bearded male wearing a Corinthian helmet, and on the reverse is a bearded
male seated in a winged chariot and holding a falcon in his outstretched hand,
with the legend *yhd* (Yahud) above. Some scholars believe that this coin was
minted by one of the satraps of the fourth century and was used to pay Judean
mercenaries in the Persian army. There has been speculation about whether the
seated figure, which is clearly a deity, might be a depiction of the God of Israel.
Interestingly, one of the coins minted in Samaria in the fourth century depicts
an enthroned god, holding a flower, who is identified by an inscription as Zeus –
perhaps the God of Israel worshiped by the Samarians on Mount Gerizim.

Recommended Reading

Joseph Blenkinsopp, *Judaism, The First Phase: The Place of Ezra and Nehemiah in the
Origins of Judaism* (Grand Rapids, MI: Eerdmans, 2009).

Diana Edelman, *The Origins of the "Second" Temple, Persian Imperial Policy and the Rebuilding of Jerusalem* (London: Equinox, 2005).

Jill Middlemas, *The Templeless Age: An Introduction to the History, Literature, and Theology of the "Exile"* (Louisville, KY: Westminster John Knox, 2007).

Ephraim Stern, *Archaeology of the Land of the Bible, Volume II: The Assyrian, Babylonian, and Persian Periods (732–332 B.C.E.)* (New York: Doubleday, 2001).

⚛ ⚛ ⚛ ⚛ ⚛

FOUR

THE EARLY HELLENISTIC PERIOD
(332–167 B.C.E.)

HISTORICAL BACKGROUND: GENERAL

After the end of the Peloponnesian War in 404 B.C.E., Greece was fragmented politically, with no major powers or power blocs. This situation changed in the middle of the fourth century with the rise of **Macedon**. Macedon was a tribal kingdom on the northeast periphery of the Greek world ruled by **Philip II**, a warrior-king. The Greeks considered the Macedonians semi-barbarians – that is, not fully Greek. The word barbarian derives from "bar-bar-bar," which was how the Greeks described the sound of other languages. In 338 B.C.E., Philip II defeated a coalition of Greek city-states at the battle of Chaeronea and united Greece under Macedonian rule. Philip II's preparations to invade the Persian Empire were cut short, however, when he was assassinated in 336 B.C.E.

Philip II was succeeded to the Macedonian throne by his 18-year-old son, Alexander. Two years later (334 B.C.E.), Alexander launched an invasion of the Persian Empire, crossing the Hellespont and landing on Persian soil in the area of Troy. From there, Alexander marched eastward with his troops. The Persian king **Darius III** led his army against the invaders; over the next four years, he fought a series of battles against Alexander. Alexander was victorious in all the battles, until finally, after the last battle (at Gaugamela in 331 B.C.E.), Darius was murdered by his own men, paving the way for Alexander to become ruler of the Persian Empire. Alexander continued to march eastward with his army, conquering lands that had not been subject to the Persians, through Bactria and Sogdiana (modern Afganistan, Uzbekistan, and Tajikistan), into southern Russia, and across the Indus River Valley into India. Alexander apparently planned to invade Arabia, but his Macedonian troops refused to go any farther, putting an end to future expansion and setting the limits of his empire.

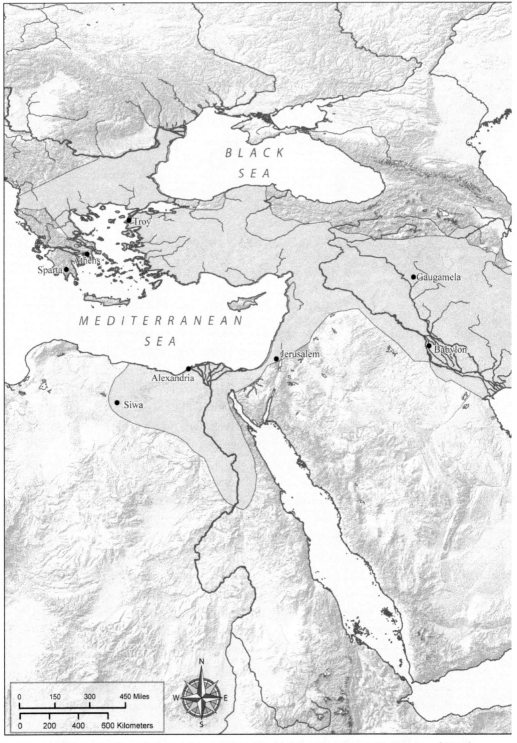

4.1 Map of Alexander's Empire. Ancient World Mapping Center, University of North Carolina at Chapel Hill (www.unc.edu/awmc).

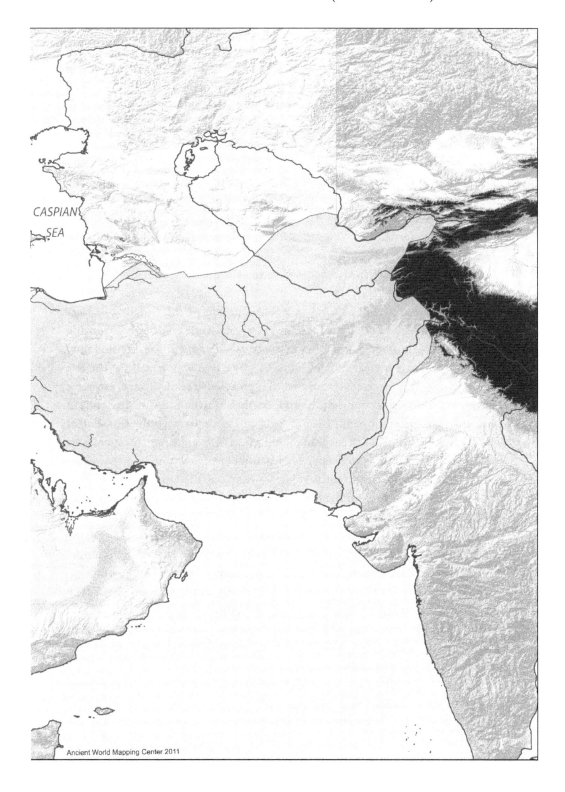

CASPIAN
SEA

Ancient World Mapping Center 2011

In 332 B.C.E., in the midst of his campaign, Alexander detoured south from Asia Minor and Syria to Egypt, bringing Palestine under his rule. Alexander was eager to take the land of the pharaohs, which was rich in gold and wheat. While in Egypt, Alexander founded a new city on the coast, which he named after himself: Alexandria. Alexander also visited an oracular shrine dedicated to **Zeus Ammon** at the remote desert oasis of **Siwa**, where the priests reportedly greeted him as a god, a concept alien to the Greeks (discussed later).

Alexander never returned to Greece, and instead set up court in **Babylon**, where he died of a fever in 323 B.C.E. Alexander's conquests had a lasting impact that changed the face of the ancient Near East for centuries. We refer to the three centuries following Alexander's conquests as **Hellenistic** ("Greek-like") because, for the first time, Greek culture was introduced directly – by Greeks – into the lands of the ancient Near East, which previously had been under Persian rule. Hellenistic comes from the word *Hellas*, which is Greek for "Greece" (similarly, *Hellenic* is an adjective that means "Greek" – for example, Hellenic culture = Greek culture). Alexander promoted the mingling of Near Eastern and Greek culture by setting up an Oriental-style court in Babylon and encouraging his Macedonian soldiers to marry native women. The intermingling of Greek and ancient Near Eastern cultures was a two-way street. On the one hand, Alexander's successors promoted the spread of Greek language, customs, religion, and styles of architecture and art through the lands of the ancient Near East. On the other hand, Near Eastern culture influenced the Greeks. For example, unlike previous Greek leaders and rulers, Alexander and his successors were worshiped or venerated as gods or godlike beings, a tradition that had a long history in the ancient Near East (as, for example, the Egyptian pharaohs).

Alexander's empire disintegrated immediately upon his death, as a 20-year-long war erupted over the succession to the throne. Eventually, Alexander's three wives and his offspring were killed and his empire was divided up among his generals. Two of Alexander's generals seized the lion's share of the empire. **Seleucus** took Asia Minor, Syria, and Mesopotamia, establishing a kingdom ruled by his successors (the **Seleucids**). **Ptolemy** established a kingdom in Egypt that was ruled by his successors (the **Ptolemies**). The Ptolemies and Seleucids fought over control of Palestine, which lay between their kingdoms. For most of the third century B.C.E. Palestine was under Ptolemaic rule; in the second century, it was under Seleucid rule.

Because the Ptolemies and Seleucids were not related to Alexander, they were concerned about establishing their legitimacy as his successors. They therefore imitated Alexander, in an attempt to make themselves appear like him in the eyes of their subjects. For example, these rulers had themselves depicted as physically resembling Alexander (in statues, in portrait busts, and on coins), with a wavy leonine mane of hair or wearing a lion skin cape – an attribute of the hero **Heracles (Hercules)**, which alluded to divine status – and with eyes directed up toward the gods. In antiquity, few people ever saw the ruler and therefore were unfamiliar with his appearance. Because coins circulated widely, they were used by rulers as vehicles of mass media to broadcast messages. The only image of the king that most people ever saw was the one on coins.

Alexander's successors also followed his example by establishing new cities around their kingdoms. For example, in the third century b.c.e., the Palestinian coastal city of **Akko** (modern **Acre**) was refounded as Ptolemais, and Rabbath-Ammon, the ancient capital of the Ammonites (modern Amman in Jordan), was renamed Philadelphia (in honor of Ptolemy II Philadelphos). Many of these cities were not established *de novo* (from scratch), but rather were towns or villages that were rebuilt as Greek cities by the king and renamed – usually after themselves, following Alexander's precedent in founding Alexandria. Greek cities (s. *polis*; pl. *poleis*) were awarded certain privileges and benefits. *Poleis* had a Greek style of government (such as a city council [*boule*]) and Greek institutions (such as theaters for the performance of Greek plays, gymnasia for the education of youth in the Greek manner, and temples for the worship of Greek gods), and were granted other advantages, such as tax benefits and the opportunity to send athletes to compete in international games. Alexander's successors used the dissemination of Greek culture as a means of unifying the diverse populations in their kingdoms. By establishing *poleis*, the Hellenistic kings also won the loyalty of the residents, who benefited from a rise in their standard of living.

Historical Background: Palestine

Alexander's conquest had little immediate impact on the population of Palestine. Most of the inhabitants would have hardly noticed Alexander's replacement of Persian officials and administrators with his own men. However, in later centuries, after Alexander's fame increased, traditions developed as native populations sought to establish a connection to this legendary figure. For example, according to the first-century c.e. Jewish historian Josephus, Alexander took a detour inland to Jerusalem on his way to Egypt, to pay homage to the God of Israel and the high priest Jaddua (*Antiquities* 11: 325–31). This story was fabricated to show that even Alexander the Great acknowledged the omnipotence of the God of Israel.

In the book of Daniel (8:1–21), the author foretells Alexander's conquests, using a secret language in which animals denote humans:

> In the third year of the reign of King Belshazzar a vision appeared to me, Daniel. . . . I looked up and saw a ram standing beside the river. It

had two horns. . . . I saw the ram charging westward and northward and southward. All beasts were powerless to withstand it, and no one could rescue from its power; it did as it pleased and became strong. As I was watching, a male goat appeared from the west, coming across the face of the whole earth without touching the ground. The goat had a horn between its eyes. It came toward the ram with the two horns that I had seen standing beside the river, and it ran at it with savage force. . . . The ram did not have the power to withstand it; it threw the ram down to the ground and trampled upon it, and there was no one who could rescue the ram from its power. . . . He [Gabriel] said, "Listen, and I will tell you what will take place later in the period of wrath; for it refers to the appointed time of the end. As for the ram that you saw with the two horns, these are the kings of Media and Persia. The male goat is the king of Greece [Alexander]." (NRSV)

The book of **Daniel** is an **apocalyptic** work – that is, a work that predicts the downfall of this world and a coming time of salvation – and it is pseudepigraphic, which means that Daniel is not the author's real name (his true identity is unknown). Although the angel Gabriel supposedly reveals that one day Alexander will defeat the Persian king, the book of Daniel was composed around 167–164 B.C.E. (the time of the Maccabean revolt), which means that it postdates Alexander's conquests by a century and a half!

Under the Ptolemies, Jerusalem and Judea were part of the province of Syria. This province (and others) included different kinds of administrative units, which were governed in different ways. For example, there were Greek cities (*poleis*), such as Akko/Acre (Ptolemais) and Gaza; Greek colonies, such as Samaria, **Beth-Shean (Scythopolis)**, and Amman (ancient Rabbath-Ammon/Philadelphia); and military colonies, such as the district of Ammon (governed by the Tobiads). Judea (with Jerusalem) was an autonomous unit governed by the Gerousia, a council of priests and elders led by the high priest. This administrative structure was retained even after the Seleucid king Antiochus III conquered Palestine in 198 B.C.E. The Judeans were classified as an *ethnos* – that is, a tribal nation in possession of its own territory. According to this definition, a Jew (Greek *Ioudaios*) was a person of Judean parentage, whose place of origin legally was Judea, and who was obligated to worship the Judean national deity – the God of Israel. Antiochus III proclaimed that "all members of this *ethnos* shall be governed in accordance with their ancestral laws." This means that the Torah had the status of royal law. In other words, the Ptolemies and Seleucids followed and preserved the policy that had been set by the Persians and implemented by Ezra, according to which Jewish law was the law of the land.

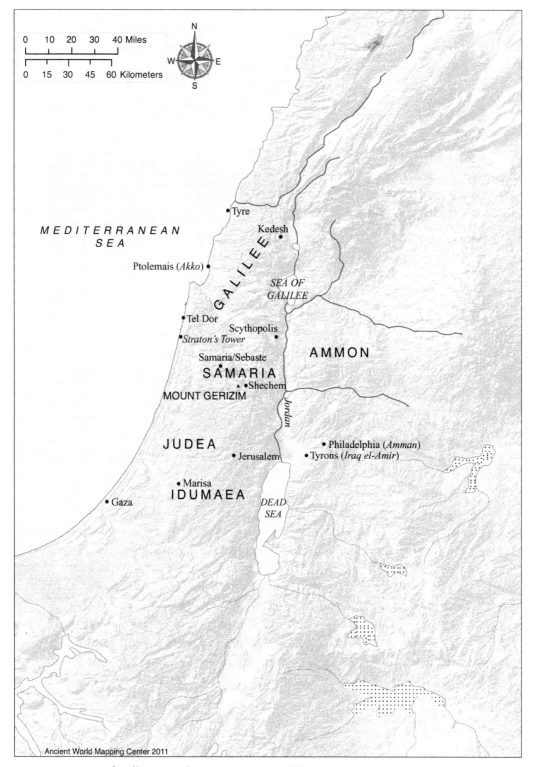

4.2 Map of Hellenistic Palestine. Ancient World Mapping Center, University of North Carolina at Chapel Hill (www.unc.edu/awmc).

4.3 Round tower at Samaria.

ARCHAEOLOGY: SITES

Samaria and Shechem

After the Samaritan revolt (see Chapter 3), Alexander banished the Samaritans from the city of Samaria – the ancient capital of the northern kingdom of Israel – and settled Macedonian veterans there. The Samaritans settled in Shechem, an ancient biblical town at the foot of their holy mountain, Mount Gerizim. The Macedonian veterans reoccupied the Israelite citadel at Samaria, adding round towers to its ancient circuit wall. The towers are distinguished by the style of **masonry** – that is, the way the stones are cut and laid. The faces of the stones are roughly smoothed, and all the stones are laid as headers (meaning that the short end faces out, in contrast to stretchers, in which the long side faces out).

Round towers are a characteristic feature of Hellenistic fortifications. They became common in the Hellenistic period in response to the introduction of a new type of offensive weapon: *ballistas*, which were torsion machines that threw large stone projectiles (cannon shot). Square towers were vunerable to ballistas because the stones could damage or break the corners. However, not all round towers are Hellenistic (some are later), and square towers continued to be built and used for centuries.

Straton's Tower

The dating of round towers figures prominently in attempts to identify archaeological remains of **Straton's Tower** (later rebuilt by Herod the Great and

4.4 Round tower at Caesarea.

renamed **Caesarea Maritima**). Straton's Tower was a small town on the Palestinian coast, located south of the modern city of Haifa. The town's name refers to the Phoenician king (Straton or Strato), who founded it in the fourth century B.C.E., when the Palestinian coast was under the rule of Tyre and Sidon. Although many different archaeological expeditions have worked at Caesarea since the establishment of the state of Israel in 1948, remains associated with Straton's Tower have proven elusive. Apparently, when Herod rebuilt the town as Caesarea, most of the earlier remains were obliterated.

The town's name suggests that a tower was a prominent feature. Therefore, attempts to identify Hellenistic period remains have focused on a round tower that is incorporated into the (later) Herodian city wall on the north side of Caesarea. The fact that the tower is round suggests an early date to some archaeologists. However, unlike at Samaria, the round tower at Caesarea is built of stones laid as both headers and stretchers. Furthermore, unlike at Samaria, at Caesarea the faces of the stones have **drafted margins** (that is, the four edges of the stone are smooth) and rough, projecting center panels (called "**bosses**"). This masonry style is characteristic of the late second and first centuries B.C.E. Therefore, most archaeologists date the round tower at Caesarea either to the time of Herod the Great or to the late Hellenistic period (ca. 100 B.C.E.).

Jerusalem

During the early Hellenistic period, Jerusalem continued to be a relatively small settlement limited to the City of David and the Temple Mount. Not

4.5 The "seam" at the southern end of the east wall of the Temple Mount, showing the earlier wall on the right and the Herodian extension on the left.

long before the outbreak of the Maccabean revolt (in 167 B.C.E.) the Seleucid king **Antiochus IV Epiphanes** erected a fortress in Jerusalem called the **Akra** (a Greek word meaning "high point"). 1 Maccabees (an apocryphal work) and Josephus (*Antiquities* 12.252) describe the Akra as a strongly fortified citadel garrisoned by Gentile soldiers. According to Josephus, the Akra overlooked the temple, and 1 Maccabees 14:36 suggests that it was located close to the temple, which the Gentiles defiled with their presence. In 141 B.C.E. **Simon**, the youngest brother of **Judah Maccabee**, captured the Akra and razed it to the ground. Where was the Akra located, and do any identifiable remains survive?

Perhaps the most logical place to seek the Akra is at the northwest corner of the Temple Mount, which is a natural high point where two later fortresses (the **Baris** and the **Antonia**) were built. However, there is no evidence that the Akra was located at this spot. Therefore, other locations around Jerusalem have been proposed, including the City of David and the western hill. The Israeli archaeologist Yoram Tsafrir suggested that the Akra was at the southeast corner of the Temple Mount. This location is attractive because of its proximity to the temple but is problematic because the ground slopes down to the Kidron Valley instead of dominating the Temple Mount from above.

Tsafrir's suggestion is based on the presence of a "seam" or "straight joint" in the east wall of the Temple Mount, close to the south corner. The wall on the south side of the "seam" clearly represents Herod the Great's extension

4.6 The Qasr el-Abd at Iraq el-Amir.

of the Temple Mount. The Herodian extension is built up against an earlier, pre-existing stretch of wall. This earlier stretch of wall is characterized by stones laid in alternating courses of headers and stretchers, which have smooth drafted margins and a roughly flattened but protruding boss. Tsafrir identifies this stretch of wall as the foundations of the Akra. However, it is equally possible that this is part of the pre-Herodian wall surrounding the Temple Mount. For example, Ecclesiasticus (the Wisdom of Ben Sira) (a work included in the Catholic canon of sacred scripture but not in the Hebrew or Protestant Bibles), which was written ca. 190–180 B.C.E., mentions repairs on the temple including the construction (or reconstruction) of a "high retaining wall of the temple precinct" (50:1–3).

IRAQ EL-AMIR

In the Persian period, the *medinah* of Ammon, which had a mixed population, was governed by a Judean named Tobiah and his descendants (the Tobiads). In the early Hellenistic period, the ancient city of Rabbath-Ammon (modern Amman) was refounded as a Greek polis named Philadelphia, and was given autonomy from Tobiad rule. The Tobiads therefore established a new capital, located approximately halfway between Jericho and Amman. The new Tobiad capital – ancient **Tyros** (modern name: **Iraq el-Amir**) – is referred to in our ancient sources as the "**Birtha** [stronghold] **of the Ammonites**." Josephus describes the buildings constructed at Tyros by a Tobiad named **Hyrcanus**, which incorporated extensive gardens watered by perennial

fresh-water springs. Some of the caves in the surrounding cliffs were modified for use as living and sleeping quarters. Josephus' description includes a
reference to a large building that dominated the complex, which he calls the
baris: "He [Hyrcanus] also erected a *baris*, and built it entirely of white stone to
the very roof, and had animals of a prodigious magnitude engraven upon it. He
also drew round it a great and deep canal of water" (*Antiquities* 12.4.11).

Josephus' *baris* is identified with the remains of a monumental building
today called the **Qasr el-Abd** (an Arabic name meaning "fortress of the slave").
As Hyrcanus committed suicide when Antiochus IV Epiphanes became king
(175 B.C.E.), this building is dated securely to the first quarter of the second
century B.C.E. The Qasr el-Abd sits in the middle of a lush valley surrounded
by cliffs. The building is preserved to its original height of two stories as a result
of its reuse as a church in the Byzantine period. The walls are constructed of
enormous blocks of stone with drafted margins and flattened but protruding
bosses. There are porches with Corinthian columns at the front and back, and
windows are still preserved at the first- and second-story levels. Part of a frieze
of lions and/or leopards carved in relief encircles the base of the second story
level, corresponding with Josephus' reference to "engraved" animals. On either
side of the building, at ground level, two leopards are carved in relief from
mottled stone that was chosen because it resembles the felines' spotted skin.
The leopards have spouts in their mouths, indicating that they were fountains.

Although scholars agree that the Qasr el-Abd should be identified with the
baris described by Josephus, the building's original function is debated. Some
scholars have suggested that it was a fortress because of the term *baris* (which
has that meaning in Greek), and because there are towers at the four corners of
the building. However, the porch entrances are unfortified, and the decoration
is not typical of a fortress. Other scholars identify this building as a temple on
the basis of similarities with a type of ancient temple in Syria-Palestine that
has corner towers. If this is correct, the Qasr el-Abd would represent the only
surviving example of an ancient Jewish temple (that is, a temple built by a Jew),
as we have no remains of the Jerusalem temple(s) or the ancient Jewish temples
at Elephantine and Leontopolis in Egypt (see Sidebar). The possibility that the
Qasr el-Abd is a temple is exciting because it might shed light on the appearance
of the Second Temple in Jerusalem. It would also be important for indicating
the use of Greek architectural styles and figured (animal) decoration in a Jewish
temple building.

Recently, however, the Israeli archaeologist Ehud Netzer suggested that the
Qasr el-Abd was a pleasure palace. He pointed out that the building sat on an
island surrounded by an artificial lake that was fed by springs (and remember
the spouted leopard fountains?). According to Netzer, the second story level
was a dining room and reception hall, with the windows allowing for cool
breezes and a view of the lake. He also noted the richly carved decoration on

4.7 Leopard with spouted mouth in the Qasr el-Abd at Iraq el-Amir.

the building would be appropriate for a palace. So far, the identification of the Qasr el-Abd as a pleasure palace is the most convincing and makes the most sense.

MARISA

After 586 B.C.E., Edomites settled in the southern part of the former kingdom of Judah (the northern Negev). Their descendants were known as Idumaeans, and the area was called Idumaea. During the early Hellenistic period, **Marisa** (Hebrew: **Maresha**) became the major city in this region, with a mixed population of Idumaeans and Hellenized Sidonians (Phoencians from Sidon). Marisa is located about four miles (6.5 kilometers) northeast of Lachish, which was the most important town in southern Judah before 586 B.C.E. Marisa's modern name in Arabic – **Tell Sandahannah** – derives from a nearby Crusader church that was dedicated to St. Anne (Santa Anna).

Marisa is a tel with remains dating to before 586 B.C.E., which are covered by the early Hellenistic town. In 1900, Frederick Jones Bliss and Robert Alexander Stewart Macalister conducted excavations at Marisa on behalf of the Palestine Exploration Fund. The Ottoman authorities granted them an excavation permit on the condition that they leave the site looking as they found it. Bliss and Macalister circumvented this restriction in a clever way. They began excavating the top of the tel, and when the tops of walls appeared, they piled the dirt on one of the walls of each room and excavated the rest. At the end of the excavation, Bliss and Macalister backfilled the site with the dirt. Therefore, there is nothing to see on top of Marisa today, and there is no point in re-excavating the buildings because Bliss and Macalister removed the finds. Bliss and Macalister's records and plans are our only source of information about the appearance of the early Hellenistic town on top of the tel. In the 1980s, the Israeli archaeologist Amos Kloner excavated part of the fortification wall and towers of Marisa, as well as **extramural** (suburban) houses on the slopes of the tel.

Bliss and Macalister's excavations brought to light a settlement with many Greek features. The town was surrounded by a fortification wall with square (not round) towers. The area enclosed within the wall was roughly rectangular, and was divided into large blocks (***insulae***) by a grid of north-south and east-west streets. Many of the blocks were occupied by spacious residences. Two large, open spaces in the town's center were an **agora**, a Greek word meaning marketplace (analogous to a Roman **forum** [pl. fora]). An agora was a large, open-air paved area where vendors could sell their wares. Agoras typically were surrounded by public buildings, such as temples, meeting halls, and theaters. Another large, open space was located on the eastern side of Marisa. In its center was a **tripartite** temple (a temple with three rooms), suggesting that it was dedicated to a triad of gods that presumably included **Qos**, the national deity of the Edomites and Idumaeans. The finds from Bliss and Macalister's excavations include several dozen fragments of stone tablets inscribed in Greek with spells and incantations, and 16 small "voodoo" type human figurines bound with fetters made of lead or iron, attesting to magical practices among the town's population.

Underlying Marisa's layout are some basic principles of urban planning: a roughly rectangular city with a grid of north-south and east-west streets creating blocks, and the idea of zoning – that is, the separation of residential, industrial, commercial, and religious quarters and activities. These principles of urban planning were applied to many cities around the Hellenistic world, and especially to newly established *poleis*. The ancient Greeks credited the invention of urban planning to an architect named **Hippodamus**, a native of Miletos in Asia Minor; therefore, this type of layout is called a Hippodamian town plan. Hippodamus lived around 500 B.C.E. and designed the layout of several cities, including the port of Athens (Piraeus). However, we do not know whether Hippodamus invented these principles of urban planning or just employed some of them in his work.

Marisa was a prosperous town with a diverse economic base, set among fertile, gently rolling hills. The extramural houses uncovered by Kloner are large and sturdily built of the local chalky stone cut into the shape of bricks. The houses are two stories high with rooms arranged around a central courtyard. A stairway provided access to one or more caves below each house. The slopes of Marisa are honeycombed with manmade caves that were hewn into the soft chalk. The caves were quarries for building stone, which, once hewn, were used for

4.8 Plan of Hellenistic Marisa. From F. J. Bliss and R. A. S. Macalister, *Excavations in Palestine during the Years 1898–1899* (London: Palestine Exploration Fund, 1902), Pl. 16. By permission of the Palestine Exploration Fund.

various purposes. Because the caves remain cool and moist even in the summer, many were used as cellars beneath houses for storing food or as cisterns for water. Other caves were used for agricultural or industrial purposes. For example, some caves contained olive presses. Oil was extracted from the olives through a two-step process that involved crushing and pressing. First, the olives were placed in a hollowed-out basin on top of a large, round stone. Another circular stone, placed on its side, was rolled around and around, over the olives, to crush them. A horizontal wooden pole attached the rolling stone to a vertical wooden pole stuck into the center of the bottom circular stone. The horizontal wooden pole

4.9   Olive press at Marisa (crushing stone). Courtesy of Zev Radovan/BibleLandPictures.com.

protruded from the rolling stone, providing a handle for people or animals to push the rolling stone around the basin. The crushed olives were collected into baskets. The baskets were piled one on top of another and pressed by a large wooden beam that was fixed to a wall at one end, and at the other end was weighted down by a series of large stones dangling by ropes wrapped around the beam. The oil that flowed out of the pressed olives was collected in a basin at the base of the baskets. Some of the caves with olive presses at Marisa have a small altar carved into the wall, presumably to hold offerings in thanks for a good harvest or to request a good harvest. It is estimated that the twenty olive presses discovered at Marisa produced up to 270 tons of oil per year, far exceeding the needs of the local population and indicating that the export of olive oil was one of the economic mainstays of this town.

4.10 Olive press at Marisa (pressing installations). Courtesy of Zev Radovan/BibleLand Pictures.com.

Some of the caves at Marisa contain columbaria (sing. **columbarium**), meaning that the walls are lined with rows of small niches. Columbaria are common at Hellenistic and early Roman sites around southern Palestine, including atop Masada (where they are installed in built structures rather than caves). The function of Palestinian columbaria has been debated. According to one theory, the niches were designed to contain cremation burials in urns. However, there is no evidence that the local populations cremated their dead, and no human remains have been discovered in any columbaria. Instead, columbaria apparently functioned as dovecotes, with each niche accommodating a bird. The niches were placed well above the ground level, out of reach of predators. Pigeons and doves were used as carrier birds, food (pigeon is still considered a delicacy by the local Arabs), as a source of guano (for fertilizer), and for cultic purposes (offerings). There are more than 60 columbaria caves at Marisa, containing a total of 50,000 to 60,000 niches. The largest columbarium cave, called es-Suk (Arabic for "the marketplace"), has a long central hall with branches at right angles. The raising of pigeons and doves – and their by-products – was another mainstay of Marisa's economy.

A few caves surrounding the tel were used for burials. In 1902, word spread that local villagers had discovered two painted tombs and were defacing the images, which they found offensive. Two scholars who were based in Jerusalem, John Peters and Hermann Thiersch, visited Marisa and commissioned a professional photographer to record the paintings. After being shown the photographs, other scholars associated with the École Biblique (a French Dominican

4.11 Columbarium (es-Suk) at Marisa. Courtesy of Zev Radovan/BibleLandPictures.com.

institute) in Jerusalem rushed to Marisa and made their own watercolors of the paintings. The photographs and watercolors from 1902 are the only surviving documentation of the paintings, which have since disappeared completely (the paintings now visible in Tomb I are recent re-creations). Tomb I is the larger and more elaborately decorated of the two tombs. A small opening in the bedrock provides entry into a small, central room, from which three elongated burial halls branch off – the main one on axis and the other two set perpendicularly on

4.12 Interior of Tomb I at Marisa looking towards back wall. Courtesy of Zev Radovan/ BibleLandPictures.com.

either side. Burial niches called *loculi* (sing. *loculus*; Hebrew **kokh**) are carved into the walls of the halls. Each loculus accommodated a single **inhumation** (whole corpse), which was wrapped in a shroud and perhaps placed in a wooden coffin. These are the earliest examples of loculi in Palestine, which are a characteristic feature of tombs in Alexandria and therefore reflect Hellenistic influence on the local population.

A raised bench carved in the shape of a dining couch at the back of the main burial hall in Tomb I marked the entrance to three burial rooms, which must have contained the remains of prominent members of the community. The area around the entrance to these rooms was painted in imitation of a Doric-style building, with Doric columns flanking the doorway and a triglyph-and-metope frieze and pediment above. Two large, lidded amphoras (jars) bedecked with ribbons were painted on either side of the Doric-style building, perhaps representing Greek cremation urns. The wall in front of this scene was flanked by paintings of three-footed tables bearing flaming incense burners. Incense often was burned in tombs, not only as an offering but also to mask the foul odors. Above the incense burners, two eagles with outstretched wings held a garland that continued along the side walls, above the loculi. Ionic columns with wreaths were painted on either side of each loculus.

Along the side walls of the main hall, the space between the garland and the top of the loculi was decorated with a continuous painted **frieze**. The frieze began with a man in ceremonial dress, blowing a long trumpet. To his left another man was depicted on horseback, with the horse rearing up as the man

4.13 Loculi and painted frieze in Tomb I at Marisa. Courtesy of Zev Radovan/BibleLand Pictures.com.

prepared to spear a leopard. This scene is reminiscent of the painting of a young man (perhaps Alexander the Great) on the façade of a royal tomb at Vergina, the capital of ancient Macedon (although there is no evidence of any direct connection, and no evidence that the figure in the Marisa tomb represented Alexander). The rest of the frieze depicts a procession of exotic animals, such as giraffes, and fantastic hybrid creatures, such as fish with elephant trunks and a lion with a bearded man's head. The ultimate source of inspiration for this animal procession was Alexandria, the cultural capital of the Hellenistic world. In addition to its famous library, ancient Alexandria had a zoo that contained a collection of exotic animals from Africa. Scenes incorporating Egyptian motifs were popular in Hellenistic and early Roman art, and picture books of these exotic animals circulated around the Mediterranean world. The animal frieze in Tomb I at Marisa therefore reflects another element of Alexandrian influence on the local population.

The animals in the frieze are labeled in Greek – for example, *pardalos* for leopard. In addition, the names of the deceased are inscribed or painted in Greek next to many of the loculi. In some cases, it is possible to identify two to three generations of a family. Whereas members of the first (older) generation tend to have Semitic names, the younger generations usually have Greek names, attesting to a process of Hellenization over time. One such example mentions the leader of the Sidonian community at Marisa: "Apollophanes, son of Sesmaios, head of the Sidonians."

4.14 Fish plate. Painter: the Black and White Stripe Painter. Greek, South Italian, Late
Classical to Early Hellenistic Period, about 340–320 B.C.E. Place of manufacture: Italy,
Apulia. Ceramic, Red-Figure. Height: 4 cm; diameter: 18 cm. Museum of Fine Arts,
Boston. Gift of Mrs. and Mrs. Cornelius C. Vermeule III in the name of Cornelius Adrian
Comstock Vermeule. 1986.1018. Photograph © [2012] Museum of Fine Arts, Boston.

Pottery

As in the Persian period, in the early Hellenistic period the largest quantities
of imported (especially Greek) pottery are found at coastal sites such as Gaza,
Ashkelon, and Tel Dor. By the early Hellenistic period, the production of Attic
red- and black-figured wares had ceased. Instead, early Hellenistic fine wares
generally have a black-slipped (coated) surface that is matte or shiny, sometimes
painted with delicate floral designs in white or light pastel colors. One common
early Hellenistic type is the "fish plate," which is represented in Palestine by
imports and locally produced imitations. Fish plates are large, shallow platters
with a depression in the center, a high ring base, and overhanging rim. They are
so called because the painted fish decorating some platters suggest they were
used for serving fish, with the depression perhaps having been designed to hold
fish sauce.

Another common early Hellenistic fine ware is mold-made "Megarian bowls"
(named after Megara in Greece). These are deep, hemispherical bowls covered
with floral designs in relief. Molds were first used for manufacturing pottery
during the early Hellenistic period, a technology that made possible the mass

Sidebar: Zenon

In 260–258 B.C.E., an official named **Zenon** traveled to Syria-Palestine on behalf of his boss, the Ptolemaic finance minister Apollonius, to assess the country's prosperity and revenues for tax purposes. Papyri from the ancient site of Philadelphia in Egypt's Fayyum document Zenon's journey, shedding important light on settlements and living conditions in Ptolemaic Palestine. Zenon sailed up the coast from Alexandria and landed at Straton's Tower. The sites that he visited included Kedesh (which provided him with food supplies and the luxury of a bath), Jerusalem, Jericho, Birtha in the "land of Tobiah" (Iraq el-Amir), and Marisa. The papyri provide evidence of a lucrative trade in olive oil, grain, and wine, and frequently mention slaves as well. For example, Zenon sent five letters to officials at Marisa concerning five young slaves that he purchased during his visit there, who had escaped and returned to their former masters. Other papyri document gifts of rare animals and young slaves sent by Tobiah to the Ptolemaic king and to Apollonius.

production of certain vessels such as bowls and oil lamps. Before the early Hellenistic period, oil lamps were wheel-made, and local Palestinian lamps were simply bowls with a pinched rim for the nozzle. Mold-made oil lamps were manufactured in two parts, upper and lower, which were joined along the sides. Mold-made pottery is easy to identify because it usually is decorated in relief, with delicate raised designs covering the surface of the vessel (an effect that is difficult to achieve on a potter's wheel). In addition to being mold-made, early Hellenistic oil lamps are characterized by a round body with a small filling hole in the center, and a long, narrow nozzle. They typically are decorated with geometric or floral designs in relief, and are covered with a black or gray slip.

The local pottery of Palestine in the early Hellenistic period continues earlier native traditions and generally is undecorated. The discovery of relatively large numbers of imported Greek wine amphoras in Jerusalem may be connected with the presence of Gentile soldiers who were stationed in the Akra. Many of these amphoras come from the City of David. Often they have inscriptions stamped on the handles, which indicate the source of the wine and the name of the official who oversaw production. Most of the amphoras found in Jerusalem contained wine from the island of Rhodes, which was exported widely around the Mediterranean in the early Hellenistic period.

Coins

Before Alexander's time, no mortals – not even kings – put images of themselves on coins. Instead, coins were decorated with the figures and attributes

4.15   Early Hellenistic mold-made oil lamp. Courtesy of Zev Radovan/BibleLandPictures.com.

of deities, or with motifs such as animals and plants, which often symbolized the minting province or city (such as the lily on the Yahud coins). The coins minted by Alexander the Great display the head of Heracles (Hercules) in profile wearing a lionskin cape on the obverse, and on the reverse Zeus (the father of Heracles) enthroned and holding an eagle and scepter, accompanied

4.16   Coin of Alexander the Great. Courtesy of Zev Radovan/BibleLandPictures.com.

by the Greek inscription "of Alexander." The lionskin cape was an attribute of Heracles, who began to wear it after slaying the Nemean lion (one of the legendary hero's twelve labors). Clearly, Alexander's intention was to associate or identify himself with Heracles, from whom he claimed descent. This is evidence of the blurring of the boundaries between Greek mortal ruler and divine status that began under Alexander. Not surprisingly, Alexander's successors followed his precedent, either minting coins with the same image (Alexander as Heracles) or depicting themselves resembling Alexander and wearing the lionskin cape or with a leonine mane of wavy hair.

Sidebar: Greek Architecture

The late seventh and sixth centuries B.C.E. witnessed the development of the classical Greek architectural styles called the Doric and Ionic orders. The Doric order is so called because it developed in the Peloponnese (the southern part of the Greek mainland), where the Doric dialect was spoken. The Ionic order is so called because it developed in Ionia (the western coast of Asia Minor). Originally these orders were restricted to temples, but soon they were applied to other types of buildings as well. Scholars agree that many of the features of the Doric and Ionic orders represent a translation into stone of elements that previously had been constructed of wood. Before the late seventh century, Greek temples were relatively modest structures constructed of mud-brick, wood, and other perishable materials. By the late seventh century, the Greeks began to experiment with large-scale construction in stone – around the same time that they began to make life-sized (or larger) stone statues instead of small bronze figurines or wooden statues. These innovations reflect Near Eastern, and especially Egyptian, influence on Greek culture, which is why archaeologists refer to the seventh century in Greece as the Orientalizing period.

In both the Doric and Ionic orders, the temple consisted of a building in which the main room was the **naos** or **cella**, which contained the cult statue of the deity. By the sixth century B.C.E., the roofing system (ceiling beams) of the *naos* was supported by two rows of columns. Most Greek temples had a porch in front of the *naos* (called a **pronaos**), generally with two columns set between the thickened ends (**antae**) of the porch walls (an arrangement called **in-antis**). Doric temples typically have a back porch (**opisthodomos**), which was added for symmetry, to give the building the same appearance at the front and back.

In both the Doric and Ionic orders, the temple building stood on a raised, stepped platform. The top step is called the **stylobate** – literally, the base for the columns (*stylos* is Greek for column). The building was surrounded on all four sides by columns, which supported the overhanging eaves of the roof (the cornice). By the sixth century B.C.E., it became common to erect two or even three rows of columns around Ionic temples (but not Doric temples). The columns surrounding the temple are called a **peristyle** (which literally means "surrounding columns"). At the tops of the columns was a decorative carved element called a **capital**, which differed in form depending on the order. The horizontal area between the column capitals and the roof eaves is called the **entablature**. In both the Doric and Ionic orders, the entablature was divided into two horizontal strips: a lower strip (**architrave**) and an upper strip (frieze [pronounced "freeze"]). By the sixth century B.C.E., Greek temples had moderately pitched (sloping) roofs covered with terra-cotta tiles, with an open triangular space called a **pediment** above the porch at either narrow end of the building.

The above features are common to the Doric and Ionic orders. Sometimes Doric and Ionic temples differ in plan, as in, for example, the presence or absence of an *opisthodomos* or the addition of more than one row of columns around the exterior, as mentioned previously. The Doric and Ionic orders also differ in decorative details. For example, whereas in the Doric order the peristyle columns sit directly on top of the stylobate, in the Ionic order the columns have carved bases. Doric capitals have the shape of a plain, inverted cushion, whereas Ionic capitals resemble a rolled-up scroll (the rolled-up elements are called volutes) separated by an egg-and-dart motif. In the Doric order, the architrave is plain, with a a **triglyph** and **metope** frieze above, which is so called because of the series of alternating panels (called metopes [pronounced met-uh-PEES]) and triple-grooved vertical elements (called triglyphs). The metope panels were sometimes left plain, sometimes were painted, and sometimes were carved with relief decoration.

By the sixth and fifth centuries B.C.E., Greek architects had developed an ideal canon of proportions for Doric temples. One of the rules of this canon dictated that there should be twice as many peristyle columns plus one along the sides of the building as along the front and back. In most Doric temples this meant thirteen columns along the sides and six columns at the front and back. The Parthenon, which is larger than most Doric temples, has seventeen columns along the sides and eight along the front and back. This canon of proportions did not apply to Ionic temples. According to another rule of the Doric canon, each column in the peristyle should be aligned with the center of a triglyph in the frieze above, and there is supposed to be a triglyph at each corner of the building. If you look at a drawing or photograph of a Doric temple, you will notice that this rule is impossible to follow, as there is no way to center a triglyph over the corner peristyle columns and have it at the corner of the frieze. Greek architects attempted to solve this problem in various ways, such as increasing the width of the metopes, which were supposed to be square (a solution called *angle contraction*). Some scholars believe that the Doric order declined in popularity after reaching its height in the fifth century because of the difficulty in observing these rules.

In the Ionic order, the architrave either is plain or is divided into three narrow, horizontal strips (**fasciae**). Instead of triglyphs and metopes, in the Ionic order the frieze is a continuous (uninterrupted) band, sometimes decorated with painting or carved reliefs. In the Doric order the pediment can contain sculpture, whereas in the Ionic order the pediment typically is empty. The so-called Corinthian order is not really an order at all, but instead is a later variant on the Ionic order, the only difference being the appearance of

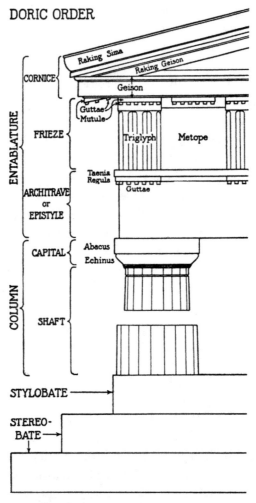

4.17 Line drawing of the Doric order. From Isabelle Hoopes Grinnell, *Greek Temples* (New York: Metropolitan Museum of Art, 1943), p. xviii. By permission of the Metropolitan Museum of Art. Image © Metropolitan Museum of Art.

the capital, which is covered with leafy decoration. The Corinthian variant became popular because the capitals look the same from all sides, as opposed to Ionic capitals, which can be viewed fully only from the front and back.

At the beginning, elements of the Doric and Ionic orders were never mixed in a single building. However, the Parthenon, which was built in the second half of the fifth century and is often cited as the prime example of the Doric order, already incorporates Ionic elements (Ionic columns in an extra interior room and a continuous Ionic frieze around the top of the building). By the Hellenistic period, when Greek styles of architecture spread throughout the Near East, Doric and Ionic elements were often combined in a single building.

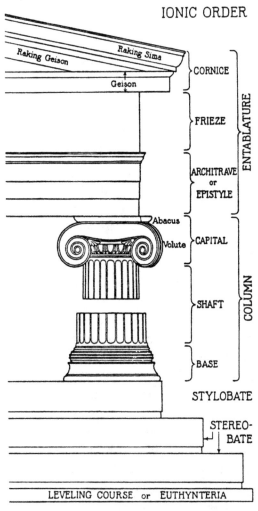

4.18 Line drawing of the Ionic order. From Isabelle Hoopes Grinnell, *Greek Temples* (New York: Metropolitan Museum of Art, 1943), p. xix. By permission of the Metropolitan Museum of Art. Image © Metropolitan Museum of Art.

Sidebar: Ancient Egyptian Jewry

There has been a Jewish Diaspora in Egypt for thousands of years. Jeremiah, who ended his life and prophetic career in Egypt after the fall of Jerusalem in 586 B.C.E., refers to Jewish communities at Migdol, Tahpanhes, Memphis, and the land of Pathros (Jeremiah 44:1). By the Late Iron Age (seventh–sixth centuries B.C.E.), Judean mercenaries employed by the pharaoh were stationed at border forts. One Jewish military colony was located at Elephantine (pronounced el-uh-fan-TEEN-ee) (Hebrew **Yeb**), an island opposite Aswan that guarded Egypt's frontier with Nubia. An archive of over 100 Aramaic papyri dating between 495 and 399 B.C.E. from Elephantine provides valuable information about the local Jewish community. For example, from the papyri we learn that this community established a temple dedicated to the God of Israel, whom they called Yahu (=YHWH), in which animal sacrifices were offered. The papyri indicate that the temple was an impressive stone structure with pillars and was furnished with vessels of gold and silver. In 411/410 B.C.E., when the local governor was away, Egyptian priests of the god Khnum or Khnub destroyed the temple of Yahu. The Elephantine papyri include letters of protest written by the local Jewish community to various officials (including the governors of Jerusalem and Samaria), pleading for assistance. Although the temple to Yahu seems to have been rebuilt, animal sacrifices were no longer offered there.

Another Jewish temple dedicated to the God of Israel was established at the site of Leontopolis, near Heliopolis in the Nile Delta, by one of the dispossessed **Oniad** high priests from Jerusalem (apparently Onias IV) (see Chapter 5 Sidebar). The descendants of the Oniads presided over a sacrificial cult at this temple until it was shut down by the Roman emperor **Vespasian** in 73 C.E., apparently because of fears of messianic or revolutionary activity in the wake of the First Jewish Revolt.

There are no archaeological remains of the temples at Elephantine and Leontopolis. Interestingly, in contrast to the Samaritan temple at Mount Gerizim, there is no evidence that Jews ever condemned the Egyptian temples as schismatic, perhaps because they made no claim to be substitutes for the Jerusalem temple. Instead, they seem to have served the local Jewish communities.

By the Hellenistic period, Jews lived around Egypt, with an especially large community in Alexandria that was home to the famous Jewish philosopher Philo in the first century B.C.E. and first century C.E. In the Hellenistic period, the Pentateuch was translated from Hebrew to Greek, apparently to serve the needs of these Greek-speaking Diaspora Jews. A pseudepigraphic work called the **Letter of Aristeas** presents a fictional account according to which the Ptolemaic king commissioned the translation of the Torah (Penta-teuch) to Greek for inclusion in the royal library at Alexandria. The Greek translation of the Torah is called the **Septuagint**, which means "the transla-tion of the Seventy" (sometimes abbreviated with the Roman numerals LXX), because, according to the Letter of Aristeas, it was done by seventy-two men (six men from each of the twelve Israelite tribes). Although this story is an obvious fabrication intended to glorify Judaism by showing the importance of the Torah, Hellenistic Alexandria is the likely setting for its translation into Greek.

Kedesh in Upper Galilee continued to function as an important administrative center in the early Hellenistic period, as indicated by the discovery of storerooms with large jars that contained wine, grain, and oil, and more than 2000 clay bullae from an archive of documents. Most of the bullae are stamped with images rather than inscriptions, including Greek gods and goddesses (such as Aphrodite, Athena, and Hermes), symbols and portraits of Hellenistic monarchs, and the sign of Tanit, the Phoenician fertility goddess. The excavators believe that this building was destroyed and burned during a battle in 145 B.C.E. In the summer of 2010, a very rare coin was discovered at Kedesh. Weighing almost an ounce, it is the heaviest gold coin ever found in an excavation in Israel. The coin was minted in Alexandria by Ptolemy V (ca. 200 B.C.E.) and depicts a queen, apparently either Arsinoe II Philadelphos (who was married to her half-brother Ptolemy II) or Cleopatra I (Ptolemy V's wife).

Recommended Reading

Andrea M. Berlin, "Between Large Forces: Palestine in the Hellenistic Period," *Biblical Archaeologist* 60.1 (March 1997): 2–51.

Elias J. Bickerman, *The Jews in the Greek Age* (Cambridge, MA: Harvard University, 1988).

Peter Green, *The Hellenistic Age: A History* (New York: Modern Library, 2007).

Marin Hengel, *Judaism and Hellenism, Vols. 1–2* (Philadelphia: Fortress, 1974).

Saul Lieberman, *Greek in Jewish Palestine, Hellenism in Jewish Palestine* (New York: Jewish Theological Seminary, 1994).

J. J. Pollitt, *Art in the Hellenistic Age* (New York: Cambridge University, 1993).

℗℗ ℗℗ ℗℗ ℗℗

FIVE

THE LATE HELLENISTIC (HASMONEAN) PERIOD (167–40 B.C.E.)

HISTORICAL BACKGROUND: GENERAL

While the eastern Mediterranean and Near East were under the rule of Alexander's successors, the western Mediterranean was caught up in a struggle between two powers: Rome and Carthage. According to tradition, Rome was founded in 753 B.C.E., when a group of villages by the Tiber River united under the rule of a king. In 509 B.C.E., the last king was expelled and the Roman Republic was founded. Rome soon embarked on a campaign of expansion, first annexing adjacent territories (including Etruria [modern Tuscany] to the north and Campania to the south), and later expanding its control throughout Italy. By the third and second centuries B.C.E., Rome had begun to extend its reach beyond the Italian peninsula.

Rome's expansion brought it into conflict with Carthage in North Africa (modern Tunisia). Carthage was established in 814 B.C.E. as a Phoenician trading colony, but it soon became a wealthy and independent power, controlling much of the sea trade around the Mediterranean. During the third and second centuries B.C.E., Rome and Carthage became embroiled in series of conflicts called the **Punic Wars** (*Punic* comes from the Latin word for Phoenician). During the Second Punic War (218–202 B.C.E.), Carthage's forces were led by **Hannibal**, a brilliant general and military strategist (whose name contains the Phoenician theophoric "Bal" [Baal]). Although Hannibal gained notoriety for leading elephants with his army across the Alps (most of the elephants died during the crossing), his real success came from defeating the Roman army at several important battles around Italy, which demonstrated that Rome was not invincible and caused the desertion of key allies. Nevertheless, Rome rallied and the Second Punic War ended with Carthage's defeat at the battle of Zama

(204 B.C.E.). After the battle, Hannibal took refuge with Antiochus III, the Seleucid king. A decade later (183 B.C.E.), after Antiochus III was defeated by Rome, Hannibal ended his life by taking poison.

After the battle of Zama, Rome imposed on Carthage harsh terms of surrender. Following another round of conflict (the Third Punic War), Rome razed Carthage to the ground and, according to tradition, sowed the ground with salt to ensure its desolation. In that same year (146 B.C.E.), Rome also destroyed Corinth, a prosperous trading city that had opposed Roman expansion into Greece. By the first century B.C.E., Rome was making significant inroads into the Hellenistic world. At the same time, the Roman Republic was beginning to dissolve, as powerful generals fought for control. These generals included **Pompey**, who annexed the Hasmonean kingdom on behalf of Rome in 63 B.C.E. (discussed later), and **Julius Caesar**, who ruled Rome as dictator from 48 to 44 B.C.E. After Caesar's assassination, his step-nephew **Octavian** (later **Augustus**) formed a ruling coalition of three men called the Second Triumvirate. By 36 B.C.E., the coalition had been reduced to two: Octavian, who was in charge of the western half of the Mediterranean, and **Mark Antony**, who ruled the eastern half of the Mediterranean. Mark Antony established his base of operations in Alexandria, where he met and fell in love with the Ptolemaic queen **Cleopatra VII**, for whom he abandoned his wife Octavia (the sister of his co-ruler Octavian).

HISTORICAL BACKGROUND: PALESTINE

Although under the Ptolemies and Seleucids the Torah continued to have the status of royal law in Judea, the impact of Hellenization caused deep divisions among the Jewish population. Many of Jerusalem's elite families (including priests) eagerly adopted Greek customs. We have already seen Greek influence on the style and decoration of the *baris* (the Qasr el-Abd) at Iraq el-Amir, which was constructed by the Tobiad Hyrcanus around 175 B.C.E. In the same year, Jason, who was serving as interim high priest on behalf of his brother **Onias III** (see Sidebar on the **Heliodorus affair**), convinced the Seleucid king Antiochus IV Epiphanes (ruled 175–164 B.C.E.) to refound Jerusalem as a Greek *polis* named Antiochia. Jerusalem's conversion to a *polis* was not imposed on the Jews but was initiated by Jason and his supporters, and our ancient sources give no indication of opposition within the Jewish community. Greek law now became the law of the land, although the practice of Judaism was still legal. The author of the apocryphal work 2 Maccabees, who was opposed to Hellenization, was scandalized by the behavior of the Jerusalem high priests:

> And to such a pitch did the cultivation of Greek fashions and the coming-in of foreign customs rise, because of the excessive wickedness of this godless Jason, who was no high priest at all, that the priests were no

longer earnest about the services of the altar, but disdaining the sanctuary and neglecting the services, they hurried to take part in wrestling school, and after the summons to the discus-throwing, regarding as worthless the things their forefathers valued, and thinking Greek standards the finest. (2 Macc. 4:13–15; NRSV)

In 167 B.C.E., Antiochus IV issued an edict requiring all inhabitants of his kingdom to adopt Greek practices and customs, including worshipping Greek gods. This edict also outlawed the practice of Judaism, including the observance of the Sabbath, dietary laws, and circumcision. The Jerusalem temple was rededicated to Olympian Zeus and was defiled through the sacrifice of pigs and the practice of sacred prostitution. Similarly, the Samaritan temple on Mount Gerizim was rededicated to Zeus Hellenios. Although Antiochus IV's reasons for issuing this edict are not entirely clear, he likely was motivated by political considerations rather than anti-Jewish sentiment. As we have seen, Hellenistic kings typically used Hellenization as a means of unifying diverse populations under their rule.

No matter what Antiochus IV's motives were, the effect was the same: practicing Judaism now became a criminal act punishable by death. Our ancient sources indicate that many Jews readily abandoned Judaism and embraced Greek customs. However, some Jews opposed Antiochus IV's edict. Trouble erupted in **Modiin**, a village midway between modern Tel Aviv and Jerusalem, when an elderly local priest named Mattathias defied the king's order to participate in a Greek sacrifice, killing a Jew who complied and executing a king's officer. Mattathias was the head of the Hasmonean clan. His third son (out of five) – Judah "Maccabee" (the hammer) – took charge of rebel bands that fled to the countryside. The rebels conducted guerilla warfare against Seleucid troops sent by Antiochus IV to enforce his edict, and attacked Hellenizing Jews (whom they considered "lawless" for having abandoned the observance of the Torah). In other words, the Maccabean revolt was also a civil war that pitted conservative Jews against Hellenizers.

Under Judah's command, the rebels scored some significant victories in battles against Antiochus IV's forces. After Antiochus IV died in 164 B.C.E., his son Antiochus V issued a new edict that rescinded the old one, permitting the practice of Judaism and returning the Jerusalem temple to the Jews. Judah and his followers cleansed and rededicated the Jerusalem temple to the God of Israel in mid-December 164 B.C.E., an event commemorated by the holiday of **Hanukkah**. Jews celebrate Judah's victory and the rededication of the temple by lighting a nine-branched candelabrum that recalls the seven-branched **menorah** (lampstand) used to light the temple's interior.

After the rededication of the temple, Judah and his followers renewed the conflict, capitalizing on the weakening condition of the Seleucid kingdom. The Jewish rebels were supported by the Romans, who were interested in undermining Seleucid power. Judah sent delegates to Rome, where they appeared before the Senate and signed a treaty of friendship and alliance. After Judah was killed in battle (160 B.C.E.), his brother **Jonathan** assumed leadership of the revolt. Jonathan exploited a quarrel between two claimants to the Seleucid throne to establish Judean independence from Seleucid rule. Jonathan also assumed the office of high priest – a controversial move that deeply divided the Jewish population, as it violated the biblical principle of separation between royal and priestly powers (a precedent first established by the appointment of Moses as leader of Israel and his brother Aaron as high priest). After Jonathan was killed (142 B.C.E.), the last surviving brother, Simon, took over. Simon renewed the treaty of friendship and alliance with the Romans, serving as ruler and high priest until his death in 134 B.C.E.

Simon was succeeded by his son, John Hyrcanus I (134–104 B.C.E.). John Hyrcanus I embarked on an aggressive campaign of expansion, conquering Idumaea, Samaria, and territories in Transjordan. He instituted a policy of Judaization, forcing non-Jewish peoples to convert to Judaism or go into exile. As a result, the Idumaeans now were converted to Judaism – among them, Antipas, the grandfather of Herod the Great. The Samaritans were dealt with differently. They were a Yahwistic population who already worshiped the God of Israel but were considered schismatics by the Judeans. Therefore, John Hyrcanus I did not convert the Samaritans, but instead destroyed their temple on Mount Gerizim. Because modern (rabbinic) Judaism prohibits forced conversion and discourages proselytizing activity, scholars debate the motives behind Hasmonean policy. Perhaps it makes the most sense to consider Hasmonean Judaization as analogous to Hellenization, with the **Hasmoneans** using Judaism as a means of unifying different peoples under their rule.

John Hyrcanus I was succeeded by his son **Aristobulus I** (104–103 B.C.E.). To eliminate the competition for the throne, Aristobulus I had one brother put to death and imprisoned his other brothers and his mother (where she died of starvation). Aristobulus I was the first Hasmonean to adopt the title of "king." He conquered Galilee and the **Golan**, forcibly converting to Judaism the native populations, including the Ituraeans of the Golan. Aristobulus I's Judaization of Galilee approximately one century before Jesus' birth should be considered as a factor in Matthew and Luke's attempts to establish a Judean (versus Galilean) origin for Jesus (because, according to Jewish tradition, the messiah will be descended from the Judean house of David).

When Aristobulus I died of an illness in 103 B.C.E., his widow, **Salome Alexandra**, freed his brothers (who were still in prison) and married one of them – **Alexander Jannaeus** (ruled 103–76 B.C.E.). Alexander Jannaeus was a cruel and ruthless ruler, whose disregard for the proper observance of Jewish law aroused much opposition among the Jewish population, especially the **Pharisees**. Eventually some of these Jews rebelled, turning to the Seleucid king

Demetrius III for help. But when Demetrius III invaded, the rebels regretted their actions and defected back to Alexander Jannaeus. Nevertheless, Alexander Jannaeus exacted revenge on them, as Josephus describes: "He [Alexander Jannaeus] brought them [the rebels] back to Jerusalem; and there he did a thing that was as cruel as could be: while he feasted with his concubines in a conspicuous place, he ordered 800 of the Jews to be crucified, and slaughtered their children and wives before the eyes of the still-living wretches" (*Ant.* 13.380).

When Alexander Jannaeus died, his widow Salome Alexandra succeeded him to the Hasmonean throne (76–67 B.C.E.). Because only men could serve in the Jerusalem temple, Salome Alexandra's older son **John Hyrcanus II** officiated as high priest in her stead. After Salome Alexandra's death, a civil war erupted between her sons, Hyrcanus II and **Aristobulus II**. The ensuing chaos and instability provided an opportunity for the Roman general Pompey to annex the Hasmonean kingdom (63 B.C.E.).

The Romans immediately dismembered the Hasmonean kingdom. Hyrcanus II was appointed high priest and put in charge of administering areas with high concentrations of Jews (Judea, Idumaea, Galilee, and Peraea [the area on the eastern side of the Jordan River and Dead Sea]). Hyrcanus was assisted by **Antipater**, an influential and well-connected Idumaean whose father, **Antipas**, had been converted to Judaism by the Hasmoneans. After Antipater was assassinated in 43 B.C.E., the Romans appointed his sons **Phasael** and Herod "tetrarchs of Judea." The most Hellenized cities in the region – those most loyal to Rome – were formed into a semiautonomous league called the **Decapolis**. The Decapolis cities, which were concentrated to the north and east of the **Sea of Galilee**, were part of the newly established Roman province of Syria, which was under the administration of a high-ranking official called a **legate** (the commander of a legion), who was based in **Antioch**.

By the middle of the first century B.C.E., Roman expansion eastward brought Rome into conflict with the **Parthians**, the successors to the ancient Persians. In 40 B.C.E. the Parthians overran Syria-Palestine and reestablished the Hasmonean kingdom, placing on the throne **Mattathias Antigonus**, the son of Aristobulus II. Mattathias Antigonus captured Phasael, who committed suicide, and Hyrcanus II, whom he disqualified for the office of high priest by disfiguring him (he bit off Hyrcanus II's ear!). Herod fled for his life, moving south through Idumaea, depositing his family for safekeeping on the fortress atop **Masada**, and pleading with the Nabataean king for assistance (Herod's mother was a Nabataean named **Cypros**). When the Nabataeans turned him down, Herod went to Egypt, where Cleopatra welcomed him and offered her assistance. However, Herod refused Cleopatra, whom he mistrusted, and sailed for Rome. In Rome, Herod appeared before the Senate, which – thanks to Mark Antony's support and encouragement – bestowed on him the title "King of Judea."

5.1 Map of the Hasmonean Palestine. Ancient World Mapping Center, University of North Carolina at Chapel Hill (www.unc.edu/awmc).

ARCHAEOLOGY: SITES

Jerusalem

First Wall

During the Hasmonean period, the settlement in Jerusalem grew and expanded onto the western hill. The wall built by Hezekiah to fortify the western hill, which had lain in ruins since 586 B.C.E., was now repaired and rebuilt. Portions of this wall survive, including inside the courtyard of the **Citadel**, a medieval and Ottoman-period fortified enclosure at the northwest corner of the western hill. Archaeologists identify the Hasmonean wall with the First Wall described by Josephus (see Chapter 7). The stones in the wall are laid in alternating courses of headers and stretchers, and have drafted margins with rough, protruding bosses, which means that the four edges (margins) are cut back and smooth, whereas the central part (the boss) is unworked. These techniques are characteristic of monumental construction in the late Hellenistic period (see, for example, the stones on the north side of the "seam" at the southeast corner of the Temple Mount described in Chapter 4's discussion of the Akra).

Jason's Tomb

In the 1950s, a monumental Hasmonean period tomb was discovered in the western Jerusalem neighborhood of Rehavia. A long, narrow, open passage (*dromos*) cut into the slope of a hill provided access to a porch in front of the tomb, which contained two separate, side-by-side underground chambers cut into bedrock. A single Doric column was set between the jambs of the porch (an arrangement called *in-antis* in Greek, meaning between the *antae* [thickened jambs]). A monumental stone pyramid was erected above the tomb. Jews of the late Second Temple period referred to a monumental grave marker as a **nefesh** (Hebrew for "soul").

One of the underground chambers (A) had loculi cut into the walls, into which the burials (individual inhumations) were placed. Whereas Marisa has the earliest examples of loculi found in Palestine so far, this is their first appearance in a Jewish tomb. The use of the Doric order and loculi (and Greek language; discussed later) reflect Hellenistic influence on the Jewish family that owned Jason's Tomb.

Graffiti were drawn in charcoal or incised into the plaster of the porch walls. The graffiti include several inscriptions in Aramaic and one in Greek. One Aramaic inscription enjoins visitors to the tomb to lament the death of Jason — hence the name given to the tomb by archaeologists. The graffiti include depictions of a stag, five seven-branched menorahs (among the earliest surviving representations of this object), and three ships with unfurled sails. One ship

5.2 Jason's Tomb. Courtesy of Zev Radovan/BibleLandPictures.com.

appears to be in pursuit of the other two, with a man at the curved prow poised to shoot a bow and arrow and another man behind him holding a spear. Human heads representing rowers are lined up along the side of the ship. The meaning of these graffiti – who made them and why – is unknown. The excavator suggested that perhaps the family that owned the tomb made its fortune through piracy at sea, as we have ancient references to Jewish pirates. Whether or not this is the case, the owners of Jason's Tomb likely were a priestly family. This is indicated by the name Jason (which was common among the Jerusalem high priests), the depiction of menorahs (alluding to the temple), the evidence of Greek influence, and the tomb's size and ostentation.

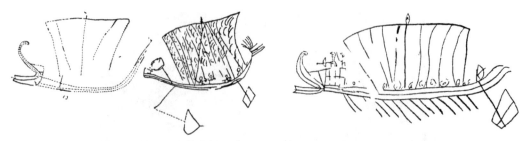

5.3 Graffiti of ships from Jason's Tomb. From L. Y. Rahmani, "Jason's Tomb," *Israel Exploration Journal* 17.2 (1967), Figs. 5a–5b. By permission of the Israel Exploration Society.

The Nabataeans

The neighbors of the Hasmoneans to the east and south were the Nabataeans. The Nabataeans were Arabs who spoke an early form of the Arabic language. Originally the Nabataeans were nomads who plied the caravan routes between the Arabian Peninsula and the Mediterranean coast. They grew wealthy trading in luxury goods such as frankincense and myrrh, which were bundled and transported across the desert on pack animals. These luxury goods were exported by ship from the port at Gaza and fetched high prices at markets around the Mediterranean. Eventually, some of the trading posts became permanent settlements (towns). By the second and first centuries B.C.E., the Nabataeans established a kingdom with a capital at **Petra** (southeast of the Dead Sea), which encompassed much of the area of modern Jordan, the Negev, and the Sinai. The Nabataean kingdom flourished until 106 C.E., when the emperor Trajan annexed it to Rome and moved the caravan routes to the north, away from Nabataean control. The Nabataeans also developed a sophisticated system of water storage, irrigation, and terracing, which enabled them to cultivate the desert. The Nabataean desert towns and cities flourished through the Byzantine period and into the early Islamic period (eighth to ninth centuries C.E.), when the Nabataeans converted to Christianity and, eventually, Islam (see Chapter 16).

Petra, the most famous Nabataean town, today is designated a World Heritage site. It is situated in a dramatic moonlike landscape of barren and rugged red sandstone mountains (hence the name Petra, which means "rock" in Greek). A broad, paved, colonnaded street (a street lined with columns) ran through the town, alongside a wadi (dry riverbed). On either side of the street and wadi were monumental buildings, including temples and, by the Byzantine period, churches. A residential quarter with spacious villas decorated with wall-paintings overlooked the colonnaded street. Farther up the wadi, a large Greek-style theater is cut into the slopes of a rocky hill. In addition to temple buildings, Petra is dotted with small shrines cut into the cliff faces. The

5.4 Theater at Petra.

Nabataeans typically represented their deities with simple **stelae** (stones), on which facial features such as eyes were sometimes represented. The deities worshiped at Petra included the goddess Allat.

Petra is best known for its extensive necropolis, with thousands of rock-cut tombs honeycombing its cliffs. Many of the tombs consist of simple, unadorned openings leading into a single, rock-cut chamber. The facades of some tombs are decorated with carved designs that imitate architectural elements; in the case of the most elaborate tombs, the façade has a porch with rock-cut columns and a Greek-style entablature. The most famous tomb at Petra, called the **Khazneh** (Arabic for "treasury"), is located at the end of a long, narrow, winding canyon called the **Siq**, which provides the main access to the site. Every visitor to Petra sees the Khazneh upon emerging from the Siq. The Khazneh was featured in the film *Indiana Jones and the Last Crusade* as the spot where the Holy Grail was found (in reality, though, the interior consists of a single rock-cut burial chamber with no connection to the Holy Grail). In addition to its prominent location, the Khazneh is distinguished from other tombs at Petra by the exceptionally high quality of the carving and the deep rose color of the sandstone. The face of the cliff was cut in imitation of a two-story-high building, with a Greek-style porch on the bottom, and a pediment with a circular structure (*tholos*) on top. Figures carved in relief decorated the spaces between the columns. The prominent location and high quality of the Khazneh leave little doubt that it originally contained the remains of one of the Nabataean kings – perhaps **Aretas IV**, who ruled around the time of Jesus (ca. 9 B.C.E.–40 C.E.).

5.5 The Khazneh at Petra. Photo by Jim Haberman.

Although Petra is the most famous Nabataean site, we have remains of many other Nabataean towns and settlements. One such site is **Oboda** (the ancient Nabataean name; the modern Hebrew name is **Avdat**), which is located in the heart of the Negev desert. Oboda is dominated by an acropolis – a fortified citadel that originally contained a Nabataean temple, which was later replaced by a Byzantine church. The remains of the settlement are spread along the slopes of the acropolis. Farmsteads dotted the terraced hills nearby, and ancient dams trapped flash-flood waters in the wadis below or channeled it into rock-cut cisterns. Piles of stones (called in Arabic *tuleilat el-enab*) on the hillsides served to clear the slopes and increased the surface runoff after rainfalls. A large wine press found at Oboda indicates that grapes grown in the area were used to make wine. In the 1950s, David Ben-Gurion, Israel's first prime minister, dreamed of making the desert bloom through cultivation. Israeli scientists attempted to

5.6 Aerial view of the acropolis of Oboda (Avdat). Courtesy of Zev Radovan/BibleLand Pictures.com.

achieve this goal by learning from the Nabataeans and reconstructing an ancient farm at the foot of Avdat, which operated for a number of years. The crops raised at the farm (replicating ancient crops) included grain, grapes, peaches, apricots, almonds, and pistachios. However, because the yields were lower than those using modern irrigation techniques, this experiment was not replicated elsewhere.

Like other native peoples of the Near East, the Nabataeans were influenced by Hellenistic and Roman culture. This is evident in the Greek style of some of the tomb façades at Petra, the incorporation of a colonnaded street and theater, the wall paintings decorating the villas, and the classicizing style of some Nabataean sculpture. In addition, the Nabataeans produced the finest pottery in the region. Nabataean bowls are distinguished by having eggshell-thin, hard-fired walls, decorated on the interior with delicate, red-painted, geometric and floral designs.

Pottery

The typical fine table ware of the Hasmonean period is called **Eastern Terra Sigillata** (or **Eastern Sigillata**). **Terra Sigillata** (Latin for "stamped clay") is so called because sometimes the potter stamped his name on the base of the plate or bowl. Eastern Sigillata was produced at centers around the eastern Mediterranean, including Phoenicia (where a variant called **Eastern Sigillata A [ESA]**

5.7 Painted Nabataean bowl. Photo by Jim Haberman.

was manufactured). Eastern Terra Sigillata is made of a pale yellow or pink clay covered with a glossy, orange-red slip. The slip tends to be uneven, with darker and lighter patches, and it flakes off easily, revealing the light-colored clay beneath. Eastern Sigillata A is found at Hasmonean period sites in Galilee – not surprising, considering the region's proximity to Phoenicia – but does not appear in Judea until the middle of the reign of Herod the Great; even then, it tends to be limited to elite contexts (such as Herod's palaces and the wealthy mansions of Jerusalem's Jewish Quarter). Much of the local pottery of Judea during the Hasmonean period is undecorated.

The typical early Hellenistic mold-made oil lamps with a long nozzle continued to be used during the Hasmonean period. In Judea, these were supplemented by two locally produced types: **cornucopia** (or folded wheel-made) lamps and Judean radial lamps. Cornucopia lamps were made by pinching the sides of a bowl to form a spout, similar to the wheel-made lamps of the Iron Age, of which perhaps they represent a revival. Judean radial lamps are mold-made, with an elongated nozzle and a round body decorated with radiating lines encircling the filling hole.

Coins

Beginning with John Hyrcanus I, the Hasmoneans minted a series of small-denomination bronze coins. Unlike other Hellenistic rulers, the Hasmoneans did not depict the figures of humans, gods, or animals on their coins. Instead, they

5.8 Cornucopia lamps. Courtesy of Zev Radovan/BibleLandPictures.com.

used symbols alluding to royalty (such as diadems), victory (such as wreaths and anchors), and prosperity (such as cornucopiae [horns of plenty]). The anchors depicted on Hasmonean coins might symbolize naval victories or the conquest of major port cities. The coins are also inscribed with the names and titles of the Hasmoneans under whom the coins were minted. The inscriptions are in Greek and Hebrew. The use of Greek by the Hasmoneans – like their adoption of Greek names early on – is interesting, considering that originally Mattathias and his sons opposed Antiochus IV Epiphanes' attempt to impose Greek culture on the Jews. The Hebrew inscriptions on the coins are written in the ancient Hebrew script (paleo-Hebrew), which had been abandoned by the Jews after 586 B.C.E. in favor of the Aramaic script. The use of the paleo-Hebrew script likely was an allusion to the revived biblical kingdom of David and Solomon.

Mattathias Antigonus put an image of the seven-branched menorah on his coins, which symbolized the Jerusalem temple and the establishment of Jewish

5.9 Coin of John Hyrcanus I. Courtesy of Zev Radovan/BibleLandPictures.com.

5.10 Coin of Mattathias Antigonus with a depiction of the menorah. Courtesy of Zev Radovan/ BibleLandPictures.com.

independence from Roman rule (as the Hasmoneans served as high priests and kings). The menorahs on these coins and those incised on the walls of Jason's Tomb are the earliest surviving depictions of the seven-branched lampstand used in the Jerusalem Temple.

Sidebar: The Heliodorus Affair and the Zadokite High Priests

From 2 Maccabees 3–4 and Daniel 11:20 we learn about a series of events that modern scholars describe as "the Heliodorus affair." These events unfolded against the backdrop of political and economic rivalries between Jerusalem's leading families during the first quarter of the second century B.C.E. These families jockeyed for power by aligning themselves with the Ptolemies or Seleucids. The Heliodorus affair was set in motion during the time of Onias III, the high priest in Jerusalem during the reign of Seleucus IV (187–175 B.C.E.). A supporter of the Tobiads named Simon, who was captain of the temple (an administrative position), accused Onias III of hiding money in the Jerusalem temple that should have been declared to the Seleucid king. Seleucus IV sent his finance minister, Heliodorus, to Jerusalem to investigate, and Onias III headed to Antioch to seek an audience with the king and clear his name. While he was away, Onias III left his brother Jason (Hebrew Jeshua) in charge as interim high priest. Although he reached Antioch, Onias III never got to meet the king, who was assassinated by Heliodorus and was succeeded to the throne by his brother, Antiochus IV Epiphanes (175–164 B.C.E.). In the meantime, Jason secured for himself the position of high priest by paying off Antiochus IV Epiphanes, and received permission from Antiochus to refound Jerusalem as a Greek *polis*.

In 172 B.C.E., Jason sent Menelaus (the brother of Simon, the former captain of the temple), to make the required annual payment to the Seleucid king. Menelaus took advantage of the opportunity to outbid Jason, offering

Antiochus IV Epiphanes more money for the position of high priest. Jason fled to Ammon and eventually to Sparta, where he died. Onias III, who was still in Antioch, was assassinated by a hit man hired by Menelaus. His son, Onias IV, fled to Egypt, where he established the Jewish temple at Leontopolis, over which the Oniads presided until it was shut down by Vespasian in 73 C.E.

The Oniads were **Zadokite** high priests. This means they traced their ancestry back to **Zadok**, the high priest appointed by Solomon to officiate in the first temple. The Zadokites controlled the high priesthood in the Jerusalem temple until it was usurped by Menelaus, who was not a Zadokite, and they never regained the high priesthood. The Oniad branch of the Zadokite family established and presided over the temple at Leontopolis in Egypt. Another branch of the Zadokites remained in Jerusalem, accommodated with the ruling powers, and eventually became known as the **Sadducees** (Zadokite and Sadducee are the same word in Hebrew). A third branch of the Zadokite family was instrumental in founding the sect that eventually became known as the **Essenes**, members of which established the settlement at **Qumran** (see Chapter 6).

Recommended Reading

Albert I. Baumgarten, *The Flourishing of Jewish Sects in the Maccabean Era: An Interpretation* (New York: Brill, 1997).

Erich Gruen, *The Hellenistic World and the Coming of Rome, Vols. 1–2* (Berkeley: University of California, 1984).

Judith McKenzie, *The Architecture of Petra* (New York: Oxford University, 1990).

Anthony J. Saldarini, *Pharisees, Scribes, and Sadducees in Palestinian Society* (Grand Rapids, MI: Eerdmans, 2001).

Stephan G. Schmid, "The Nabataeans: Travellers between Lifestyles," in Burton MacDonald, Russell Adams, and Piotr Bienkowski (eds.), *The Archaeology of Jordan* (Sheffield, UK: Sheffield Academic, 2001), 367–426.

@@ @@ @@ @@

SIX

THE ARCHAEOLOGY OF QUMRAN AND THE DEAD SEA SCROLLS

Qumran is a small ruin located on a natural **marl** (chalk) terrace by the northwest shore of the Dead Sea, 8 miles (13 kilometers) south of Jericho. In this chapter, we explore the site of Qumran and the nearby caves in which the Dead Sea Scrolls were found, beginning with an account of the discovery of the Dead Sea Scrolls.

THE DISCOVERY OF THE DEAD SEA SCROLLS

The first Dead Sea Scrolls were discovered by accident in the winter-spring of 1946–1947, when a Bedouin boy entered a cave (Cave 1) in the limestone cliffs behind Qumran and found a row of tall, cylindrical ceramic jars covered with bowl-shaped lids. Most of jars were empty, but at least a couple reportedly contained ancient scrolls. Eventually the Bedouins removed seven complete or nearly complete scrolls from Cave 1. Because the scrolls were written on **parchment** (processed animal hide) and resembled pieces of old leather, the Bedouins sold them to a cobbler in **Bethlehem** named Kando. Kando could not read the scrolls, but thought the writing on them might be ancient Syriac (the language used by the Syrian Orthodox church, to which Kando belonged). Kando therefore offered four of the scrolls to the patriarch of the Syrian Orthodox church in Jerusalem, Mar Athanasius Yeshua Samuel, who purchased them for the sum of 24 British pounds sterling (about $100 at that time).

Kando offered to sell the other three scrolls to Eleazar Lipa Sukenik, an Israeli biblical scholar and archaeologist at the Hebrew University of Jerusalem. Sukenik traveled to Bethlehem and arranged to purchase these scrolls from Kando on November 29, 1947, coincidentally the same day that the United Nations voted in favor of the establishment of the State of Israel. Sukenik

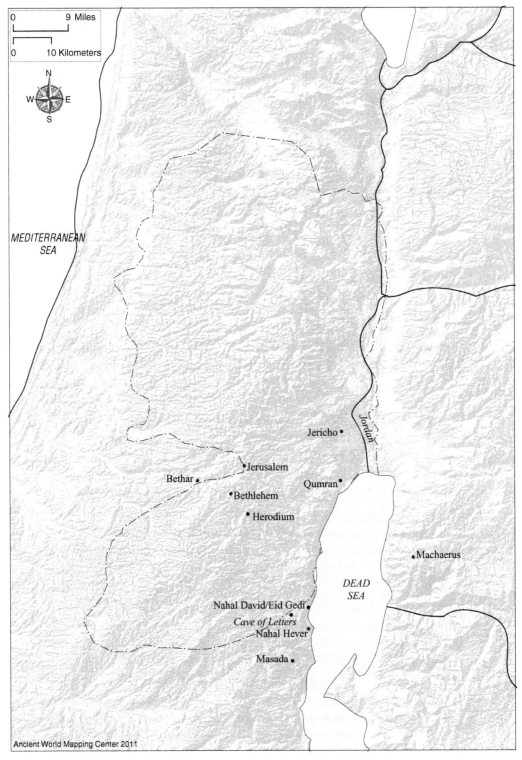

6.1 Map of the Dead Sea region. Ancient World Mapping Center, University of North Carolina at Chapel Hill (www.unc.edu/awmc).

6.2 Aerial view of Qumran looking south. Courtesy of Zev Radovan/BibleLandPictures.com.

seems to have been the first scholar to recognize the date and importance of the scrolls, which had surfaced on the antiquities market without any archaeological context. In the meantime, Samuel tried – without success – to sell his four scrolls for a profit. Eventually he put them up for sale in the United States, placing an advertisement in the *Wall Street Journal* on June 1, 1954. When the ad appeared, Yigael Yadin, who was Sukenik's son (and later became a famous archaeologist and chief of staff of the Israeli army), was in the United States on a fundraising mission. Through the aid of a middleman, Yadin purchased the four scrolls from Samuel (who received $250,000 – a handsome profit on his investment!). Thus, eventually all seven scrolls from Cave 1 came to be in the possession of the state of Israel, which subsequently built the Shrine of the Book at the Israel Museum in Jerusalem to house and display the scrolls.

Once the significance of the scrolls was recognized, scholars attempted to ascertain their origin. By the end of the 1940s, the caves around Qumran had been pinpointed, and in the early 1950s an archaeological expedition was organized to Qumran. After the establishment of the state of Israel in 1948 and until the 1967 Six-Day War, Qumran was in Jordanian territory (the "West Bank"). Therefore, the archaeological expedition to Qumran was organized under the auspices of the Jordanian government. The expedition was led by Roland de Vaux (pronounced deh-VOH), a French biblical scholar and archaeologist

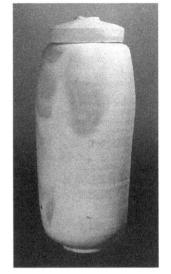

6.3 Cylindrical jar with lid from Qumran. Courtesy of Zev Radovan/BibleLandPictures.com.

affiliated with the Dominican École Biblique et Archéologique Française in Jerusalem. From 1951 to 1956, de Vaux excavated the site of Qumran and searched the caves in the area for additional scrolls. Eventually scrolls were discovered in 11 caves in the vicinity of Qumran, which are numbered Caves 1–11. Altogether these caves yielded the remains of more than 900 different scrolls. Most of these are not complete scrolls, but small fragments surviving from what originally were complete scrolls. Perhaps the most important cave – which was discovered by Bedouins, not archaeologists – is Cave 4, located in the marl terrace on which the site of Qumran sits. Cave 4 (which actually is two caves, 4a and 4b), yielded the remains of more than 500 scrolls, which were found lying strewn on the floor of the cave and had disintegrated into thousands of fragments. The delays in publication of the Dead Sea Scrolls, which caused considerable controversy in the 1980s and 1990s, were the result of the time scholars spent sifting through these fragments, determining which pieces belonged to the same scrolls and what kinds of literature they represented, long before the advent of computer technology. Now all the Dead Sea Scrolls are published, and they have been fully accessible to the public for well over a decade.

THE CHRONOLOGY OF QUMRAN

De Vaux's excavations at Qumran brought to light a settlement with many unique and peculiar features. The site is small and compact, and unlike contemporary settlements and villages, it contains no private houses or dwellings. Instead, all the rooms at Qumran were used for communal purposes (such as communal dining rooms) or as workshops. If there were no private dwellings in the settlement, where did the inhabitants live – that is, where were the sleep-ing quarters? Some of the rooms in the settlement originally had two stories. It may be that some of the second-story rooms were used as bedrooms. If all the members of the Qumran community lived (slept) inside the settlement, the population must have been very small – perhaps only ten to twenty people – because there is so little space for sleeping in the second-story rooms. However, de Vaux likely was correct in suggesting that most, if not all, of the members of this community lived (slept) not inside the settlement but outside it – in tents, huts, and in some of the surrounding caves. In this case, the population could have been as many as 100 to 150 people, a number suggested by the size of the communal dining room (discussed later). It is also likely that the population fluctuated over the long term and even seasonally, although archaeology does not provide the resolution necessary to distinguish such fluctuations.

Qumran is distinguished not only by the small and compact size of the settlement but also by the simplicity of the architecture. The walls are built of unworked or roughly cut field stones with mud mortar or sometimes are made of of mud brick, and the floors are of packed dirt (sometimes plastered) or are paved with rough **flagstones**. The flat roofs were made of thick layers of rushes and reeds bound with mud set on top of pieces of wood that spanned the walls. Unlike contemporary villas and palaces, there is no evidence of interior decoration such as **frescoes** and **stucco** (molded plaster) on the walls or **mosaics** on the floors.

De Vaux distinguished several occupation phases at Qumran. The sectarian settlement (which is the focus of our discussion) was preceded by a late Iron Age phase dating to the seventh century B.C.E. (ending ca. 586 B.C.E.). After an abandonment of several centuries, the sectarian settlement was established during the Hasmonean period (ca. 100 B.C.E.), and existed until its final destruc-tion by the Romans at the time of the First Jewish Revolt (68 C.E.). After 68 C.E. a small Roman garrison occupied the site, probably until the fall of Masada in 73/74 C.E. De Vaux referred to the occupation phases of the sectarian settlement as Periods I and II. In the second half of the first century B.C.E., the settlement suffered two destructions: by earthquake (31 B.C.E.) and by fire (ca. 9/8 B.C.E.). After the earthquake, the inhabitants cleaned up the site and repaired the build-ings. After the fire, which seems to have been the result of an enemy attack, the inhabitants abandoned the settlement briefly before reoccupying it.

THE BUILDINGS AT QUMRAN

The northern side of the settlement is dominated by a two-story-high watch-tower, so placed because the main approach to Qumran is from the north (Jerusalem and Jericho). The tower was accessed at the second-story level by

6.4 Cave 4 at Qumran.

wooden gangways from the surrounding buildings, which could be raised in times of trouble, providing protection for those taking refuge inside.

South of the tower, in the heart of the settlement, is a room that de Vaux identified as a **scriptorium**, or writing room. Mixed in with the collapse from the second-story level, de Vaux found pieces of long, narrow tables and benches made of mud brick and covered with plaster. He identified this room as a scriptorium because of the presence of inkwells among the debris, which are

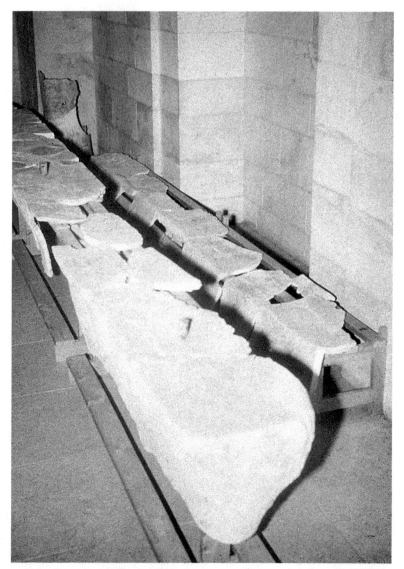

6.5 Table and bench from the "scriptorium" at Qumran. From Roland de Vaux, *Archaeology and the Dead Sea Scrolls* (Schweich Lectures, Oxford, 1973), Pl. XXIa. © The British Academy. Courtesy of the Israel Antiquities Authority.

rarely found on archaeological excavations in Israel. De Vaux's identification has been the subject of debate, because in the ancient Mediterranean and Near East scribes typically squatted when they wrote, holding the materials in their laps. The custom of sitting on a chair to write at a table (as we do today) developed later, in medieval monasteries. Some scholars have suggested that the scribes sat on top of the tables and rested their feet on the benches, holding the materials on their laps. This is unlikely because the tables, which are made of mud brick and are concave on the bottom, would have cracked under the weight. Therefore,

6.6 Broken dishes in the pantry at Qumran. From Roland de Vaux, *Archaeology and the Dead Sea Scrolls* (Schweich Lectures, Oxford, 1973), Pl. Xa. © The British Academy.

some scholars have suggested that the room was not a scriptorium but was used for some other purpose, such as a **triclinium** (dining room) in which diners reclined on the benches and the food was set on the tables. The problem with this theory is that the benches are so narrow (only about 15 inches wide) that anyone trying to recline on them would have rolled off!

Although we do not understand how the furniture was used, de Vaux's interpretation seems the most likely because of the inkwells, which are difficult to explain otherwise. Furthermore, the long, narrow tables would have been well suited for the preparation of scrolls, providing a surface on which to lay the pieces of parchment. In this case, some of the Dead Sea Scrolls might have been written or copied in this room. It is important to note that some of the Dead Sea Scrolls must have been brought to Qumran from elsewhere, because some of them antedate (were written before) the establishment of the settlement. However, some of the Dead Sea Scrolls are contemporary with the settlement, and therefore might have been written or copied in the scriptorium.

De Vaux identified the largest room in the settlement as an assembly hall. He identified it also as a communal dining room because in the adjacent room he found a pantry of more than 1000 pottery dishes. Originally the dishes were stacked on wooden shelves lining the walls of the pantry, but the shelves collapsed in the earthquake of 31 B.C.E. After the earthquake the broken dishes were left lying where they had fallen, and that part of the room was sealed off by a wall. Nearly all of the dishes in the pantry are open shapes – plates, cups, and bowls – that is, table ware, the kinds of dishes used for dining (as opposed to cooking pots and storage jars, for example). The discovery of hundreds of dining dishes in the pantry led de Vaux to suppose that the large adjacent room was used for communal meals.

One peculiar phenomenon at Qumran is the animal bone deposits. In the open-air spaces outside and around the buildings, de Vaux found deposits of animal bones. An analysis of the bones indicated that they all belong to **kosher** species of animals – that is, species that are permitted according to biblical Jewish law: sheep, cows, and goats, but no pigs. There is also no poultry, although it is permitted by biblical law. The animals had been slaughtered and butchered, and the meat had been cut into chunks, which were boiled or roasted. The chunks of cooked meat were eaten, and the bones were deposited on top of the ground outside the buildings, covered with pieces of broken pottery or placed inside pots.

It is difficult to explain this phenomenon because no analogous animal bone deposits have been discovered at other sites. The suggestion made by some scholars that the bones were deposited in this manner because of a fear of predators makes no sense, as it would have been easier to dispose of them by tossing them over the cliff into Wadi Qumran, and because the bones would have attracted predators. And if this was an effective means of keeping away predators, why are similar deposits not found at other sites – were predators a problem only at Qumran? Another possibility is that these bones represent the remains of animal sacrifices. However, we have no indication that the Jewish sect that inhabited Qumran rejected the biblical (Deuteronomic) injunction requiring all sacrifices to be offered in the Jerusalem temple (although members of this sect apparently chose not to participate in the sacrifices). There is also no archaeological evidence of an altar for animal sacrifices at Qumran. De Vaux suggested that the animal bone deposits were the remains of special, ritual meals that were eaten by the Qumran community. Although de Vaux's suggestion makes the most sense, it lacks explanatory power – that is, it does not explain *why* the inhabitants deposited or disposed of the bones in this peculiar manner. To understand the animal bone deposits, we must acquaint ourselves with the Qumran community.

The inhabitants of Qumran were members of a sect that was founded by dis-possessed Zadokite priests (see the Sidebar in Chapter 5). This sect believed that the current Jerusalem priesthood was illegitimate and unfit to serve because they were not Zadokites. They therefore considered the Jerusalem temple and the sacrifices offered there to be polluted (impure). The sect withdrew from the temple, apparently refusing to participate in the sacrificial cult, and awaited the day when they would regain control of the priesthood. In the interim, the sect constituted itself as a substitute temple (or, more precisely, as a wilderness tabernacle), with each full member living his everyday life as if he were a priest.

6.7 Deposit of animal bones covered by potsherds found at Qumran. From Roland de Vaux, *Archaeology and the Dead Sea Scrolls* (Schweich Lectures, Oxford, 1973), Pl. XIb. © The British Academy.

Participation in the sect's communal meals seems to have been considered a substitute for participation in the temple sacrifices.

What happened during sacrifices in the Jerusalem temple and other ancient temples? Throngs of people gathered to watch as the priests slaughtered and butchered dozens of sacrificial animals. In some cases (such as in a holocaust offering), all the meat was burned on the altar, feeding the deity as the smoke rose to the heavens. In other cases, some of the meat was burned on the altar, and the rest was cooked and consumed on the spot by the priests and pilgrims. In other words, Jerusalem's Temple Mount was an enormous precinct where crowds congregated to feast on sacrificial meat. Because of the warm climate and lack of refrigeration, once an animal was slaughtered, the meat had to be consumed immediately. The inedible parts of sacrifices, such as bones, apparently were disposed of in specially designated areas around the outside of the Temple Mount. Because the members of the Qumran community conceived of themselves as a substitute temple, it may be that they disposed of the remains of their communal meals in a manner analogous to the remains of sacrifices in the

Jerusalem temple – in this case, around the outside of the settlement. If this is so, although the animal bone deposits from Qumran are not the remains of sacrifices, conceptually they are analogous.

Among the many workshops that dot the settlement at Qumran is a potters' workshop, located in the southeast corner of the site. The workshop included two kilns, oriented with their openings in different directions to take advantage of changing winds. Some of the pottery manufactured in the workshop is similar to pottery found elsewhere in Judea in the late Second Temple period. However, some types are distinctive to Qumran, such as the cylindrical jars with bowl-shaped lids that are found by the dozens in the settlement and in the surrounding caves. Analyses indicate that some pottery vessels were made of clay brought from Jerusalem.

THE WATER SYSTEM AND RITUAL BATHS (*MIQVA'OT*)

An extensive water system runs through the Qumran settlement, consisting of a series of pools fed by an **aqueduct** (channel). The pools were dug into the marl terrace, and were lined with stone and plastered. Some of the pools were used as cisterns for storing drinking water, a necessity in Qumran's arid environment. They include a round cistern on the western side of the settlement that dates to the Iron Age and was reused in the sectarian occupation phases. Ten of the pools were used as Jewish ritual baths (Hebrew **miqveh**; pl. *miqva'ot*), as indicated by a broad set of steps running along the width of the pool, from top to bottom, which facilitated immersion in the water. Many of the ritual baths have other features, such as low partitions running down the steps (to separate pure from impure), staggered broad and narrow steps (with the broad steps being used as bathing platforms, depending on the level of the water), and a deep basin at the bottom to enable immersion when the water reached its lowest level.

The concept of ritual purity, which was central to the lifestyle of the Qumran sect, is poorly understood by many people today. According to the Torah, people become ritually impure as a result of coming into contact with certain things or experiencing certain natural processes. The causes of ritual impurity appear quite random to us – ranging, for example, from touching mildew on the walls of a house to touching a lizard to touching a corpse, or having a menstrual period (for a woman) or a nocturnal emission (for a man). Ritual impurity in Judaism is a mechanical category, meaning that it does not make a person bad or sinful (in the Christian sense of the word), or dirty or unhygienic. All people become impure at various times. The method of purification varies, depending on the status of the affected person (layperson versus priest) and the nature of the impurity (corpse impurity is the worst, and requires a complicated purification procedure). But for most people and most types of impurity, purification is effected by immersing in a pool of undrawn water, and, after immersion, waiting

6.8 *Miqveh* with earthquake crack at Qumran. Photo by Jim Haberman.

for the passage of a certain amount of time (usually until sundown). Undrawn water means that the pool cannot be filled by mechanical means, such as a hose or bucket (although the pool can be filled by allowing water to flow through a channel). Natural bodies of water, such as lakes, rivers, streams, and pools of rainwater, are permissible.

The need to observe ritual purity laws was limited to certain times or situations – mostly when one entered the presence of the God of Israel. Many religions in the Mediterranean world and Near East had similar purity laws. In ancient Judaism, the focal point for entering the presence of God was the Jerusalem temple. Therefore, everyone – including Jesus and Paul – took it for granted that ritual purification was required first. But the fact is that most Jews usually were in a state of ritual impurity, and did not worry about being ritually pure on an everyday basis. Only priests had to be concerned with a more regular observance of the ritual purity laws, because of their service in the temple. Judaism was distinguished from other ancient religions in that some groups or sects in the late Second Temple period extended the observance of ritual purity beyond the boundaries of the temple cult, reflecting their belief that God's presence was not limited to the Jerusalem temple. Full members of the Qumran sect observed ritual purity laws at the highest level and on an everyday basis because they lived as though they were priests in the temple or

6.9 Aqueduct cut as a tunnel through a cliff at Qumran.

wilderness tabernacle, with God's presence and angels dwelling in their midst. The large number of ritual baths at Qumran and their large sizes relative to the size of the community are a clear expression of this community's concern with the observance of ritual purity.

All of the pools at Qumran (cisterns and ritual baths) were filled by an aqueduct that brought flash flood water from the nearby riverbed (Wadi Qumran). The edge of the marl terrace on which Qumran sits overlooks Wadi Qumran. Like most other riverbeds along the shores of the Dead Sea, Wadi Qumran is usually dry. However, once or twice a winter, when enough rain falls in the mountains behind (to the west of) Qumran, the ground becomes saturated with water and flash floods flow through the riverbeds into the Dead Sea. The flood waters flow as a torrent but usually last for less than twenty-four hours. Because the pools at Qumran were replenished only once or twice a year, the water in the ritual baths became dirty as members immersed themselves repeatedly and the water level dropped – highlighting the fact that the concept of ritual purity has nothing to do with cleanliness or hygiene. To feed the pools, the inhabitants of Qumran dug or cut a channel in the ground leading from Wadi Qumran to the site. The channel originated at the base of a (usually dry) waterfall in the riverbed, by a dam. In times of a flash flood, water rose behind the dam and filled the channel, flowing to the site and filling each pool in succession. One flash flood filled all the pools in the settlement. The dam long ago washed away, but much of the channel is still visible, including a section alongside Wadi Qumran where it is cut as a tunnel through a cliff.

6.10 Heaps of stones covering graves in the Qumran cemetery.

THE CEMETERY

A large cemetery containing approximately 1,100 graves is located on top of the plateau to the east of the settlement. De Vaux excavated forty-three graves. All the burials are inhumations, meaning that the body was buried whole (not cremated), and nearly all contained single burials. The graves are similar to our own graves today, consisting of a trench dug six feet deep into the ground. The corpse, wrapped in a shroud and sometimes placed in a wooden coffin, was laid at the base of the trench, and the space was sealed with stone slabs or mud bricks. The trench was filled in with dirt, and stones were heaped on top of the grave, with headstones marking each end. Most of the graves are located on top of the plateau, with others scattered on hills to the north, east, and south. The graves on top of the plateau are lined up in neat rows, with the bodies placed so that the head lies to the south and the feet are to the north. The graves on the hills to the north and east are oriented the same way. However, the graves on the hills to the south (south of the plateau and south of Wadi Qumran) are more randomly scattered, with many oriented east–west. Of the graves that de Vaux excavated, all but three in the main part of the cemetery and the hills to the north and east contained adult men; the three exceptions are burials of adult women, with no children or infants represented. The graves to the south, which contained large numbers of women and children, apparently are relatively recent (modern) Bedouin burials. This evidence, although based on a small number of excavated graves proportionate to the cemetery, suggests that the Qumran community was not an ordinary settlement of families, but consisted overwhelmingly of adult men.

What are the Dead Sea Scrolls and What Is Their Connection to Qumran?

I use the term *Dead Sea Scrolls* to refer to the remains of more than 900 scrolls from the eleven caves around Qumran, but not ancient scrolls and documents found in caves elsewhere around the Dead Sea (such as the Bar-Kokhba documents from Nahal Hever and Wadi Murabbat). No scrolls were discovered in the settlement at Qumran; instead, all of them come from caves around Qumran. It is precisely this fact that has made it possible for some scholars to suggest that Qumran was not a sectarian settlement (as de Vaux thought), but was a villa, manor house, fort, commercial entrepôt, or pottery manufacturing center. To identify Qumran as anything but a sectarian settlement, one must divorce the scrolls from the site, which means that the inhabitants of the site were not responsible for depositing the scrolls in the nearby caves. There are many problems with these alternative theories, including the fact that none adequately explains how the scrolls came to be deposited in the caves around Qumran if they were not deposited by the inhabitants of the site. For example, one theory posits that the scrolls originated in the library of the Jerusalem temple and were deposited in the caves around Qumran on the eve of the temple's destruction in 70 C.E. Aside from the fact that it is difficult to accept such a coincidence – that whoever carried the scrolls from Jerusalem bypassed the thousands of other caves along the way and happened to choose the caves around Qumran – we have no idea what kind of literary collection or library the Jerusalem temple housed. Moreover, much of the literature from Qumran expresses opposition to the sacrificial cult in the Jerusalem temple and the Jerusalem priesthood, so presumably could not have originated there.

The alternative theories also ignore the clear connection between the scroll caves and the site of Qumran. First is an archaeological connection: the same types of pottery, including types unique to Qumran such as the cylindrical jars, are found in the scroll caves and in the settlement. Second is the physical connection: some of the scroll caves are in the marl terrace on which the settlement sits and could be accessed only by walking through the site. It is also possible that originally there were scrolls at Qumran, but if so, they burned in the fires that destroyed the settlement around 9/8 B.C.E. and in 68 C.E. The scroll caves, of course, were unaffected by these fires. In short, one cannot divorce the scrolls from the settlement, with the conclusion being that the inhabitants of Qumran were sectarians (members of a Jewish sect).

The Dead Sea Scrolls are a collection of Jewish religious literature that belonged to the community that lived at Qumran. No examples of historical

6.11   The Isaiah scroll from Cave 1 at Qumran. Courtesy of Zev Radovan/BibleLandPictures
.com.

works such as 1 and 2 Maccabees are represented among the Dead Sea Scrolls,
and there are no personal documents such as deeds to property, marriage con-
tracts, or personal correspondence. Approximately one-quarter of the Dead Sea
Scrolls are copies of the Hebrew Bible (Old Testament). All of the books of the
Hebrew Bible are represented among the Dead Sea Scrolls by at least one copy,
and some in multiple copies, except for the book of Esther. It is not clear whether
Esther was represented by a copy that has not been preserved, or whether it
was not included at all. These are the earliest copies of the Hebrew Bible that
have survived, written centuries earlier than the ninth- and tenth-century C.E.
copies that we had before the discovery of the Dead Sea Scrolls. The copies of
the Hebrew Bible from Qumran are important because they are much closer in
date to the time when the biblical text was first composed and edited (a process
that, according to conservative estimates, began with the Pentateuch in the late
eighth to sixth centuries B.C.E. and ended with Daniel ca. 167–164 B.C.E.).

Do the copies of the Hebrew Bible from Qumran differ from the text used
today – that is, have any changes been made over the course of the centuries?
The answer is yes *and* no, for the following reason. Today all Jews use the
same version of the Hebrew Bible, which is called the **Masoretic Text** (MT),
from the Hebrew word for tradition. However, in the late Second Temple period,
different variants of the text of the Hebrew Bible were used by Jews. Most of the
variations are relatively minor (differences in a sentence here or sentence there,
or individual words), but there were variations. It was only after the Second
Temple period that Jews decided to use only one version of the Hebrew Bible, at
which point the other variants ceased to be copied and disappeared. The Dead

Sea Scrolls include copies of the Proto-Masoretic Text, as well as variant texts that had not been preserved. They therefore contribute to our understanding of the compositional and transmission history of the Hebrew Bible.

The Dead Sea Scrolls also include a few fragments of the Septuagint (see the Sidebar in Chapter 4), which serves as the basis for the text of the Old Testament used by some denominations today (including the pre-1943 Catholic church by way of early Latin translations, and the Armenian and Coptic churches). In contrast, the Protestant Old Testament is translated from the Hebrew text (Hebrew Bible). No copies of the New Testament or any other early Christian works were found at Qumran.

The Dead Sea Scrolls include other types of literature related to the Hebrew Bible. For example, there are Aramaic translations of the biblical text (**Targums**) and commentaries on or interpretations of prophetic books (**Pesharim**; sing. **Pesher**). There are apocryphal works, such as Tobit and Ecclesiasticus or the Wisdom of Ben Sira. There are also works called Pseudepigrapha, such as the books of Enoch and Jubilees, which were not included in the Jewish, Protestant, or Catholic canons of sacred scripture but sometimes were preserved in the canons of other churches.

The Dead Sea Scrolls include works that are sectarian in nature, meaning they describe or reflect the peculiar outlook, beliefs, and practices of the community that lived at Qumran (and the wider movement of which it was a part). Sectarian works include the **Damascus Document** (copies of which were found at the end of the nineteenth century in the Cairo **Geniza**, a repository of damaged Jewish sacred writings in a Cairo synagogue), the **Community Rule** (sometimes called the **Manual of Discipline**), the **War Scroll**, and perhaps the **Temple Scroll**. The sect might have formed in the first half of the second half of the second century B.C.E. (between ca. 200-150 B.C.E.), under a leader or founder called "the **Teacher of Righteousness**." One of the peculiarities of the Dead Sea Scrolls is that they usually refer to historical figures (people) not by their real names but by nicknames, such as the Teacher of Righteousness, his opponent the **Wicked Priest**, the Man of Lies, and the **Lion of Wrath**. In some cases we can identify these nicknamed figures with some confidence (for example, the Lion of Wrath is Alexander Jannaeus). However, the identity of the Teacher of Righteousness remains elusive, although he could not be **John the Baptist**, Jesus, **James the Just**, or anyone else in Jesus' circle, because the scrolls referring to the Teacher were composed well before Jesus' time. In fact, the Teacher's name indicates that he was a Zadokite priest, as the nicknames are puns in Hebrew: Righteousness (Hebrew *zedek*) is a pun on Zadok. Although not all (or even most) sectarians were priests, they lived a priestly lifestyle, and priests (especially Zadokites) occupied prominent positions.

Members of this sect lived in towns and villages around Palestine, including in Jerusalem, but some practiced desert separatism – that is, some lived apart in the desert. Qumran was one such desert community; we do not know whether there were others because so far none has been found. Only physically and mentally unblemished adult men could apply for full membership (the same qualifications required for priests serving in the Jerusalem temple), which involved undergoing a process of initiation that lasted two to three years. After passing the initial stages of initiation, the candidate was required to surrender all personal property, as the sect practiced the pooling of possessions.

Belonging to this sect was a hardship because of the rigorous observance of ritual purity laws, which affected all aspects of daily life, even toilet habits (discussed later). Nevertheless, the sect attracted members because it promised salvation to them alone, for this was an apocalyptic sect that anticipated the imminent arrival of the end of days. They believed that the end of days would be ushered in by a forty-year-long apocalyptic war between the Sons of Light (= good = the sect) and the Sons of Darkness (= evil = everyone else). One of the peculiarities of this sect compared with other Jewish groups is that they believed in predeterminism, meaning that everything is preordained by God and there is no human free will at all. Therefore, the forty-year-long war and its outcome – victory for the Sons of Light – were preordained by God. This victory would usher in a messianic era. Another peculiarity of this sect is that it anticipated the arrival of not one but two messiahs: to the usual royal messiah of Israel descended from David, they added a second, priestly messiah descended from Aaron – not surprising, considering the priestly orientation of the sect (some scholars think the sect also expected a third, prophetic messiah).

THE ESSENES

Many scholars (including myself) identify the Qumran community and the wider sectarian movement of which it was a part with the Essenes. However, nowhere in the Dead Sea Scrolls are Essenes mentioned, at least not by that name. Instead, we learn about the Essenes from contemporary outside authors – that is, authors who lived in the late first century B.C.E. and first century C.E. Our most important sources on the Essenes are Flavius Josephus (who provides the longest and most detailed account and is the only author who claims a personal familiarity with the Essenes), Philo Judaeus (the Jewish philosopher who lived in Alexandria), and **Pliny the Elder** (the Roman author who died during the eruption of Mount Vesuvius in 79 C.E.). All these authors describe a Jewish sect called the Essenes, with beliefs and practices that overlap with information from the Dead Sea Scrolls (for example, holding communal meals, pooling possessions, and a long initiation process). Although Pliny's description is the shortest and is somewhat confused (because he never visited Judea but derived his information from an unknown source), Pliny is the only author who situates the Essenes on the northwest shore of the Dead Sea – that is, in the same geographical area where Qumran is located.

Furthermore, the lack of reference to Essenes in the Dead Sea Scrolls is far from decisive in arguing against their identification with the Qumran community. Some scholars have suggested that Essenes are mentioned in the scrolls, but by a Hebrew or Aramaic term that was translated or transliterated in Greek and Latin as "Essene" (Josephus, Philo, and Pliny wrote in Greek and Latin, whereas the majority of the scrolls are in Hebrew and a smaller number are in Aramaic). Suggestions of an original Hebrew or Aramaic term for the Greek and Roman word Essene include **hasid** ("pious one") and 'osay ("the doers," meaning those who observe the Torah). Or, it may be that Essenes are not mentioned in the Dead Sea Scrolls because this was a name given to the sect by outsiders, whereas members called themselves by other names, such as the Sons of Light, the sons of Zadok, and the **yahad** (the "unity" or "community").

WAS JESUS AN ESSENE?

By now it should be clear that Jesus was not an Essene. True, there are some similarities between Jesus' movement and the Essenes, including holding communal meals, pooling possessions, a dualism of light versus darkness, and an apocalyptic outlook. On the other hand, there are also important differences, including the Qumran sect's anticipation of at least two messiahs and its belief in predeterminism. And nowhere is Jesus mentioned in the Dead Sea Scrolls. Perhaps the most important differences between Jesus and his movement and the Essenes concern their approaches to ritual purity observance and membership. Because the Qumran sect constituted itself as a substitute temple, it extended the observance of priestly purity laws to all full members on an everyday basis. In contrast, Jesus is portrayed as coming into contact with the most impure members of Jewish society, including lepers, hemorrhaging women, and even corpses – people whom the Essenes would have avoided. Furthermore, whereas the Essenes were an exclusive sect, barring large sectors of the population from applying for admission and requiring a long process of initiation, Jesus's movement was inclusive and welcomed everyone.

Was John the Baptist an Essene? Of all of the figures who reportedly were associated with Jesus, John the Baptist seems closest to the Essenes. After all, he was the son of a priest, was active in the wilderness near Qumran at the same time the settlement existed, performed purification rites involving immersion in water, and lived an ascetic lifestyle. Thus, it may be that John was an Essene at some point in his life, or at least was acquainted with the sect. However, by the time we hear about John in the Gospel accounts, he could not have been an Essene, as his food, clothing, and purification practices are different. Whereas Essene men apparently wore linen clothing and consumed only the pure food

6.12 Roman luxury latrine at Ephesus.

and drink of the sect, John is described as wearing camel-hair garments and eating grasshoppers and wild honey. In other words, even if John was an Essene at some point (a big if!), our sources suggest that he did not end his life as an Essene.

TOILETS AND TOILET HABITS IN THE ANCIENT WORLD: THE TOILET AT QUMRAN

Because of their strict observance of purity laws, the Essenes' lifestyle differed from that of other Jews even in details such as toilet habits. De Vaux's discovery of a toilet at Qumran provides an opportunity to discuss ancient toilets and toilet habits in general and those of the Essenes in particular. Despite sophisticated aqueduct systems and other technologies, the Roman world was a filthy, malodorous, and unhealthy place, certainly by contemporary Western standards. If we could be transported back in time, it is unlikely that most of us would survive exposure to the widespread dirt and diseases, to which we lack immunity. The streets and sidewalks of Roman streets were littered with garbage, human and animal feces, and even carcasses of animals and birds. Scavenging dogs, birds, and swarms of flies spread diseases. Even the emperor was not insulated from these conditions, as indicated by a passage from **Suetonius**' *Life of Vespasian* (5:4): "Once when he was taking breakfast, a stray dog brought in a human hand from the cross-roads and dropped it under the table." The streets of the most advanced cities, such as Pompeii, were marginally better in having raised sidewalks with stepping stones for pedestrians, which provided some protection when heavy rains caused flooding.

The Romans developed the most sophisticated toilet facilities in the ancient Mediterranean world. These toilets, called *Roman luxury latrines*, were usually in a room attached to a bath house. A constant stream of running water brought by an aqueduct circulated through the various rooms of the bath house before reaching the latrine. The water flowed in an underground channel along the sides of the latrine room. A row of stone or wooden toilet seats pierced by holes was placed above the channel, and the waste was carried away by the water. A shallow channel at the base of the seats collected spillage and was used to hold and dip a sponge on a stick, which the Romans used to clean themselves (like toilet paper). The arrangement of side-by side toilet seats in a luxury latrine – which could accommodate up to sixty people – shows that there was no expectation of toilet privacy in the Roman world.

When individuals had no access to built toilet facilities, they relieved themselves anywhere they could, including in streets and alleys, staircases of dwellings, bath houses and other public buildings, and tombs. Public urination and even defecation do not appear to have been unusual sights, as indicated by signs and graffiti found in cities around the Roman world requesting that individuals relieve themselves elsewhere. Chamber pots or broken jars were used in houses that were not equipped with built toilet facilities, with the waste emptied into the streets.

When built toilet facilities are found in private dwellings in the Roman world, they usually consist of a stone or wooden seat set over a cesspit. Other household waste such as garbage was also thrown into the cesspit, which is why toilets in Roman houses often were located in or next to the kitchen. Most cesspits were not connected to a drainage or sewer system and had no outlet. Instead, Roman sewers drained runoff water or overflow (and with it, the accumulated waste) from the main streets. Once the cesspit of a toilet was full, a manure merchant was paid to empty it, selling the contents as fertilizer ("night soil"). A toilet installation of this type was discovered in the late Iron Age house of Ahiel in the City of David (see Chapter 2). A stone seat pierced by a hole was still set above the cesspit. An analysis of the contents of the cesspit provided evidence about the diet of the house's residents and the diseases and parasites from which they suffered. Similarly, the toilet that de Vaux found at Qumran consists of a cesspit that was dug into the dirt floor of a room (L51), which was lined with caked, hardened mud. According to de Vaux, the cesspit was filled with layers of dirty, smelly soil. A terra-cotta pipe set into the middle of the pit might have been connected with a toilet seat, which was not preserved. The only doorway in the room with the toilet opened onto a ritual bath that was damaged by the earthquake of 31 B.C.E.

The Dead Sea Scrolls and Josephus indicate that the Qumran sect differed from other Jews and Romans in being concerned with toilet privacy and modesty. Their permanent, built toilet facilities (such as the one at Qumran) were enclosed,

6.13 Toilet in the house of Ahiel in the City of David. Courtesy of Jane Cahill West.

roofed rooms with doors that could be closed to shield the user from view. Furthermore, sectarian law required that the excrement be buried in a pit. When they did not have access to built toilet facilities, the Essenes did not relieve themselves in full view as others did, but instead did so in the manner described by Josephus:

> [On the Sabbath they do not] even go to stool. On other days they dig a trench a foot deep with a mattock – such is the nature of the hatchet which they present to neophytes – and wrapping their mantle about them, that they may not offend the rays of the deity, sit above it. They then replace the excavated soil in the trench. For this purpose they select the more retired spots. And though this discharge of the excrements is a natural function, they make it a rule to wash themselves after it, as if defiled. (*War* 2.147–149)

According to Josephus, when they did not have access to built toilet facilities, the sectarians sought a secluded spot, dug a small pit in the ground, wrapped their cloaks around them, squatted, and after they finished, filled the pit with soil. This practice displays the peculiar sectarian concerns with toilet privacy, modesty, and burying excrement in a pit.

The toilet habits of the Qumran sect derived from their interpretation of biblical Jewish law – specifically, Deuteronomy 23:9–14. This passage mandates the placement of the toilets outside the wilderness camp (during the desert wanderings of the Israelites), with the excrement being buried in a pit, because it is indecent and must be kept hidden from God's view:

> When you are encamped against your enemies you shall guard against any impropriety. If one of you becomes unclean (impure) because of a nocturnal emission, then he shall go outside the camp; he must not come within the camp. When evening comes, he shall wash himself with water, and when the sun has set, he may come back into the camp. You shall have a designated area outside the camp to which you shall go. With your utensils you shall have a trowel; when you relieve yourself outside, you shall dig a hole with it and then cover up your excrement. Because the Lord your God travels along with your camp, to save you and to hand over your enemies to you, therefore your camp must be holy, so that he may not see anything indecent among you and turn away from you. (NRSV)

Because the Qumran sect constituted itself as a substitute temple or wilderness tabernacle and believed that God and his angels dwelled in their midst, they extended the laws of the desert camp to their everyday life. This is the reason they buried excrement in a pit and were concerned with toilet privacy and modesty. The sectarians also differed from other Jews in considering excrement to be ritually impure, which explains why the only doorway in the room with a toilet at Qumran opens onto a ritual bath. Perhaps most peculiarly, the sectarians seem to have refrained from defecating on the Sabbath, as Josephus describes, probably to avoid profaning the Sabbath through pollution (ritual impurity).

Sidebar: Women at Qumran

Some scholars have described the Qumran settlement as "monastic," meaning that all the inhabitants were adult men. This is suggested by the excavated burials in the cemetery, which consist overwhelmingly of adult males, and by the testimony of Josephus, Philo, and Pliny, who describe the Essenes as a sect consisting of celibate men (although in one passage Josephus mentions a group of Essenes who marry and have children). The problem is that none of the sectarian scrolls from Qumran mandate celibacy, and, in fact, many include legislation concerning women and children (including marriage, childbirth, divorce, etc.). Because of such contradictory information, some scholars claim that the inhabitants of Qumran should not be identified with the Essenes described by outside sources (Josephus, Philo, and Pliny), but must belong to another (unidentified) Jewish sect.

In my opinion, the apparent contradiction is due to the different nature of our sources. The Dead Sea Scrolls represent the sect's own literature and contained their interpretation of biblical law, including the regulations that governed their everyday lives and shaped their beliefs and practices. This literature was intended for internal consumption. In contrast, Josephus,

Philo, and Pliny wrote for a nonsectarian audience. Let us consider Josephus and Philo, who were Jewish authors (Pliny's somewhat garbled account reflects the fact that he never visited Judea and derived his information about the Essenes second- or third-hand). Both Josephus and Philo can be considered as Diaspora Jews; Philo lived in Alexandria his entire life, and, although Josephus was a Judean, he composed his works after settling in Rome after 70 C.E. Therefore, both Josephus and Philo were members of a Jewish minority living in a world where Greco-Roman culture and religions were the norm for the majority of the population. Although Josephus and Philo composed different kinds of literature, they used their writings to try to influence their readers. Specifically, both attempted to demonstrate that Judaism was superior to Greco-Roman culture and religions. This message was intended for Jews (Judaism offers everything the others have, so there is no need to look elsewhere) and non-Jews (whatever Greco-Roman culture and religions have to offer, Judaism did it first and does it better). The writings of Josephus and Philo were shaped, at least in part, by this agenda.

Although the Essenes were the smallest and most marginal of the major Jewish sects, Josephus and Philo devoted to them a disproportionate amount of attention. For example, Josephus's description of the Essenes is much longer than his accounts of the Pharisees and Sadducees, who were far more numerous and influential. This is because as an ascetic sect, the Essenes served Josephus' and Philo's purpose of demonstrating the superiority of Judaism. The **ascetic** lifestyle – denying oneself physical or bodily pleasures in order to devote one's time to study – was one of the Greco-Roman philosophical ideals. Physical and bodily pleasures included diet, clothing, and sexual relations. Women were considered inferior to men in the ancient world and were viewed as a distraction from philosophical study. The Essenes served Josephus's and Philo's purpose because they lived an ascetic lifestyle (they pooled possessions, wore coarse clothing, shared meals, ate a simple diet, and constantly engaged in study [but of Jewish law, not Greek philosophy]) that approximated the Greco-Roman philosophical ideal. But does this mean that the Essenes were celibate?

The Dead Sea Scrolls indicate that the sect included women and children, and some members were married. However, the scrolls do not tell us whether women could join the sect voluntarily and undergo a process of initiation as men did, or whether women became part of the sect through marriage or by being born into it. Furthermore, the scrolls do not indicate whether women could become full members. There are hints that although some women might have attained some degree of status within the sect, their position was inferior to that of men. This makes sense because full members lived as if they were priests, and only Jewish men could be priests. Women, children, and men with physical or mental defects could not serve as priests in the Jerusalem temple and therefore could not be full members in the Qumran sect.

Biblical Jewish law does not mandate celibacy. To the contrary, Jews consider the injunction to be fruitful and multiply (Genesis 1:28) as God's first commandment. Ancient Jewish priests were married with families and lived in towns and villages throughout Palestine. The priests who officiated in the Jerusalem temple were divided into groups ("courses") that rotated on a weekly basis. During their course of service the priests stayed in the temple and had no contact with their families because of purity concerns. Because full members of the Qumran sect lived a priestly lifestyle, many must have been married with families. However, it may be that some members practiced occasional celibacy, by which I mean that like the priests serving in the temple, they left their families at certain times and had no contact or relations with them. Furthermore, although it is nowhere mandated, it may be that some members of the Qumran sect practiced permanent celibacy because of purity concerns.

Either way, it is the practice of occasional and perhaps permanent celibacy that Josephus and Philo described, because it served their purpose (although Josephus acknowledged that some Essenes were married). In other words, Josephus and Philo presented a partial picture of the Essenes, highlighting only the beliefs and practices that made it appear as though this Jewish sect lived according to the Greco-Roman philosophical ideal. They downplayed or ignored Essene beliefs and practices that did not serve this purpose. For example, the observance of biblical purity laws, which is so central to the sectarian lifestyle, is hardly mentioned by our authors. Pliny picked up information about the Essenes from an unknown source and included it as piece of exotica in his encyclopedic *Natural History*.

Recommended Reading

George J. Brooke, *The Dead Sea Scrolls and the New Testament* (Minneapolis: Fortress, 2005).

Philip R. Davies, George J. Brooke, and Phillip R. Callaway, *The Complete World of the Dead Sea Scrolls* (London: Thames and Hudson, 2002).

Weston W. Fields, *The Dead Sea Scrolls, A Full History, Volume 1* (Boston: Brill, 2009).

Jodi Magness, *The Archaeology of Qumran and the Dead Sea Scrolls* (Grand Rapids, MI: Eerdmans, 2002).

Lawrence H. Schiffman and James C. VanderKam (eds.), *Encyclopedia of the Dead Sea Scrolls, Vols. 1–2* (New York: Oxford University, 2002).

James C. VanderKam, *The Dead Sea Scrolls Today* (Grand Rapids, MI: Eerdmans, 2010).

James C. VanderKam and Peter Flint, *The Meaning of the Dead Sea Scrolls* (New York: HarperSanFrancisco, 2002).

Roland de Vaux, *Archaeology and the Dead Sea Scrolls* (London: Oxford University, 1973).

Geza Vermes, *The Complete Dead Sea Scrolls in English* (New York: Penguin, 2004).

@@ @@ @@ @@

SEVEN

THE EARLY ROMAN (HERODIAN) PERIOD (40 B.C.E.–70 C.E.)

JERUSALEM

HISTORICAL BACKGROUND: GENERAL

After dividing between them the lands under Roman rule, escalating tensions between Octavian and Mark Antony erupted at the battle of **Actium** (31 B.C.E.), a naval engagement fought off the coast of Greece. Antony and Cleopatra were defeated and fled to Egypt, where they committed suicide. Octavian became sole ruler of Rome, and in 27 B.C.E. the Roman Senate awarded him the title Augustus, marking the transition from the Roman Republic to the Roman Empire. Despite being sickly, Augustus outlived a number of designated heirs, ruling until his death in 14 C.E. Augustus promoted the arts and literature, and initiated a massive building program that transformed Rome's appearance. Augustus's successors (the **Julio-Claudian dynasty**) were **Tiberius** (14–37), Gaius Caligula (37–41), Claudius (41–54), and **Nero** (54–68).

After Nero committed suicide, a civil war erupted, with a rapid succession of four emperors over the course of a year (69). Order was restored with the accession to the throne of the general Vespasian, who established the **Flavian dynasty** (consisting of **Vespasian** [69–79] and his sons **Titus** [79–81] and Domitian [81–96]).

HISTORICAL BACKGROUND: PALESTINE

After being appointed king of Judea by the Roman Senate in 40 B.C.E., Herod returned to Palestine to fight Mattathias Antigonus, who surrendered with the fall of Jerusalem in 37 B.C.E. and was beheaded by Mark Antony. Ironically, during the first part of his reign, Herod's greatest threat came from his supporter,

@@ 133

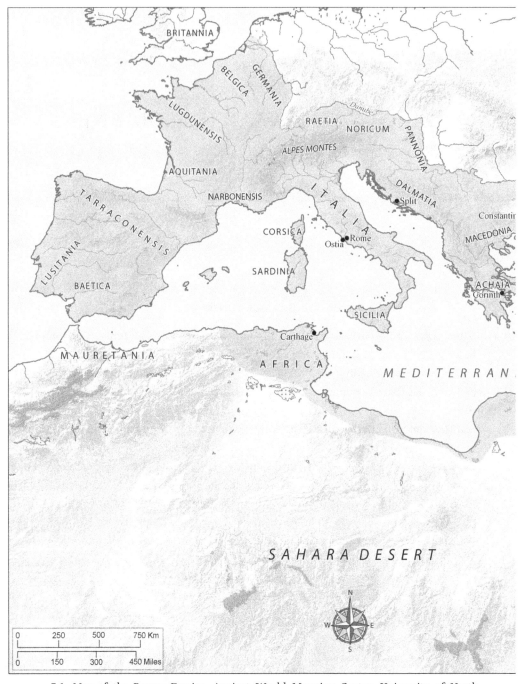

7.1 Map of the Roman Empire. Ancient World Mapping Center, University of North
Carolina at Chapel Hill (www.unc.edu/awmc).

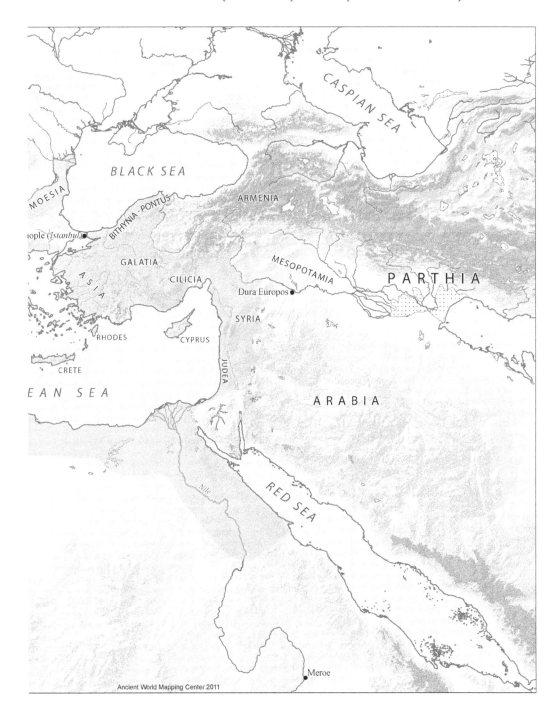

Ancient World Mapping Center 2011

Mark Antony – or, more specifically, from Antony's lover (and later wife), Cleopatra VII. As a Ptolemaic queen, Cleopatra coveted the territories ruled by Herod, which once had been part of the Ptolemaic kingdom. She persuaded Antony to give her parts of Herod's kingdom, including the Decapolis cities, most of the Palestinian coast, the eastern shore of the Dead Sea, and the lucrative plantations at Jericho, which produced an expensive perfume from the opobalsam plant. The battle of Actium removed the threat of Cleopatra, but Herod feared that his friendship with Antony would cost him the throne – and perhaps his life. Herod therefore hastened to meet with Octavian, to whom he now pledged loyalty. Octavian was persuaded; he not only reconfirmed Herod as king of Judea but also increased the size of his kingdom, which eventually included the Golan and extended even farther to the north and east.

Herod was an unusually cruel ruler, even by ancient standards. He dealt ruthlessly with all opposition (real and imagined), including members of his own household. Herod's paranoia was perhaps partially justified, as he was unpopular among much of the Jewish population, which considered him – an Idumaean Jew who was not a Hasmonean – a usurper to the throne. Herod's marriage to the beautiful Hasmonean princess **Mariamne**, one of his nine wives (many of whom were not Jewish) complicated matters, as from Herod's point of view the greatest threat to his rule came from the Hasmonean family. Eventually Herod had Mariamne (who was his favorite wife), as well as her younger brother Aristobulus III and their mother Alexandra, put to death. Later in his reign, Herod had two of his grown sons by Mariamne (Aristobulus and Alexander) strangled, and just five days before his death, Herod ordered the execution of his oldest son, Antipater (by his first wife, Doris). No wonder Augustus reportedly quipped, "It is better to be Herod's pig than his son." This is a clever pun on the Greek words for pig (*hus*) and son (*huios*), and it suggests that Herod might have observed the biblical Jewish dietary laws by abstaining from pork. Herod's elimination of several family members, including his own sons, might underlie the story of the massacre of the innocents (Matthew 2:16–18), according to which Herod ordered the slaughter of all children under the age of two around Bethlehem. Ironically, Herod is perhaps best remembered for this atrocity, despite the fact that many scholars believe it is fictitious.

In archaeological circles, Herod is known for having been the single greatest builder in the history of Palestine. Herod's projects include the reconstruction of the Jerusalem temple, the rebuilding of Straton's Tower (Caesarea) and Samaria, the construction of a winter palace at Jericho, and the establishment of fortified palaces in the Judean Desert, including those at **Herodium** and Masada. Herod died at Jericho in 4 B.C.E., after suffering from an agonizing illness (perhaps syphilis?), and was buried at Herodium.

7.2   Map of Herod's kingdom. Ancient World Mapping Center, University of North Carolina
at Chapel Hill (www.unc.edu/awmc).

Herod's kingdom was divided among three of his sons (all named Herod), although they were awarded a lesser title than "king":

- **Herod Archelaus** received Judea, Samaria, and Idumaea. A cruel and ineffective ruler, he was removed from his post and banished to Gaul in 6 C.E.
- **Herod Antipas** received Galilee and **Peraea** (a Judaized territory east of the Jordan River and Dead Sea). He rebuilt **Sepphoris** in Galilee and established a new capital city at **Tiberias** on the Sea of Galilee (named in honor of the emperor Tiberius). He is perhaps best known for having John the Baptist beheaded. According to the Gospel accounts, John condemned Antipas' marriage to his brother's wife Herodias, a union that is prohibited by biblical law. Josephus attributed the execution to Antipas' fears that John's movement would cause political unrest. Antipas was removed from his post and banished to Gaul in 39 C.E.
- **Herod Philip** received Gaulanitis, Trachonitis, Batanea, and Panias, which were northern territories inhabited mostly by Gentile populations. Philip was married to Herodias (the daughter of Herod's sister), until she divorced him to marry Antipas. Philip was the only son of Herod to rule until his death (33/34 C.E.).

The Romans (like the Ptolemies and Seleucids) did not have a monolithic system of government, but instead employed different administrative models that varied across time and space. Whereas the province of Syria was under the direct administration of a legate, up to this point Judea had been ruled by a client king (Herod) and his sons. When Archelaus was removed from his post in 6 C.E., the Romans replaced the native (Herodian) dynasty with governors (**prefects** or **procurators**), who were outranked by the legate in Syria. The Roman governors moved the capital of Judea from Jerusalem to Caesarea Maritima. Philo describes **Pontius Pilate**, the fifth prefect (26–36 C.E.), as "naturally inflexible, a blend of self-will and relentlessness," and speaks of his conduct as full of "briberies, insults, robberies, outrages and wanton injuries, executions without trial constantly repeated, ceaseless and supremely grievous cruelty" (*Embassy to Gaius* 301–2). It was during Pilate's administration that Jesus was arrested and crucified. Pilate was removed from office after executing a group of Samaritans who had followed their leader to Mount Gerizim in search of tabernacle treasures.

After Herod Philip died (37 C.E.), the emperor Gaius Caligula gave his territories to **Herod Agrippa I**, the grandson of Herod the Great and Mariamne. Herod Agrippa I had been raised in Rome and, as a child, became friends with the young Caligula. When Antipas was deposed in 39 C.E., Herod Agrippa I received his territories as well. After Caligula was assassinated, Herod Agrippa I helped convince the Roman Senate to appoint Claudius as the next emperor. In return, Claudius granted Herod Agrippa I Judea, Samaria, and Idumaea. Therefore, by 41 C.E., all of Herod the Great's former kingdom was under the rule of his grandson. Although Herod Agrippa I was not an observant Jew, he was popular among the Jewish population. Christian tradition describes Herod Agrippa I as a persecutor of the early church who had James the son of Zebedee beheaded and Peter arrested (Acts 12:1–3). Herod Agrippa I ruled only briefly, until his death in 44 C.E., when his kingdom reverted to the administration of Roman governors. His son, **Herod Agrippa II**, was granted the small kingdom of Chalcis in Lebanon and was given oversight of the Jerusalem temple. Herod Agrippa II remained a faithful vassal of Rome until his death (ca. 92 C.E.).

After Herod Agrippa I died, conditions in Palestine deteriorated, thanks to the inept and corrupt Roman governors and an increasingly polarized population. Escalating tensions pitted rich against poor, rural against urban, Jews against Samaritans, Jews against Gentiles, and members of various Jewish sects and movements against one another. Gangs of bandits roamed the countryside, robbing victims and making travel unsafe. An urban terrorist group called the **Sicarii** (literally, the "dagger men") assassinated their opponents in broad daylight by circulating among dense crowds and stabbing victims in the back, then hiding their daggers under their robes and disappearing amid the ensuing panic. The escalating unrest culminated with the outbreak of the First Jewish Revolt against the Romans in 66 C.E. The Jews established an independent government and divided the country into seven administrative districts. After the Syrian legate Cestius Gallus was defeated in battle by the Jewish insurgents, Nero appointed Vespasian as general. Vespasian assembled his troops at Antioch and marched south, first taking Galilee and then Peraea (including Jericho and apparently Qumran in late spring–early summer of 68). Vespasian's strategy of isolating Jerusalem by subduing the rest of the country first was delayed by Nero's death and the civil war in Rome, as he awaited orders from the emperor. After Vespasian was proclaimed emperor in 69, he departed for Rome and left his older son Titus in charge.

By the time Titus undertook the siege of Jerusalem, the city's population was swollen with refugees. A dire shortage of food was exacerbated by the burning of granaries during the course of infighting among various rebel factions. The Romans tried to intimidate the Jews into submission by returning prisoners to the city with their hands cut off and by crucifixion near the walls: "The soldiers out of rage and hatred amused themselves by nailing their prisoners in different postures; and so great was their number, that space could not be found for the crosses nor crosses for their bodies" (Jos., *War* 5:451). Despite stiff Jewish resistance, the Romans managed to breach the city's walls on the north and took the Antonia fortress. According to Josephus, the daily sacrifices in the temple ceased on that day, probably because of lack of lambs. Fighting then spread onto the Temple Mount, where some Jews took refuge inside the temple, which had its own fortifications. The temple was set on fire and burned to the ground on the tenth day of the Jewish month of Av (August of 70; according to rabbinic chronology, the ninth of Av). Titus and his men entered the burning building and removed its treasures. Fighting continued on the western hill for another month. The Jews made their last stand in Herod's palace, where the rebel leaders Simon bar Giora and John of Gischala (Gush Halav) were captured.

The First Jewish Revolt ended with the fall of Jerusalem in 70. Back at home in Rome, Vespasian and Titus celebrated their victory with a parade of prisoners and treasures from Jerusalem. The treasures included the menorah (seven-branched candelabrum) and showbread table from the Jerusalem temple, which are depicted on the arch of Titus in the Roman Forum and were put on display in a temple that Vespasian dedicated to Peace. The victory parade culminated at the temple of Capitoline Jupiter, where Simon bar Giora was taken to be scourged and executed, while John of Gischala was sentenced to life in prison.

JERUSALEM

Herod's Palace and the Three Towers

When Jerusalem fell to Herod in 37 B.C.E., the walled settlement consisted of the Temple Mount (with the second temple), the City of David, and the western hill. The Temple Mount and City of David had been resettled after the return from Babylonian exile and fortified under Nehemiah, whereas the wall surrounding the western hill (the First Wall) was constructed in the Hasmonean period (following the line of the late Iron Age wall). On the northwest side of the western hill, Herod built a palace for himself, as he could not use the existing palace, which belonged to the Hasmonean family. Josephus describes Herod's palace as consisting of two wings separated by pools and gardens. Herod named the wings the Caesareum, in honor of Augustus, and the Agrippaeum, in honor of **Marcus Agrippa**, Augustus' son-in-law and designated heir (who died in 12 B.C.E., predeceasing Augustus). Herod formed a close friendship with Marcus Agrippa, who visited Judea and toured Herod's kingdom in 15 B.C.E. Although excavations have been conducted in the area where Herod's palace was located (the modern Armenian Garden), almost no remains of the superstructure have survived.

At the northwest corner of the First Wall and on the north side of his palace, Herod erected three large towers. These towers served two purposes: (1) to reinforce the city's vunerable northern flank, which was not bounded by a deep natural valley as the other sides were; and (2) to protect Herod's palace, which was surrounded by its own fortification system. Josephus tells us that Herod named the largest tower Phasael (in honor of his older brother, who committed suicide in 40 B.C.E.), the middle-sized tower Hippicus (after a friend), and the smallest tower Mariamne (in honor of his beloved Hasmonean

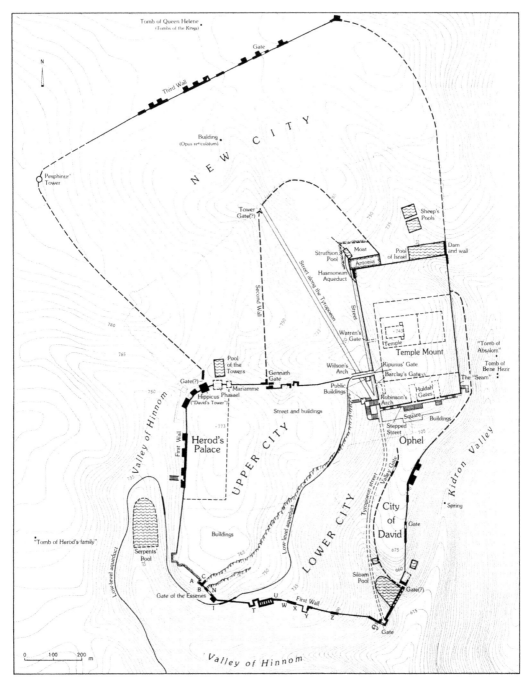

7.3 Plan of Jerusalem at the end of the Second Temple period. From E. Stern (ed.), *The New Encyclopedia of Archaeological Excavations in the Holy Land* (New York: Simon and Schuster, 1993), vol. 2, p. 718. By permission of Hillel Geva and the Israel Exploration Society.

7.4   David's Tower and the First Wall. Courtesy of Zev Radovan/BibleLandPictures.com.

wife, whom he executed). When Jerusalem fell to the Romans in 70 C.E., Titus had two of the towers razed to the ground but left one standing.

Today, the surviving Herodian tower lies inside a large fortified enclosure (the Citadel) next to Jaffa Gate, in the middle of the western wall of the modern Old City. Most of the remains in the Citadel are much more recent than the Roman period, dating to medieval and Ottoman times. However, some earlier remains are enclosed within the Citadel, including the northwest corner of the First Wall, into which the Herodian tower is set. Only the lower part of

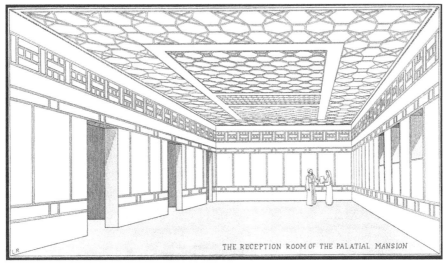

THE RECEPTION ROOM OF THE PALATIAL MANSION

7.5   Stucco room in "the mansion." Reconstruction by Leen Ritmeyer ©.

the tower has survived, which is constructed of characteristic Herodian-style masonry: large ashlar stones with smooth, drafted margins and a flat, paneled boss. The upper part of the tower was reconstructed later using much smaller stones. The current moniker, **David's Tower**, reflects a popular (and incorrect) association with King David that stems from a later tradition. The tower is visible immediately to the right after entering Jaffa Gate, within the walls of the Citadel, as well as inside the courtyard of the Citadel. Sometimes modern visitors confuse David's Tower with the minaret of an Ottoman mosque that is also located inside the courtyard of the Citadel. Because of its large size, many scholars identify the tower as Phasael. However, an Israeli archaeologist, Hillel Geva, has suggested that it is Hippicus, based on Josephus' description of the location of the tower relative to the line of the First Wall.

The Western Hill

In the late Second Temple period, the western hill was Jerusalem's upper-class residential quarter. This is where the Hasmonean and Herodian palaces were located, and where Jerusalem's wealthiest Jews lived. In addition to offering a stunning view across the Tyropoeon Valley to the Temple Mount, the western hill remains cooler in summer thanks to its relatively high elevation. Although the Hasmonean palace has not been found, Avigad's excavations in the Jewish Quarter in the 1970s brought to light densely packed urban villas belonging to the Jerusalem elite. The largest villa, which Avigad dubbed "the mansion," covers an area of some 600 square meters. Each villa consisted of two or three stories of rooms (including a basement for storage) surrounding a central courtyard.

7.6 Mosaic floor and stone table from the Jewish Quarter. Courtesy of Zev Radovan/ BibleLandPictures.com.

Unlike contemporary houses in North America, which have large windows opening onto lawns and gardens surrounding the house, in the ancient Mediterranean and Near East houses focused on a central courtyard surrounded by rooms. This arrangement provided privacy for the house's residents, with windows and doorways in the walls facing the courtyard providing light and air to the surrounding rooms.

The urban villas discovered by Avigad were decorated in Roman fashion with mosaic floors, wall paintings (frescoes) in the Second Pompeian Style (a style popular in Italy in the first century C.E.), and stucco (plaster molded in imitation of marble panels and other architectural shapes). Some rooms had been repainted or remodeled more than once, to keep up with changing styles of interior decoration. The villas also were furnished elaborately with expensive Roman-style stone tables (carved of local Jerusalem chalk) and sets of imported Eastern Terra Sigillata pottery dishes. One family owned a beautiful mold-made glass vase that was signed by **Ennion**, a famous Phoenician master craftsman. (A complete glass vase manufactured in the same mold is in the collection of New York's Metropolitan Museum of Art [it was acquired on the antiquities market, so its provenance is unknown].) The discovery of the vase in the Jewish Quarter excavations provides a context for dating Ennion's products to the first century C.E.

The size and lavish decoration of these urban villas indicates that the residents were members of the Jerusalem elite. Clearly these wealthy Jews were "Romanized" – that is, they had adopted many aspects of the Roman lifestyle.

7.7 Ennion's glass vase from the Jewish Quarter, mold blown, signature inscription in Greek, Jerusalem, first century C.E. Collection of the Israel Antiquities Authority. Photo © The Israel Museum, Jerusalem.

At the same time, there is evidence that they also observed Jewish law. For example, the interior decoration is Roman in style but lacks the figured images that characterize Roman art (such as deities, humans, and animals). Instead, these wealthy Jews apparently understood the Second Commandment, which prohibits the making of images for worship, as meaning that it is forbidden to portray any figured images in art. Furthermore, each villa was equipped with one or more *miqva'ot* (ritual baths) and yielded large numbers of stone (chalk) dining dishes and other stone vessels, attesting to the observance of purity laws. Many Jews of the late Second Temple period believed that stone cannot contract ritual impurity (based on their interpretation of a biblical passage). In contrast, if a pottery vessel comes into contact with something that is ritually impure, it cannot be purified and must be smashed. Although stone is more difficult and therefore more expensive to work than pottery, the investment paid off for Jews who were concerned about the observance of purity laws and could afford to purchase stone vessels. The stone vessels found in the Jewish Quarter villas include knife-pared stone "mugs" – which are common at sites around Palestine

7.8 Stone vessels from the Jewish Quarter. Courtesy of Zev Radovan/BibleLandPictures .com.

and may have been used for ritual hand-washing before meals – as well as sets of more expensive lathe-turned dining dishes and large jars. The stone dining dishes might have been used for offerings of produce (Hebrew *terumah*) given to priests, which had to be consumed in a state of ritual purity. John (2:1–11) describes Jesus turning water stored in stone jars into wine at a wedding at Cana in Galilee: "Now standing there were six stone water jars for the Jewish rites of purification, each holding twenty or thirty gallons."

The archaeological evidence for purity observance suggests that some of the wealthy residents of the Jewish Quarter villas were priests, which is not surprising, as we know that priestly families (and especially high priestly families) were members of the Jerusalem elite. Avigad discovered additional evidence of priestly presence in a villa that he dubbed "the **Burnt House**." This villa is so called because the basement rooms (the only part of the house that survived) were covered with layers of ashy soot, from the destruction of the house by the Romans in 70 C.E. The vats, ovens, tables, and other installations suggest that this was a workshop, perhaps for the manufacture of a product used in the Jerusalem temple. A stone weight found in one of the rooms is inscribed with the name of a known priestly family – **Bar Kathros** – presumably the villa's owners. On a step leading down into the basement, Avigad found the skeletal arm of a young woman about 20 years of age, who was crushed when the burning house collapsed on top of her. These are the only human physical remains that have been discovered until now connected with Jerusalem's destruction by the Romans in 70 C.E.

7.9 Skeletal arm of a young woman in the Burnt House. Courtesy of Zev Radovan/ BibleLandPictures.com.

The Temple Mount

The centerpiece of Herod's building program in Jerusalem was his reconstruction of the second temple, which had been consecrated in 516 B.C.E. Herod rebuilt the temple itself, as well as the esplanade or open platform surrounding it (the Temple Mount). Although no remains of the temple survive, today's

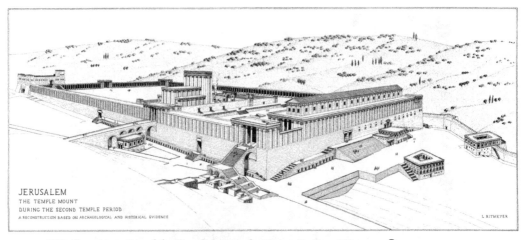

JERUSALEM
THE TEMPLE MOUNT
DURING THE SECOND TEMPLE PERIOD
A RECONSTRUCTION BASED ON ARCHAEOLOGICAL AND HISTORICAL EVIDENCE

L. RITMEYER

7.10 Reconstruction of the Herodian Temple Mount. By Leen Ritmeyer ©.

Temple Mount is a product of Herod's building program. Work on the temple building was carried out between ca. 23/20 and 15 B.C.E., but construction on the massive complex surrounding it continued until 64 C.E., a situation alluded to by the author of the Fourth Gospel: "Jesus answered them, 'Destroy this temple, and in three days I will raise it up.' The Jews then said, 'This temple has been under construction for forty-six years, and will you raise it up in three days?'" (John 2:18–19). Josephus reports that the construction of the temple, which was carried out by priests, took ten years, during which time rain fell only at night.

Herod monumentalized the temple building by expanding the esplanade on which it stood (the Temple Mount), creating one of the largest sacred precincts in the ancient world (ca. 140,000 square meters). To make the platform level, the bedrock had to be cut back on the north, where it rises. To the south, where the bedrock drops toward the City of David, the expanded platform was supported on a series of underground arches or vaults called a **cryptoporticus**. The cryptoporticus supported the pavement and buildings above, but without the outward pressure and danger of collapse that would have been created had the area simply been filled in with a mass of dirt and stones. The arches of the cryptoporticus still survive (although the area is closed to the public). They are now called **Solomon's Stables**, a name that originated when Jerusalem was part of the Crusader kingdom in the Middle Ages. At that time, different orders of knights occupied or were given different parts of the city. One order of knights occupied the Temple Mount, and therefore became known as the Knights Templar. They attributed the cryptoporticus to Solomon (because the Temple Mount had been the site of Solomon's temple) and used the area for stabling their horses.

7.11 The Western Wall. Courtesy of Zev Radovan/BibleLandPictures.com.

Herod enclosed the expanded platform with a *temenos* wall (the Greek word *temenos* refers to a sacred precinct). Herod's extension is visible on the south side of the "seam" at the southeast corner of the Temple Mount, where Herodian style masonry abuts earlier construction (see Chapter 4). The upper part of the *temenos* wall was decorated with engaged pilasters (square pillars built into the wall), which broke up the monotony of the masonry by creating a play of light and shadow in the bright sunlight. Pieces of broken pilasters can be seen lying among the heaps of stones that fell from above onto a paved Herodian street on the southwest side of the Temple Mount, evidence of the violence wrought by the Roman destruction of 70 C.E. The bases of a few pilasters are preserved **in situ** (in their original position) in an underground tunnel at the northwest side of the Temple Mount (under the basements of later buildings abutting the *temenos* wall). One of the stones in the Herodian *temenos* wall (on the western side of the Temple Mount) is about 40 feet long and weighs approximately 400 tons! The Western ("Wailing") Wall is part of Herod's *temenos* wall around the Temple Mount, not part of the temple building itself (which was located on top of the platform, approximately where the Dome of the Rock sits today). The Jewish tradition ascribing special sanctity to the site of the Western Wall (as opposed to other sections of the Herodian *temenos* wall) probably developed because this was the closest spot to the temple building outside the Temple Mount. After the temple's destruction, it became customary for Jews to congregate here to mourn its loss.

7.12 Wilson's Arch. Courtesy of Zev Radovan/BibleLandPictures.com.

A number of gates in the *temenos* wall provided access to the Temple Mount, several of which are still visible today, specifically (from north to south) **Wilson's Arch**, **Barclay's Gate**, **Robinson's Arch** (all on the western side of the Temple Mount) and the **Hulda Gates** (on the south side of the Temple Mount). Wilson's Arch is part of a bridge carried on arches that provided access across the Tyropoeon Valley from the western hill to the Temple Mount (for recent discoveries that suggest a different picture, see the Sidebar on Wilson's

7.13 Robinson's Arch. Courtesy of Zev Radovan/BibleLandPictures.com.

Arch). Today, the underside of the bridge's first (easternmost) arch abuts the north side of the Western Wall, in an underground area reserved for men's prayers (but open to everyone for visits at certain times). The remains of Barclay's Gate are preserved on the south side of the Western Wall (in the women's section), consisting of part of the doorpost and lintel, with the original passage blocked by smaller stones. Robinson's Arch is located at the southwest corner of the Temple Mount, visible as the beginning of a large arch projecting from the *temenos* wall. Originally, Robinson's Arch was considered analogous to Wilson's Arch – a bridge across the Tyropoeon Valley carried on arches. However, excavations conducted by the Israeli archaeologist Benjamin Mazar after 1967 around the southern and western sides of the Temple Mount brought to light part of a staircase, which indicated that Robinson's Arch turned a ninety-degree angle and led into the Tyropoeon Valley below. This was a busy commercial area with a broad paved street lined by shops (the same street crushed in 70 c.e. by falling stones from the *temenos* wall above).

The Hulda Gates are two gates, each originally with double doors, in the south wall of the Temple Mount. They provided the main access for pilgrims to the Temple Mount, who could purify themselves first in the large *miqva'ot* outside the gates or in the pool of Siloam to the south. Unlike the other gates just described, which are named after nineteenth-century British explorers, Hulda is an ancient name (perhaps referring to the nearby tomb of the prophetess Hulda, or perhaps deriving from the Hebrew word for mole, as the gates led to underground passages). The Hulda Gates worked as a pair, with the eastern

7.14 Hulda Gate with steps. Courtesy of Zev Radovan/BibleLandPictures.com.

set used for entrance to the Temple Mount and the western set used as the exit. Both sets led to passages below the Royal Stoa (discussed in the following paragraph), which brought visitors into the Temple Mount. Part of one of the doorways of the western set of gates is still visible today, including the doorpost and lintel (with a flat arch above). The passage through the door is blocked by smaller stones, and the rest of the gate is covered by a Crusader tower that is built up against the southern *temenos* wall. The underground passages, which

7.15   The Temple Mount in the Holyland Model. Courtesy of Zev Radovan/BibleLandPictures .com.

today lie underneath the **al-Aqsa mosque**, were decorated with stucco molded with delicate geometric designs.

The Temple Mount esplanade was a huge, open paved space surrounded on the east, north, and west sides by colonnaded porches (porches with columns that supported the wooden beams of a roof), which provided shelter from sun and rain for the masses of pilgrims. A monumental, two-story-high building called the **Royal Stoa** or **Royal Basilica** occupied the southern end of the Temple Mount (encompassing the area occupied today by the al-Aqsa mosque, but much larger). As its name suggests, this rectangular structure with rows of columns inside was an all-purpose public building that could be used for various kinds of gatherings and transactions.

The temple – of which nothing survives – stood in the center of the Temple Mount, on a natural outcrop of bedrock that is enshrined today in the Dome of the Rock. The temple was surrounded by its own fortification wall and tow-ers. Scholars disagree about whether the building was oriented toward the east or west (the Holyland Model, which is a scale model of Herodian Jerusalem on display at the Israel Museum, depicts the temple oriented toward the east). The building was approached through two courtyards. The first was the Women's Court, which is where Jewish women congregated (although men and women were not segregated, as men had to pass through the Women's Court).

Nicanor's Gate – named after a wealthy Jew who donated this gate to the temple – marked the passage from the Women's Court to the Court of the Israelites, which was in front of the temple building. Jewish men congregated around the altar in the Court of the Israelites, where the sacrifices were offered by the priests. Only priests were allowed beyond this, into the temple itself.

The only surviving remains associated with the temple itself consist of two Greek inscriptions that originally were set into a low stone fence (called a *soreg*) that surrounded the temple's fortifications. Greek and Latin inscriptions in the fence prohibited non-Jews (Gentiles) from entering the temple on pain of death. The two surviving Greek inscriptions were discovered in fills to the south of the Temple Mount. The more complete inscription is in the Istanbul Archaeological Museum in Turkey (where it was taken after being found when Palestine was still under Ottoman rule). The second, fragmentary inscription is in the Israel Museum in Jerusalem. The complete inscription says: "No man of another nation is to enter within the fence and enclosure round the temple. And whoever is caught will have himself to blame for his death which will follow." Notice that the agent of death is not mentioned – only that trespassers will die. Josephus provides a remarkably similar description of the *soreg* inscriptions: "Proceeding across this [the open court] towards the second court of the temple, one found it surrounded by a stone balustrade, three cubits high and of exquisite workmanship; in this at regular intervals stood slabs giving warning, some in Greek, others in Latin characters, of the law of purification, to wit that no foreigner was permitted to enter the holy place, for so the second enclosure of the temple was called" (*War* 15:417).

Paul was arrested and taken into protective custody after the Jews charged him with taking a Gentile into the temple – apparently the area marked off by the *soreg*:

> Then Paul took the men, and the next day, having purified himself, he entered the temple with them, making public the completion of the days of purification when the sacrifice would be made for each of them. When the seven days were almost completed, the Jews from Asia, who had seen him in the temple, stirred up the whole crowd. They seized him, shouting, "Fellow Israelites, help! This is the man who is teaching everyone everywhere against our people, our law, and this place; more than that, he has actually brought Greeks into the temple and has defiled this holy place." For they had previously seen Trophimus the Ephesian with him in the city, and they supposed that Paul had brought him into the temple. Then all the city was aroused, and people rushed together. They seized Paul and dragged him out of the temple, and immediately the doors were shut. While they were trying to kill him, word came to the tribune of the cohort that all of Jerusalem was in an uproar. (Acts 21: 26–31; NRSV)

7.16   Soreg inscription in the Istanbul Archaeological Museum. Photo by Jim Haberman.

Notice that Paul purified himself before entering the temple, indicating that he observed this requirement of Jewish law. Paul was recognized not by the Judeans (who did not know him), but by the Jews from Asia (=Asia Minor, not the Far East), because he was from Tarsus. They also recognized the Gentile with the Greek name Trophimus, who came from Ephesus (also in Asia Minor). Finally, notice that the Romans took Paul into protective custody to prevent a lynching, suggesting that otherwise the Jewish mob would have been the agents of death. Paul was imprisoned at Caesarea Maritima for a couple of years (see Chapter 8) before being shipped off to Rome for a trial.

Although today we tend to think of the Temple Mount exclusively in religious terms, it was a center of commercial activity as well. The thousands of visitors to Jerusalem's Temple Mount included not only Jewish pilgrims but also Gentiles (who could enter the Temple Mount but not the temple itself). The enormous esplanade, with the Royal Stoa and porticoes, bustled with merchants and vendors, many of them selling sacrificial animals and birds. In fact, Herod's Temple Mount was analogous to ancient agoras or fora (marketplaces), which typically consisted of a large open paved space surrounded by public buildings such as **stoas**, **basilicas**, theaters, and temples. Although placing the temple in the center of the marketplace (instead of to one side) is unusual, it is not unparalleled in the Roman world. For example, the **Capitolium** (temple of Capitoline Jupiter) dominated the center of the forum at Pompeii, with Mount Vesuvius towering above in the distance.

The commercial activity on the Temple Mount is the setting for an episode described in the Gospels – Jesus' cleansing of the temple:

> Then they came to Jerusalem. And he entered the temple [the Greek word *hieron* denotes the Temple Mount in general rather than the temple building specifically] and began to drive out those who were selling and those who were buying in the temple, and he overturned the tables of the money changers and the seats of those who sold doves; and he would not allow anyone to carry anything through the temple. He was teaching and saying, "Is it not written, 'My house shall be called a house of prayer for all the nations'? But you have made it a den of robbers." (Mk 11:15–17; also see Mt 21:12–15; Lk 19:45–46; Jn 2:13–16)

Today this episode is often understood as stemming from Jesus' objection to commercial activity in the temple. However, the notion that Jesus opposed buying and selling on the Temple Mount is anachronistic, as commercial activity associated with temples was taken for granted in the ancient world. Instead, this episode likely was motivated by Jesus' concern for the poor, as suggested by his singling out of money changers and dove sellers. Pigeons and doves were the cheapest form of sacrifice, offered by impoverished people who could not afford more expensive animals such as sheep and goats. The money changers served pilgrims who needed to pay the temple tax, which helped pay for cultic and sacrificial expenses. The Hebrew Bible requires a one-time payment or tax on Israelites who reached adulthood. Shortly before Jesus' time, this requirement was changed to an annual payment for the maintenance of the Temple cult. Furthermore, the tax had to be paid in only one kind of currency – Tyrian tetradrachmas (silver sheqels) – which apparently was preferred by the temple authorities because of the high quality of the silver (92 percent silver or better). Money changers exchanged currency for Jewish pilgrims so they could pay the tax in Tyrian tetradrachmas. Scraping together the cash needed to exchange and purchase the Tyrian silver coins annually must have been a great hardship on the poor. Some other Jewish groups of the late Second Temple period, including the Qumran sect, also opposed the institution of an annual temple tax.

The Antonia Fortress and Via Dolorosa

At the northwest corner of the Temple Mount, Herod erected a massive fortress that he named the Antonia, in honor of Mark Antony (indicating that it was built before the battle of Actium in 31 B.C.E.). The fortress, which was garrisoned with gentile soldiers, sat on a natural high point overlooking the Temple Mount. Herod knew that he was not liked by the Jewish population, and he considered the masses of pilgrims on the Temple Mount as a source of potential unrest.

7.17 Lithostratos pavement. Courtesy of Zev Radovan/BibleLandPictures.com.

The Antonia was a deterrent (message to the Jews: you are being watched!), and housed troops to quell any uprisings or trouble.

Although Josephus provides a description of the Antonia, its dimensions have been the subject of debate. Today, the area where the Antonia was located is bisected by a road called the **Via Dolorosa**, which runs parallel to the northern side of the Temple Mount. The Via Dolorosa (Italian for "Way of Sorrow") is so called because, according to Christian tradition, this is the route along which

Jesus carried his cross, beginning with his sentencing by Pontius Pilate and ending with his crucifixion and burial (now enshrined within the Church of the Holy Sepulcher). A convent called the **Church of the Sisters of Zion** lies along the north side of the Via Dolorosa today. During the construction of the convent in the late nineteenth century, a series of ancient remains came to light. The remains consist of large pools or cisterns called the **Struthion** (Greek for "sparrow") **Pools**, which are overlaid by a stone pavement (today identified as the **Lithostratos pavement**), and a monumental, triple-arched gateway sitting on top of the pavement (today called the **arch of Ecce Homo**). The pavement and arched gateway are identified with places where, according to the Gospel of John, Jesus was sentenced by Pontius Pilate and clothed with a purple robe and a crown of thorns:

> When Pilate heard these words, he brought Jesus outside and sat on the judge's bench at a place called The Stone Pavement (*lithostratos*). (John 19:13; NRSV)

> So Jesus came out, wearing the crown of thorns and the purple robe. Pilate said to them, "Behold the man [*ecce homo*]!" (John 19:5; NRSV)

These remains were long thought to be part of the Antonia, with the pools used for water storage inside the fortress, the pavement belonging to an inner courtyard, and the arched gateway providing access to the fortress. If these remains were part of the Antonia, there would be no contradiction with Christian tradition, as the Antonia was built more than half a century before Jesus' death. However, scholars now agree that the Antonia was much smaller than previously thought, and did not extend to the area north of the Via Dolorosa, thereby excluding the remains in the Church of the Sisters of Zion. Furthermore, only the Struthion pools antedate 70 C.E., and they were located in an open moat outside the Antonia fortress. The arch and pavement were part of a forum that the emperor Hadrian established on this spot in the second century C.E. (see Chapter 13). The so-called Lithostratos pavement and arch of Ecce Homo cannot be identified with the places mentioned by John because they did not exist in the time of Jesus.

Today, the Via Dolorosa begins on the north side of the Temple Mount because, according to modern Christian tradition, this is where Jesus took up the cross after being sentenced to death by Pontius Pilate. In other words, modern Christian tradition identifies the Antonia as the place where Jesus was sentenced to death. However, the Gospel accounts mention the **praetorium**, not the Antonia: "Then the soldiers of the governor took Jesus into the praetorium" (Matt. 27:27). The *praetorium* – the palace of the Roman governor in Jerusalem – was Herod's palace, not the Antonia fortress. Therefore, Jesus was sentenced to death and took up the cross not in the area to the north of the Temple Mount,

7.18 Arch of Ecce Homo. Courtesy of Zev Radovan/BibleLandPictures.com.

but on the western side of the city. This means that the route walked by Jesus is different from the one walked by modern pilgrims (the Via Dolorosa). Today's route is based on a relatively late Christian tradition.

The Second and Third Walls

Josephus tells us that by the time Jerusalem was destroyed by the Romans in 70 C.E., the city had expanded beyond the line of the First Wall. The suburbs to the north were enclosed by two successive fortification walls, called the Second Wall and the Third Wall. The First Wall was built by the Hasmoneans, following the line of the late Iron Age wall around the western hill. According to Josephus, the Third Wall – the latest and northernmost of the three walls – was begun by Herod Agrippa I and completed on the eve of the outbreak of the First Jewish Revolt. Although Josephus not does mention who built the Second Wall, most scholars believe that Herod is the best candidate because of the chronology (the First Wall is earlier and the Third Wall is later), and because there was so much growth and construction during his reign.

Josephus also describes the routes of the First, Second, and Third Walls. There is no controversy about the First Wall, which ran along the northern end of the western hill (just above the Transverse Valley), as indicated by archaeological remains. However, scholars disagree about the routes of the Second and Third Walls, with two main schools of thought: minimalists (represented mainly by British, German, French, and Australian archaeologists) and

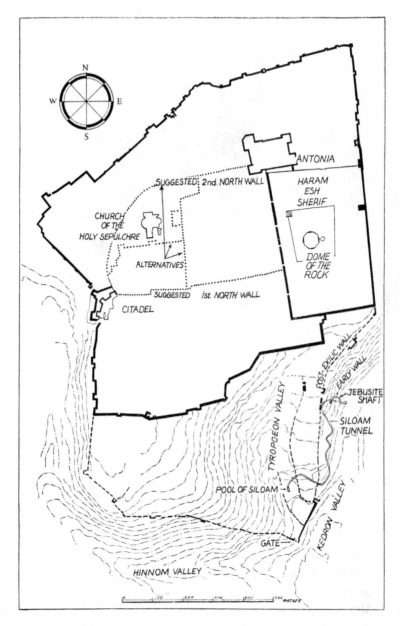

7.19 Plan showing alternative lines for the second north wall of Jerusalem, according to the minimalists. From K. M. Kenyon, *Digging Up Jerusalem* (London: Ernest Benn Ltd., 1974), p. 233 Fig. 38. By permission of A&C Black Publishers.

maximalists (represented mainly by Israeli archaeologists and American followers of William Foxwell Albright). The problem is that the landmarks that Josephus mentions along the Second and Third Walls disappeared long ago and their exact locations are unknown, although Josephus' description makes it clear that Third Wall enclosed a much greater area than the Second Wall.

7.20 Remains of the Third Wall.

According to the minimalists, the Third Wall is the same line marked by the north wall of the Old City today (in the center of which is the Damascus Gate), whereas the maximalists place the Third Wall to the north of the Old City.

The maximalists identify the Third Wall with the remains of a fortification wall that has been discovered about 1300 feet to the north of the Old City. This fortification wall – sometimes called the Meyer-Sukenik line after two Israeli archaeologists who excavated part of it – seems to be a convincing candidate for the Third Wall because it is built of Herodian-style stones. The minimalists have advanced no convincing explanation for the Meyer-Sukenik line if it is not the Third Wall. For example, they have proposed that perhaps it is a fourth line of wall built by the Jews at the time of the First Jewish Revolt, but Josephus mentions no such wall. Some have suggested that it was a circumvallation wall built by Titus when he besieged Jerusalem in 70 C.E., despite the fact that the towers project to the north, rather than south toward the city. In my opinion, although the Meyer-Sukenik line might be the Third Wall, it likely was built or rebuilt by Hadrian when he founded Aelia Capitolina (see Chapter 13).

The Second Wall is just as problematic as the Third Wall. According to the minimalists, the Second Wall reached only as far north as the area of the Antonia fortress whereas, according to the maximalists, it extended to the area of the Damascus Gate. In other words, according to the minimalists, the area of the Damascus Gate was part of the Third Wall, whereas according to the maximalists it was part of the Second Wall. Nevertheless, despite the lack of agreement and absence of unequivocal archaeological remains, both the minimalists and

7.21 Early Roman pottery including Eastern Sigillata A and Herodian oil lamps. Courtesy of Zev Radovan/BibleLandPictures.com.

maximalists reconstruct a dogleg on the west side of the Second Wall, at exactly the same spot. This is because of reconstructions that take into account the location of the Church of the Holy Sepulcher, which, according to Christian tradition, enshrines the site where Jesus was crucified and buried. The Gospel accounts describe Jesus' crucifixion and burial as taking place outside the city wall. If the Church of the Holy Sepulcher enshrines the spot where Jesus was crucified and buried, it must lie outside the city wall at the time of Jesus' death. This wall would be the Second Wall (if we assume that it was built by Herod), because the Third Wall was not begun until after Jesus' death. Although the Church of the Holy Sepulcher was built about 300 years after the time of Jesus, most scholars accept the authenticity of the tradition (because it is one of the earliest Christian churches built anywhere – see Chapter 15). Therefore, to leave the Church of the Holy Sepulcher – the supposed site of Jesus' crucifixion and burial – outside the city wall at the time of Jesus' death, both minimalists and maximalists reconstruct the Second Wall with a dogleg (despite the lack of archaeological remains of a wall at this spot).

MATERIAL CULTURE

Pottery

By the Herodian period, red-slipped dishes (Terra Sigillata) were the most popular table wares in the Roman world. Eastern Terra Sigillata was produced

7.22 Jerusalem painted bowls. Courtesy of Zev Radovan/BibleLandPictures.com.

at centers in the eastern Mediterranean (Phoenicia and Asia Minor) beginning around 125 B.C.E. Over the next century or two, centers in the western Mediterranean (Italy and Gaul) began manufacturing their own fine red ware (**Western Terra Sigillata**). The western products are distinguished by being made of fine, deep red clay covered with a glossy dark red slip, often applied over molded (relief) designs. Western Terra Sigillata is rare at sites in Palestine.

Although most of the local pottery is plain (undecorated), in the Herodian period a distinctive series of plates and shallow bowls was produced in the Jerusalem area. They have thin, hard-fired walls and are decorated with delicate geometric and floral designs. Because these Jerusalem painted bowls appear to imitate Nabataean ware, they are sometimes referred to as **Pseudo-Nabataean** ware.

Oil Lamps

Roman oil lamps are mold-made and have round bodies with short, splayed nozzles, usually flanked by volutes. The top of the lamp is closed (this part of the lamp is called a **discus**) and typically is decorated in relief, often with figured images (such as gods and goddesses, gladiators, and animals). Lamps of this type are common around the Mediterranean and were produced in various centers, including workshops in Syria-Palestine.

Another type – the so-called Herodian or wheel-made lamp – was popular among the Jewish population of Palestine, who probably avoided using the

7.23 Roman discus lamp. Courtesy of Zev Radovan/BibleLandPictures.com.

Roman lamps because they considered the figured decoration offensive. Herodian lamps are the same shape as the Roman lamps – a round body with short, splayed nozzle – but have a large filling hole in the middle of the discus and lack decoration. Herodian lamps are found in large numbers at sites around Palestine. Recent analyses have indicated that the Herodian lamps found at sites such as Gamla were manufactured in Jerusalem, and were apparently transported for sale to the northern part of the country. It is not clear why the Jews of Galilee and the Golan preferred to purchase Jerusalem products rather than manufacture their own imitations.

Glass

Although glass had been invented centuries earlier, it was an expensive and rare product before the Herodian period. During the Hellenistic period, mold-made glass bowls became common (similar to mold-made pottery bowls). However, late in the first century B.C.E., the invention of glass blowing revolutionized glass production. Blown glass is made by blowing hot glass through a tube

7.24 Herodian (wheel-made) lamps. Courtesy of Zev Radovan/BibleLandPictures.com.

into the desired shape. This invention made glass vessels much less costly and therefore more common. Phoenicia (where Ennion worked) and Palestine were centers of glassmaking in the Hellenistic and Roman periods. In the Jewish Quarter excavations, Avigad discovered refuse (waste) from a glassmaking workshop. The refuse, consisting of lumps of glass, unfinished vessels, and glass rods and tubes, had been dumped into a ritual bath that was paved over during the reign of Herod. This is the earliest archaeological evidence of blown glass found anywhere. This discovery indicates that Jerusalem was a center of glass production, which is surprising because we would not expect this sort of industrial activity in an urban center.

Coins

Herod minted his own bronze coins, many of which bear symbols similar to those used by the Hasmoneans (anchors, cornucopiae, and wreaths). He might have been concerned not to offend the Jewish population by putting figured images on his coins. However, one series of coins minted by Herod bears symbols that appear to be pagan in nature, such as an altar or table on top of which is a cap with a star – perhaps the cap of the **Dioscuri**, the sons of Zeus. This series was minted for a short time, possibly at the non-Jewish site of Samaria-Sebaste, and had limited circulation. Herod Agrippa I and Herod Agrippa II minted coins bearing figured images (including busts of the emperor, their own heads, and perhaps other family members) for circulation in non-Jewish territories.

7.25 Coin of Herod showing a cap with a star. Courtesy of Zev Radovan/BibleLandPictures
.com.

During the First Revolt, the Jews minted their own coins as a proclamation of
independence. These coins – minted in silver and bronze – carry symbols and
slogans alluding to Jerusalem and the temple. The symbols include a chalice
(a vessel used in the temple) and a branch with three pomegranates (perhaps a
staff used by the priests). The coins are inscribed in the paleo-Hebrew script
with Hebrew-language slogans alluding to Jerusalem and the temple (and the
revival of an independent Jewish kingdom), such as "Jerusalem the holy" and
"for the freedom of Zion." The designation of these coins as sheqels – an ancient
system of weights – also alludes to the revival of the biblical kingdom. The coins
carry dates, from Year One to Year Five (of the revolt), with the establishment of
a new calendar being another proclamation of independence from Roman rule.

To commemorate their victory over the Jews, the Flavian emperors minted a
special series of coins. The head of the emperor is depicted on the obverse, and

7.26 Coin of the First Jewish Revolt. Courtesy of Zev Radovan/BibleLandPictures.com.

7.27 Judea Capta coin. Courtesy of Zev Radovan/BibleLandPictures.com.

the reverse shows a young woman (symbolizing the Jewish people) mourning under a date palm (symbolizing the province of Judea), and a man with hands bound behind his back standing on the other side of the tree. These images are accompanied by the inscription **Judea Capta**, meaning "Judea has been conquered."

Sidebar: Wilson's Arch

Recent excavations by the western wall are revolutionizing our understanding of the function and date of Wilson's Arch. Israeli archaeologists conducting the excavations claim to have found evidence that Wilson's Arch was part of a Herodian period staircase that turned 90 degrees and provided access from the Tyropoeon Valley to the Temple Mount, similar to Robinson's Arch. This staircase abutted an earlier Hasmonean-period dam across the Tyropoeon Valley that was put out of use when Herod expanded the Temple Mount. The excavators also suggest that the First Wall did not terminate on the east at Wilson's Arch, but was located farther to the north. After Hadrian rebuilt Jerusalem as Aelia Capitolina in the second century C.E., the remains of the Herodian period staircase (Wilson's Arch) were incorporated into a bridge carried on arches across the Tyropoeon Valley. Jerusalem's main *decumanus* originated on the western side of the city in the area of the Citadel (Jaffa Gate), and was connected by the bridge with the Temple Mount to the east (see Chapter 13).

7.28 The Bethesda (Sheep's) pools. Courtesy of Zev Radovan/BibleLandPictures.com.

Sidebar: Herodian Jerusalem's Water Supply

Jerusalem's expansion in the late Second Temple period increased the demand for water. The sacrificial cult on the Temple Mount, and the masses of pilgrims who poured into the city, also required huge quantities of water. The Gihon spring and cisterns in houses, which in earlier periods had sufficed, were now supplemented in various ways. A series of enormous open pools or reservoirs that surrounded the city not only stored water but also created defensive barriers (like a moat). On the north side of the city these pools included (from east to west) **Birket Isr'il** (the **pool of Israel**) at the northeast corner of the Temple Mount, the **Sheep's pools** (or **Bezetha** or **Bethesda pools**; see John 5:2–4), and the Struthion pool (associated with the Antonia fortress). To the west (from north to south), were **Hezekiah's pool** (the **Amygdalon pool** or **pool of the Towers**, by Herod's three towers), the **Mamila pool** (outside the modern Jaffa Gate), and the **Sultan's pool** (in the Ben-Hinnom valley). Another large pool (**Birket el-Hamra**) was located near the junction of the Kidron, Tyropoeon, and Ben-Hinnom valleys.

The Temple Mount literally was honeycombed with rock-cut cisterns that stored water used by the cult. These cisterns were filled with rain water as well as by means of aqueducts that brought the water from sources outside the city. The earliest aqueduct apparently was constructed by the Hasmoneans, and the system was expanded by Herod. The aqueducts brought water from large collection pools (called **Solomon's pools**) south of Bethlehem, where the Judean mountains are higher in elevation than in Jerusalem. Water that was collected and stored in Solomon's pools flowed (by gravity) through channels and tunnels to the Temple Mount (a distance of about 13 miles). This water system is similar to the one at Qumran (although the water came from collection pools rather than flash floods), but is much larger in scale.

Recommended Reading

Nahman Avigad, *Discovering Jerusalem* (Nashville: Thomas Nelson, 1993).

Oleg Grabar and Benjamin Z. Kedar (eds.), *Where Heaven and Earth Meet: Jerusalem's Sacred Esplanade* (Austin: University of Texas, 2009).

Lee I. Levine, *Jerusalem, Portrait of the City in the Second Temple Period (538 B.C.E.– 70 C.E.)* (Philadelphia: Jewish Publication Society, 2002).

Benjamin Mazar, *The Mountain of the Lord, Excavating in Jerusalem* (Garden City, NY: Doubleday & Company, 1975).

Emil Schürer, *The History of the Jewish People in the Age of Jesus Christ, Vols. 1–3* (Revised and edited by Geza Vermes, Fergus Millar, and Martin Goodman; Edinburgh: T & T Clark, 1986).

EIGHT

THE EARLY ROMAN (HERODIAN) PERIOD (40 B.C.E.–70 C.E.)

CAESAREA MARITIMA, SAMARIA-SEBASTE, HERODIAN JERICHO, AND HERODIUM

Caesarea Maritima

History of the Town

The small town of Straton's Tower was established during the Persian period, when the Palestinian coast was governed by the Phoenician kings of Tyre and Sidon. The town was part of the territory that Herod received from Octavian (Augustus Caesar) after the battle of Actium in 31 B.C.E., when Octavian reconfirmed Herod as king of Judea and increased the size of his kingdom. Herod rebuilt Straton's Tower as a showcase Greco-Roman port city and renamed it Caesarea. Herod's establishment of Caesarea followed the precedent of Alexander the Great and his Hellenistic successors, but instead of naming it after himself he named it in honor of Octavian – a brilliant move that demonstrated Herod's loyalty to his new patron. Herod's city of Caesarea had two components: the settlement (on land), called Caesarea Maritima, and the harbor, called Sebaste (**Sebastos** is Greek for Augustus). A glance at a map of Palestine reveals that the coastline is relatively even and lacks large natural harbors and anchorages. Herod's new harbor filled this gap, and the city quickly became Palestine's major port city.

Caesarea had a long history and flourished for centuries. Its importance increased after Herod Archelaus was removed from rule in 6 C.E., when it became the seat of the local Roman governor (prefect or procurator) in Palestine (although Herod had a palace at Caesarea, Jerusalem was the capital of his kingdom). After Paul was arrested, he was imprisoned in the Roman governor's palace at Caesarea for two years before being shipped off to Rome for trial and (presumably) execution (Acts 23:23–24, 33). Caesarea was a Greco-Roman city

8.1   Aerial view of Caesarea. Courtesy of Zev Radovan/BibleLandPictures.com.

with a large Gentile population and a minority of Jews. By Paul's time, the inhabitants also included some members of the early church: "The next day we left and came to Caesarea; and we went into the house of Philip the evangelist, one of the seven, and stayed with him. . . . After these days we got ready and started to go up to Jerusalem. Some of the disciples from Caesarea also came along and brought us to the house of Mnason of Cyprus, and early disciple, with whom we were to stay" (Acts 21:8, 15–16). Tensions between Jews and Gentiles at Caesarea contributed to the outbreak of the First Jewish Revolt in 66 C.E., when a pagan ceremony conducted on the Sabbath near the entrance to a synagogue sparked riots.

Vespasian made Caesarea the headquarters of his operations during the First Revolt. After the revolt, Vespasian raised Caesarea to the rank of a Roman colony, a status that conveyed certain benefits to the population, which now included Roman military veterans. In the centuries that followed, Caesarea continued to grow, reaching its maximum extent during the fifth and sixth centuries C.E. (the Byzantine period). Caesarea was the last major city in Palestine to fall to the Muslims, surrendering in 640 C.E. after a seven-month-long siege. Although Caesarea contracted in size after the Muslim conquest, it continued to be an important commercial hub, as indicated by large quantities of imported pottery from around the Mediterranean. Caesarea was conquered during the First Crusade (1101) and became a key stronghold of the Crusader kingdom in the Holy Land. The Genoese found a green-colored glass vessel in the city and declared it to be the **Holy Grail**, the goblet used by Jesus at the Last Supper. It was taken to Genoa and placed in the Church of San Lorenzo. Caesarea fell to Saladin in 1187 and was retaken by the Crusaders in 1191.

When the Mamluke ruler Baybars conquered Caesarea in 1265, he razed it to the ground, bringing to an end the city's long history. In the 1870s and 1880s, the Ottomans settled Bosnian refugees at Caesarea (Kaisariyeh). This settlement existed until the establishment of the state of Israel in 1948; some descendants of the Bosnian families still live in the nearby Israeli town of Hadera. After 1948, the Israeli authorities cleared and restored the Crusader fortification walls and moat.

The Harbor

Herod's harbor at Caesarea (ca. 23–15 B.C.E.) was an amazing engineering feat that resulted in the largest artificial harbor ever built in the open sea up to that point. It consisted of a large outer harbor and a smaller, more sheltered, inner harbor. The harbor was created by building two breakwaters extending out into the sea. The breakwaters protected boats from rough waters and created a barrier against the prevailing currents, which come from the south and bring silt from the Nile Delta. For this reason, the southern breakwater was much longer (ca. 2000 feet) than the northern one (ca. 800 feet). Passage through the breakwaters was from the northwest. Silting was a constant problem, kept at bay in antiquity only by the repeated dredging of the harbor. By the early Islamic period, the inner harbor had silted up and was covered with buildings. Since then, earthquakes, the rising level of the Mediterranean, and a possible tsunami have submerged both breakwaters.

Underwater excavations at Caesarea indicate that the breakwaters were constructed using the latest innovations in Roman concrete technology. Herod imported hydraulic concrete from Italy, which contained a special type of volcanic ash that allowed the concrete mixture to harden underwater. To make the breakwaters, Herod's engineers constructed enormous wooden boxes or formworks, which were towed out into the open sea. The concrete mixture was poured into the wooden formworks, causing them to sink to the sea floor, where the concrete hardened. A series of buildings was constructed on top of the breakwaters, including *horrea* (sing. **horreum**), warehouses to store the goods brought in and out of the harbor. Towers at the ends of the breakwaters marked the entrance to the harbor. One of them was a lighthouse that Herod modeled after the **Pharos of Alexandria** – one of the seven wonders of the ancient world – and that he named the Drusion, in honor of Augustus' stepson Drusus (father of the emperor Claudius).

8.2 Reconstruction of Herod's harbor at Caesarea. National Geographic Image ID 18651, by Robert J. Teringo/National Geographic Stock.

Caesarea's Temples

Towering over Caesarea's harbor, Herod built a temple dedicated to Roma (the goddess of the city of Rome) and Augustus – another demonstration of Herod's loyalty to his new patron. The temple stood on an elevated artificial platform (now called the Temple Platform) overlooking the inner harbor. Similar to the southern end of Jerusalem's Temple Mount, the Temple Platform at Caesarea was supported on a series of underground vaults (arches). At Caesarea, the vaults served as *horrea* (warehouses) that opened toward the inner harbor. The *horrea* continued to the south of the harbor, where one was converted into a **Mithraeum** in the second century C.E. (a Mithraeum is a shrine dedicated to **Mithras**, a Near Eastern deity whose cult was especially popular among Roman soldiers; see Chapter 13).

Herod's temple to Roma and Augustus was constructed in an Italic rather than a Hellenistic style. The Italic features include the placement of the temple on a tall, raised podium that was accessed by steps only on the west (with the porch facing the harbor), creating an axiality and a frontality that differed from Greek temples. The few surviving fragments of the superstructure indicate

8.3 Vault in the Temple Platform at Caesarea.

that the temple was built of kurkar (local sandstone) covered with stucco. The column capitals were Corinthian.

Herod's reconstruction of the Jerusalem temple presumably was motivated by genuine piety as well as by political considerations (an attempt to win the loyalty of the Jewish population). Similarly, Herod's dedication of the temple at Caesarea was intended to demonstrate his loyalty to Augustus and Rome. Although we tend to think of Herod as a Jewish (or, at least, half-Jewish) king, he apparently had no qualms about establishing a pagan temple. In fact, Herod dedicated another temple to Roma and Augustus at Samaria (discussed later), and, according to Josephus, he built or restored pagan temples in Tyre, Berytus (Beirut), and Rhodes (the temple of Pythian Apollo). In other words, Herod dedicated numerous temples within his kingdom and abroad, to the Jewish God as well as to pagan deities and the Roman emperor. All these projects likely were motivated as much by piety as by political concerns; they hint at Roman influence on Herod's worldview, as the Romans believed that all gods should be treated with respect.

Statues discovered around Caesarea indicate that there were other temples, the locations of which are still unknown. For example, excavations by an Israeli archaeologist in 1951 brought to light a Byzantine (fifth–sixth century C.E.) street flanked by two colossal but headless statues. Both statues depict seated, robed males and date to the second or third centuries C.E., which means that they were already ancient by the time they were set up by the street. One of the statues is of porphyry, a hard red stone from Egypt. Many scholars believe that

8.4 Byzantine street at Caesarea flanked by Roman statues.

it represented the Roman emperor Hadrian (117–138 C.E.), who reconstructed Caesarea's aqueduct system (discussed later). An inscription found elsewhere at Caesarea mentions a Hadrianeum (a temple dedicated to Hadrian), perhaps the source of the porphyry statue.

In 1961, an Italian expedition made a chance discovery in the ancient theater (discussed later). During the course of excavations, they dislodged a stone that was in secondary use (reused). The stone's underside bears a dedicatory inscription referring to an otherwise unknown temple to the emperor Tiberius, which was dedicated by Pontius Pilate, prefect of Judea. As the Roman governor of Judea from 26 to 36 C.E., Pontius Pilate's main palace and administrative base were at Caesarea. According to the Gospel accounts, Pilate sentenced Jesus to death by crucifixion. The Caesarea inscription is the only archaeological artifact discovered so far that is associated directly with Pontius Pilate, aside from small bronze coins that he minted (but do not bear his name).

By the fifth and sixth centuries, most of Caesarea's population was Christian. At this time, Herod's temple to Roma and Augustus was replaced by an octagonal church, perhaps dedicated to St. Procopius, the city's first martyr. At some time during the early Islamic period, this church was destroyed or abandoned. Later, when the Crusaders occupied Caesarea, they established the Cathedral of St. Peter on the Temple Platform, the **apses** of which still stand today. Jerusalem's Temple Mount and the Temple Platform at Caesarea illustrate a well-known archaeological phenomenon: the continuity of cult. Continuity of cult means that once a spot becomes holy or sacred, it tends to retain its sanctity over

8.5 The Pontius Pilate inscription from Caesarea. Courtesy of Zev Radovan/BibleLand
Pictures.com.

time even if the religions change. Scattered remains associated with one or more
Jewish buildings dating to the fifth and sixth centuries – perhaps a synagogue –
have been discovered on the northern side of the city.

The Palaces

A palace built by Herod or the earliest Roman governors was spectacularly
situated on a natural promontory jutting out into the sea south of the harbor
and the Crusader city. The centerpiece of the promontory palace was a large
pool that apparently was stocked with fish. Rows of columns surrounded the
pool on all four sides, creating a peristyle porch with the open-air pool in the
center. The pool was on the lower part of the promontory, with another part of
the palace located on a higher terrace to the east.

The area between the Crusader city and the promontory palace was filled with
spacious, richly decorated villas or mansions that belonged to the Roman and
Byzantine governing elite. The villas were abandoned after the Muslim conquest
and buried under sand dunes. Long before large-scale excavations began in this

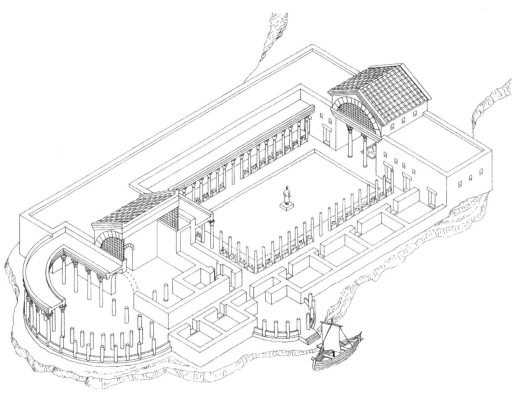

8.6   Reconstruction of Herod's promontory palace. By Leen Ritmeyer ©

8.7   Inscription in the "archives building" at Caesarea.

area in the 1990s, the discovery of an "archives building" immediately to the south of the Crusader city hinted that this was an elite quarter. The "archives building" consists of seven rooms surrounding a central courtyard. Inscriptions in the mosaic floors identify this as the office where accountants of the imperial governor's tax department kept their records. The inscriptions remind citizens of their civic duty by citing passages from the New Testament, such as Paul's Letter to the Romans (13:3): "Do you wish to have no fear of the authority [the governor]? Then do what is good, and you will receive its approval." Another villa nearby was paved with a beautiful mosaic floor depicting personifications of the four seasons. During the Byzantine period, new buildings were erected in this quarter, including a large public bath house, a palace, and a basilica (perhaps a church).

The Entertainment Arenas and City Walls

Large-scale excavations undertaken in the 1990s by the Israel Antiquities Authority to the south of the Crusader city brought to light a **hippodrome** from the time of Herod the Great. The hippodrome was located alongside the sea, north of and adjacent to the promontory palace. It was bordered on the east by the palatial villa quarter, which overlooked it – an arrangement reminiscent of Rome, where the imperial palaces on the Palatine Hill overlooked the Circus Maximus. The hippodrome was a long, narrow arena with starting gates (*carceres*) at the northern end and a curved southern end, surrounded by banks of seats. It was used for chariot races and perhaps footraces as well.

In the second century C.E., apparently during Hadrian's reign, a new hippodrome was built at some distance to the east (the Herodian hippodrome continued to function but was used for various purposes, including as an amphitheater for animal and gladiator fights). Although it is now covered by agricultural fields of the local kibbutz, the outline of the Hadrianic hippodrome is clearly visible in aerial photographs. Parts of the *spina* (spine) – the wall that ran down the middle of the racecourse and around which the horses and chariots raced – still survive in the kibbutz fields, together with stone monoliths and obelisks (the Romans typically erected monuments and lap counters on top of the *spina*). Limited excavations have revealed some of the seating and floor of this hippodrome.

To the south of the promontory palace, Herod built a Roman-style theater overlooking the sea. The theater seated about 5,000 people on banks of seats supported by stone arches and vaults (in contrast to Greek theaters, which typically had seating on natural slopes or hillsides). The theater and hippodrome were an integral part of Caesarea's elite quarter, which included the palaces of the Roman and Byzantine governors. Although most of the Herodian city is still unexcavated, there are indications that it had an orthogonal layout, with a grid of north-south and east-west streets. The fortification wall of the Herodian city

Sidebar: Roman Places of Entertainment and Spectacle

Roman entertainment arenas varied depending on the nature of the spectacle, just as today we have different kinds of arenas depending on the nature of the event (e.g., football stadiums, baseball fields, hockey arenas). Some types of Roman arenas originated in the Greek world. For example, theaters first developed in Greece in the sixth and fifth centuries B.C.E. Originally they consisted of simple wooden bleachers on the natural slope of a hill, arranged in a semicircle around a circular area below that was called an orchestra, where the chorus chanted. A modest wooden scene building was located behind the orchestra. By the Roman period, concrete technology made it possible to place seats on artificial vaulted structures anywhere, not just on natural hillsides. Roman orchestras were cut in half by a raised wooden stage in front of the scene building, which was two to three stories high and had elaborate decoration, including projecting columns and niches framing statues. The scene building was a false façade that created a backdrop for the actors performing on the stage.

Whereas theaters originated in the Greek world and were used for the performance of plays, amphitheaters were a purely Italic invention. The word *amphitheater* comes from a Greek word referring to the fact that the oval arena was completely encircled by seats (usually supported by a built, vaulted structure). Amphitheaters were used for gladiator and animal fights. Perhaps the most famous example is the Flavian amphitheater in Rome, popularly known as the Colosseum because the emperor Vespasian built it near the site of a colossal statue of his predecessor Nero.

Other types of arenas included stadiums for footracing, which had a long tradition in the Greek world going back at least to the first Olympic games in 776 B.C.E., and hippodromes, which were horse and chariot racecourses. Hippodromes were long and narrow, with one curved end and a flat end with the starting gates. Banks of seats, set on natural hillsides or on built vaulted structures, lined the sides of Roman hippodromes. A wall called a *spina* (Latin for spine) bisected the middle of the course and typically had obelisks, lap counters, and other monuments set atop it. The Romans called a hippodrome (Greek for "horse-racing course") a *circus*. The most famous Roman hippodrome was the Circus Maximus, located at the foot of the Palatine Hill in Rome.

The Romans also developed a sophisticated culture of baths and bathing. Most Roman cities had one or more public bath houses, and the palaces and villas of the wealthy were equipped with private bath houses. No matter what their size, Roman bath houses typically contained the same types of rooms: a dressing room (**apodyterium**), a cold-water plunge bath (**frigidarium**), a warm room (*tepidarium*), and the hot room or steam bath (**caldarium**). The *caldarium* usually was heated by a hypocaust system, in which hot air from a furnace outside the room circulated below a raised floor and through pipes along the walls. Steam was created by throwing water from bathtubs onto the floor and walls (see Chapter 10). A constant supply of fresh water was brought to the bath house by aqueduct. It was common for bath houses to include a latrine, with rows of stone or wooden seats lining the walls and a channel with water underneath to carry away the waste.

extended from the round towers on the north (see the discussion of Straton's Tower in Chapter 4) to the theater on the south. By the fifth century, a new wall encompassing a much larger area was built, attesting to the continued growth of the city. After the Muslim conquest, the elite quarter was abandoned and covered with sand dunes, as mentioned earlier. By the Crusader period the settlement had contracted to a fraction of the Herodian city, centering on the Temple Platform and inner harbor.

On the northeast side of the city, the outlines of an unexcavated **amphitheater** are visible among the agricultural fields. The amphitheater lies at the edge of the Herodian city, but well within the expanded walls of the fifth century C.E. The oval arena must have been used for animal and gladiator fights.

Aqueducts

Roman cities were characterized by an abundance of fresh running water, sometimes brought from great distances by aqueducts. Fountains dotted the streets of Roman cities, and the water that overflowed swept garbage and debris into sewers. Water also supplied the public and private bath houses that were a feature of Roman life. Although many people visualize Roman aqueducts as huge bridges carried on arches (such as the famous Pont du Gard in France), in reality an aqueduct is simply a water channel. Although sometimes Roman aqueducts employed siphons to pump water upward, in most cases the water flowed naturally through the channel along a gentle downward slope. To maintain the level of the flow (in cases where the ground level dropped), an arched bridge was built to support the channel. If there were hills or mountains in the way, the channel could be cut as an underground tunnel, as in a short section of the aqueduct at Qumran. Water channels usually were covered with stone slabs, which could be removed from time to time to clean out accumulations of silt and lime.

Like a typical Roman city, Herod provisioned Caesarea with plenty of fresh water brought by aqueduct. The water came from springs in the Carmel Mountains to the northeast. To maintain a gentle downward slope, with the steep drop

8.8 View of the Herodian theater and hippodrome at Caesarea. Courtesy of Zev Radovan/ BibleLandPictures.com.

from the mountains to the sea, Herod's aqueduct (the "high-level aqueduct") was carried on an arched bridge built of stone. Long stretches of this aqueduct still survive on the beach north of Caesarea. The aqueduct entered the city as a water channel running under the gate between the two round towers.

As Caesarea's population grew, so did the need for water. In the second century C.E., Hadrian doubled the amount of water by building a second channel alongside Herod's, supported by another arched bridge that abutted Herod's original aqueduct. Dedicatory inscriptions set into Hadrian's aqueduct indicate that it was constructed by Roman legionary soldiers stationed in the vicinity.

In the fourth century C.E., a new aqueduct (the "low-level aqueduct") was constructed. Unlike the high-level aqueduct, this channel originated in the marshy delta of the Tanninim (Crocodile) River, just a few miles north of Caesarea. The low-level aqueduct was created by damming the river, which was diverted into the channel. The aqueduct is so called because an arched bridge was not necessary in this case to maintain the level of the water. Instead, the channel ran just above ground level.

Sprawling country villas belonging to wealthy families dotted the rich agricultural landscape outside Caesarea's walls. Part of one such villa was discovered accidentally and excavated in 1950 to the northeast of Caesarea. It included a lavish mosaic with medallions containing depictions of exotic animals, apparently the floor of a large peristyle courtyard. In the same area a luxurious bath house dating to the end of the Byzantine period was found, which included a

8.9 The high-level aqueduct at Caesarea showing the two construction phases. Courtesy of Zev Radovan/BibleLandPictures.com.

fish pond (*piscina*) for fresh-water fish that could be caught and served to the bathers.

SAMARIA-SEBASTE

Alexander the Great banished the Samaritans from the city of Samaria, the former capital of the northern kingdom of Israel, and settled Macedonian veterans there. Therefore, by Herod's time Samaria, like Caesarea, was inhabited by a non-Jewish population. And, as he did with Caesarea, Herod rebuilt Samaria after the battle of Actium, naming it Sebaste (Sebastos) in honor of Augustus. There are many other parallels between Herod's cities of Caesarea and Samaria. For example, on top of the ancient acropolis Herod established an Italian-style temple dedicated to Roma and Augustus. The temple stood on an elevated podium with steps along the front, and was oriented to the south like typical Roman temples. The temple was located in the center of a large, open platform, which was supported along the sides by underground arches and vaults. A small theater on the north side of the acropolis had seating on the natural slope of the hill. Another temple dedicated to Kore was located on a terrace to the north, just below the acropolis. **Kore** (or **Persephone**) was the daughter of the goddess Demeter, and her cult was associated with fertility.

The city was surrounded by a wall, with a main gate on the west flanked by round towers. The gate led to a colonnaded street that bisected the city from

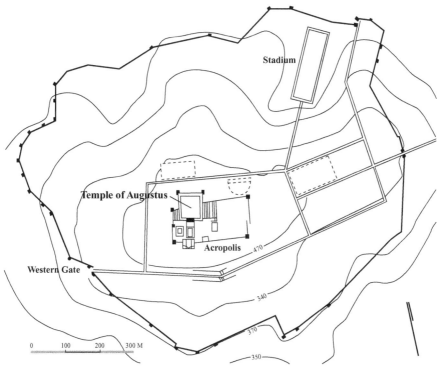

8.10 General plan of Sebaste. From E. Netzer, *The Architecture of Herod the Great Builder* (Grand Rapids, MI: Baker Academic, 2008), p. 83 Fig. 20. © Mohr Siebeck Tübingen, 2006, by permission of Mohr Siebeck.

8.11 The steps of Herod's temple to Rome and Augustus at Samaria.

8.12 The colonnaded street at Samaria.

west to east and was overlooked by the acropolis to the north. A stadium (or, according to a more recent theory, a peristyle courtyard) lay in a flat plain at the northern edge of the city. An inscription on an altar found in the stadium or courtyard was dedicated to Kore by a high priest. To the east of the acropolis was a forum, with a basilica along the western side. An aqueduct brought water into the city from springs to the east.

HERODIAN JERICHO

Jericho is a desert oasis just to the northwest of the Dead Sea. The Hasmonean kings established a series of winter palaces at Jericho because of its warm climate, abundance of fresh water springs, and proximity to Jerusalem (only 17 miles away). The Hasmonean palaces included luxuriously appointed living quarters (including frescoes, stucco, and mosaics), lush gardens, and swimming pools, as well as numerous *miqva'ot* − not surprising because the Hasmonean kings also served as high priests. Herod followed suit by establishing three successive palace complexes adjacent to the Hasmonean palaces. Herod's Third Palace at Jericho − the largest and most elaborate of the series − straddled the banks of Wadi Qelt, a riverbed fed by perennial fresh water springs. The palace itself was located on the north bank, and included a Roman-style bath house and an enormous reception hall decorated with frescoes and mosaics, and **opus sectile** (colored tile) pavements. Across the riverbed, on the south bank, was a large garden overlooked by stoas (porches) on either side, which was connected to

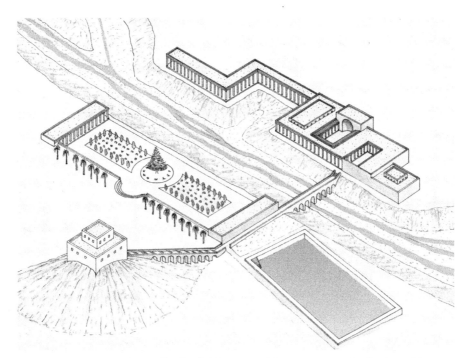

8.13 Reconstruction of Herod's Third Palace at Jericho. Reconstruction by Leen Ritmeyer ©.

the north bank by a bridge. Flowerpots with holes in the base for drainage were discovered in the excavations in the garden. A huge swimming pool lay to the east of the garden, overlooked by a building on a nearby hill, the function of which is unknown.

Herod's Third Palace at Jericho was constructed by combining Roman concrete technology with the local building material – mud brick. The walls were built of mud brick or concrete faced with sandstone blocks laid in a distinctive net pattern called **opus reticulatum** (reticulate work) (see the Sidebar). The walls would have been covered with plaster and then painted with frescoes. *Opus reticulatum* has been discovered in only three places in Israel: Herod's Third Palace at Jericho, a Herodian palace at Banyas (in Upper Galilee), and a mausoleum (apparently associated with Herod's family) north of the Damascus Gate in Jerusalem. Because Roman concrete technology was unfamiliar to the local population, architects or workmen from Italy must have participated in these construction projects. Ehud Netzer, who excavated the Hasmonean and Herodian palaces at Jericho, suggested that this exchange occurred in the wake of Marcus Agrippa's visit to Herod's kingdom in 15 B.C.E.

About one mile from the palaces, Herod established a public arena that included a stadium with theatral seating at one end. To protect the palaces, Herod built a fortress on top of a mountain overlooking the outlet of **Wadi**

8.14 Aerial view of the northern wing of Herod's Third Palace at Jericho. Courtesy of Zev Radovan/BibleLandPictures.com.

Qelt, which he named Cypros in honor of his mother. Like Herod's other fortified desert palaces (such as Masada and Herodium), Cypros was equipped with lavishly decorated palatial quarters, storerooms for food and cisterns for water, and a Roman-style bath house.

8.15 *Opus reticulatum* in the bath house of Herod's Third Palace at Jericho.

HERODIUM

Unlike the other sites we have discussed, Herod named Herodium after himself, apparently because he planned it as his final resting place and everlasting memorial (the location of another Herodium mentioned by Josephus is unknown). Indeed, the distinctive, cone-shaped mountain (which Josephus described as breast-shaped), still dominates the landscape around Bethlehem and is visible even from Jerusalem. Herodium was a sprawling complex consisting of a fortified palace atop the mountain (Upper Herodium) and another palace and administrative complex at its base (Lower Herodium).

Herodium is a feat of engineering: an artificial mountain created by piling huge quantities of earth around two concentric stone walls that were built on a natural hill. The concentric walls were several stories high, with vaulted stone passages one above another inside them. Four stone towers oriented toward the cardinal points were set into the towers, the eastern one round and the others semicircular. The palace atop Upper Herodium was set into a huge depression inside the circular walls, resembling the mouth of a volcano. Within the depression, the palace was laid out axially, with the eastern half consisting of a large peristyle garden with exedrae (semicircular niches that perhaps contained statues) in the north, east, and south walls. The western half of the palace was divided into two equal parts: a bath house on the north and palace rooms on the south. The bath house is a modest-sized but well-equipped Roman style facility with a **hypocaust** heating system (see Chapter 10), and the centerpiece of the palace rooms was a large triclinium. At the time of the First Revolt, Jewish rebels

8.16 Aerial view of Herodium. Courtesy of Zev Radovan/BibleLandPictures.com.

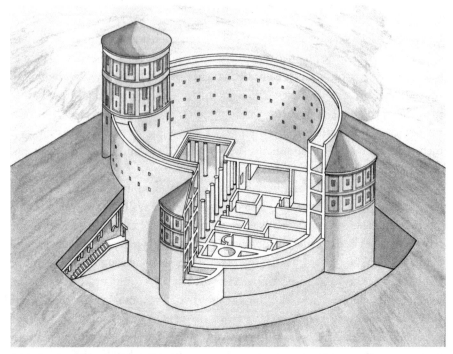

8.17 Section through Upper Herodium. Reconstruction by Leen Ritmeyer ©.

converted the triclinium into a synagogue (see Chapter 14). Only bits and pieces of the original decoration of the palace – frescoes, stucco, and mosaics – survive. However, the **tepidarium** (warm room) of the bath house is still covered by the original stone dome.

On the lower slope of Herodium facing Jerusalem is a large administrative palace complex. The palace was built on a terrace above a long, narrow hippo-drome that was dominated by a monumental building at one end. The complex overlooks a gigantic pool (ca. 225 by 150 feet) that was surrounded by a peri-style with extensive gardens. The pool had a circular pavilion in the center, and was used for boating as well as bathing. It was supplied by aqueducts that brought water from springs in the area of Bethlehem. The lush green of the gardens and sparkling water in the pool created a stark contrast with the arid desert environment – a visual statement of power and abundance.

Upper and Lower Herodium were connected by a staircase that ascended the northwest side and was enclosed by stone walls and a vaulted ceiling. Josephus relates that when Herod died in his palace at Jericho in 4 B.C.E., a procession brought his body to Herodium for burial. Ehud Netzer, an Israeli archaeologist who began excavating at Lower Herodium in the 1980s, spent decades searching for Herod's tomb, the location of which remained a mystery. Some scholars believed that Herod was buried at the top of the mountain or inside it, whereas Netzer thought it might be in or around the monumental

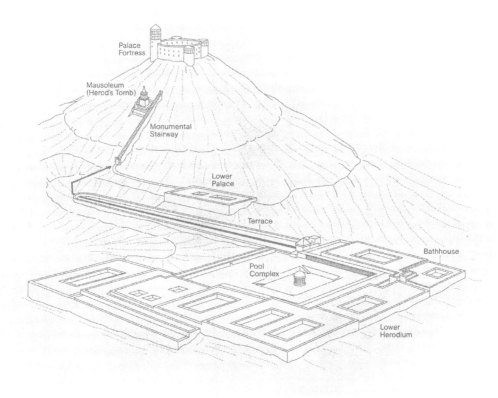

Palace Fortress

Mausoleum (Herod's Tomb)

Monumental Stairway

Lower Palace

Terrace

Bathhouse

Pool Complex

Lower Herodium

8.18 Reconstruction of Herodium including Herod's tomb. National Geographic Image ID 1198441, by Hiram Henriquez/National Geographic Stock.

building by the hippodrome. Finally, in 2007, Netzer found the tomb about midway down the northern slope of the mountain – the side facing toward Jerusalem. The tomb was marked by a massive *tholos* (circular structure) on a raised square podium. The high quality of the carved stone decoration of the *tholos* and stone **sarcophagus** (coffin) fragments found nearby is unparalleled elsewhere in Israel, leaving little doubt that this is the tomb of Herod (despite the absence of inscriptions so far).

Netzer's excavations on the slope around the tomb have indicated that this was part of a much larger complex of buildings that included a small theater. One room behind the theater was decorated with an exquisite fresco depicting figures in a sacro-idyllic landscape, painted in a **trompe l'oeil** window on the wall – a Roman-style painting of the highest quality that has no parallels in Israel. According to Netzer, the structures on the side of the mountain were buried in earth shortly before Herod's death – apparently preplanned. Netzer also suggested that Herod's sarcophagus was smashed to bits by disgruntled Jews shortly after his death. Josephus' failure to refer to the exact location of Herod's burial – or, indeed, to provide any description of the *tholos* marking it – suggests that it may have been forgotten by his time.

Sidebar: Roman Concrete Technology

Early temples in Italy were constructed of mud-brick and stone, sometimes covered with painted terra-cotta plaques or decoration. Eventually, in an attempt to monumentalize temples and other buildings, the Romans began to use other building materials. Although the Romans adopted and adapted classical Greek styles of architecture, Italy is poorer than Greece in high-quality marble. Therefore, the Romans tried to make marble go as far as possible by slicing it into thin slabs used as the covering (veneer) for walls and other surfaces, in contrast to classical Greek monuments, which usually were constructed entirely of marble. By the late Republican period (second and first centuries B.C.E.), the Romans began constructing buildings using concrete. Although it was poured into a frame like modern concrete, Roman concrete was a much chunkier mixture. It utilized the natural volcanic materials that abound in Italy, specifically volcanic ash and tufa, a friable, spongy stone that otherwise is not well suited for building purposes.

Greek architecture often is described as post-and-lintel construction, referring to a series of horizontal and vertical elements (such as columns, walls, and entablatures) created by the use of marble or other types of stone. In contrast, the liquid nature of concrete, which is poured into a frame, makes it easy to create curvilinear shapes such as arches, domes, and vaults. Today, concrete usually is poured into a wooden frame, which is removed after the concrete hardens. In Roman architecture, concrete typically was poured into a brick or stone frame, with the courses of bricks or stones built up little by little as the concrete was poured. Unlike modern wood frames, the bricks or stones were embedded in the concrete and could not be removed after it hardened. Despite the fact that the bricks or stones frequently were laid in decorative patterns – such as the *opus reticulatum* (net) pattern found at Herodian Jericho – they were not seen after construction was completed, because the surfaces were covered with plaster (sometimes painted), marble veneer, or mosaics.

Only three examples of buildings using Roman concrete have been discovered in Israel (not including the breakwaters of Herod's harbor at Caesarea). The architects and craftsmen who worked on these structures, as well as the concrete itself, almost certainly came from Italy. Roman influence is evident in Herod's other monuments, which incorporate arches, domes, and vaults, but use cut stone instead of concrete. In fact, it is more costly and difficult to manufacture curvilinear shapes in stone than in concrete, because the stones must be cut precisely and carefully to fit together.

Sidebar: Ehud Netzer (1934–2010)

Ehud Netzer was an Israeli archaeologist who taught at the Hebrew University of Jerusalem. He was trained as an architect and worked in that capacity on Yigael Yadin's excavations at Masada in the mid-1960s. Netzer was known for his work on the architecture of Herod the Great, having conducted excavations at Masada, Herodian Jericho, Cypros, Caesarea Maritima, and Herodium. In addition to publishing the results of these excavations, Netzer produced several authoritative studies of Herod's architecture. In October 2010, Netzer died suddenly and tragically at Herodium, where he was conducting excavations, when he tumbled down the slope after a railing on which he was leaning collapsed. Only a couple of years before his death, Netzer had discovered Herod's tomb at Herodium after decades of searching.

Recommended Reading

Kenneth G. Holum et al., *King Herod's Dream, Caesarea on the Sea* (New York: W. W. Norton, 1988).

Ehud Netzer, *The Architecture of Herod the Great Builder* (Grand Rapids, MI: Baker Academic, 2006).

Ehud Netzer, *The Palaces of the Hasmoneans and Herod the Great* (Jerusalem: Yad Ben-Zvi, 2001).

Peter Richardson, *Herod, King of the Jews and Friend of the Romans* (Minneapolis: Fortress, 1999).

NINE

THE EARLY ROMAN (HERODIAN) PERIOD (40 B.C.E.–70 C.E.)

Jesus' Birth and Galilean Setting

Roman Palestine was an **agrarian**, preindustrial society. Nearly all the wealth and power were concentrated in the hands of a small percentage of the population. Most of this elite population – which included the high priestly families – lived in and around Jerusalem and Jericho. Roman Galilee was overwhelmingly rural, with a population consisting of farmers, fishermen, craftsmen, and artisans who had little disposable income and lived just above the subsistence level. The New Testament indicates that Jesus came from a lower-class Galilean family. As the New Testament scholar John Meier remarks, "He [Jesus] was in one sense poor, and a comfortable, middle-class urban American would find living conditions in ancient Nazareth appalling. But Jesus was probably no poorer or less respectable than almost anyone else in Nazareth, or for that matter in Galilee."

Lower-class Jews populate the Gospel accounts and seem to have been Jesus' target audience. Typically they were villagers who owned houses and had a few possessions but were not destitute like the leper who begs Jesus to heal him in Mark 1:40. The agrarian nature of rural Galilee is reflected in Jesus' parables and teachings, which mention picking and sowing grain, netting fish, herding sheep, and so on. References to patched clothing (Mark 2:21), hired laborers in vineyards (Matthew 20:1–16), and debtors sold into slavery (Matthew 18:23–35) must have resonated with Jesus' audience. This chapter reviews the archaeology of Bethlehem and Galilee – which the Gospels describe as the setting for Jesus' birth and ministry – in the time of Jesus.

BETHLEHEM

Of the four canonical Gospels, only Matthew and Luke begin with Jesus' birth. Matthew opens with a genealogy that traces Jesus' lineage from King David, and then describes astrologers' arrival in Bethlehem to pay homage to the infant Jesus. Luke's birth narrative opens with parallel announcements of the conception and birth of Jesus and John the Baptist. In Luke, Jesus' birth is announced to Mary in Nazareth by the angel Gabriel. Because (according to Luke) Joseph was descended from the house of David, he had to go to Bethlehem to be counted in the census of Quirinius, the governor of Syria.

Many scholars have discussed the differences between the birth narratives in Matthew and Luke. For our purposes, it is important to note that both accounts go to great lengths to connect Jesus with Bethlehem and establish his relationship to King David. The reason is simple: according to Jewish tradition, the messiah will be descended from David. Therefore, if Jesus really was the Jewish messiah, he had to be related to David, who, according to the Hebrew Bible, was born in Bethlehem. As the author of the Fourth Gospel puts it: "Surely the Messiah does not come from Galilee, does he? Has not the scripture said that the Messiah is descended from David and comes from Bethlehem, the village where David lived?" (John 7:41–42). It is interesting that Mark, which many scholars believe is the earliest of the canonical Gospels (ca. 60–70 C.E.), does not contain a birth narrative but instead opens with Jesus' baptism by John the Baptist. Collectively, the canonical Gospels provide very little information about Jesus before adulthood.

None of this is surprising when we consider that Jesus was a lower-class Galilean whose life and activities would have gone unnoticed before he began his ministry and attracted a following. The efforts of Matthew and Luke to establish Jesus' connection to Bethlehem and David are understandable in light of the messianic claims made about Jesus after his death. Jesus' Galilean origins would have posed a problem to followers who believed in his messianic status, as this precluded a connection to Judea, where Bethlehem is located. This accounts for the different birth narratives in Matthew and Luke, which present scenarios connecting Jesus to Bethlehem and David, bolstered by numerous biblical allusions and quotations.

Even if we accept the birth narratives in Matthew and Luke as fictitious attempts to establish Jesus' messianic status, is it possible that Jesus was of Judean descent? In my opinion, although we cannot rule out this possibility, it is unlikely. First, had Jesus' family been Judean, there would have been no need for Matthew and Luke to construct different narratives that go to great lengths to connect Jesus' birth and lineage with Bethlehem. We might also expect Mark to mention Jesus' Judean origins rather than omit this information altogether. Second, remember that the Hasmonean kings had "Judaized" the inhabitants of Galilee. Prior to this forced conversion, Galilee's population consisted of a mixture of native non-Jewish peoples, such as the Ituraeans, together with descendants of the biblical Israelites, many of whom had intermarried with Gentiles after 722 B.C.E. Although some Judean colonists settled in Galilee after the Hasmonean conquest, the Gospel writers do not associate Jesus' family with them and there is no other evidence supporting such a connection. In other words, Jesus likely was a native Galilean – that is, a person of mixed origins whose family had been Judaized by the Hasmoneans approximately a century before his time.

In the fourth century C.E., **Constantine** erected the **Church of the Nativity** over a grotto that had come to be venerated as Jesus' birthplace (see Chapter 16). However, few archaeological remains of the first century B.C.E. and first century C.E. survive in Bethlehem, which seems to have been a small village surrounded by scattered farms. The closest major site was Herod's fortified palace, administrative center, and final resting place at Herodium (see Chapter 8), located three miles southeast of Bethlehem. We shall therefore proceed to Galilee, which was the setting for most of Jesus' life and ministry.

SEPPHORIS

Roman Galilee was overwhelmingly agrarian and rural, with a landscape of rolling hills dotted by villages, hamlets, and farmsteads. Most locals supported themselves through agriculture (cultivating wheat, barley, olives, and grapes), fishing in the Sea of Galilee (which is actually a brackish water lake), and crafts production – including Jesus' family. There were only two large towns (sometimes inaccurately described as "cities") in Galilee in Jesus' time: Sepphoris and Tiberias. Tiberias was established on the western shore of the Sea of Galilee by Herod Antipas (ruled 4 B.C.E.–39 C.E.), the son of Herod the Great, as the capital of his tetrarchy, which consisted of Galilee and Peraea. Following his father's example, Antipas named the town in honor of his patron, the Roman emperor Tiberius.

In contrast, Sepphoris was founded long before Antipas' time. Under the Hasmoneans, it served as the administrative capital of Galilee. Josephus informs us that after Antipas inherited Sepphoris as part of his tetrarchy, he fortified it "to be the ornament of all Galilee" (*Ant.* 18:27). Antipas resided at Sepphoris until he founded Tiberias. During the First Jewish Revolt (66–70 C.E.), Sepphoris was pro-Roman and surrendered early to Vespasian. Although in the following centuries Sepphoris had a mixed population of Jews and Gentiles, it became a rabbinic center and was the seat of the **Sanhedrin** (the Jewish law court) under **Rabbi Judah ha-Nasi** (ca. 200 C.E.).

Sepphoris is not mentioned in the Gospel accounts, suggesting that Jesus' ministry focused especially on the rural, agrarian, and largely lower-class population of Roman Galilee. Nevertheless, scholars who study the historical Jesus have devoted much attention to Sepphoris because it is only four miles from Nazareth. Many scholars believe that Jesus must have visited Sepphoris, where he would have been exposed to Greco-Roman urban culture. Perhaps, some

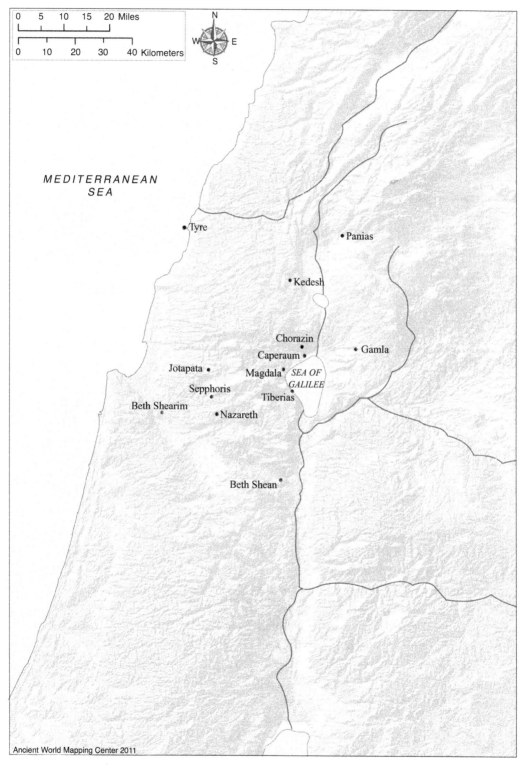

9.1 Map of Roman Galilee. Ancient World Mapping Center, University of North Carolina at Chapel Hill (www.unc.edu/awmc).

scholars speculate, Jesus and his family even worked on the construction of some of the town's monuments. Scholars who identify Greco-Roman influence (such as the philosophy of the Cynics) on Jesus' teachings argue that Sepphoris is the most likely setting for such interaction.

We cannot know for sure whether Jesus ever visited Sepphoris. Even if he did, there are serious questions about the degree to which the town was Romanized in Jesus' time (under Herod Antipas). The town of Sepphoris included an upper city (acropolis) and a lower city. Despite extensive excavations by American and Israeli expeditions, nearly all the remains discovered so far postdate the time of Jesus (late first century and second century C.E. on). Most of the remains from the time of Jesus (early first century) are located on the acropolis, consisting of a residential quarter of houses, many of which are equipped with small *miqva'ot*. Scholarly interest in Jesus has been attracted especially to a theater built into the steep northern side of the acropolis. It is a Greek-style theater that could accommodate up to 4,500 spectators, with seats laid out on the natural slope of the hill. The theater has been dated differently by different teams of archaeologists. In the past, some argued that Antipas built the theater, which would have indicated that Sepphoris was Romanized in Jesus' time. However, scholarly consensus now dates the establishment of the theater to the early second century C.E., which means that it did not exist in Jesus' time – even assuming he did visit Sepphoris.

In other words, even if Jesus visited Sepphoris, there is little evidence of Romanization in his time, with the exception of fragments of Roman style (but non-figured) wall paintings found in one of the early Roman houses on the acropolis. On the other hand, there is a great deal of evidence of Romanization after Jesus' time, including the theater, a grid of streets, and monumental public buildings decorated with wall paintings, stucco, and mosaics, most of which date to the fourth to sixth centuries C.E. Around 200 C.E. a mansion was erected on the acropolis, just above the theater. The excavators dubbed the mansion "the **Villa of Dionysos**" because it has a Roman-style dining room (triclinium) decorated with an exquisite mosaic floor depicting the drinking contest between **Dionysos** (the god of wine) and the hero Heracles/Hercules. Although some archaeologists argue that this villa may have belonged to a prominent Jewish family, perhaps even that of Judah ha-Nasi, I agree with those who believe it belonged to a Gentile family. Mosaic floors with Dionysiac scenes are common in rooms associated with the mystery cult of Dionysos, who was worshiped in connection with expectations of life after death (as grapevines and other vegetation die and are renewed annually). The villa's location suggests an association with the cult of Dionysos, who was also the god of theater performances (as theater performances blur the boundaries between reality and fantasy, which also happens after drinking too much wine).

9.2 Aerial view of Sepphoris' theater and acropolis. Courtesy of Zev Radovan/BibleLand Pictures.com.

GALILEAN VILLAGES

Capernaum

The village of **Capernaum** by the northwest shore of the Sea of Galilee was the center of Jesus' Galilean ministry. Matthew (9:1) calls Capernaum Jesus' "own town," for it was here that Jesus reportedly preached and performed many miracles, and where five of the twelve apostles – Peter, Andrew, James, John, and Matthew – were chosen. According to the Gospel accounts, Jesus stayed many times in the house of Peter and taught in the synagogue built by the Roman centurion. No remains of a synagogue from the time of Jesus have been found, but there is a monumental late antique synagogue building (see Chapter 14).

Capernaum was a modest village about 10 to 12 acres in size. The villagers supported themselves through fishing, agriculture, and some commerce and trade. During the reign of Herod Antipas, Capernaum was a border village with a customs house, and Jesus' disciple Matthew reportedly was a customs official here (see Matthew 9:9). The village had an orthogonal layout, with streets and alleys dividing residential areas into quarters. The houses were built sturdily of local **basalt**, a hard, black volcanic rock. Each house contained small

9.3 Mosaic floor in the Villa of Dionysos at Sepphoris. Courtesy of Zev Radovan/BibleLand Pictures.com.

9.4 House at Capernaum with a window wall.

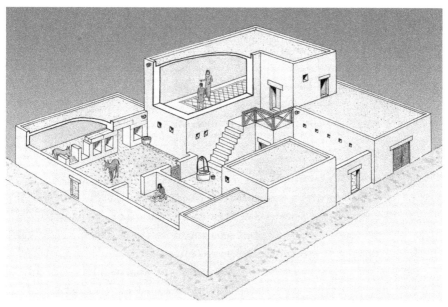

9.5 Reconstruction of a house at Capernaum. By Leen Ritmeyer ©.

dwelling rooms arranged around a courtyard. Sometimes the dwelling rooms were separated from the courtyard by a wall pierced by a continuous row of windows. This common device in ancient houses in northern Palestine, called a **window wall**, allowed air and light to enter the interiors of rooms. Family life centered on the courtyard, where there were ovens and stoves for cooking, a staircase providing access to the roof (or sometimes a second story), and an exit to the street. The flat roofs of the houses were used for sleeping (in warm weather), drying fruits, and other activities. Typical of the ancient Mediterranean and Near East, the village houses focused on the courtyard, with only one door opening to the street and few (if any) windows in the outer walls.

Chorazin

The village of **Chorazin** is contemporary with Capernaum and is located a short distance away, just 2.5 miles north of the Sea of Galilee. It is one of the three towns (together with Bethsaida and Capernaum) mentioned in the Gospels as having been upbraided by Jesus for failing to accept his teachings: "Alas for you, Chorazin! Alas for you, Bethsaida! For if the wonders that have been done in you had been done in Tyre and Sidon, they would have repented in sackcloth and ashes long ago! But I tell you, Tyre and Sidon will fare better on the day of judgment than you will! And you, Capernaum! Are you to be exalted to the skies? You will go down among the dead!" (Matthew 11:21–23) A monumental synagogue that is several centuries later than the time of Jesus is located in the middle of the village (see Chapter 14).

The houses in the village follow the topography – that is, they are laid out along the natural contours of the hill on which the village is built. The houses are similar to those at Capernaum – sturdily built of basalt, with small rooms grouped around a central courtyard, and arranged in residential quarters divided by streets and alleys. *Miqva'ot* attest to the observance of purity laws by at least some of the villagers, and olive presses indicate that the production of olive oil was an important part of the local economy.

Gamla (Gamala)

Gamla is a town in the southern Golan Heights that flourished in the first century B.C.E. and first century C.E. The name Gamla/Gamala comes from the Hebrew and Aramaic word for "camel" and refers to the steep rocky ridge on which the town was built, which resembles a camel's hump. Josephus provides a dramatic account of Gamla's fall to the Romans in 67 C.E. during the First Jewish Revolt, when intense fighting ended with a mass suicide of inhabitants who threw themselves over the cliffs rather than surrender to the Romans.

The town was protected on all sides by deep riverbeds (wadis) that flow into the Sea of Galilee, with the only approach from the east, along a natural spur or ridge. A fortification wall – almost 20 feet thick! – was erected only on the eastern side of the town. The wall and other buildings in the town are constructed of basalt. Square towers projected from the wall and flanked the main gate, and a circular tower was erected at the crest of the hill.

The layout of the town followed the natural contours of the steep hills, with the structures supported on artificial terraces and arranged in quarters separated by stepped streets. Just inside and abutting the fortification wall is a Jewish public building (synagogue), consisting of a single hall surrounded by stone benches, with columns to support the roof (see Chapter 14). A *miqveh* located in a room adjacent to the synagogue apparently was used by congregants. Other *miqva'ot*, some in private dwellings and others for public use, are scattered around the town.

Excavations inside the town have concentrated on several areas. The western area seems to have been a wealthy residential quarter consisting of houses built of ashlar masonry and evidence of Roman style (but non-figured) wall paintings. A large olive press was found nearby, installed in a room with a column supporting two stone arches that were roofed with basalt slabs. A *miqveh* adjacent to the press suggests that the inhabitants produced olive oil according to biblical law, which dictated that the first fruits must be donated to priests, who were required to consume these offerings in a state of ritual purity. The eastern area contained two blocks of densely packed rooms and dwellings

9.6 View of Gamla looking west. Photo by Jim Haberman.

separated by a narrow street. Midway between the western and eastern areas, a mansion was uncovered that was built on three different levels. The mansion had a beautifully cut stone façade, with columns from the second story level that had fallen to the ground.

Nazareth

Few archaeological remains from Jesus' time have survived in Nazareth, although farms have been discovered in its vicinity. In December 2009, Israeli archaeologists announced the discovery of the first dwelling in Nazareth dating to Jesus' time. The dwelling is described as a modest house belonging to a "simple Jewish family." Based on this evidence, the archaeologists conclude that Nazareth was "an out-of-the-way hamlet of around 50 houses on a patch of about four acres . . . populated by Jews of modest means."

CONCLUSION

The picture of Roman Galilee provided by archaeology is consistent with that presented in the New Testament and other ancient sources. Most of the population consisted of lower-class Jews who lived in simple but sturdy houses in farms and small villages, and supported themselves through farming, fishing, and craft production. A small number of more prosperous Jews lived in

9.7 The Sea of Galilee boat. Courtesy of Zev Radovan/BibleLandPictures.com.

the largest settlements – towns such as Sepphoris, Tiberias, and Gamla. They emulated the lifestyle of the Jerusalem elite by building spacious houses decorated with Roman-style wall paintings, and acquired small quantities of fine imported pottery and cooking wares. The "trickle-down" effect of Romanization on these local elites is evident in the much less impressive quality and quantity of interior decoration and imported goods compared to Jerusalem. At the same time, the discovery of *miqva'ot* and stone vessels in Galilean towns and villages attests to the observance of Jewish purity laws among much of the local population.

Sidebar: The Sea of Galilee Boat (the "Jesus boat")

The Sea of Galilee boat is a modest fishing boat dating to the Herodian period that came to light in 1986, when a drought caused the shoreline of the Sea of Galilee to recede. Two members of a local kibbutz (communal farm) noticed ancient pieces of wood sticking out of the mud and alerted archaeologists. The lack of oxygen in the mud preserved the wood for 2,000 years – the same type of **anaerobic** conditions that preserved the so-called Bog People in northern Europe. The excavation of the boat involved treating the wood with special chemicals to prevent it from disintegrating upon exposure to air. The boat is now on permanent display at Kibbutz Ginnosar on the northwest shore of the Sea of Galilee.

Measuring 27 feet long and 7.5 feet wide, the boat is a shallow vessel with a flat bottom, a design that facilitated fishing close to the shoreline. Radiocarbon dating of the wood and pottery found inside the boat indicate that it was in use some time between 50 B.C.E. and 50 C.E. The boat was manufactured from scraps of wood of different types, and had been repaired many times. When it could no longer be repaired, the useful parts were removed and the hull sank to the bottom of the lake.

Despite the popular moniker, there is no evidence that this boat has any direct connection to Jesus and his disciples. Nonetheless, it provides valuable information about fishing boats used on the Sea of Galilee in Jesus' time.

Recommended Reading

Mark A. Chancey, *Greco-Roman Culture and the Galilee of Jesus* (New York: Cambridge, 2005).

Sean Freyne, *Jesus, A Jewish Galilean: A New Reading of the Jesus-Story* (New York: T & T Clark, 2004).

John P. Meier, *A Marginal Jew: Rethinking the Historical Jesus, Vols. 1–3* (New York: Doubleday, 1991).

Rebecca Martin Nagy et al., *Sepphoris in Galilee, Crosscurrents of Culture* (Raleigh: North Carolina Museum of Art, 1996).

Jonathan L. Reed, *Archaeology and the Galilean Jesus: A Re-examination of the Evidence* (Harrisburg, PA: Trinity Press International, 2000).

Shelley Wachsmann, *The Sea of Galilee Boat* (College Station: Texas A & M University, 2000).

TEN

THE EARLY ROMAN (HERODIAN) PERIOD (40 B.C.E.–70 C.E.)

MASADA

Masada is the most famous of Herod's fortified desert palaces, both because of its spectacular natural setting and because it was the site of a reported mass suicide of Jewish insurgents seventy-five years after Herod's death. We begin this chapter by reviewing the remains of Herod's palaces atop Masada, and end with a discussion of the mass suicide story.

HEROD'S PALACES AT MASADA

Masada is a mesa – a flat-topped mountain with steep cliffs on all sides – overlooking the southwest shore of the Dead Sea (see Figure 6.1). The name *Masada* derives from the Hebrew word for "fort" or "fortress," reflecting the mountain's natural suitability for that purpose, which was exploited by Herod. Early in his reign, Herod sought to protect the southern and eastern borders of his kingdom from Cleopatra's ambitions by constructing a series of fortresses. Like Masada, some of these were built over fortified palaces that had been established by the Hasmonean kings, such as Alexandrium-Sartaba (in the Jordan Valley north of Jericho) and Hyrcania (west of Qumran). Although Josephus tells us that Masada was first fortified by a Hasmonean king named Jonathan (referring either to Judah Maccabee's brother or to Alexander Jannaeus, whose Hebrew name was Jonathan), archaeologists have not succeeded in identifying any buildings at Masada from the Hasmonean period. Apparently Herod's construction projects at Masada obliterated earlier remains. When Herod fled Judea in 40 B.C.E. in the wake of the Parthian invasion, he deposited his family for safekeeping in the Hasmonean fortress at Masada before proceeding south to the Nabataean kingdom.

10.1 Aerial view of Masada from the northwest. Courtesy of Zev Radovan/BibleLandPictures
.com.

Masada's steep cliffs make the 1300-foot climb to the top difficult, even treacherous. There have always been two main routes of access: the narrow, winding Snake Path on the east slope (seen from above by visitors riding in the cable car today), and a route on the west side that is buried under the Roman siege ramp (discussed later). Herod fortified the top of the mountain with a casemate wall and towers encircling the edge of the cliff. The casemate wall consisted of two parallel walls divided into a row of rooms, which were used for garrisoning soldiers and storing supplies and military equipment. Gates furnished with guardrooms provided access through the wall at the top of the Snake Path and the western route.

Herod's main buildings inside the fortifications consisted of two palace complexes, one on the north and one on the west. Both complexes included palace rooms (living rooms, dining rooms, etc.), administrative offices, servants' quarters, workshops, bath houses, and storage rooms. Herod apparently intended the two palaces to serve different functions: the western palace included Herod's throne room and was used for official ceremonies, whereas the northern palace contained Herod's private living quarters. All of Herod's buildings at Masada were constructed of large, well-cut blocks of stone that were quarried on top of the mountain.

10.2 View of the northern palace complex looking south. Courtesy of Todd Bolen/BiblePlaces
.com.

The Northern Palace Complex: The Palace

The rooms of the northern palace are situated spectacularly on three terraces
supported by retaining walls that spill over the northern edge of the cliff.
A large, white-plastered stone wall that broadened at the base separated the
northern palace from the rest of the mountain. The only access to the rooms of
the northern palace was through a guardroom at the eastern end of the wall,
effectively creating a fortress within a fortress. Graffiti depicting a ship and
garden enclosure on the wall above a bench may have been incised into the
plaster by a bored guard. The guard room opened onto the uppermost terrace of
the northern palace, which contained a modest suite of bedrooms with simple
black-and-white mosaics of geometric designs resembling a honeycomb pattern.
A semicircular porch in front of the bedrooms provides a breathtaking view of
the rugged desert landscape and the Dead Sea, including the oasis at **Ein Gedi**,
which is visible as a dark patch in the haze at the foot of the mountains some 11
miles to the north. The area between the base of Masada and the Dead Sea shore
is filled with badlands created by the erosion of soft marl (chalk) deposits.

The three terraces of the northern palace originally were connected by
enclosed staircases, with steps that wound around a square stone pillar. Today,
visitors to Masada climb down a modern wooden staircase that runs along the
side of the mountain. The middle terrace of the northern palace was constructed
of two concentric walls, the inner one partly hewn out of the bedrock of the
cliff and partly built of stone, and the outer one built of stone. The walls served

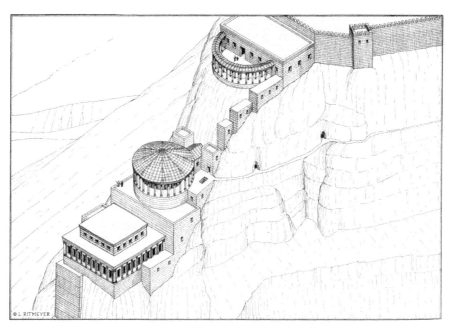

10.3 Reconstruction of the northern palace. By Leen Ritmeyer ©.

to extend the terrace beyond the edge of the cliff and would have been covered by a floor. Columns along the edge of the terrace supported a roof, creating a covered patio with a spectacular panoramic view. A row of vertical niches in the back wall of the terrace (the bedrock side) might have been a library, if the small holes inside the niches held wooden shelves for scrolls.

The lowest terrace of the northern palace was used as a reception hall (triclinium). The terrace is rectangular in plan and had an outer peristyle surrounding an inner rectangle created by a low wall with columns at intervals, mirroring the outer peristyle. From the center of the inner rectangle, the desert landscape would have been visible by looking over the low wall, with the view framed by columns. Much of the original interior decoration of the reception hall is preserved, thanks to having been buried for more than 2,000 years. The columns consisted of stone drums covered with molded stucco to give the appearance of fluted marble shafts, and they were topped with stuccoed and painted Corinthian capitals. The low walls of the inner rectangle and the lower part of the cliff wall of the outer rectangle were plastered and decorated with paintings in the Second Pompeian Style. Typical of this style, the paintings depict colorful panels imitating colored stone and marble plaques. An illusion of depth was created on the cliff face by constructing engaged half-columns in the middle of each panel, which seem to cut off and block the view of the panels behind. Interestingly, Josephus' description of the northern palace inaccurately refers to **monolithic** stone columns and colored stone panels. We do not know whether Josephus ever visited Masada or whether he merely relied on the descriptions of others.

A small bath house was located below the east side of the lowest terrace. Although much of it has eroded and collapsed over the edge of the cliff, a stepped and plastered pool is still visible, with a poorly preserved mosaic on the floor in front of it. It was here that Yadin made a stunning discovery, which he interpreted in light of Josephus' account of the mass suicide at Masada:

> When, however, we came to clear the formidable pile of debris which covered the chambers of the small bath-house, we were arrested by a find which it is difficult to consider in archaeological terms, for such an experience is not normal in archaeological excavations. Even the veterans and the more cynical among us stood frozen, gazing in awe at what had been uncovered; for as we gazed, we relived the final and most tragic moments of the drama of Masada. Upon the steps leading to the cold-water and on the ground nearby were the remains of three skeletons. One was that of a man of about twenty – perhaps one of the commanders of Masada. Next to it we found hundreds of silvered scales of armour, scores of arrows, fragments of a prayer shawl (*talith*), and also an ostracon (an inscribed potsherd) with Hebrew letters. Not far off, also on the steps, was the skeleton of a young woman, with her scalp preserved intact because of the extreme dryness of the atmosphere. Her dark hair, beautifully plaited, looked as if it had just been freshly coiffeured. Next to it the plaster was stained with what looked like blood. By her side were delicately fashioned lady's sandals, styled in the traditional pattern of the period. The third skeleton was that of a child. There could be no doubt that what our eyes beheld were the remains of some of the defenders of Masada. In describing the last moments, Josephus writes:

> "And he who was the last of all, took a view of all the other bodies lest perchance some or other among so many that were slain, should want his assistance to be quite dispatched; and when he perceived that they were all slain, he set fire to the palace, and with the force of his hand ran his sword entirely through himself, and fell down dead near to his own relations."

> Could it be that we had discovered the bones of that very fighter and of his kith? This, of course, we can never know for certain.

The Northern Palace Complex: The Service Quarters

The northern palace was serviced by buildings located just outside (south) of the large, white-plastered stone wall, one of which is a large, Roman-style bath house. Bath houses were a characteristic feature of Roman life, not just providing facilities for bathing but also serving as cultural centers, with entertainment,

10.4 Lowest terrace of the northern palace with wall-paintings and stuccoed columns. Courtesy of Zev Radovan/BibleLandPictures.com.

dining, and exercise facilities. Roman cities typically had one or more public bath houses, and the villas and mansions of the wealthy were equipped with private bath houses, analogous to having a swimming pool or exercise room in one's home today.

The large bath house at Masada was entered through a peristyle courtyard decorated with a mosaic floor with black-and-white geometric designs, and Second Pompeian Style paintings on the walls. The first room in the bath house was the *apodyterium* or dressing room, where guests undressed before proceeding to the baths. The walls of the *apodyterium* were decorated with Second Pompeian Style wall paintings, and the floor was paved with black and white triangular tiles (*opus sectile*). Although most of the tiles were later robbed out, their impressions are still visible in the plaster bedding underneath. Seventy years after Herod's death, the Jewish rebels who occupied Masada (discussed later) built a square plastered installation (perhaps for storage?) in one corner of the *apodyterium*, covering the tile floor and wall paintings. Against the opposite wall they added a bench made of column drums laid side by side and covered with plaster.

An arched doorway led from the *apodyterium* to the *tepidarium*, a moderately heated room. At one end of the *tepidarium* is a small, stepped and plastered pool that was a cold-water plunge bath (*frigidarium*). A doorway in the opposite wall provided access to the largest room in the bath house: the *caldarium* or hot (steam) room. Modern visitors to Masada are immediately struck by the small pillars covering the floor of the room, which are made of round (cut) stones that were plastered. Originally these small pillars, which are called **suspensura**, were not visible. Instead they supported another floor, which was covered with black and white triangular tiles as in the *apodyterium* (as indicated by remains of plaster with impressions of robbed-out tiles on top of the *suspensura*). Hot air from a furnace just outside the *caldarium* would have circulated among the small pillars and heated the tiled floor. An arched opening leading to the furnace can still be seen in the wall of the *caldarium*, below the level of the tiled floor. The walls were also heated by rectangular terra-cotta pipes that carried hot air from under the tile floor. The pipes were covered by plaster and painted, and, like the *suspensura*, would not have been visible. Niches at either end of the room contained bathtubs with water. Steam was created by sprinkling water from the tubs onto the floor and walls. The *caldarium* was roofed with a stone vault, whereas the other rooms in the bath house had flat ceilings and roofs. Here we see Herod's adoption of Roman architectural forms using local building materials (stone instead of concrete). The *caldarium* at Masada also represents an early example of this kind of heating system (called a **hypocaust**), which became a hallmark of the Roman world.

Surrounding the large bath house to the east and south are long, narrow storerooms, which contained supplies for the northern palace. Ancient storerooms typically display this kind of layout, as only short wooden beams were needed for roofing a narrow room, whereas the elongated shape maximized the room's size. Yadin found dozens of ceramic storage jars buried in the collapse of the storerooms. These originally contained food supplies such as wine, oil, grain, and fruit, as indicated by inscriptions on the jars and analyses of their contents. In some cases, the remains of seeds, nuts, and fruits were still preserved because of the arid desert climate. Some inscriptions date to the time of the First Jewish Revolt against the Romans and mention tithes, indicating that the Jewish rebels at Masada observed biblical laws requiring the tithing of produce to priests.

The Synagogue

One of the rooms in the casemate wall was converted to a synagogue by the rebels who occupied Masada at the time of the First Jewish Revolt against the Romans. In Herod's time, this room seems to have been used as a reception hall. It was larger than the other casemate rooms, with a porch in front and a main hall with five columns to support the roof. The Jewish rebels who occupied Masada seventy years after Herod's death removed the porch wall to enlarge the hall, and added benches to accommodate a congregation (see Chapter 14).

Proceeding south from the synagogue, one reaches the top of the Roman siege ramp (discussed later), and just to the east of it, the entrance to Herod's western palace complex.

10.5 *Caldarium* in the large bath house. Courtesy of Zev Radovan/BibleLandPictures.com.

The Western Palace Complex

The western palace complex was entered through a guardroom, which, like the other guardrooms at Masada, had benches along the walls and was decorated with stucco molded in imitation of marble panels. From the guardroom, an elongated hall bisected the administrative offices, servants' quarters/workshops, and storerooms (long, narrow rooms as in the northern palace complex). The hall provided access to the royal wing of the western palace, which consisted of a large courtyard surrounded by rooms that were decorated with Second Pompeian Style wall paintings. The throne room was located on the far side of the courtyard. Holes sunk into the floor at one end of this room show where the legs of the throne had been placed.

A waiting room or reception hall adjacent to the throne room was decorated with the most elaborate mosaic floor found at Masada. The mosaic is made of colored **tesserae** (cut stone cubes), and displays a **rosette** surrounded by bands decorated with geometric and floral motifs. The floral motifs include olives, pomegranates, and grapes, which are among the **seven species** of agricultural produce that symbolized the fertility of the Land of Israel, according to biblical tradition. The seven species are depicted frequently in Jewish art of the late Second Temple period, when many Jews refrained from using the figured images that are so common in Roman art, in strict observance of the Second Commandment, which prohibits the making of images for worship. It is interesting that despite Masada's remote location, Herod chose typically "Jewish" motifs to decorate his palaces and refrained from using figured images. This

10.6 Mosaic floor in the western palace. Courtesy of Zev Radovan/BibleLandPictures.com.

likely reflects Herod's concern not to offend Jewish visitors to Masada rather than his own religious observance or leanings, as outside of Judea he dedicated pagan temples (at Caesarea and Samaria, for example).

Across the courtyard from the throne room was a two-story suite of rooms that included another bath house. Instead of a hypocaust, this bath house had an earlier type of heating system, consisting of a bathtub supplied with heated water. The rooms of the bath house were paved with simple colored mosaics. One mosaic depicts a rosette and is located by the entrance to a deep but narrow stepped pool that apparently was a *miqveh*. During the First Jewish Revolt, the rebels who occupied Masada installed a small, square bin (for storage or rubbish?) in the corner of this room, which cut through the mosaic with the rosette.

The Southern Part of Masada

Just south of the western palace complex is a large, wide, deep stepped and plastered pool that dates to the time of Herod. It is enclosed by stone walls containing rows of square niches. Although this pool could be a *miqveh*, it is more likely a swimming pool, analogous to the larger swimming pools in Herod's

10.7 Southern cistern. Courtesy of Todd Bolen/BiblePlaces.com. Credit: Matt Floreen/ www.mattfloreen.com.

palaces at Herodium and Jericho. In this case the niches in the surrounding walls would have been a cabana – a place for bathers to leave their clothes while swimming. Another large swimming pool is located close to the southern tip of the mountain.

The southern half of Masada is less built-up than the northern part. To the south of the western palace complex and swimming pool are structures with low walls made of small stones that are dwellings erected by the rebels at the time of the First Jewish Revolt. Yadin also found evidence – including hearths, stoves, and other domestic installations – that rebel families lived in the casemate rooms. In Herod's time, the southern half of Masada was cultivated with gardens and food crops, as Josephus describes. Today the top of Masada is barren and brown, with rocky outcrops of rock and the bare stone walls, but two thousand years ago the open spaces were green and the outsides of the buildings were plastered and whitewashed.

A peculiar structure located to the south and east of the swimming pool consists of a circular stone wall with no openings. Inside, the walls contain rows of small square niches. This structure is a columbarium (dovecote), similar to those at Marisa (see Chapter 4). Columbaria are common at Hellenistic and early Roman sites in southern Palestine (Idumaea and Judea). A casemate room just north of the Roman siege ramp contains another columbarium.

Close to the southern tip of Masada is a large underground cistern. Accessed by means of a narrow, steeply descending staircase, it is hewn entirely out of the natural hard limestone. The inside of the cistern is an enormous cavern with the staircase on one side. The staircase and the walls and floor of the cistern are covered with thick coats of plaster that prevented seepage into the cracks of the hard stone. Horizontal lines visible on the walls of the cistern reflect fluctuations in the water level over time. The steps made it possible to descend and draw water as the level dropped, and facilitated access to clean out silt from time to time. The bottom of the cistern is still covered with a thick layer of silt.

There are approximately eighteen large cisterns at Masada (and numerous smaller pools for storing water), but this is the only one on top of the mountain. The largest group of cisterns is located on the northwest side of the mountain (below the northern palace complex), where they are arranged in two rows, one above the other, which were filled by an aqueduct that brought flash flood waters from the riverbeds on the cliffs opposite. The aqueduct was at the same level as the rows of cisterns, but was buried and put out of use when the Romans constructed the ramp. In other words, the water system at Masada operated in a manner similar to the water system at Qumran, but on a much larger scale. There are also cisterns on the eastern and southeastern side of the mountain (one is by the top of the Snake Path). The cisterns on the eastern and southeastern sides of the mountain, and the one on top, were too high in elevation to be filled by aqueduct. Plastered channels led rainwater into these cisterns, but there is so little rainfall in this region that most of the water was brought manually, carried by people and pack animals from other cisterns and pools.

According to Yadin, each of the large cisterns at Masada had a capacity of up to 140,000 cubic feet, with a total capacity of almost 1,400,000 cubic feet of water. It has been estimated that each cistern held enough drinking water to sustain 1,000 people for one year! This bounty of water on the top of a remote desert mountain made it possible for Herod to equip his palaces with bath houses, swimming pools, and lush gardens.

During the First Jewish Revolt, the rebels at Masada installed a *miqveh* in a casemate room on the southeast side of the mountain. A similar *miqveh* was installed by the rebels in the administrative building of the northern palace complex. These were among the earliest *miqva'ot* to be recognized as such. At the time of Yadin's excavations, little was known about ancient *miqva'ot*. In his popular book, Yadin describes bringing to Masada two rabbis, who examined the pools and certified that they complied with the requirements for *miqva'ot* according to Jewish law. Today, dozens of ancient *miqva'ot* are known from sites around Palestine. More recently, Netzer identified other stepped pools at Masada as *miqva'ot*, including the narrow stepped pool in the bath house of the western palace, and perhaps the swimming pool just south of the western palace complex.

The two *miqva'ot* identified by Yadin have an unusual feature: an additional pool for storing rain water (identified by some scholars as an *'otsar*, or "treasury") adjacent to the larger, stepped immersion pool. According to biblical law, water used for immersion must be living (undrawn), which means that the pool cannot be filled mechanically. Following this law atop Masada would have been difficult, as there is little rain and no springs or riverbeds from which water could be channeled (simply by gravity) to fill the pools. The *'otsar* may have been designed to facilitate the observance of biblical law by storing rain water or other undrawn water. The immersion pool was filled mechanically to a certain level (that is, water was brought by bucket or skins from other pools and cisterns on the mountain). Unplugging a hole in the wall separating the *'otsar* from the immersion pool would have allowed a small amount of undrawn water from the *'otsar* to flow into the immersion pool, thereby purifying the drawn water. The innovation of the *'otsar* was accepted by the rabbis (and perhaps the Pharisees before them), but was rejected by some groups such as the Qumran sect. Although large numbers of ancient *miqva'ot* are now known, only a few are equipped with an *'otsar*. Because they are so rare, some scholars now question the identification of these additional pools as *'otsarot*, and suggest they might have served other purposes (for example, for immersion instead of water storage).

After Herod's Death: The Roman Siege of Masada

After Herod's death, Masada was occupied by a small garrison of soldiers. When the First Revolt erupted in 66 C.E., Jewish rebels took over the mountain and remained there for the duration of the revolt. According to Josephus, these rebels were members of a ruthless band of assassins called the Sicarii (see Chapter 7; Yadin inaccurately referred to the rebels at Masada as Zealots, a different Jewish group). The Sicarii probably were joined by other Jews during the revolt, including (probably) some members of the Qumran community, who fled after the settlement was destroyed by the Romans in 68 C.E.

In 70 C.E., the First Revolt ended with the destruction of Jerusalem and the second temple. However, three former Herodian fortified desert palaces were still occupied by Jewish rebels: Herodium, **Machaerus** (in Peraea, on the eastern side of the Dead Sea), and Masada (see Figure 6.1). Vespasian and Titus sent troops to take these last holdouts, beginning with Herodium, which capitulated quickly. Machaerus was taken after a siege. Finally, in the winter–spring of 72–73 or 73–74 (there is a debate about the exact year), the Romans arrived at the foot of Masada – the last Jewish stronghold. According to Josephus, there were now 967 Jews holding out atop Masada. These were not 967 soldiers, but families of men, women, and children. The Romans arrived at the foot of Masada with approximately 8,000 soldiers, a disproportionate force for the task at hand. Apparently, it was important to the Romans to take Masada, both to set an example for other subject peoples (do not even think about rebelling!), and because they wanted to stamp out every last spark of Jewish resistance, to ensure that the rebels would not restart the revolt.

When the Romans arrived at the foot of Masada, they set up a siege. Masada's siege works are among the best-preserved examples in the Roman world, thanks to the fact that they are constructed of stone (whereas in Europe siege walls and camps usually were made of perishable materials such as wood and sod), and because of the remote desert location, which was never built over or destroyed. Masada therefore provides an opportunity to examine how the Roman army operated during a siege. Incidentally, because this episode is so famous, many modern visitors have the mistaken impression that the siege of Masada lasted for three years. In fact, the siege took place during the course of one winter season (72–73 or 73–74), and lasted no more than six months – and possibly as little as two months.

There are three main elements in the Roman siege works at Masada: a **circumvallation wall**, camps, and a ramp. A circumvallation wall is a standard component of Roman siege works. Its purpose was to cut off the besieged by making both escape and assistance impossible. The circumvallation wall at Masada was made of stone and was about 10 to 12 feet high, with watchtowers for guards along the more level tracts of ground to the east of Masada. It completely encircles the base of the mountain, even climbing the steep cliffs, for a distance of some 4,000 yards! The Romans also established eight camps to house their troops (labeled A–H by archaeologists, beginning with A on the east and running counterclockwise from there). The camps are distributed around the base of the mountain, guarding potential routes of escape.

By the first century C.E., the Roman army was a professional force consisting of career soldiers who enlisted for a lifetime of service. The soldiers were trained to operate in an efficient and highly standardized manner. This standardization is reflected in the camps at Masada, which all have a square plan with the sides oriented toward the four cardinal points. Gates in the center of each side provided access to two main roads that bisected the camps from north to south and east to west. The most important units, including the headquarters, officer's mess, and commander's living quarters, were placed around the intersection of the two roads in the center of the camp. The rest of the units, including the living quarters of the enlisted soldiers, were located farther from the center.

Although all the camps at Masada have a similar plan, they vary in size. Two of the camps – B and F – are much larger than the others. The variations in size reflect the composition of the troops that participated in the siege. The Roman army included different kinds of soldiers – specifically, legionaries and auxiliaries. The legionaries served mainly as heavy infantry. Only Roman citizens could enlist as legionaries in the first century C.E. The auxiliaries were

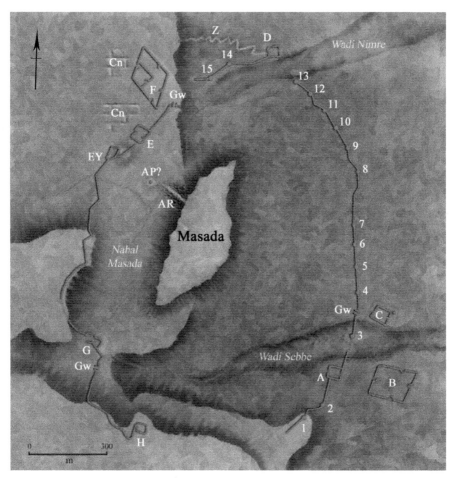

10.8 Plan of the Roman siege works at Masada. Courtesy of Gwyn Davies.

the more mobile troops that protected the flanks of the heavy infantry in battle, including light infantry, cavalry, and archers. Auxiliaries were drafted from among non-Roman citizens, with Roman citizenship being awarded at the end of a lifetime of service. Legionaries served in units called legions, each consisting of approximately 5,000 men. One legion – the Tenth Legion – participated in the siege of Masada. This legion was involved in putting down the Jewish revolt before 70, including participating in the sieges of Gamla and Jerusalem. The large camps – B and F – apparently housed the legionary soldiers at Masada, including the commander, whose name was **Flavius Silva**. The smaller camps housed auxiliary troops. Camp B was situated on the eastern side of the mountain in order to supervise the distribution of supplies, which were brought by boat on the Dead Sea from Ein Gedi, Jericho, Nabataea, and other sites around Palestine. Camp F was located on the northwest side of the mountain, positioned so Flavius Silva could oversee the construction of the ramp and the attack on the mountain.

10.9   View of Camp F looking west.

Although Yadin was an expert on ancient warfare and served as chief of staff of the Israel Defense Forces (see the Sidebar), his excavations at Masada focused on the top of the mountain and largely ignored the Roman siege works. In the summer of 1995, I was invited to codirect the first and only ever excavations in the Roman siege works at Masada, together with three Israeli colleagues (Professor Gideon Foerster, Dr. Haim Goldfus, and Mr. Benny Arubas). For six weeks in June and July, we conducted excavations with student volunteers from the United States. We decided to focus our efforts on the ramp (discussed later) and Camp F, which is the better-preserved of the two legionary camps.

Camp F has a typical square plan, although when drawn it appears trapezoidal because it was laid out on ground that slopes steeply down toward the edge of the cliff to the east. The square enclosure (F2) in the southwest corner of Camp F is an unusual feature, representing an encampment of soldiers who remained for a short period after the end of the siege, to ensure that the area was fully subdued. All the stone walls at Masada are built of dry field stones with no mortar, indicating that the Romans invested a minimal effort in construction. Originally the stone enclosure walls of Camp F were 10 to 12 feet high. The area inside the camp is filled with low stone walls (originally 3–4 feet high), which were the bases for leather tents. Each tent unit consisted of one or more "rooms," many of which were lined by low stone benches that were used for dining as well as sitting and sleeping. The rooms were filled with pieces of broken pottery, belonging mostly to storage jars that originally contained food and water.

10.10 The *praetorium* and tribunal in Camp F.

Our excavations in Camp F focused on the center, where the most important units were concentrated. To the east of the later wall of F2, we excavated the commander's unit (*praetorium*), so identified on the basis of its location within the camp. This identification was confirmed by the discovery of luxury items in this unit, including imported glass from Italy and eggshell-thin, painted Nabataean bowls (see Figure 5.7). My personal favorite is an *amphoriskos* (table amphora) with painted ivy-leaf decoration, from which I like to imagine Flavius Silva's wine was poured. Clearly Flavius Silva dined well in the field! Adjacent to the *praetorium* is the tribunal – a square stone podium from which Flavius Silva could review or address his troops. In front of the tribunal is an open space where the soldiers could muster.

Near the *praetorium* and tribunal is a large triclinium (dining room), which served as the officers' mess. Shaped like the Greek letter *pi* (or Hebrew letter *het*) and with the open end facing toward Masada, only the foundations survive. The rest of the stones were stripped for reuse in the later enclosure wall of Camp F2, which overlies the rear wall of the triclinium. Originally, dining couches lined the three walls of the triclinium, arranged so the officers had a view of Masada while they reclined and enjoyed their meals.

Just inside the enclosure wall of Camp F2, and partly covered by it, is the camp headquarters (**principia**). This was the only unit we excavated that had white plaster-covered walls and floors. However, there were few finds, as the rooms seem to have been emptied of their contents before the wall of Camp F2 was constructed.

10.11 Painted *amphoriskos* from the *praetorium* in Camp F. Photo by Jim Haberman.

10.12 *Contubernium* in Camp F, with a book on the bench for scale.

10.13 Arrowhead from Yadin's excavations at Masada. Photo by G. Laron, Hebrew University of Jerusalem.

Inside Camp F2, we excavated a row of *contubernia*, which are tent units that housed the enlisted soldiers. To operate and maneuver in the field, legions were subdivided into smaller units, the smallest of which was a group of eight men called a **contubernium**. During campaigns, these eight soldiers marched together and shared a tent. The *contubernia* that we excavated were modest units, each consisting of a single room encircled by a stone and dirt bench used for dining and sleeping, and a small porch or courtyard in front. The tent could accommodate only about half the members of the *contubernium* at once, as at any given time the others would have been on active duty (similar to sleeping in shifts on modern submarines). In the corner of each front porch we found a hearth with signs of burning, where the men prepared their meals using mess kits.

We found natural river pebbles, about the size of large eggs, piled conspicuously in and around the tent units. These had been gathered for use as slingshot stones and were left behind after the siege ended. The rest of the military equipment was taken by the soldiers when they departed Masada. However, in his excavations atop Masada, Yadin found a great deal of military equipment associated with the fighting during the siege. Most of the finds consist of iron arrowheads – hundreds of them – representing the characteristic Roman

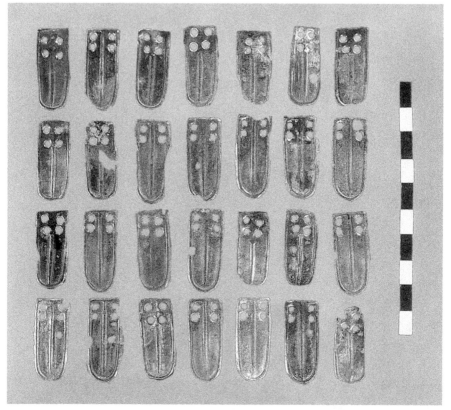

10.14 Scales of armor from Yadin's excavations at Masada. Photo by G. Laron, Hebrew University of Jerusalem.

type with three barbed wingtips (to stick into the flesh) and a long tang that originally was set into a wooden shaft. Arrows provided cover fire while the ramp was erected and the siege machinery was winched into place. Hundreds of small bronze scales were also found in Yadin's excavations, which belonged to scale armor. Each has four tiny holes punched through the top, so they could be sewn in an overlapping manner onto a leather or cloth backing. During the first century C.E., scale armor typically was worn by auxiliary soldiers, whereas legionaries wore segmented armor, which consisted of overlapping metal strips. The other finds from Yadin's excavations included an almost complete iron sword (a rare find), with a strip of bronze still adhering to the blade, which indicates that it had been in a leather scabbard. The leather disintegrated, but the metal reinforcement along the sides was still stuck to the blade. Yadin also discovered a scabbard chape, which is the bronze reinforcement for the tip of a leather scabbard (to prevent the tip of a sword from piercing the leather). The chape found by Yadin was decorated with delicate cutout designs that would have created a contrast between the bronze and the dark leather backing of the

10.15 Scabbard chape from Yadin's excavations at Masada. Photo by G. Laron, Hebrew
University of Jerusalem.

scabbard. This ornate scabbard chape has parallels in Italy and must have been
brought to Masada by an officer.

The siege was in place once the mountain was sealed off and escape was
impossible. At this point, the Romans might have waited, starving the besieged
into surrender. However, this was not an option, because the Jewish rebels atop
Masada had large stores of food and water. In contrast, the Roman army had
to provide food, water, firewood, and animal fodder on a daily basis at this
remote desert location for some 8,000 soldiers plus slaves, pack animals, and
camp followers. Once the siege works were in place they had to mount an attack,
which meant scaling the mountain and breaching Herod's fortification wall at
the top. Trying to carry out such an attack by climbing the existing paths (the
Snake Path and the western route) was not feasible, because the steepness and
narrowness of these paths would have required a difficult, single-file climb for
the soldiers. In addition to their own military equipment, the soldiers needed
to carry siege machinery to break through the fortification wall.

Flavius Silva ordered his men to construct a ramp on the western side, filling
the space between the top of the mountain and a low white hill nearby. The
ramp created a gentle slope that was easy to climb and could accommodate a
number of soldiers in formation rather than in single file, and up which siege
machinery could be carried. Contrary to a popular misconception, the ramp was

constructed by soldiers, not Jewish slaves, as this is what the Roman army was trained to do. It would have been inefficient and counterproductive to employ Jewish slaves in the construction of the ramp, although Josephus reports that they carried supplies during the siege. At the top of the ramp (which fell short of the top of the mountain and has dropped more in the past 2,000 years as a result of earthquake activity), the Romans built a large stone platform. On top of this platform they placed a battering ram sheathed in iron. While the ramp was being completed and the battering ram erected, cover fire was provided by archers shooting volleys of arrows and **ballistas** flinging large round stones (like cannon shot). Large numbers of ballista stones and arrowheads found in Yadin's excavations ringing the area around the top of the ramp attest to the fierce battle that took place 2,000 years ago.

Josephus reports that after the Romans breached the wall, the Jewish rebels repaired it with a wooden wall filled with dirt, which absorbed the blows of the battering ram. However, the Romans set this wall on fire and prepared to enter the mountain. At this point, according to Josephus, the rebel leader, whose name was **Eleazar Ben-Yair**, convened the men together, perhaps in the synagogue. In a speech reported by Josephus, Eleazar Ben-Yair convinced the men to commit suicide, to rob the Romans of their hard-won victory and prevent their wives and children from becoming enslaved. Accordingly, the families gathered together, and the men killed their wives and children. After drawing lots, ten of the men then killed the others. The ten remaining men drew lots again, and one of them killed the other nine and then committed suicide. Notice, by the way, that technically there is thus only one suicide at Masada — that is, only one person who died by his own hand. It was the remains of this last rebel and his family who Yadin thought he found on the lowest terrace of the northern palace. By the time the Romans entered the mountain, everyone was dead.

But if everyone committed suicide, how do we know about Eleazar Ben-Yair's speech and the drawing of the lots? According to Josephus, not everyone committed suicide. A couple of old women overheard the suicide plans, and hid with some children in a cave on the side of the mountain. They surrendered and told the Romans the story, which was then reported, directly or indirectly, to Josephus.

JOSEPHUS

Josephus has been an important source of information for many of the sites we have examined, including Masada. Josephus was an aristocratic Jew from a priestly family in Judea. He was born in 37 C.E. as **Joseph ben Mattityahu** (Joseph son of Mattathias). When the First Revolt erupted in 66, the provisional Jewish government appointed Josephus commander of Galilee. Galilee was the first part of the country subdued by Vespasian, as he marched south from Antioch at the head of a huge Roman force. The towns and fortresses under Josephus' command were captured or capitulated quickly, until only one fortress called Jotapata (Hebrew Yodefat) remained under Josephus' control. Here Josephus prepared to make his last stand, holed up in a cistern with forty soldiers under his command. When the soldiers decided to make a suicide pact, Josephus had no choice but to go along. They drew lots, but somehow, as he himself later reported, through fate or contrivance he drew the last lot. Instead of committing suicide Josephus surrendered to the Romans, which is why many Jews consider him a traitor.

When led to Vespasian, Josephus predicted that Vespasian would one day be emperor of the Roman Empire. This was a clever move on Josephus' part in light of contemporary events in Rome. It was 67 C.E. and Nero, the emperor at the time, was very unpopular in the aftermath of the great fire in Rome three years earlier ("Nero fiddled while Rome burned"). Josephus knew that Nero likely would not last much longer, and he suspected that Vespasian was ambitious. And Josephus was right. Instead of ordering Josephus' execution, Vespasian had him taken into captivity. The following year (68) Nero committed suicide, and a year later (69) Vespasian was proclaimed emperor by his troops and seized power, at which point he released Josephus from captivity.

After his release, Josephus became a client of the imperial family. He was given Roman citizenship and property and he Latinized his name to Flavius Josephus, adopting his imperial patron's family name (Vespasian founded the Flavian dynasty). Josephus was present at the Roman siege of Jerusalem in 70, where he tried to persuade the city to surrender. After 70 Josephus moved to Rome, where he spent the rest of his life as a Diaspora Jew until his death around 100 C.E.

Josephus spent his years in Rome writing history books that were commissioned by his imperial patrons. His first work, **The Jewish War**, completed around 80 C.E., is a seven-book account of the First Revolt. Josephus began his story with the Maccabean revolt, which he viewed as putting into motion the events that culminated with the First Jewish Revolt. He ended his account with a dramatic account of the mass suicide and fall of Masada. Around 93–94, Josephus completed his second massive work, **Jewish Antiquities**, which is a history of the Jewish people beginning with creation and ending with the outbreak of the First Revolt, and which overlaps with *The Jewish War*.

Although Josephus is an important source of information (and sometimes our only source) about historical events in Judea in the late Second Temple period, he is often biased and sometimes unreliable. Of course, Josephus did not have first-hand knowledge of many of the events he describes (including the fall of Masada). His account is based on other sources, most of which are lost. For example, much of Josephus' information about Herod comes from **Nicolaus of**

Damascus, Herod's court biographer, whose writings are not preserved. Not only can we not gauge the accuracy of Nicolaus' information, but we also cannot evaluate how faithfully Josephus reported that information, and whether he did so partially or fully. Furthermore, typical of ancient writers, Josephus freely plagiarized his sources, meaning he usually did not cite them. Thus, in many cases we do not know the sources of Josephus' information.

Josephus' accounts are also colored by biases, self-justification, and apologetic tendencies. For example, in *War*, Josephus portrays the Jewish rebels as extreme fringe elements – fanatics and criminals – because he did not want his readers to know that the revolt was supported by some members of the Jewish aristocracy. Josephus also presents the Romans as perfect gentlemen. For example, according to Josephus, Titus did his best to prevent the destruction of the Jerusalem temple and even wept when it burned! By the time Josephus wrote *Antiquities*, the trauma of the revolt was less immediate. Therefore, the apologetic tendencies of *War* (trying to excuse the Jews for the revolt) are less pronounced in *Antiquities*, which instead seeks to exalt the Jews and Judaism (not surprising considering that Josephus had been living for over two decades as a minority in a Diaspora context).

It has been estimated that only about 1 percent of all ancient writings have survived. Josephus' works were preserved by Christians who considered these works important because they provide testimony about the time of Jesus and especially the destruction of the second temple, which Jesus reportedly foretold (see Mark 13:1–2; Matthew 24:1–2; Luke 21:5–6). Furthermore, in a controversial passage in *Antiquities*, Josephus refers to Jesus Christ. Although this passage might be a later interpolation by Christians (and at the very least was reworked and altered), there are other authentic but reworked passages concerning John the Baptist and James the Just (the brother of Jesus). Interestingly, Josephus' writings were not preserved in the Jewish tradition. The rabbis of the period after 70 viewed the rebels as crazed fanatics who brought disaster on Israel. They had no interest in preserving writings that were not sacred scripture and were not part of the rabbinic tradition of **Oral Law**.

JOSEPHUS AND THE MASS SUICIDE AT MASADA

Some scholars have suggested that Josephus fabricated the story of the mass suicide at Masada, as he describes similar mass suicides in other, unrelated episodes. For example, according to Josephus the inhabitants of Gamla flung themselves over the cliffs to escape the Romans, and at Jotapata the soldiers under Josephus' command committed suicide. Were there so many cases of mass suicide, or is it possible that Josephus fabricated some of them as a literary device to enhance his story and make it more exciting? Indeed, Masada is famous today because of the mass suicide.

It is impossible to determine whether Josephus fabricated the mass suicide story at Masada, for several reasons. First, Josephus is our only source on the mass suicide. No other ancient author, including Tacitus, describes the fall of Masada. In other words, there is no independent confirmation of the story of the mass suicide from other sources. Second, the possibility that Josephus fabricated the mass suicide story cannot be contradicted on the grounds that the Romans would have objected because it was not true. The Romans read history books to be entertained, not with the expectation of objective history in the modern sense of the word. This is why Josephus and other ancient authors focused on people and events that were exotic and different rather than on the mundane (for example, Josephus devoting so much attention to the small and marginal Essene sect versus the Pharisees and Sadducees). Therefore, the Romans would not have objected had Josephus invented a fantastic ending to his story of the siege of Masada. Third, the possibility that Josephus fabricated the mass suicide cannot be contradicted on the grounds that the Romans would have objected because the story presents the Jewish rebels as noble in defeat, preferring death at their own hands. To the contrary, by making the Jews appear heroic Josephus elevated the Romans' victory over them, as there is much greater glory in defeating a strong enemy than a weak one. For example, Hellenistic period sculptural groups of the Dying Gaul and the Gaul Committing Suicide, which were erected on the acropolis of Pergamon (a city in northwest Asia Minor), elevated the Pergamene victory over invading Gallic tribes by depicting the enemy as sympathetic and noble in death.

Archaeology also cannot confirm or disprove the historicity of Josephus' mass suicide story at Masada because the remains can be interpreted differently, depending on how one understands Josephus. For example, Yadin's excavations did not turn up the physical remains of the approximately 960 rebels who supposedly took their lives at Masada. Instead, Yadin found three skeletons on the lowest terrace of the northern palace, which he identified as the remains of a Jewish family (see above), and another 5 to 25 skeletons in a cistern on the southeast side of the mountain, which could be the remains of Jews, Romans, or even Byzantine monks (there was a Byzantine monastery atop Masada in the fifth and sixth centuries C.E.). Yadin, who interpreted Josephus' account literally, assumed that most of the rebels had been buried in a mass grave or cremated by the Romans. Certainly the Romans would have disposed of any corpses immediately, as they left a garrison stationed atop Masada for a couple of decades after the siege. On the other hand, the picture would be the same even if no mass suicide had occurred; there was a battle, some Jews were killed and their remains disposed of, and the rest were taken into captivity. Another example: Yadin claimed to have found a group of "lots" in a room next to the large bath house in the northern palace complex. The "lots" consist of ostraca – potsherds inscribed with names in Hebrew, including the name "Ben Yair"

Sidebar: Yigael Yadin (1917–1984)

Yigael Yadin was the son of the Israeli archaeologist and biblical scholar Eleazar Sukenik. As a youth, Yadin served in the Haganah (Hebrew for "defense"), a Jewish paramilitary organization in British Mandatory Palestine that became the core of the Israel Defense Forces (IDF). Yadin was Head of Operations during Israel's War of Independence (1948) and served as chief of staff of the IDF from 1949 to 1952. For the next three decades Yadin devoted himself to archaeology. He wrote a dissertation on the War Scroll from Qumran and later published the Temple Scroll – both of which remain the definitive studies of these works. Yadin conducted excavations at some of the most important archaeological sites in Israel, including Hazor, Megiddo, and Masada. He also made spectacular discoveries dating to the time of the Bar-Kokhba Revolt in caves near Ein Gedi (see Chapter 12). Yadin taught at the Institute of Archaeology at the Hebrew University of Jerusalem and served as its head.

In 1976 Yadin left academia for politics, forming a new party called the Democratic Movement for Change (Dash). Although the party won some seats in the Israeli parliament (Knesset) and joined the government coalition, ultimately it was a failure. Yadin retired from politics in 1981 and returned to teaching, but died just three years later. Yadin was a charismatic teacher and brilliant scholar who had a lasting influence on archaeology in Israel.

Sidebar: How Were Roman Legionaries Equipped?

Roman legionaries were equipped so they could fight effectively as heavy infantry. The upper part of their body was protected with armor, including helmets with large cheek-pieces worn on the head and segmented armor (overlapping strips of metal) covering the torso. Legionaries wore short (knee-length) **tunics** to allow for mobility, shin guards, and heavy nailed sandals called *caligae*. Several items were attached to a belt worn around the waist: an apron of studded leather strips in front to protect the genitals (because nothing was worn under the tunic), and on either side a short dagger and a sword. The dagger and the sword were housed in reinforced leather sheaths attached to the belt.

In their left hands, legionaries carried a large rectangular shield that protected the unarmored lower parts of their bodies. In their right hands, legionaries carried a six-foot long javelin called a *pilum*, which consisted of an iron point set into a wooden shaft. The legionaries would throw the *pilum* while advancing toward the enemy and then use their swords for hand-to-hand combat.

(perhaps the same rebel leader mentioned by Josephus). The problem is that there are twelve ostraca, not ten, in this group of "lots." Yadin discounted one because it was incomplete, but that still leaves eleven. Joseph Naveh, an epigrapher who published these ostraca, was unable to determine whether they were in fact "lots," because ostraca are not uncommon at Masada and were used for various purposes, such as meal ration tickets.

More recently, Netzer noted an interesting phenomenon at Masada. Many of the rooms in the western palace complex show no signs of the burning that is attested elsewhere at Masada (for example, burnt wooden beams were found on the floors of storerooms in the northern palace complex). Netzer connected this with Josephus' account, postulating that because of the western palace's proximity to the ramp, the Jewish rebels took wooden beams from these rooms to construct the replacement wall. Netzer argued that this evidence confirmed the accuracy of Josephus' testimony, including the historicity of the mass suicide story. On the other hand, an Israeli archaeologist, Hillel Geva, has pointed to another interesting phenomenon at Masada: a huge mound of chalky dirt mixed with large numbers of artifacts was piled against the outside of the white plastered, stone wall that separated Herod's palace rooms from the rest of the northern palace complex. According to Geva, the pile of dirt and artifacts is a siege ramp or mound that the Romans erected when Jewish rebels took refuge inside the rooms of the northern palace. If Geva is correct, it would mean that there was intense fighting rather than a mass suicide at Masada.

Maybe there is some truth in both points of view: perhaps some of the Jews took their own lives while others fought to the death. In my opinion, we will never know for sure. Archaeology cannot prove or disprove the historicity of Josephus' mass suicide story, as the archaeological remains are ambiguous and can be interpreted in different ways. Whether the mass suicide story is true or not ultimately depends on how one evaluates Josephus' reliability as an historian.

Recommended Reading

Amnon Ben-Tor, *Back to Masada* (Jerusalem: Israel Exploration Society, 2009).

Shaye J. D. Cohen, *Josephus in Galilee and Rome* (Boston: Leiden, 2002).

Tessa Rajak, *Josephus, The Historian and His Society* (London, Duckworth, 1983).

Jonathan P. Roth, *Roman Warfare* (New York: Cambridge University, 2009).

Neil Asher Silberman, *A Prophet from Amongst You: The Life of Yigael Yadin: Soldier, Scholar, and Mythmaker of Modern Israel* (Reading, MA: Addison-Wesley, 1993).

Yigael Yadin, *Masada, Herod's Fortress and the Zealots' Last Stand* (New York: Random House, 1966).

ELEVEN

ANCIENT JEWISH TOMBS AND BURIAL CUSTOMS (TO 70 C.E.)

By the first century C.E., Jerusalem was surrounded by a necropolis of rock-cut tombs.

These tombs are characterized by the following features:

1) The rock-cut tombs are artificially hewn, underground caves cut into the bedrock slopes around Jerusalem.
2) With few exceptions, the tombs were located outside the walls of the city.
3) Each tomb was used by a family over the course of several generations, as reflected by the biblical expression "he slept with [or was gathered to] his fathers" (for example Judges 2:10; 2 Chronicles 32:33; 2 Chronicles 33:20; 2 Chronicles 34:28).
4) When a member of the family died, the body was wrapped in a shroud and sometimes placed in a coffin, and was then laid in the tomb as an individual inhumation, even if the bones were later collected and placed elsewhere.
5) Because of the expense associated with hewing a burial cave into bedrock, only the wealthier members of Jerusalem's population – the upper classes – could afford rock-cut tombs. The lower classes apparently disposed of their dead in a manner that has left fewer traces in the archaeological record – for example, in individual trench graves or cist graves dug into the ground.
6) From the earliest periods, the layout and decoration of Jerusalem's rock-cut tombs exhibited foreign cultural influences and fashions. Evidence for such influence – and indeed, for the use of rock-cut tombs – is attested only in times when Jerusalem's Jewish elite enjoyed an autonomous or semi-autonomous status; that is, in the late First Temple period (late Iron Age) and the late Second Temple period (Herodian period). During these periods the Jerusalem elite adopted foreign fashions that were introduced by the rulers or governing authorities. We begin with a brief review of rock-cut tombs in the late Iron Age.

11.1   Burial cave at Ketef Hinnom with rock-cut benches.

Rock-Cut Tombs in Jerusalem: The Late First Temple Period/Late Iron Age (Eighth to Early Sixth Centuries B.C.E.)

Rock-cut tombs of the late First Temple period have been discovered to the west, north, and east of the Old City. They include tombs at Ketef Hinnom (on the northwest side of the Ben-Hinnom Valley), St. Étienne (the École Biblique, to the north of the Old City), and in the Silwan (Siloam) village (across the Kidron Valley from the City of David). These tombs typically consist of one or more burial chambers that were entered through a small, unadorned opening cut into the bedrock. Each burial chamber was surrounded on three sides with rock-cut benches, on which the bodies of the deceased were laid. When the benches were filled and space was needed for new burials, the earlier remains (bones and burial gifts) were moved onto the floor or were placed in a pit (repository) hewn under one of the benches. An undisturbed repository in the Ketef Hinnom cemetery contained large numbers of skeletons as well as accompanying burial gifts, including ceramic vases and oil lamps, jewelry, seals, a rare early coin, and two silver **amulets**. One of the amulets is inscribed with the priestly blessing (Numbers 6:24–26), which is the earliest citation of a biblical text ever found. Many of the decorative elements in late Iron Age burial caves, such as the benches with carved headrests and parapets, and the cornices carved around the top of the burial chambers (as, for example, at St. Étienne) reflect Phoenician influence (or Egyptian styles transmitted directly from Egypt or through Phoenician intermediaries). Phoenician influence on the tombs of

Jerusalem's elite in the First Temple period is hardly surprising in light of the biblical accounts of Phoenician involvement in the construction of Solomon's Temple, as well as later contacts between the Israelites and their neighbors to the north.

ROCK-CUT TOMBS IN JERUSALEM: THE LATE SECOND TEMPLE PERIOD

After 586 B.C.E., Jerusalem's rock-cut tombs ceased to be used because the elite families who owned them were dead or dispersed. Rock-cut tombs reappeared only in the Hasmonean period (second half of the second century B.C.E.), when Jerusalem again came under Jewish rule and an autonomous Jewish elite reemerged. In the meantime, in 353 B.C.E., a local dynast named **Mausolus** of Caria died and was buried in a monumental tomb in his capital city of Halicarnassos (modern Bodrum on the southwest coast of Turkey). Although little survives of this tomb because of the ravages of humans and nature, ancient literary accounts and depictions on coins indicate that it consisted of a Greek-temple-style building surrounded by columns with a pyramidal roof on a tall, raised podium (in which the burial chamber was located). The tomb was decorated with hundreds of statues and reliefs carved by the most famous Greek sculptors of the day (most of the surviving sculpture is now in London's British Museum). In fact, it was because of the high quality and lavishness of the decoration that the tomb of Mausolus became one of the seven wonders of the ancient world. Since then, it has become conventional to refer to all monumental tombs as mausolea (singular: mausoleum).

The **Mausoleum at Halicarnassos** inspired rulers and elites around the Mediterranean to construct their own tombs in imitation, including the Mausoleum of Augustus in Rome. When an autonomous Jewish elite emerged in Judea after the Maccabean revolt, its members, too, adopted this type of monumental tomb. Ironically, although the Maccabees were renowned for their opposition to the imposition of Greek customs on the Jews, the Hasmonean rulers showed signs of Hellenization soon after the establishment of their kingdom. Nowhere is this better illustrated than by the monumental family tomb and victory memorial built by Simon in their hometown of Modiin, in which he interred the remains of his parents and brothers. Although no remains of this tomb survive, ancient literary sources leave little doubt that it was inspired by the Mausoleum at Halicarnassus:

> And Simon built a monument over the tomb of his father and his brothers, he made it high so that it might be seen, with polished stone at the front and back. He also erected seven pyramids, opposite one another, for his father and mother and four brothers. For the pyramids he devised an

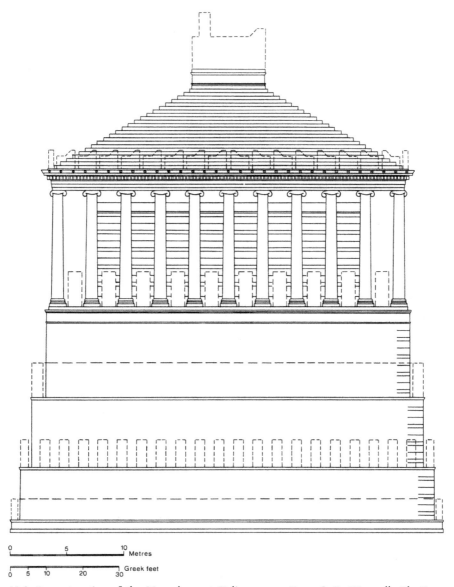

0   5   10 Metres

0   5   10   20   30 Greek feet

11.2   Reconstruction of the Mausoleum at Halicarnassos. From G. B. Waywell, *The Free-Standing Sculptures of the Mausoleum at Halicarnassus in the British Museum* (London: British Museum, 1978), p. 58 Fig. 8. By permission of the Trustees of the British Museum.

elaborate setting, erecting about them great columns, and on the columns he put suits of armor for a permanent memorial, and beside the suits of armor he carved ships, so that they could be seen by all who sail the sea. This is the tomb that he built in Modein; it remains to this day. (1 Macc. 13:27–30; NRSV)

However, Simon sent some to the city Basca to bring away his brother's bones, and buried them in their own city Modin; and all the people made great lamentation over him. Simon also erected a very large monument for his father and his brethren, of white and polished stone, and raised it to a great height, and so as to be seen a long way off, and made cloisters about it, and set up pillars, which were of one stone apiece; a work it was wonderful to see. Moreover, he built seven pyramids also for his parents and his brethren, one for each of them, which were made very surprising, both for their largeness and beauty, and which have been preserved to this day. (Josephus, *Ant.* 13:210–11; Whiston's translation)

These descriptions indicate that like the Mausoleum, the tomb of the Maccabees consisted of a tall podium with a temple-like building surrounded by columns and capped by a pyramidal roof (or in the case of the tomb of the Maccabees, seven pyramids, one for each family member). In contrast, late Iron Age rock-cut tombs typically had plain, undecorated exteriors.

Jason's Tomb in Jerusalem indicates that the Jewish elite soon began to imitate the new tomb style introduced by Simon, which was inspired by the Mausoleum at Halicarnassos (see Chapter 5). Jason's Tomb continues the earlier tradition of rock-cut burial caves in Jerusalem but with several innovations. On the one hand, the Jerusalem elite revived the ancient tradition of interring their dead in rock-cut family tombs consisting of one or more burial chambers that were used over the course of several generations. Furthermore, the custom of making space for new burials by depositing the earlier remains elsewhere in the tomb continued. On the other hand, newly introduced elements reflect foreign influence and fashions. These elements included the use of loculi instead of benches to accommodate the bodies inside the burial chamber(s), and decorating the tomb's exterior, sometimes with a Greek-style porch and a pyramid or other monument marking the site of the tomb.

The features that appeared in Jason's Tomb remained characteristic of Jewish rock-cut tombs in Jerusalem until the end of the Second Temple period. The differences between individual rock-cut tombs of the late Second Temple period in Jerusalem mostly concern their size and degree of elaboration – that is, the number of burial chambers, the presence or absence of a porch (with or without columns), the addition of decoration (typically around the entrance to the burial chambers and/or on the porch façade), and the presence or absence of one or more monumental tomb markers. Many burial chambers are encircled by rock-cut benches just below the loculi, on which the bodies of the deceased could be placed as they were prepared for interment. Herod's tomb and memorial to himself – the mountain of Herodium – displays the same features as others but on a much larger scale: a tomb structure containing a burial chamber and a monumental conical marker (see Chapter 8).

Rock-cut tombs of the late Second Temple period surround Jerusalem on the north, east, and south. Well-known examples include the **tomb of Bene Hezir**, the **tomb of Queen Helena of Adiabene** (the so-called **Tombs of the Kings**),

11.3 The Tomb of Bene Hezir (left) and the Tomb of Zachariah (center), looking east.

the **Sanhedria tombs**, and **Nicanor's tomb** (all discussed later). Most of Jerusalem's rock-cut tombs are more modest than these examples, having an undecorated or simply decorated entrance and a single burial chamber with loculi.

The Kidron Valley Tombs

A series of monumental tombs of the late Second Temple period are located in the Kidron Valley, at the foot of the slope of the Mount of Olives. These tombs are positioned so as to be visible from the Temple Mount above. Their size, location, and decoration indicate that they belonged to some of the wealthiest and most prominent members of Jerusalem's elite. There are three monuments in a row, from north to south: the **tomb of Absalom** (and associated **cave of Jehoshaphat**), the tomb of Bene Hezir, and the **tomb of Zachariah**.

The tomb of Bene Hezir is cut into the bedrock cliff at the foot of the Mount of Olives. It has a porch with two Doric columns and a Doric entablature with a triglyph and metope frieze, which gives access to several burial chambers with loculi. The tomb is so called because an inscription on the porch's architrave states that this is the tomb and *nefesh* of the family of Bene Hezir, who are known to have been priests. It is not surprising that the elite families who owned rock-cut tombs included priests, many of whom were among the wealthiest Jews.

A passage cut through the rock cliff on one side of the porch of the tomb of Bene Hezir connects it with the tomb of Zachariah, just to the south. The "tomb of Zachariah" is a misnomer, however, as it is not a tomb and was not connected with that prophet. Instead, the tomb of Zachariah is a solid rock cube hewn from the bedrock cliff at the foot of the Mount of Olives. The stepped base of the cube, the Ionic columns carved around its sides, and the pyramidal roof recall the Mausoleum at Halicarnassos. The tops of the columns (just under the Ionic capitals) are encircled by carved notches that indicate the beginning of fluting, instead of having fluting along the entire length of the columns. This feature long ago suggested to scholars that the tomb of Zachariah was modeled after a lost building of late Second Temple period Jerusalem. And indeed, in the 1970s, Avigad's excavations in the Jewish Quarter brought to light the remains of an enormous Ionic capital (and matching column base) with this same peculiar treatment. Although we do not have the remains of the building with which the column found by Avigad was associated, this discovery confirmed that the columns on the tomb of Zachariah were inspired by a contemporary monument. The tomb of Zachariah is not a tomb because the rock cube has no burial chambers within. Apparently it served as the *nefesh* (monumental marker) for the nearby tomb of Bene Hezir, to which it is connected by a passage.

The tomb of Absalom is the northernmost of the monuments in the Kidron Valley. Like the tomb of Zachariah, it is a free-standing cube, not a rock-cut tomb. The lower half of the tomb of Absalom is cut from the cliff of the Mount of Olives, whereas the upper part is built of stone. The sides of the cube are encircled by Ionic columns with a Doric triglyph and metope frieze, capped by a cone topped with a lotus flower instead of a pyramidal roof. The tomb of Absalom has no connection with the biblical figure of that name, but unlike the tomb of Zachariah, the cube contains burial chambers (holes in the sides were made by grave robbers who plundered the tomb's contents long ago). A large rock-cut tomb (the cave of Jehoshaphat) cut into the cliff immediately behind the tomb of Absalom provided additional space for burials and presumably belonged to the same family. In other words, the tomb of Absalom served as both a tomb and as a *nefesh* for the burial cave behind it.

The Tombs of the Kings (the tomb of Queen Helena of Adiabene)

To the north of the Old City, near the current American Colony Hotel, is a monumental tomb of the late Second Temple period. Popularly known as the Tombs of the Kings because of a mistaken association with the burials of the last kings of Judah, this is, in fact, the family tomb of Queen Helena of Adiabene, a kingdom in northern Syria-Mesopotamia. In the middle of the first century C.E., Queen Helena, the ruler of the kingdom, converted to Judaism and moved to Jerusalem with her family.

11.4 Tomb of Absalom. Courtesy of Zev Radovan/BibleLandPictures.com.

The tomb of Queen Helena is the only Judean tomb singled out for mention by the second century C.E. Greek author Pausanias, who wrote a series of travelogues: "I know of many wonderful graves, and will mention two of them, the one at Halicarnassus and one in the land of the Hebrews. The one at Halicarnassus was made for Mausolus, king of the city, and it is of such vast size, and so notable for all its ornament, that the Romans in their great admiration of it call remarkable tombs in their country 'Mausolea.' The Hebrews have a grave, that of Helen, a native woman, in the city of Jerusalem, which the Roman Emperor razed to the ground" (*Graeciae Descriptio* 8.16:4–5; translation from M. Stern, *Greek and Latin Authors on Jews and Judaism*).

In front of the tomb of Queen Helena is an enormous open courtyard that was hewn out of bedrock, which was accessed by a monumental rock-cut staircase. A large *miqveh* at the base of the staircase was used by visitors to the tomb. The tomb consists of a porch that originally had two columns, and a rock-cut entablature with a triglyph and metope frieze decorated with vegetal designs including bunches of grapes. The entrance to the burial chambers was sealed by a large round stone in a slot, enabling it to be rolled. The burial chambers, loculi, and benches in the tomb of Queen Helena are cut more finely and evenly than

11.5 Tomb of Queen Helena with monumental rock-cut staircase in the foreground. Courtesy of Zev Radovan/BibleLandPictures.com.

most other Judean tombs. This tomb also yielded a large, exquisitely decorated stone sarcophagus (coffin), carved in relief with wreaths and vegetal designs and bearing an inscription indicating that it belonged to Queen Helena.

The Sanhedria Tombs

At some distance to the northwest of the tomb of Queen Helena is a group of rock-cut tombs known as the Sanhedria tombs. They are so called because the largest and most elaborate tomb contains approximately seventy loculi, which suggested to early visitors the number of members of the Sanhedrin. This is a mistaken identification, as members of the Sanhedrin would have been buried in family tombs, not as a separate group. The surrounding modern Jerusalem neighborhood of Sanhedria takes its name from this group of tombs. Some of the tombs are modest in size and scale, whereas others have porches with columns and are decorated with carved designs. The largest tomb, with approximately seventy loculi in an unusual double-tiered arrangement, has a beautifully carved pediment containing vegetal designs above the porch (but no columns), and a smaller but similar pediment above the entrance to the burial chambers. There was a large courtyard in front of the porch, where visitors could gather to mourn and perhaps hold commemorative meals and other ceremonies for the dead.

11.6 Interior of a rock-cut tomb with loculi and ossuaries. Courtesy of Zev Radovan/ BibleLandPictures.com.

The Tomb of Nicanor

The tomb of Nicanor came to light in the early 1970s, during construction work on the Hebrew University's Mount Scopus campus. Today the tomb is located in the university's botanical garden. The burial chambers are located at different levels underground. The tomb had a porch with square piers but no signs of a decorated entablature. An inscription on one of the ossuaries found inside the tomb mentions Nicanor of Alexandria – apparently the same wealthy Jew from Alexandria in Egypt who donated Nicanor's Gate to the Jerusalem temple (see Chapter 7).

Ossuaries

In the middle of Herod's reign, around 20–15 B.C.E., ossuaries first appeared in Jerusalem's rock-cut tombs. Ossuaries were used as containers for bones removed from loculi (after the flesh had decayed), in contrast to sarcophagi (coffins), which accommodated corpses still with the flesh (inhumation). Ossuaries are much smaller than sarcophagi – only big enough to accommodate individual bones gathered together – whereas sarcophagi were designed to contain whole corpses. Most ossuaries from Jerusalem are made of locally quarried stone, usually soft chalk and, rarely, harder limestone. They have flat, rounded, or gabled lids. The ossuaries can be plain or decorated (most decoration consists of incised or chip-carved designs, rarely in relief, and sometimes with painting).

Sometimes the name(s) of the deceased (and infrequently other information, such as the person's title or occupation) were incised on the front, back, side, or lid of the ossuary. Most of the inscriptions are in Aramaic, Hebrew, or Greek, and usually they are crudely executed, having been added inside the tomb by family members involved in collecting the remains.

There is no correlation between the relative wealth and status of the deceased and the ornamentation of the ossuary; plain and uninscribed ossuaries have been found in tombs belonging to some of ancient Jerusalem's most prominent families. The same is true of the tombs themselves, as indicated by the modest size and appearance of a tomb belonging to the Caiaphas family. This tomb was discovered in 1990 to the southwest of the Old City, and was excavated by Israeli archaeologists. Two of the ossuaries from the tomb are inscribed with the name **Caiaphas** (Aramaic "Capha"), including one inscribed "Joseph son of Caiaphas." Because Caiaphas is an unusual name and Joseph son of Caiaphas is known to have served as high priest from 18–36 C.E., this tomb likely belonged to the family of the same high priest who presided over the trial of Jesus (according to the Gospel accounts). Interestingly, some of the largest and most lavishly decorated tombs belonged to émigré families living in Jerusalem, including the tomb of Queen Helena of Adiabene (which, according to Josephus, was crowned by three pyramidal markers) and Nicanor's tomb (which contains more burial chambers than any other Jerusalem tomb). Perhaps these families constructed especially large and lavish tombs to establish their standing among the local elite.

Whereas there is no doubt that ossuaries were used as containers for bones removed from loculi, scholars question why they were introduced into Jerusalem's rock-cut tombs around 20–15 B.C.E. and why they disappeared from Jerusalem after 70 C.E. (with evidence of their use on a smaller and more modest scale in southern Judea and Galilee until the third century). An Israeli archaeologist named Levi Yitzhak Rahmani connects the appearance of ossuaries with the Pharisaic belief in the individual, physical resurrection of the dead. The anticipation of a future, physical resurrection of the dead is accepted today as part of normative, rabbinic Judaism. This doctrine became popular among the Pharisees in the late Second Temple period. However, the Sadducees rejected the belief in individual, physical resurrection of the dead on the grounds that such a doctrine is nowhere explicitly stated in the Pentateuch (Torah). Rahmani suggests that the introduction of ossuaries is connected with the spread of the belief in a future, physical resurrection of the dead. As we have seen, prior to the introduction of ossuaries, the remains of burials in rock-cut tombs were collected in pits, repositories, or charnel rooms. The skeletons therefore were mingled and susceptible to separation, breakage, and even loss. This means that in the event of a physical resurrection, an individual would be restored to life missing vital body parts. According to Rahmani, ossuaries were introduced into

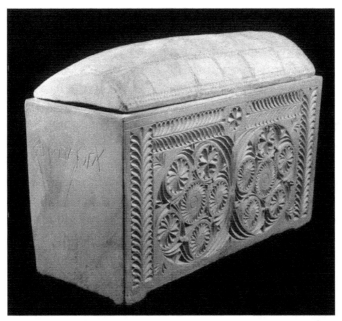

11.7 Inscribed ossuary from the Caiaphas family tomb. Courtesy of Zev Radovan/BibleLand Pictures.com.

Jerusalem's rock-cut tombs to preserve the remains of each individual. Rahmani also argues that the collection of bones in an ossuary corresponds with the Pharisaic notion that the decay of the flesh is connected with the expiation of sin. In other words, each individual's remains were preserved intact in an ossuary, in a sinless state, awaiting future resurrection.

Many scholars have pointed to difficulties with Rahmani's explanation. For example, ossuaries frequently contain the bones of more than one individual, and sometimes parts of the skeleton are missing. In fact, according to rabbinic law it was not necessary to collect all the bones. Furthermore, even in tombs with ossuaries some skeletons continued to be deposited in pits or repositories. Another difficulty with Rahmani's explanation is that the monumental rock-cut tombs with ossuaries belonged to Jerusalem's elite, many of whom were Sadducees, who reportedly rejected the doctrine of individual, physical resurrection of the dead. In fact, some of these tombs and ossuaries belonged to high priestly families, such as the tomb of Bene Hezir and the tomb and ossuaries of the Caiaphas family. In other words, ossuaries were used by some of the same members of Jerusalem society who reportedly rejected the concept of the resurrection of the dead. It is not a coincidence that outside of Jerusalem, the largest cemetery with rock-cut loculus tombs containing ossuaries is at Jericho, which was the site of the Hasmonean and Herodian winter palaces and the center of a priestly community.

Instead of associating ossuaries with expectations of an afterlife or other religious beliefs, their appearance should be understood within the context of foreign (specifically, Roman) influence on the Jerusalem elite – just as the other features of rock-cut tombs. In the late first century B.C.E. and first century C.E., cremation was the prevailing burial rite among the Romans. The ashes of the deceased were placed in small stone containers called *cineraria* (cinerary urns), which are usually casket-shaped and have gabled lids. Sometimes they have carved decoration and/or inscriptions. Cinerary urns were in widespread use around the Roman world, including Rhodes, Asia Minor, and North Africa. Small stone containers or chests used for the secondary collection of bones (called *ostothecai*) are also found in Asia Minor. Like their Judean counterparts, these stone boxes can have carved decoration and sometimes contain the remains of more than one individual. This evidence suggests that the appearance of ossuaries in Judea is related to funerary customs and fashions that were prevalent in the Roman world instead of to Jewish expectations of resurrection.

Rahmani has objected to the possibility that ossuaries were inspired by Roman cinerary urns on the grounds that Jerusalem's elite could not have imitated a practice with which they were unacquainted. However, other Hellenized features in tombs and burial customs were adopted by Jerusalem's elite without personal contact or familiarity (as were other aspects of Hellenistic and Roman culture). Monumental tombs marked by a pyramid became a raging fashion after Simon constructed the family tomb at Modiin. The ultimate source of inspiration for these tombs was the Mausoleum at Halicarnassus, which presumably none of Jerusalem's elite in the Hasmonean period – not even Simon – ever saw. Loculi, which also originated in the Hellenistic world, quickly became universal in Jerusalem's rock-cut tombs. The spread of these features has little or nothing to do with religious beliefs in the afterlife and everything to do with social status. Jerusalem's elite were prohibited by Jewish law from cremating their dead. Instead, they could, and did, adopt the external trappings of cremation by depositing the bones of the deceased in ossuaries (urns). Like loculi, once ossuaries appeared, they quickly became universal in rock-cut tombs.

The disappearance of ossuaries supports the suggestion that they were inspired by Roman cinerary urns. If the use of ossuaries was connected with the concept of the individual, physical resurrection of the dead, they should have become even more popular after 70 C.E., when this belief became normative in Judaism. In fact, the opposite is true. After 70, ossuaries disappeared from Jerusalem because the Jewish elite who used the rock-cut tombs were now dead or dispersed. The appearance of crude ossuaries in Galilee and southern Judea probably is connected with the emigration or displacement of members of Jerusalem's elite to these regions after the First Revolt. By the mid- to late third century, ossuaries ceased to be used.

The production of ossuaries (and other stone vessels) was one component of Jerusalem's economy during the late Second Temple period. It is not a coincidence that ossuaries first appeared during Herod's reign. This period is characterized by a heavy dose of Roman influence on other aspects of the lifestyle of Jerusalem's elite, with a wide range of imported and locally produced consumer goods appearing around 20–10 B.C.E. Their mansions were decorated with Roman-style wall paintings, stucco, and mosaics, and were furnished with locally produced stone tables modeled after Roman prototypes. As in the case of the tombs, these fashions were introduced to Judea by the ruler (in this case, Herod) and were imitated or adopted by the Jerusalem elite.

The heavy dose of Roman cultural influence evident in Jerusalem around 20–10 B.C.E. should be understood within the context of contemporary events. It was during these years that Herod undertook the reconstruction of the Jerusalem Temple. He established a theater and an amphitheater (or hippodrome) in Jerusalem in which athletic competitions, chariot races, and musical and dramatic contests were held. Herod also maintained close contacts with Augustus. In 22 B.C.E., Herod sent his sons Alexander and Aristobulus (by his Hasmonean wife Mariamne) to Rome to be educated. Alexander and Aristobulus remained in Rome for five years, staying first with Pollio and then with Augustus. A couple of years later (20 B.C.E.), Augustus traveled to Syria, where he was hosted by Herod. In 17 B.C.E., Herod traveled to Rome to visit Augustus, returning to Judea with his sons, who were now young men about nineteen and eighteen years of age. Two years later, Herod entertained Augustus' son-in-law and heir apparent Marcus Agrippa, taking him on a tour of his kingdom. The appearance of ossuaries and other Romanized elements in Jerusalem is a result of the close contacts and interactions between Augustus and his family on the one hand, and Herod and his family on the other. It is not surprising that beginning around 20 B.C.E., the lifestyle – and death style – of Jerusalem's elite was heavily influenced by Roman culture.

TOMBS AND BURIAL CUSTOMS OF THE LOWER CLASSES AND THE QUMRAN COMMUNITY

We have seen that in the late Second Temple period, the upper classes of Jerusalem and Jericho buried their dead in rock-cut family tombs that were used over the course of several generations. When a family member died, the body was wrapped in a shroud and placed in a loculus. When the loculi became filled, space was made for new burials by clearing out the earlier remains and placing them in a pit or on the floor of the tomb. In the middle of Herod's reign, small bone boxes called ossuaries were introduced into rock-cut tombs as containers for the remains removed from loculi.

This picture is skewed and incomplete because only the more affluent members of Jewish society, who comprised only a small percentage of the population, could afford rock-cut tombs. The association of rock-cut tombs with the upper classes is indicated by several factors. First, rock-cut tombs are concentrated in areas of elite presence, primarily around Jerusalem and Jericho, with scattered examples elsewhere. Second, rock-cut tombs are attested in Jerusalem only in the late First Temple period and late Second Temple period – that is, only when there was an autonomous Jewish elite in the city. The flourishing of the necropolis at Beth Shearim is connected with the displacement and relocation of the Judean elite to Lower Galilee after 70 (see the Sidebar).

The fact that rock-cut tombs accommodated only a small proportion of the population can be demonstrated on the basis of numbers and distribution. Approximately 900 rock-cut tombs of the late first century B.C.E. to the first century C.E. are known from Jerusalem. No more than five to seven people per generation were buried in most of these tombs. If we take the maximum possible estimate (three generations of seven people each buried in all these tombs), the number of burials (over the course of a century) would total 18,900. During this period, Jerusalem's population at any given time was at least 60,000, and sometimes much larger (for example, during the major pilgrimage festivals). Even if we double, triple, or quadruple the number of rock-cut tombs, they would still fall far short of accommodating the majority of Jerusalem's population. The concentration of rock-cut tombs around Jerusalem (with smaller numbers in Jericho and scattered examples elsewhere) reflects the concentration of wealth and attests to their connection with the Jerusalem elite. If rock-cut tombs were used also by members of the lower classes, they should be widespread throughout Judea and Galilee and not limited to the late First Temple and late Second Temple periods. The association of rock-cut tombs and ossuaries with the elite is borne out by inscriptions, some of which name these families.

The numbers, chronology, and distribution of rock-cut tombs indicate that the majority of the ancient Jewish population must have been disposed of in a manner that left few traces in the archaeological landscape, as is true of other ancient societies in the Mediterranean world. For example, John Bodel estimates that known tombs and burials account for only 1.5 percent of ancient Rome's population. In late Republican Rome, large pits called *puticoli* located outside the city walls contained thousands, and sometimes tens of thousands, of corpses belonging to commoners. Public funerary pyres (*ustrinae*) adjoined the area where public executions took place. The bodies of the poorest members of society, including executed criminals, were thrown into pits in potter's fields or were disposed of randomly. Similarly, according to tradition, Judas' blood money was used to pay for a potter's field in Jerusalem (Matthew 27:5–8).

Many ancient Jews apparently buried their dead in individual graves dug into the ground, analogous to the way we bury our dead today. In the Iron

Age kingdoms of Israel and Judah, non-elite burials consisted of individual inhumations in simple pit or cist (stone-lined) graves. The practice of burial in pit graves or trench graves continued through the Second Temple period. The body of the deceased, wrapped in a shroud and sometimes placed in a wooden coffin, was laid in a pit or a trench dug into the ground. Sometimes the burial at the base of the trench was sealed off with stone slabs or mud bricks (as at Qumran), before the trench was filled in with dirt. Often, a headstone was erected to mark the site of the grave. The necropolis at Beth Shearim attests to a diversity of burial customs used by the Jewish population, which inside the catacombs included interment in *arcosolia* (arched niches), loculi, or in stone, lead, terra-cotta, or wood sarcophagi, sometimes with secondary collection of bones in pits or ossuaries, and outside the catacombs included burials in trench graves, cist graves, shaft graves, and even a mausoleum (see the Sidebar).

Because pit graves and trench graves are poor in finds and are much less conspicuous and more susceptible to destruction than rock-cut tombs, relatively few examples are recorded, and the lack of grave goods makes those that are found difficult to date. Qumran provides the best evidence for the use of trench graves in late Second Temple period Judea, where the cemetery is preserved and visible because it is in the desert and was never built over, covered up, or plowed. When graves of this type are found at other sites, scholars often identify them as Essene burials. Although it is possible that some or all of those buried in these cemeteries were Essenes, there is no archaeological evidence to support this assumption. Unlike those at Qumran, the trench graves at other sites are not associated with identifiable remains of Essene settlements, and they contain proportionate numbers of men, women, and children. In fact, the presence of thousands of trench graves in the first- and second-century C.E. Nabatean cemetery at Khirbet Qazone (on the southeast side of the Dead Sea) demonstrates that they are not associated only with Essenes.

The Death and Burial of Jesus

In the ancient world, the method of execution used for capital crimes varied, depending on the nature of the crime and the status of the criminal. Those found guilty by the Sanhedrin (Jewish law court) of violating Jewish law were executed by stoning, burning, decapitation, or strangulation, depending on the crime. Because he was a Roman citizen, Paul was entitled to a trial in Rome (where he apparently was sentenced to death and executed). In contrast, as a lower class Jew from Galilee, Jesus was sentenced to death by Pontius Pilate (the Roman governor of Judea from 26–36 C.E.) and executed by crucifixion. The Romans used crucifixion to punish non-Roman citizens for incitement to rebellion and acts of treason. Roman crucifixion involved using ropes or nails to affix the victim to a wooden stake and crossbeam, a type of hanging that caused slow asphyxiation. This method of execution was generally reserved for lower-class criminals because it was a painful process that could last for days.

According to the Gospel accounts, Jesus was nailed to the cross and expired on the eve of the Sabbath (Friday afternoon; John seems to place the crucifixion on Thursday). A wealthy, prominent Jewish follower of Jesus named Joseph of Arimathea received permission from the Roman governor, Pontius Pilate, to inter Jesus' body in his own family's tomb. The synoptic Gospels (Mark, Matthew, and Luke) are in broad agreement in their description of this event:

> Although it was now evening, yet since it was the Preparation Day, that is, the day before the Sabbath, Joseph of Arimathea, a highly respected member of the council, who was himself living in expectation of the reign of God, made bold to go to Pilate and ask for Jesus' body.... And he [Joseph] bought a linen sheet and took him down from the cross and wrapped him in the sheet, and laid him in a tomb that had been hewn out of the rock, and rolled a stone against the doorway of the tomb. (Mark 15:42–46; NRSV)

> In the evening a rich man named Joseph of Arimathea, who had himself been a disciple of Jesus, came. He went to Pilate and asked him for Jesus' body.... Then Joseph took the body and wrapped it in a piece of clean linen, and laid it in a new tomb that belonged to him, that he had cut in the rock, and he rolled a great stone over the doorway of the tomb, and went away. (Matthew 27:57–60; NRSV)

Joseph of Arimathea seems to have been motivated by a concern for the observance of Jewish law. On one hand, biblical law requires burial within twenty-four hours of death, even for those guilty of the worst crimes. On the other hand, Jewish law prohibits burial on the Sabbath and festivals. Because Jesus expired on the cross on the eve of the Sabbath, he had to be buried before sundown on Friday because waiting until after sundown on Saturday would have exceeded the twenty-four-hour time limit. Because there was no time to prepare a grave, Joseph of Arimathea placed Jesus' body in his family's rock-cut tomb.

In 1968, a rock-cut tomb was discovered in a northern neighborhood of Jerusalem. One of the ossuaries (inscribed with the name Yohanan [John]), contained the remains of a man who had been crucified, as indicated by a nail that was stuck in his heel bone:

> The most dramatic evidence that this young man was crucified was the nail which penetrated his heel bones. But for this nail, we might never have discovered that the young man had died in this way. *The nail was preserved only because it hit a hard knot when it was pounded into the olive wood upright of the cross.* The olive wood knot was so hard that, as the blows on the nail became heavier, the end of the nail bent and curled. We found a bit of the olive wood (between 1 and 2 cm) on the tip of the nail.

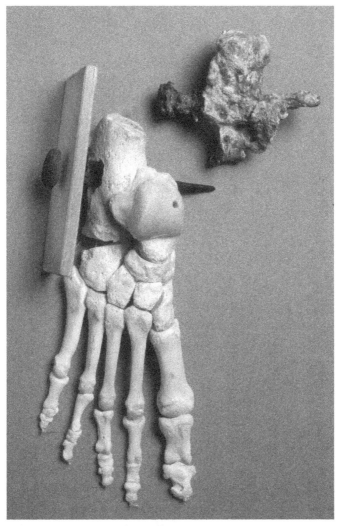

11.8 Heel bone and nail of a crucified victim from Jerusalem (upper right), next to a modern reconstruction. Courtesy of Zev Radovan/BibleLandPictures.com.

This wood had probably been forced out of the knot where the curled nail hooked into it. When it came time of the dead victim to be removed from the cross, the executioners could not pull out this nail, bent as it was within the cross. The only way to remove the body was to take an ax or hatchet and amputate the feet. (Vassilios Tzaferis, "Crucifixion – The Archaeological Evidence," *Biblical Archaeology Review* 11/1 [1985]: 50)

This is an extraordinary discovery because the means by which victims were affixed to crosses usually leave no discernable traces in the physical remains or archaeological record. Some victims were bound with ropes, which were untied when the body was removed from the cross. When nails were used, they were pulled out when the body was removed from the cross. The nail in Yohanan's heel bone was preserved only because it bent after hitting a knot in the wood and therefore could not be removed from the body.

The Gospel accounts of Jesus' burial appear to be largely consistent with the archaeological evidence. In other words, although archaeology does not prove there was a follower of Jesus named Joseph of Arimathea or that Pontius Pilate granted his request for Jesus' body, the Gospel accounts describing Jesus' removal from the cross and burial accord well with archaeological evidence and with Jewish law. The source(s) of these accounts were familiar with the manner in which wealthy Jews living in Jerusalem during the time of Jesus disposed of their dead. The circumstances surrounding Jesus' death and burial can be reconstructed as follows.

Jesus expired on the cross shortly before sundown on Friday. Because Jesus came from a lower-class family that did not own a rock-cut tomb, under ordinary circumstances he would have been buried in a pit grave or trench grave. However, there was no time to prepare (dig) a grave before the beginning of the Sabbath. Joseph of Arimathea, a wealthy follower of Jesus, was concerned to ensure that Jesus was buried before sundown, in accordance with biblical law. Therefore, Joseph hastened to Pilate and requested permission to take Jesus' body. Joseph laid Jesus' body in a loculus in his own rock-cut tomb – an exceptional measure due to the circumstances, as rock-cut tombs were family tombs. When the women entered the tomb of Joseph of Arimathea on Sunday morning, the loculus where Jesus' body had been laid was empty. The theological explanation for this phenomenon is that Jesus was resurrected from the dead. However, once Jesus had been buried in accordance with Jewish law, there was no prohibition against removing the body from the tomb after the end of the Sabbath and reburying it elsewhere. It is therefore possible that followers or family members removed Jesus' body from Joseph's tomb after the Sabbath ended and buried it in a pit grave or trench grave, as it would have been unusual to leave a non-relative in a family tomb. No matter which explanation one prefers, the fact that Jesus' body did not remain in Joseph's tomb means that his bones could not have been collected in an ossuary, at least not if we follow the Gospel accounts.

THE DEATH AND BURIAL OF JAMES

After Jesus' death, his brother James became the leader of Jerusalem's early Christian community (technically these were not early Christians, but rather a Jewish sect of Jesus' followers). James apparently was an observant Jew whose pious and ascetic lifestyle earned him the nickname "the Just." We have little direct information about James, as he was marginalized in later western Christian tradition. The New Testament contains the **Epistle** or **Letter of James**, although scholars debate whether James was the author of this work or whether someone else wrote it and attributed it to James (in which case it is a pseudepigraphic, or falsely attributed, work). Either way, the attribution of this work to James suggests that he was known for his opposition to the accumulation of wealth and the lifestyle of the wealthy, as illustrated by the following passages (all from the NRSV):

> Let the believer who is lowly boast in being raised up, and the rich in being brought low, because the rich will disappear like a flower in the field. For the sun rises with its scorching heat and withers the field; its flower falls, and its beauty perishes. It is the same way with the rich; in the midst of a busy life, they will wither away. (1:9–11)

> Has not God chosen the poor in the world to be rich in faith and to be heirs of the kingdom that he has promised to those who love him? But you have dishonored the poor. Is it not the rich who oppress you? Is it not they who drag you into court? (2:5–6)

> Come now, you rich people, weep and wail for the miseries that are coming to you. Your riches have rotted, and your clothes are moth-eaten. Your gold and silver have rusted, and their rust will be evidence against you, and it will eat your flesh like fire. You have laid up treasure for the last days. Listen! The wages of the laborers who mowed your fields, which you kept back by fraud, cry out, and the cries of the harvesters have reached the ears of the Lord of hosts. You have lived on the earth in luxury and in pleasure. (5:1–5)

The negative views on wealth expressed in the Letter of James are consistent with the nature of the early Christian community in Jerusalem, which Acts describes as having a communal and impoverished lifestyle, although some members came from wealthy families. In this regard, the early Christian community in Jerusalem resembled the Qumran community.

In 62–63 C.E., the Roman governor of Judea died suddenly while in office, and several months passed before his successor arrived from Rome. In the interim, the Jewish high priest Ananus took advantage of the opportunity to condemn James on charges of violating Jewish law and had him executed by stoning. James' opposition to the wealthy, who of course included the high priests, might explain why Ananus had him put to death, as James was otherwise known as a pious and law-abiding Jew. The possibility that the charges were trumped up is also suggested by the fact that the Pharisees protested James' execution when the new Roman governor arrived, and Ananus was removed from office. Josephus provides a contemporary account of this episode: "so he [Ananus the high priest] assembled the sanhedrin of the judges, and brought before them the brother of Jesus, who was called Christ, whose name was James, and some others [or some of his companions;] and when he had formed an accusation against them as breakers of the law, he delivered them to be stoned" (*Ant.* 20:200).

According to a slightly later source – the second century C.E. church historian **Hegesippus** – James was buried just below the Temple Mount (presumably in the area of the Kidron Valley or Mount of Olives). Hegesippus mentions that in his time the headstone (Greek *stele*) marking the grave could still be seen:

> So they went up and threw down the Just one, and they said to one another, 'Let us stone James the Just,' and they began to stone him since the fall had not killed him. . . . And a certain man among them, one of the laundrymen, took the club with which he used to beat out the clothes, and hit the Just on the head, and so he suffered martyrdom. And they buried him on the spot by the temple, and his gravestone (*stele*) still remains by the temple. (*apud* Eusebius, *Hist. Eccl.* 2.23:15–18; Loeb translation)

Although we do not know whether the grave that Hegesippus mentions contained James' remains, his testimony indicates that within a century of James' death, Christian tradition recalled that he had been buried in a pit grave or trench grave marked by a headstone. This tradition is supported by other evidence. James came from a family of modest means that presumably could not afford a rock-cut tomb. James was the leader of a community whose members lived in communal poverty, and he was known for his ascetic lifestyle and his opposition to the accumulation of wealth and the lifestyle of the wealthy. And unlike Jesus, James did not expire on the cross on the eve of the Sabbath but was executed by the Sanhedrin by stoning, which means there would have been a full twenty-four hours to dispose of his remains. This review of the deaths and burials of Jesus and James concludes our discussion of ancient Jewish tombs and burial customs.

Sidebar: The Talpiyot Tomb

The so-called **Talpiyot tomb** is a modest, single-chamber loculus tomb that was discovered in 1980 during construction work in Jerusalem's East Talpiyot neighborhood. The tomb was excavated on behalf of the Israel Department of Antiquities by Joseph Gat, and a final (scientific) report was published in 1996 by Amos Kloner. Ten ossuaries were found in the tomb, four of which are plain and the other six inscribed (five in Hebrew and one in Greek). The tomb has attracted attention because some of the names on the inscribed ossuaries correspond with figures mentioned in the New Testament in association with Jesus, specifically Yeshua (Jesus), Mariamene (Mary), and Yosé (Joseph). It is mainly on this basis that the claim has been made that this is the [lost] tomb of Jesus and his family – a claim that was the subject of a Discovery

Channel program that was broadcast in March 2007. If the Talpiyot tomb is the tomb of Jesus and his family, it would mean that the Church of the Holy Sepulcher does not enshrine the site of Jesus' crucifixion and burial, a tradition that goes back at least to the time of Constantine (early fourth century C.E.; see Chapter 15). Furthermore, if true, this claim would mean that Jesus was married and had an otherwise unknown son named Judah (as one ossuary is inscribed "Yehudah son of Yeshua"), and that Jesus was not resurrected (as his remains were gathered in an ossuary).

The identification of the Talpiyot tomb as belonging to Jesus' family flies in the face of all available evidence and contradicts the Gospel accounts, which are our earliest sources of information about Jesus' death and burial. This claim is also inconsistent with evidence from these sources indicating that Jesus was a lower-class Jew. Even if we accept the unlikely possibility that Jesus' family had the means to purchase a rock-cut tomb, it would have been located in their hometown of Nazareth, not in Jerusalem. For example, when Simon, the last of the Maccabean brothers and one of the Hasmonean rulers, built a large tomb or mausoleum for his family, he constructed it in their hometown of Modiin, not in Jerusalem. In fact, the Gospel accounts indicate that Jesus' family did not own a rock-cut tomb in Jerusalem – for if they had, there would have been no need for Joseph of Arimathea to take Jesus' body and place it in his own family's rock-cut tomb! If Jesus' family did not own a rock-cut tomb, it means they also had no ossuaries.

A number of scholars, including Kloner, have pointed out that the names on the ossuaries in the Talpiyot tomb were very common among the Jewish population of Jerusalem in the first century. Furthermore, the ossuary inscriptions provide no indication that those interred in this tomb were Galilean (not Judean) in origin. On ossuaries in rock-cut tombs belonging to Judean families it was customary to indicate the ancestry or lineage of the deceased by naming the father, as, for example, Judah son of John (Yohanan); Shimon son of Alexa; and Martha daughter of Hananya. But in rock-cut tombs owned by non-Judean families (or which contained the remains of family members from outside Judea), it was customary to indicate the deceased's place of origin, as, for example, Simon of Ptolemais (Akko/Acre); Papias the Bethshanite (of Beth Shean); and Gaios son of Artemon from Berenike. If the Talpiyot tomb indeed belonged to Jesus' family, we would expect at least some of the ossuary inscriptions to reflect their Galilean origin, by reading, for example, Jesus [son of Joseph] of Nazareth (or Jesus the Nazarene), Mary of Magdala, and so on. However, the inscriptions provide no indication that this is the tomb of a Galilean family and instead point to a Judean family.

The claim that the Talpiyot tomb belongs to Jesus' family is based on a string of problematic and unsubstantiated claims, including adding an otherwise unattested Matthew (Matya) to the family of Jesus (as one ossuary is inscribed with this name); identifying an otherwise unknown son of Jesus named Judah (and assuming that Jesus was married); and identifying the Mariamene named on one of the ossuaries in the tomb as Mary Magdalene by interpreting the word *Mara* (which follows the name Mariamene) as the Aramaic term for "master" (arguing that Mariamene was a teacher and leader). To account for the fact that Mary/Mariamene's name is written in Greek, the filmmakers who produced the Discovery Channel documentary transform the small Jewish town of **Migdal/Magdala/Tarichaea** on the Sea of Galilee (Mary's hometown) into an important trading center where Greek was spoken. Instead, as in other Jewish towns of this period, generally only the upper classes knew Greek, whereas lower class Jews spoke Aramaic as their everyday language. Individually, each of these points weakens the case for the identification of the Talpiyot tomb as the tomb of Jesus' family, but collectively they are devastating.

To conclude, the identification of the Talpiyot tomb as the tomb of Jesus and his family contradicts the canonical Gospel accounts of the death and burial of Jesus and the earliest Christian traditions about Jesus. This claim is also inconsistent with all available information – historical and archaeological – about how Jews in the time of Jesus buried their dead, and specifically the evidence we have about lower-class, non-Judean families such as that of Jesus. Finally, the fact that not a single ancient source preserves any reference to or tradition about any tomb associated with Jesus aside from Joseph of Arimathea's is a loud silence indeed, especially as Paul's writings and some sources of the synoptic Gospel accounts antedate 70 C.E. Had Jesus' family owned a rock-cut tomb in Jerusalem, presumably some of his followers would have preserved the memory of its existence (if not its location), and venerated the site. In fact, our earliest sources contradict the identification of the Talpiyot tomb as the tomb of Jesus and his family. For example, Hegesippus refers to James' grave in the second century C.E. – but he seems to describe a pit grave or trench grave marked by a headstone (as discussed earlier), and makes no reference to James having been interred with his brother Jesus in a rock-cut family tomb.

Sidebar: The James Ossuary

The so-called **James ossuary** is an ossuary with an Aramaic inscription that reads, "James son of Joseph brother of Jesus." Whereas there is little doubt that the ossuary is authentic and ancient, the inscription is the subject of an ongoing controversy. The problem is that the ossuary was not discovered by archaeologists, but surfaced in 2002 in the hands of an antiquities collector

11.9 The "James ossuary." Courtesy of Zev Radovan/BibleLandPictures.com.

in Israel. Put into "CSI" terms, this means that there is no chain of custody. The ossuary presumably was looted (illegally excavated) and was purchased by the collector on the antiquities market. Without scientific documentation describing the ossuary's original appearance and context, it is impossible to determine whether the inscription is authentic and ancient, or whether all or part of the inscription is a modern forgery – added to enhance the value of the ossuary after its discovery or purchase.

The evidence that James was buried in a pit grave or trench grave renders moot the controversy surrounding the James ossuary. Even if the inscription is authentic, it could not refer to James the Just, the brother of Jesus. Ossuaries were introduced into rock-cut tombs to collect the remains removed from loculi. Ossuaries are not associated with pit graves or trench graves, as there was no reason to exhume the remains and place them in an ossuary in order to make space for new burials. Instead, new graves were dug as the need arose. In other words, if the inscription on the James ossuary is authentic and ancient, it must refer to another individual, not James the Just, the brother of Jesus. This is certainly possible, as the names James (Hebrew Yaakov/Jacob), Jesus (Hebrew Yeshua/Joshua), and Joseph (Hebrew Yosef or Yose) were common among the Jewish population of the late Second Temple period. In fact, it has been estimated that at least twenty different individuals in first-century C.E. Jerusalem could have had this combination of names.

Sidebar: Beth Shearim

The ancient Jewish town of **Beth Shearim** in lower Galilee is known for its extensive necropolis of rock-cut catacombs, which were excavated by the Israeli archaeologists Benjamin Mazar (in the 1930s) and Nahman Avigad (in the 1950s). Rabbi Judah ha-Nasi, the editor of the Mishnah (the corpus of Jewish oral law), resided at Beth Shearim (where the Sanhedrin met) for much of his life, and was brought to Beth Shearim for burial after he died at Sepphoris. Thanks to Judah ha-Nasi's presence (and the fact that Aelia Capitolina was off-limits to Jews; see Chapter 13), during the third and fourth centuries Beth Shearim became the largest and most prestigious Jewish cemetery in Palestine. Inscriptions found in the catacombs indicate that wealthy Jews were brought to Beth Shearim for burial from as far away as Mesopotamia and Syria. Some of the individuals mentioned in the inscriptions have titles such as "rabbi," "priest," and "leader of the synagogue," indicating their high status.

The necropolis of Beth Shearim includes dozens of catacombs (large burial caves), which were hewn into the slopes of the nearby hills. The catacombs contain numerous halls that held hundreds of burials. Many of the catacombs at Beth Shearim belonged to individual families, but some contained burials of different elite families. The use of loculi and the custom of collecting bones in ossuaries are still attested in the burial halls, although on a limited basis. The prevailing burial rite consists of individual inhumation in large stone sarcophagi placed on the floors of the burial halls or in troughs cut into the walls and floors of the caves. Most of the sarcophagi are made of local limestone, with a few imports of marble. Some of the sarcophagi are decorated with crude figured reliefs, including depictions of bulls, lions, birds, fish, and winged Victories. Jewish symbols and ritual objects such as menorahs are also carved on some of the sarcophagi and on the walls of the burial halls.

An extensive necropolis consisting of catacombs that is similar to and contemporary with Beth Shearim was recently excavated at Beth Guvrin (near Marisa) in southern Judea. Around 200 C.E., **Beth Guvrin** was refounded as a Roman city called **Eleutheropolis**. Although by this time most of the Jewish population of Palestine lived in Galilee and the Golan, there was a significant concentration of Jews in the towns and villages of southern Judea – a region they called the *Darom* ("south"). The burial customs at Beth Shearim and Beth Guvrin parallel contemporary developments in Rome and the provinces during the second and third centuries, when inhumation in large stone sarcophagi in catacombs supplanted cremation as the preferred burial rite. In other words, just as Jewish tombs and burial customs before 70 C.E. reflect foreign influence on the wealthy Jews of Jerusalem, after the Bar-Kokhba Revolt the Jewish elites of Galilee and southern Judea adopted prevailing Roman rites and fashions.

Recommended Reading

Elizabeth Bloch-Smith, *Judahite Burial Practices and Beliefs about the Dead* (Sheffield, UK: Sheffield Academic, 1992).

Raymond E. Brown, *The Death of the Messiah from Gethsemane to the Grave: A Commentary on the Passion Narratives in the Four Gospels, Vols. 1–2* (New York: Doubleday, 1994).

David Chapman, *Ancient Jewish and Christian Perceptions of Crucifixion* (Tübingen, Germany: Mohr Siebeck, 2008).

Craig A. Evans, *Jesus and the Ossuaries: What Jewish Burial Practices Reveal about the Beginning of Christianity* (Waco, TX: Baylor University, 2003).

Amos Kloner and Boaz Zissu, *The Necropolis of Jerusalem in the Second Temple Period* (Leuven, the Netherlands: Peeters, 2007).

Jodi Magness, *Stone and Dung, Oil and Spit: Jewish Daily Life in the Time of Jesus* (Grand Rapids, MI: Eerdmans, 2011).

Byron McCane, *Roll Back the Stone: Death and Burial in the World of Jesus* (Harrisburg, PA: Trinity Press International, 2003).

TWELVE

FROM 70 C.E. TO THE BAR-KOKHBA REVOLT (132–135/136 C.E.)

THE SECOND JEWISH REVOLT AGAINST THE ROMANS

Historical Background: General

The Julio-Claudian dynasty, which was established by Augustus, came to an end with Nero's death in 68 C.E. Vespasian was proclaimed emperor in 69 C.E. and established the Flavian dynasty. He was succeeded by his sons Titus (who had overseen the siege of Jerusalem) and Domitian. The Flavians used their victory over the Jews to legitimize their newly founded dynasty. They filled Rome with victory monuments commemorating the "Jewish war," including the Colosseum (Flavian amphitheater) and the arch of Titus. They also broadcast their victory on a special series of coins bearing the legend "Judea Capta," which depict the province of Judea as a mourning woman (see Chapter 7). After the destruction of the Jerusalem temple, the Jews were required to pay the annual temple tax to the Capitolium in Rome.

The Flavian dynasty came to an end with Domitian, an unpopular ruler who was assassinated in 96 C.E. The Roman Senate nominated the next emperor, an elderly but highly regarded statesman named Nerva. Nerva established the long-lived **Antonine dynasty**, but ruled only two years before dying of natural causes. He was succeeded by his adopted heir, **Trajan**, the first Roman emperor from the provinces (Spain), although he was born to an Italian family. Trajan was a popular emperor who enjoyed a long and successful reign (98–117 C.E.). An accomplished general, Trajan spent much of his time on military campaigns. He added the province of Dacia (modern Romania) to the Roman Empire, using the spoils to fund a building program in Rome that included a sprawling marketplace complex. Trajan also added to the Roman Empire the province of Arabia, which included the Nabataean kingdom (106 C.E.). To remove the lucrative trade in incense and spices from Nabataean control, the Romans shifted the caravan trade routes to the north, out of Nabataean territory. As a result, many former Nabataean trading posts became permanent settlements surrounded by desert farms, as the Nabataeans turned to agriculture for their livelihoods.

Trajan was succeeded to the throne by a relative named Hadrian, who was also born to an Italian family living in Spain (ruled 117–138 C.E.). Hadrian was a Philhellene – a lover of Greek culture and philosophy – so much so, that he was sometimes referred to by the Latin nickname "Graeculus" (Little Greek). He lavished monuments and other benefactions on Athens, which had lost its claim to cultural supremacy and was a relatively impoverished, provincial backwater. Athens reciprocated by proclaiming Hadrian a "second Theseus" – that is, a second founder or refounder of the city.

Hadrian was an amateur architect who enjoyed designing his own buildings. His most famous monument, the **Pantheon**, or temple of all gods, still stands in Rome today. The Pantheon literally turned the concept of an ancient temple inside out. Using the latest innovations in Roman concrete technology, Hadrian created a huge domed space, shifting the focus of temples from the exterior to the interior. The dome had a large opening (*oculus*) in the center, through which the sun and heavens were visible above. Hadrian also designed a sprawling country villa at Tivoli outside Rome, periodically adding new buildings that were inspired by his travels. Although Hadrian is known for constructing a fortification wall in Britain that bears his name (Hadrian's Wall), aside from the Bar-Kokhba Revolt, his reign was generally peaceful.

Historical Background: Palestine

After 70 C.E., Jerusalem lay in ruins. To strengthen their hold over the country, the Romans changed the structure of the administration. The province of Judea was made independent of Syria and placed under the control of its own legate, and the Tenth Legion was stationed in Jerusalem. These measures ensured that a legate commanding a legion were always present to keep order. Because Josephus' accounts end with the First Revolt, we have much less information about Judean life for the period after 70 C.E. For information we must rely on rabbinic literature and incidental references by classical (Greek and Roman) authors and the Church Fathers.

After Jerusalem's destruction, Jewish scholars (experts in Jewish law) established an academy in the southern coastal town of **Jamnia** (Hebrew **Yavneh**), under the leadership of Rabbi **Yohanan Ben Zakkai** (ca. 1–80 C.E.) and his successor, Gamaliel II (ca. 80–120). Yohanan Ben Zakkai is said to have faked his own death during the siege of Jerusalem and was smuggled out of the city in a coffin. He became the first *Nasi* (Prince or **Patriarch**) of the academy, which replaced the Sanhedrin as the body responsible for administering Jewish law.

After 70, the Jews awaited permission from the Romans to rebuild the Jerusalem temple. They expected this to happen soon, and never imagined Judaism without a temple 2,000 years later. After all, only sixty years had passed between the destruction of the first temple and its replacement by the second temple. But as the decades passed after 70 and Roman permission was not forthcoming, the Jews of Palestine and the Diaspora became increasingly anxious.

The Diaspora Revolt (115–117 C.E.)

Toward the end of Trajan's reign, a Jewish revolt erupted among Jewish communities in the Diaspora. In contrast to the First Jewish Revolt against the Romans, we have little information about the **Diaspora Revolt**. The unrest started in Egypt and spread to Cyrene (North Africa), Cyprus, and Mesopotamia. The revolt seems to have been fueled by messianic expectations, perhaps under the leadership of a messianic figure named Lucas. Pent-up hostilities between Jews and Gentiles were also a factor. The uprising lasted for three years and seems to have been brutally suppressed. The Jews of Egypt, including the large and well-established community at Alexandria, were especially hard hit.

The Bar-Kokhba Revolt (Second Jewish Revolt against the Romans) (132–135/136 C.E.)

Historical Background

Hadrian spent much of his reign traveling around the Roman provinces. In 129–130 C.E. he toured Syria-Palestine and visited Jerusalem, which was still in ruins. Hadrian decided to rebuild Jerusalem, but as a pagan Roman city called Aelia Capitolina (see Chapter 13), with a temple to Capitoline Jupiter on the Temple Mount. Hadrian's decision was a crushing blow to Jewish expectations. In 132 C.E., the Jews of Judea rose up in revolt. The Second Jewish Revolt against the Romans was led by a messianic figure – **Simeon bar Kosiba** (Bar-Kokhba) – who reportedly was supported by the highly respected Rabbi Akiba.

Most of the limited historical information that we have about the Bar-Kokhba Revolt comes from a third-century C.E. Roman author named **Cassius Dio**. In fact, before the discovery of documents from the Judean Desert (discussed later), we did not even know Bar-Kokhba's real name. His followers called him Bar-Kokhba – the son of a star – alluding to his messianic status. But rabbinic literature refers to him as Bar-Koziba – the son of a liar or deceiver – because he was a false messiah who led a failed revolt.

The Jewish rebels learned the lessons of the First Revolt and enjoyed early success against the Romans. Instead of engaging the Romans in open battle

Sidebar: Capitoline Jupiter and the God of Israel

Although the Romans worshiped a pantheon of gods, their chief deity was Capitoline Jupiter (who they identified with the Greek Olympian Zeus). Capitoline Jupiter is so called because his ancient temple was located on the Capitoline Hill in Rome. The Jews were similar to the Greeks and Romans in having a supreme deity – the God of Israel – whom they worshiped as their national god. However, unlike other ancient peoples, Jews believed that the God of Israel would not tolerate the worship of other gods alongside him. Therefore the Jews worshiped only one god, whereas other ancient peoples worshiped numerous gods. Many Greeks and Romans equated or identified the God of Israel with their supreme deity. This explains why Antiochus IV Epiphanes rededicated the second temple to Olympian Zeus (sparking the outbreak of the Maccabean revolt), and why Hadrian established a shrine or temple to Capitoline Jupiter on Jerusalem's Temple Mount.

or attempting to hold out under siege, they conducted a campaign of guerilla warfare. The Jewish population dug warrens of underground tunnels and took advantage of natural caves around the countryside. Whole villages could disappear from view in these hiding places, which also served as bases from which Jewish insurgents could ambush Roman troops under cover of night. The Roman army was not trained in this kind of warfare, and as a result suffered many casualties, including the loss of an entire legion (the XXII Deiotariana). Hadrian ended up sending a third of the Roman army to Judea to suppress the revolt.

Inevitably, the tide turned against the Jews. The Roman historian Cassius Dio reported that 580,000 Jews were killed, and 50 fortified towns and 985 villages were destroyed. Although it is impossible to assess the accuracy of these numbers, they give an impression of the revolt's impact. Most of the fighting took place in Judea, with the Jews in other parts of Palestine participating little or not at all (although recent archaeological discoveries suggest the possible involvement of Jews in Galilee). One of the long-term consequences of the Bar-Kokhba Revolt is that many of the Jewish settlements in Judea were obliterated, and in the following centuries most of the Jewish population of Palestine was concentrated in the north (Galilee and the Golan). The Bar-Kokhba Revolt ended when the last stronghold, **Bethar** (near Bethlehem) fell to the Romans and Bar-Kokhba was killed. Although according to Jewish tradition this occurred on the ninth of Av (August) in 135 C.E., recent studies suggest that the revolt ended the following year.

The Bar-Kokhba Revolt was as disastrous for the Jews as the First Revolt. First, it took a terrible toll in human lives, with Judea hit especially hard. Second, the revolt sealed the fate of the Jerusalem temple, ensuring that it would not be rebuilt in the foreseeable future. Hadrian proceeded to rebuild Jerusalem as a pagan Roman city with a shrine or temple to Capitoline Jupiter on the Temple Mount, and prohibited Jews from living in the city and its environs (a prohibition that seems to have been in force at least through the reign of the emperor Antoninus Pius, who died in 161). To further punish the Jews, Hadrian instituted bans restricting or prohibiting some Jewish practices, such as circumcision and sabbath observance. For the first time, Jews living under Roman rule were subject to persecution under the law for practicing their religion. Finally, to obliterate the memory of this troublesome people, Hadrian changed the name of the province from Judea to Syria-Palaestina, reviving the name of the ancient kingdom of Philistia.

Archaeology

Archaeology provides valuable information about the Bar-Kokhba Revolt, supplementing the meager information from our historical sources. The most important finds were made in the wake of the discovery of the Dead Sea Scrolls (see Chapter 6). After the discovery of the first scrolls in caves around Qumran, Bedouins broadened their search for scrolls around the Dead Sea, eventually crossing into Israeli territory around Ein Gedi. As a result, an Israeli expedition was organized in 1960–61 to explore the southwest shore of the Dead Sea between Ein Gedi and Masada (see Figure 6.1). The rugged cliffs along the shoreline are cut by deep riverbeds (canyons) that empty into the Dead Sea. The Israelis divided the canyons among different teams of archaeologists. Yigael Yadin was assigned the great canyon of **Nahal Hever**, which yielded spectacular finds from the time of the Bar-Kokhba Revolt. These finds came from two caves: the **Cave of Letters** on the north bank of the canyon, and the **Cave of Horror** on the south bank. Access to both caves is difficult and sometimes treacherous, along narrow, uneven paths perched above steep drops of hundreds of feet to the riverbed below. As former chief of staff, Yadin used his connections

12.1 View of Nahal David at Ein Gedi, looking west.

with the Israeli army to have equipment airlifted to the remote desert location by helicopters. Excavation inside the caves was just as challenging because of the stifling heat, lack of air, and suffocating clouds of fine dust and bat guano churned up by even the slightest movement.

During the Bar-Kokhba Revolt, Jewish families from Ein Gedi fled their homes and hid from the Romans in nearby caves. Nahman Avigad, another member of the Israeli team whose assignment was to explore **Nahal David** at Ein Gedi, discovered a cave in the uppermost reaches of this canyon. Avigad called it the **Cave of the Pool** because the refugees constructed a cistern for storing water by the entrance. Thanks to the water supply and the cave's remote, well-hidden location, the refugees left the cave while still alive and took with them their personal possessions. For this reason, the Cave of the Pool was relatively poor in archaeological finds. The Jewish families who took refuge in the Cave of Letters and Cave of Horror in Nahal Hever were not so lucky. Their location was discovered by the Romans, who besieged the caves. Without a water supply (as in the Cave of the Pool) or access to water, the refugees starved to death inside the caves. Their physical remains and personal belongings remained in the caves, discovered 2,000 years later. In fact, the Cave of Horror is so called because when Yadin's team first entered it, they found ancient woven baskets filled with skulls and other skeletal parts. Apparently these remains were collected by relatives of the refugee families, who presumably visited the caves after the revolt ended.

12.2 Wooden plate and bowl from the Cave of Letters, Judean desert, second century C.E. Collection of the Israel Antiquities Authority. Photo © The Israel Museum, Jerusalem.

When Yadin began his excavations in the Cave of Letters and Cave of Horror, he found that the Bedouins had preceded him, as indicated by cigarette wrappers and other modern litter. We do not know what the Bedouins removed from these caves. Fortunately, however, the Jewish refugees had carefully deposited their most prized possessions in hiding places around the caves. These were discovered by Yadin's team, and they include a wide range of artifacts that shed light on everyday Jewish life during the Roman period. Thanks to the arid desert environment, artifacts made of perishable organic materials, such as wood, cloth, woven baskets, and leather, survived (the same conditions preserved the Dead Sea Scrolls in the caves around Qumran farther to the north).

Most of the finds – and the most important finds – come from the Cave of Letters. They include wooden bowls and plates, the shapes of which resemble the pottery vessels so commonly found on archaeological excavations. The wooden dishes were well used, as indicated by the knife marks showing they had been scraped clean repeatedly. There was also a set of kitchen knives in different sizes, with their wooden handles still attached. Exquisite glass plates that had been treasured by their owners were wrapped carefully in palm fibers. Thanks to the arid environment the surface is transparent, not encrusted with the shimmery patina that commonly covers ancient glass. A rare cache of nineteen bronze vessels, including bowls, jugs, and incense shovels, was wrapped and

12.3 Glass plates from the Cave of Letters, Judean desert with their original palm fiber wrapping, second century C.E. Collection of the Israel Antiquities Authority. Photo © The Israel Museum, Jerusalem.

hidden in a woven basket. The high quality and figured decoration indicate that these vessels were made in Italy and brought to Judea, presumably by a Roman soldier. Yadin suggested that a Jewish contingent took the vessels as spoils after ambushing Roman troops. The Jews then defaced the figures by rubbing out the features. This ancient damage is evident on a bronze *patera* (a handled bowl for pouring liquid offerings called *libations*) from the cache, which has a medallion showing Thetis, the sea nymph who was the mother of the Greek hero Achilles.

The finds from the Cave of Letters also included women's toiletry items, such as a wooden jewelry box closed with a small latch (which unfortunately was empty), and a mirror in its original wooden case. Like other ancient mirrors, this one is not made of glass but instead consists of a polished, thin bronze disc. One of the most poignant discoveries is a set of keys, indicating that these Jewish families had locked their houses before taking refuge in the cave. The keys are crooked and have teeth because they worked by lifting a deadbolt on the inside of the door out of its place.

A number of pieces of clothing were also found in the Cave of Letters, consisting mostly of tunics and **mantles**. Tunics and mantles were the standard articles of clothing worn by men and women throughout the Roman world. The mantle – a type of cloak worn over the tunic – consisted of a large rectangular sheet (Greek

12.4 Bronze jugs from the Cave of Letters, Judean desert, second century C.E. Collection of the Israel Antiquities Authority. Photo © The Israel Museum, Jerusalem.

himation; Latin *pallium*; Hebrew *tallit* or *me'il*). In contrast, the Roman **toga** had a curved hem and was a ceremonial garment restricted to male citizens. The tunic (Greek *chiton*; Hebrew *haluq*) was a rectangular piece of cloth with two parallel bands or stripes (*clavi*) of a different color that descended from the shoulder and indicated the wearer's rank. The length of the tunic varied depending on the wearer. For example, soldiers and slaves wore tunics at or above the knee to allow for mobility, whereas women and priests wore ankle-length tunics. Slits were left in the tunic for the head and arms. Sleeves could be added separately or formed by making the tunic wide and baggy. Tunics could be worn loose or belted at the waist (usually with cord, except for soldiers, who had leather belts). Wearing a belt allowed the tunic to be draped at different lengths.

Except for one linen child's shirt or tunic, the tunics and mantles from the Cave of Letters are made of wool, some of them dyed in different colors and patterns. Although both men and women wore the same articles of clothing, women tended to dress more colorfully. Women also gathered their hair into hairnets, remains of which were found in the Cave of Letters. The clothing from the Cave of Letters provides a valuable glimpse into the appearance of the local Jewish population. There are even examples of footwear, consisting of strapped leather sandals with a thong separating the large toe from the others, which appear strikingly contemporary in design.

12.5 Wool mantle from the Cave of Letters, second century C.E. Collection of the Israel Antiquities Authority. Photo © The Israel Museum, Jerusalem.

Whereas the Jews who took refuge in the Cave of Letters wore wool garments, full members of the Qumran sect seem to have clothed themselves in linen tunics and mantles. Linen garments are usually plain (white) because linen is difficult to dye. The clothing of the Essenes – like other aspects of their lifestyle – was adopted from the priests in the Jerusalem temple, who wore all-linen garments. The Essenes even wore a linen loincloth under the tunic, an item that was worn by the Jerusalem priests to prevent the exposure of the genitals when they ascended the altar to offer sacrifices. Most people in the Roman world – including Jews – wore nothing under their tunics (similar to Scottish kilts).

The finds from the Cave of Letters include ancient scrolls that provide valuable information about the Bar-Kokhba Revolt. In contrast to the Dead Sea Scrolls

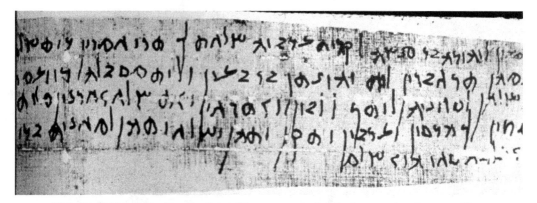

12.6 Bar-Kokhba letter from the Cave of Letters, requesting the four species. Courtesy of Zev Radovan/BibleLandPictures.com.

from Qumran, the scrolls from the Cave of Letters are personal documents that belonged to individuals who took refuge in the cave. Most are written on papyrus (whereas nearly all of the Dead Sea Scrolls are of parchment), and they are in a variety of languages, including Hebrew, Aramaic, Nabataean, and Greek. Among the documents are letters that were written by Bar-Kokhba to his commanders and followers at Ein Gedi and elsewhere. For example, one letter opens: "From Simeon Bar Kosiba to the people of Ein Gedi, shalom (peace)." In another letter, Bar-Kokhba requests that palm branches, citrons, myrtles, and willows – the four species used for celebrating the holiday of **Sukkot (Feast of Tabernacles)** – be sent to him. These documents supplement our meager historical information about the Bar-Kokhba revolt and shed light on the revolt's leader. In fact, it was from these documents that we first learned his real name, as historical sources use nicknames (Bar-Kokhba [son of a star] or Bar-Koziba [son of a liar or deceiver]).

The scrolls from the Cave of Letters also shed light on the lives of the individuals who took refuge in the cave and ultimately died there. They include a remarkable woman named **Babatha**, who came from a village at the southern end of the Dead Sea, in Nabataea. Babatha's second husband, Yehudah (Judah), was from Ein Gedi, which is the reason she ended up in the Cave of Letters with the other refugees. Babatha was an educated and an illiterate but savvy woman who kept all her personal documents (thirty-five documents, including a marriage contract and deeds to land) neatly organized and tied in a bundle. Yehudah had died several years before the Bar-Kokhba Revolt broke out. From the documents we learn that Babatha was involved in lengthy litigation with members of Yehudah's family (including his other wife, Miriam) over his property. The Babatha archive helps fill a gap in our knowledge about the lives of women in the Roman East.

The families that took refuge in the Cave of Letters seem to have been prosperous villagers, judging from their possessions and personal documents.

12.7 *Darom* oil lamps. Courtesy of Zev Radovan/BibleLandPictures.com.

After the Romans discovered the caves, they established two siege camps at the edges of the cliffs just above each cave. Not only did these camps block potential escape routes, but they also provided views of the cave in the opposite cliff, enabling the Romans to monitor the movements of the besieged. Unable to escape the caves or bring in food and water, the families starved to death, only to have their remains and personal possessions discovered by Yadin's team two thousand years later.

Material Culture

Oil Lamps

The pottery types that were common in Judea before 70 C.E. continued with few changes in the following decades. However, Herodian oil lamps were replaced by a new type: *Darom* (southern) oil lamps. *Darom* lamps are similar in shape to Herodian oil lamps, having a round body with short, flaring nozzle. But unlike Herodian oil lamps, which are wheel-made and plain, *Darom* lamps are mold-made and decorated. The decoration consists of delicate, linear designs, including floral and geometric motifs such as grapevines and grape bunches, and objects from everyday life such as agricultural implements and household vessels. Jewish ritual objects such as menorahs (seven-branched candelabra) are also depicted. A small, raised round handle is attached to the back of the lamp.

12.8 Bar-Kokhba coins. Courtesy of Zev Radovan/BibleLandPictures.com.

Coins

As was the case of the First Revolt, during the Bar-Kokhba Revolt the Jews minted their own coins as a proclamation of independence. And like the coins of the First Revolt, the Bar-Kokhba Revolt coins carry symbols and slogans

12.9 Bar-Kokhba coin showing the temple façade. Courtesy of Zev Radovan/BibleLand Pictures.com.

Sidebar: The Green Line

After the British Mandate ended in 1947, Palestine was partitioned. The state of Israel was established in 1948, encompassing the area from Galilee on the north to the Negev desert in the south. The territory along the western side of the Jordan River and the northwest shore of the Dead Sea was under Jordanian rule from 1948 until 1967, when Israel took this territory during the Six-Day War. This territory is sometimes called the West Bank (referring to the west bank of the Jordan River), the Occupied Territories (occupied by Israel since 1967), and Judea and Samaria (a revival of the ancient names of these districts that is preferred by some Jews and Israelis). The border between the territories that were under Israeli and Jordanian rule between 1948 and 1967 is called the Green Line. The Green Line divided Jerusalem into two halves, and terminated to the south just above Ein Gedi. In other words, between 1948 and 1967 Jerusalem was a divided city: East Jerusalem belonged to Jordan and West Jerusalem belonged to Israel.

Archaeology is inextricably bound up with complex, current political realities. For example, the site of Qumran was excavated (and most of the Dead Sea Scrolls were found) when the West Bank was under Jordanian rule, and de Vaux's excavations were conducted under the auspices of the Jordanian government. Therefore, any eventual political settlement will have to decide who has the legal rights to the Dead Sea Scrolls and the archaeological finds from de Vaux's excavations at Qumran: Israel (which currently has possession of the site of Qumran and most of the scrolls), the Palestinians (assuming a Palestinian state is established in this region), or Jordan. Protestors at a recent exhibit of the Dead Sea Scrolls at the Royal Ontario Museum in Toronto, Canada, claimed that Israel has no legal right to the scrolls and therefore is not entitled to export them for exhibit. Another example: excavations conducted by Israelis in parts of East Jerusalem, such as the City of David and the area around the Temple Mount, have been the subject of controversy because some argue that the Israelis do not have legal rights to this land, as it was taken during war and was not ceded to them as part of a negotiated settlement.

alluding to Jerusalem and the temple. The Bar-Kokhba rebels increased the insult to Rome by overstriking (reminting) Roman coins. Frequently the original Roman designs and inscriptions are visible beneath those added by the Jewish rebels. These coins, decorated with sacred vessels such as chalices and kraters, instruments such as trumpets and lyres, and ritual objects such as the *lulav* and *ethrog* clearly proclaimed the revolt's goal – the overthrow of Roman rule, the reestablishment of Jewish independence under the leadership of a messianic figure, and the rebuilding of the Jerusalem temple. One series of coins is decorated with the earliest surviving depiction of the Jerusalem temple. Some Jews living at the time of the Bar-Kokhba Revolt would have remembered the appearance of the temple, which had been destroyed a little more than sixty years earlier. Therefore, scholars assume that this depiction accurately depicts the main features of the second temple. The coin shows a flat-roofed building with four columns in front, framing an arched element that might be a doorway or the showbread table inside.

Like the coins of the First Revolt, the Bar Kokhba coins are inscribed in the paleo-Hebrew script with Hebrew-language slogans alluding to Jerusalem and the temple, such as "for the freedom of Jerusalem" or "Jerusalem" (the latter surrounds the depiction of the temple façade). Some coins are inscribed with the name of the revolt's leader, Simeon. Others are inscribed "Eleazar the priest," implying that Bar-Kokhba was planning ahead and had appointed a high priest to officiate in the rebuilt temple. However, there is no evidence that construction of a temple building commenced before the revolt ended. In fact, recent studies suggest that the Jewish rebels never managed to gain control of Jerusalem (which was occupied by the Tenth Legion when the revolt began).

Recommended Reading

Hanan Eshel, "The Bar Kochba Revolt, 132–135," in Steven T. Katz (ed.), *The Cambridge History of Judaism, Volume IV, The Late Roman–Rabbinic Period* (New York: Cambridge University, 2006), 105–27.

Miriam Pucci Ben Zeev, *Diaspora Judaism in Turmoil, 116/117 C.E.: Ancient Sources and Modern Insights* (Leuven, the Netherlands: Peeters, 2005).

Peter Schäfer (ed.), *The Bar Kokhba War Reconsidered* (Tübingen, Germany: Mohr Siebeck, 2003).

Yigael Yadin, *Bar-Kokhba: The Rediscovery of the Legendary Hero of the Second Jewish Revolt against Rome* (London: Weidenfeld and Nicholson, 1971).

THIRTEEN

AELIA CAPITOLINA (HADRIANIC JERUSALEM) (135 TO CA. 300 C.E.)

After brutally suppressing the Bar-Kokhba Revolt, Hadrian proceeded with his plans to rebuild Jerusalem as a pagan Roman city called Aelia Capitolina. Hadrian, whose full name was Publius Aelius Hadrianus, followed the precedent established by Alexander the Great centuries earlier and gave the refounded city his own name. Capitolina refers to Capitoline Jupiter, who replaced the God of Israel as the city's patron deity. The name Aelia stuck for centuries; even under Muslim rule (after 640 C.E.), the city sometimes was referred to as "Ilya." Aelia Capitolina was a pagan city in more than name alone. In punishment for the Bar-Kokhba Revolt, Hadrian prohibited Jews from living in Aelia Capitolina and its environs, a ban that remained in effect for at least a couple of generations. Instead, Hadrian populated the city with Roman military veterans. The Tenth Legion was stationed in Aelia Capitolina until the emperor **Diocletian** transferred it to Aila (modern ʿAqaba) on the Red Sea around 300 C.E.

Hadrian gave Aelia Capitolina a typical Roman city plan: a roughly square layout, with the four sides of the square oriented toward the cardinal points, and one main gate in the center of each side. These gates gave access to two main roads that bisected the city from north to south and east to west, and intersected in the center. Other roads were laid out parallel to the two main roads, creating a grid of streets running north-south and east-west. The Romans called a north-south road a *cardo*, and an east-west road a *decumanus*. The main north-south road was the **cardo maximus**, and the main east-west road was the **decumanus maximus**. This type of city plan is related to the layout of Roman military camps, like those at Masada. It represents an adaptation of the Hippodamian town plan common in the Hellenistic world, which had a grid of streets running north-south and east-west, but did not have a regular (square) layout or two main roads bisecting the city.

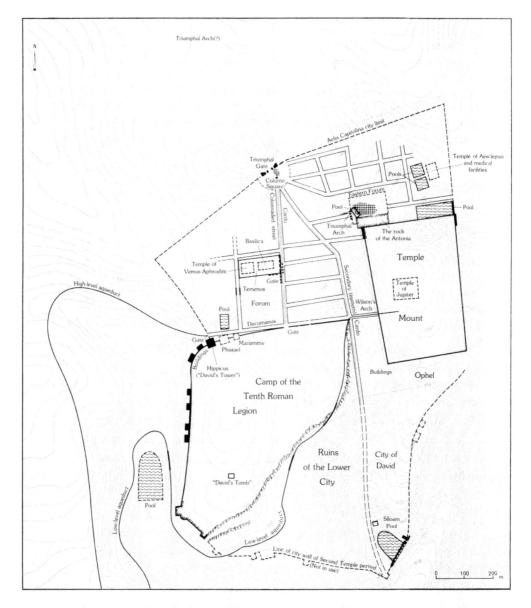

13.1 Plan of Aelia Capitolina. From E. Stern (ed.), *The New Encyclopedia of Archaeological Excavations in the Holy Land* (New York: Simon and Schuster, 1993), vol. 2, p. 758. By permission of Hillel Geva and the Israel Exploration Society.

Valuable evidence for the layout and appearance of Aelia Capitolina comes from the **Madaba map**, a map of the Holy Land that decorates the mosaic floor of a Byzantine church in the town of Madaba in Jordan. Jerusalem is prominently depicted in the center of the map in some detail (but without the City of David, which is not preserved). Although the map depicts the Holy Land around 600 C.E., when the mosaic was laid (and therefore depicts monuments

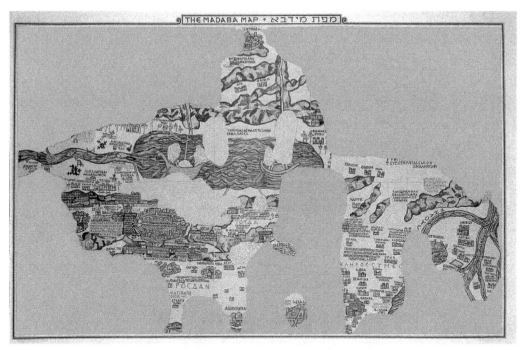

13.2 The Madaba map. Courtesy of Zev Radovan/BibleLandPictures.com.

and features that were added after Hadrian's time), it is an important source for Aelia Capitolina because the city did not experience any major destructions or reconstructions in the intervening 400 to 500 years. In fact, the modern Old City of Jerusalem still preserves the main elements of Aelia Capitolina, because never again was the city razed and rebuilt from scratch. These elements, which can be seen on the map, include the main gate at the northern end of the city, the *cardo maximus* and a second main *cardo*, and the *decumanus maximus*. Because the city has been occupied continuously, the ground level has risen, so that the Roman period northern gate and streets lie buried beneath those of the modern Old City. These elements are preserved in the layout of the modern Old City because city gates and streets are public property. Although the encroachment of shopkeepers over the centuries transformed the broad Roman colonnaded boulevards into narrow Middle Eastern alleys, the streets could not be taken over by private individuals. Over time the ground level rose as debris accumulated and the streets were repaved, but the lines of the streets have remained the same.

THE NORTHERN GATE AND MAIN STREETS OF AELIA CAPITOLINA

Typical of ancient maps, the Madaba map is oriented with east (the direction of the rising sun) at the top. It shows the northern entrance to the city (on the

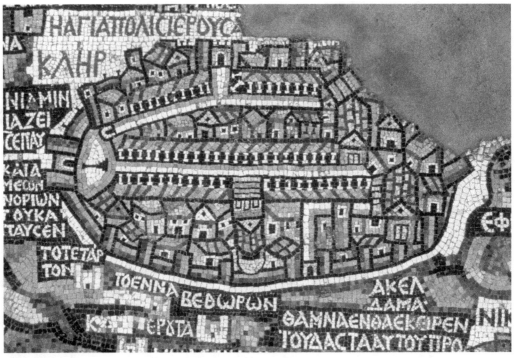

13.3 Jerusalem in the Madaba map. Courtesy of Zev Radovan/BibleLandPictures.com.

left) dominated by a gate with an arched passageway flanked by two towers. This is the site of the modern (Ottoman) Damascus Gate, which is built over the remains of the Roman gate. In Hadrian's time the gate consisted of three arched passageways – a large central passage flanked by two smaller ones, with towers on either side – but by the time the map was made, the side passages were blocked and only the central one was still in use. Today, the remains of the Hadrianic gate are visible under the modern Damascus Gate. Steps leading from the street on the north side of the Old City show how much the ground level has risen since the sixteenth century, when the current gate was constructed.

Out of the three original (Hadrianic) arched passageways, only the small eastern one has survived, with its flanking tower. The gate and tower are constructed of Herodian style stones (large ashlars with drafted margins and flat paneled bosses) in secondary use. Aelia Capitolina's monuments typically incorporate reused Herodian stones, which were readily available because they belonged to buildings that had been lying in ruins since 70 C.E. One stone just above the keystone of the passageway's arch bears a battered Latin inscription on its lower margin that reads, "by the decree of the city council of Aelia Capitolina." The Hadrianic triple-arched gate was originally a free-standing monument, and only later (in the fourth century C.E.) was it incorporated into a city wall (discussed later). The Romans often erected free-standing gates to

13.4 Remains of the Hadrianic gate at the Damascus Gate (lower left). Courtesy of Zev Radovan/BibleLandPictures.com.

mark entrances to public spaces or as commemorative monuments. For example, the arch of Titus is a free-standing victory monument that straddles the Sacred Way at the entrance to the Roman Forum.

The Madaba map shows a large oval plaza just inside the Hadrianic gate on the north side of the city. Although the ground level has risen since then, there is still an open area inside the modern Damascus Gate. Originally, the oval plaza (which was paved with large flagstones) was dominated by a monumental column carrying a statue of Hadrian. By the time the map was made, the statue had been removed, but the column was still standing and is depicted in the center of the oval area. In fact, the modern Arabic name of Damascus Gate – *Bab al-ʿAmud* (the Gate of the Column) – takes its name from the monumental column, although it disappeared long ago. A similar oval plaza is preserved at **Gerasa** (modern **Jerash** in Jordan), one of the Decapolis cities that, like Jerusalem, was rebuilt by Hadrian (see Chapter 16).

The Madaba map shows two main streets radiating from the oval plaza, bisecting the city from north to south. The more prominent of the two streets, which runs due south, is the main *cardo* (*cardo maximus*). The other street, a

13.5 Reconstruction of the Hadrianic gate at the Damascus Gate. By Leen Ritmeyer ©.

second main *cardo*, follows a more easterly course. Roman cities typically did not have two main *cardos*. In this case, Hadrian gave Jerusalem a second main *cardo* because there was a prominent topographic feature that he could not ignore: the Tyropoeon Valley. In fact, the modern street (which lies above and follows the line of the Hadrianic secondary *cardo*) is called "the street of the valley" (Arabic: *tariq al-wad[i]*; Hebrew: *rehov ha-gai*). The Madaba map indicates that originally both streets were broad, stone-paved boulevards, with columns lining the curbs of the sidewalks on either side. The columns supported pitched, red-tiled roofs that covered the sidewalks and provided shelter for pedestrians browsing in the shops on either side (similar to a modern mall!). There was plenty of space in the broad paved thoroughfares for animals, carts, chariots, and other vehicular traffic. The main east-west street (*decumanus maximus*) of Aelia Capitolina is not depicted as prominently on the Madaba map due to lack of space in the mosaic. However, part of it can be seen originating at a small arched gate in the middle of the western side of the city (the site of the modern Jaffa Gate), running east to the intersection with the main cardo. This main *decumanus* (modern David Street) follows the line of the Transverse Valley, along the north side of the western hill.

THE FORA OF AELIA CAPITOLINA

The Northern Forum

Hadrian established two fora (marketplaces) in Aelia Capitolina, one to the north of the Temple Mount and the other on the western side of the city. Both were

13.6 Oval plaza at Jerash.

large, open, paved spaces surrounded by temples and public monuments, with the entrances marked by free-standing triple-arched gates similar to the one at the Damascus Gate. The northern forum was located in the area that had been occupied by Herod's Antonia fortress before 70 C.E. Today this area is bisected by the Via Dolorosa, on the north side of which is a convent called the Church of the Sisters of Zion. The ancient stone pavement (Lithostratos) and triple-arched gate (arch of Ecce Homo) preserved inside the convent, which were once thought to belong to the Antonia fortress and are associated in modern Christian tradition with Jesus' passion, instead are part of Hadrian's northern forum (see Chapter 7). Specifically, the triple-arched gateway was a free-standing monument marking the entrance to the forum, and the Lithostratos was the flagstone pavement of the forum. The pavement was laid above the Struthion pools, which originally were open-air pools in the moat outside the Antonia fortress. The triple-arched gateway was erected on top of the pavement.

The meager archaeological evidence suggests that the Via Dolorosa was a center of cultic activity in Aelia Capitolina. In the Herodian period this side of the city was protected by the Sheep's Pools (or Bethesda or Bezetha pools) (see Chapter 7). Today the pools lie on the grounds of the Crusader-period **Church of St. Anne**. The pools are so called because they were used for washing animals brought for sacrifice in the second temple. After 70 C.E., a sanctuary of **Asclepius** was established by the pools. Asclepius was the Greco-Roman god of healing and medicine, and his cult typically required those seeking help to undergo ritual washing and incubation (a procedure involving sleeping and

13.7 Mithraic vase from Clermont-Ganneau's excavations by the Via Dolorosa. Photo of PEF-AO-4149 and PEF-AO-4150–51 by Rupert Chapman. By permission of the Palestine Exploration Fund.

the interpretation of dreams by priests). Interestingly, John (5:1–9) describes Jesus' miraculous cure of an invalid at the Sheep's Pools, suggesting that either these pools were associated with healing even before 70, or this story (which is reported only in the Fourth Gospel) originated after 70.

In the nineteenth century, a French explorer named Charles Clermont-Ganneau conducted excavations in caverns beneath the basements of houses on the north side of the Via Dolorosa, to the west of the Sheep's Pools. Among his discoveries were two unusual vases decorated with figured images in relief. A brilliant scholar, Clermont-Ganneau correctly dated the vases to the time of Aelia Capitolina. I have identified the images decorating these vases (which are now in the Palestine Exploration Fund in London) as Mithraic. Mithraism was a cult that originated in the Near East but became popular among Romans, especially soldiers, during the first to third centuries C.E. The cult centered on a mythical figure named Mithras, and promised salvation and an afterlife to its adherents (all of whom were men; women were prohibited from joining). Mithraism was a mystery cult, meaning that only initiates could participate in the rituals, which were conducted in cavelike shrines. The discovery of vases decorated with Mithraic imagery in underground caverns by the Via Dolorosa

13.8 The remains in the Russian Alexander Hospice showing the steps of the Hadrianic/Constantinian basilica (right) and adjacent threshold with image of the crucified Jesus. Library of Congress Catalogue number LC-M32-124; Repository: Library of Congress Prints and Photographs Division Washington, D.C. 20540 USA. From the G. Eric and Edith Matson Photograph Collection.

suggests that this was the site of a Mithraeum (a shrine of Mithras), a possibility supported by the cult's popularity among Roman soldiers.

The Western Forum

Hadrian's second forum was located on the western side of the city, in the area today occupied by the Church of the Holy Sepulcher. It was entered by passing through a free-standing, triple-arched gate, which marked the passage from the main *cardo* to the northeast corner of the forum. Two buildings were erected on the northern side of the forum: a basilica (on the east) and a temple (on the west). The basilica – a multifunctional public hall – was arranged with the long axis of the building running east-west, so the long side faced the forum (an arrangement typical of Roman basilicas). A staircase on the eastern façade provided access to the basilica from the direction of the main *cardo*. The temple was located to the west of the basilica. It probably was dedicated to **Aphrodite/Venus** (the Greek and Roman goddess of love), or, less likely, to Capitoline Jupiter (ancient literary sources are unclear on this point). According to Christian tradition, this temple was built over the spot where Jesus was crucified and buried. Two centuries after Hadrian's time, Constantine demolished it to expose Jesus' tomb, which he enshrined in the Rotunda of the Church of the Holy Sepulcher (see Chapter 15).

Today the remains on the northeastern side of the forum, including columns lining the original *cardo*, the triple-arched gate, the staircase and façade of the basilica, and the forum's stone pavement are preserved in the **Russian Alexander Hospice**. This building, which belongs to the White (pre-revolutionary Tsarist) Russian Church, was constructed in the late nineteenth century (a period when the various colonial powers were grabbing pieces of land from the weakening Ottoman rulers). The ancient remains were discovered during the course of construction and originally caused quite a stir, as it was thought they were associated with the Second Wall of the Herodian period (see Chapter 7). Specifically, the south wall of the basilica was identified as the line of the Second Wall because it is built of Herodian-style stones (which actually are in secondary use, typical of Hadrianic construction in Jerusalem). If these remains belonged to the Second Wall, it would have proved that the Church of the Holy Sepulcher (which is located to the west) was outside the city walls at the time of Jesus. This is important because according to the Gospel accounts, Jesus was crucified and buried outside the city walls, but the Church of the Holy Sepulcher was not built until 300 years after his death. In addition, a stone threshold adjoining the south wall of the basilica at first was identified as the gate through which Jesus was taken to be crucified. A huge image of Jesus on the cross is still displayed on top of the threshold. Nevertheless, scholars agree that these remains did not exist in the late Second Temple period but instead are part of Hadrian's western forum.

THE CAMP AND KILN WORKS OF THE TENTH LEGION

Ancient sources inform us that after 70 C.E., the Tenth Legion camped at the northwest corner of the western hill, in the area of the modern Citadel and Jaffa Gate. The camp was located by the only tower remaining of the three towers that Herod built to protect his palace (see Chapter 7). Titus razed the other two towers after the siege of Jerusalem ended. Indeed, terra-cotta roof tiles and pipes stamped with the name and symbols of the Tenth Legion have been discovered in excavations in the Citadel and the Armenian Garden to the south (the area of Herod's palace). However, these remains are scattered and are not associated with the remains of barrack buildings, which is surprising considering that the legion was stationed permanently in Jerusalem for more than two centuries, before being transferred to Aila around 300 C.E.

More substantial remains associated with the Tenth Legion, including a Roman-style bath house (with hypocaust and latrine) and hundreds of stamped legionary roof and floor tiles have been discovered in Israeli excavations southwest of the Temple Mount. These finds – some of which are coming to light in ongoing excavations – suggest that the Tenth Legion was stationed in temporary barracks in the area of the Citadel for a relatively short period (perhaps between 70 and 135?), before establishing a more substantial, permanent camp southwest of the Temple Mount (discussed later).

The kiln works of the Tenth Legion have been excavated to the west of the city (in an area called **Giv'at Ram**), close to Jerusalem's central bus station and convention center (**Binyanei Ha'uma**). Terra-cotta roof and floor tiles and pipes stamped with the name and symbols of the Tenth Legion were manufactured in the kiln works for use in legionary buildings, such as barracks and bath houses. The kiln works at Binyanei Ha'uma also produced pottery that is distinctively Roman in type and alien to the native Palestinian tradition (analyses demonstrate that the clay is local, indicating that the vessels are not imports). Roman legions typically manufactured their own stamped terra-cotta tiles and pipes, but they rarely produced their own pottery. Instead, legions would import some vessels and purchase the rest from local potters. However, Jerusalem's remote location (relative to the major Roman pottery production centers in the western Mediterranean) made it too costly to import pottery, and the native potters lacked experience in manufacturing Roman types. Therefore, the Tenth Legion in Jerusalem commissioned military potters to produce the vessels they needed.

The pottery produced in Jerusalem's legionary kiln works consists of fine table wares and cooking vessels. The soldiers used these vessels to prepare and serve Roman types of cuisine such as frittatas (which were cooked in shallow pans over a fire), and to offer guests wine at symposia (drinking parties). The table wares include fine red-slipped dishes in the tradition of Western Terra Sigillata, and unslipped, eggshell-thin cups and beakers covered with delicate relief designs. Many of the table wares are decorated in relief with Roman deities such as Dionysos (**Bacchus**), the god of wine – the first time figured images such as this are depicted on pottery made in Jerusalem. Dionysos and symbols associated with his cult (such as grapes and grapevines) were appropriate motifs for decorating vessels used for serving and drinking wine. After the legionary kiln works ceased pottery production around 200 C.E., local potters began manufacturing types that imitated the Roman wares, but usually without the figured decoration. The legionary kiln works had a long-lasting impact on the local pottery of Jerusalem, as imitation Roman wares continued to be produced for centuries.

THE *CARDOS*

Aelia Capitolina – corresponding with the roughly square area enclosed within the walls of the Old City today – is visible at the core of the Madaba map's depiction of Jerusalem, with the later (Byzantine period) expansion of the city to the south. The two *cardos* are prominently represented bisecting the city, with the main *cardo* terminating at Mount Zion (the southern end of the western hill). Because Jerusalem has not experienced another catastrophic destruction and renewal since Hadrian's time, scholars long assumed that the area of the modern Old City corresponds with Aelia Capitolina, as seen in the Madaba map. However, it was not until the 1970s that archaeologists had an opportunity to excavate the main *cardo*, which is located in the middle of the densely occupied Old City. This opportunity arose when Nahman Avigad was invited to conduct excavations on the western hill as part of Israel's reconstruction of the Jewish Quarter. Avigad discovered important remains from various periods around the Jewish Quarter, including the Herodian mansions (Chapter 7) and the "broad wall" (Chapter 2).

Avigad also excavated beneath the modern street that follows the line of Aelia Capitolina's main *cardo*. Some distance below the modern street, Avigad discovered a broad, stone-paved street, with columns lining the curbs of the sidewalks, corresponding with the depiction of the main *cardo* in the Madaba map. However, Avigad was surprised to find coins and pottery dating to the sixth century C.E. in the fills sealed by the stone pavement of the ancient street. There are no signs of an earlier street dating to Hadrian's time below this. Avigad concluded that the street he found represents a sixth century C.E. extension of the Hadrianic *cardo* to the south of the intersection with the main *decumanus*. In other words, according to Avigad, Aelia Capitolina occupied only the northern half of the modern Old City, with the area to the south uninhabited in Hadrian's time. Avigad noted that the concentration of legionary inscriptions in the northern half of the Old City supports this picture. This means that Hadrian's city was laid out not as a square but as a narrow elongated strip, with a truncated main *cardo* and second main *cardo* terminating at the intersection with the main *decumanus* (instead of intersecting in the middle of the city). Avigad proposed that only in the Byzantine period did the settlement spread to the south, at which time the main *cardo* was extended.

13.9   Remains of Jerusalem's main *cardo*. Courtesy of Todd Bolen/BiblePlaces.com.

Avigad's discovery caused scholars to reconsider previous assumptions about Aelia Capitolina's layout. I have suggested that perhaps the fortification wall to the north of the Old City, which Israeli archaeologists identify as the Third Wall, is the north wall of Hadrianic Jerusalem (it is not clear whether this wall was built in the first century C.E. as the Third Wall and reused by Hadrian, or was newly established by Hadrian). This means that the triple-arched gate and oval plaza at Damascus Gate were located in the middle of Aelia Capitolina rather than at the northern end, and the Transverse Valley (with the "main *decumanus*") marked the southern end of the city. Although other evidence seems to support my suggestion (such as the presence of a Hadrianic triple-arched gate on the line of the Third Wall and a concentration of Roman burials north of this line), one problem is that few remains dating to the time of Aelia Capitolina have been found in the area between the north wall of the Old City and the Third Wall. Even if I am correct, by ca. 300 C.E. the line of the Third Wall was abandoned in favor of the current northern line of the Old City, when a fortification wall was built which incorporated Hadrian's triple-arched gate at the site of the Damascus Gate.

Within the last decade, Israeli excavations west of the Temple Mount (by the Western Wall) have brought to light remains of the original second main *cardo* in the Tyropoeon Valley (see also the Sidebar on Wilson's Arch in Chapter 7). Like the main *cardo*, the second main *cardo* was a broad paved thoroughfare with columns lining the curbs of sidewalks, although the paving stones are laid differently. However, unlike the parts of the main *cardo* excavated by Avigad, pottery and coins date the establishment of the second main *cardo* to the time of Hadrian. In addition, the area to the west and southwest of the Temple Mount has yielded a greater concentration of legionary remains (including pottery and stamped tiles) than anywhere else in the Old City, including the Citadel. These finds suggest that from Hadrian's time or even earlier, this area was a center of legionary activity, and perhaps even the site of the Tenth Legion's camp. Future excavations and new discoveries undoubtedly will continue to revolutionize our understanding of Aelia Capitolina.

Sidebar: The Temple Mount and the Capitolium

Hadrian apparently established a shrine or temple to Capitoline Jupiter on the Temple Mount that was dedicated to Jerusalem's new patron deity, the supreme god of the Roman pantheon. No remains survive of this building. In fact, because of the confused nature of ancient literary accounts, some scholars believe that Hadrian erected only a cult statue on the Temple Mount, whereas others identify the temple by the western forum as the Capitolium. Recent excavations by the Western Wall have revealed a massive bridge carried on arches dating to the time of Aelia Capitolina, which spanned the Tyropoeon Valley and led to the Temple Mount (see the Sidebar on Wilson's Arch in Chapter 7). This discovery supports the view that Hadrian constructed a temple or shrine on the Temple Mount, as otherwise there would be little reason to provide such monumental access.

Sidebar: Hamilton's Excavations by the North Wall of Jerusalem

Robert W. Hamilton worked as an archaeologist in Jerusalem under the British Mandate. In 1937–38, he excavated several small areas ("soundings") by the north wall of the Old City. The most valuable evidence comes from Hamilton's Sounding A, which was bounded by the corner of the current Old City wall and the tower on the west side of the Damascus Gate. Hamilton's excavation methods were ahead of their time and exemplary even by today's standards. An analysis of his published report indicates that the line of the north wall of the Old City was established around 300 C.E. (in other words, the current wall, which dates to the Ottoman period, was built on top of an earlier line of wall). The need to fortify the northern side of the city with a new line of wall probably resulted from Diocletian's transfer of the Tenth Legion to Aila, or perhaps occurred with the rapid growth of the city's population after Constantine's legalization of Christianity in 313 C.E.

Recommended Reading

Nicole Belayche, *Iudaea-Palaestina: The Pagan Cults in Roman Palestine (Second to Fourth Century)* (Tübingen, Germany: Mohr Siebeck, 2001).

Herbert Donner, *The Mosaic Map of Madaba: An Introductory Guide* (Kampen, the Netherlands: Kok Pharos, 1992).

Yaron Z. Eliav, *God's Mountain: The Temple Mount in Time, Place, and Memory* (Baltimore: Johns Hopkins University, 2005).

Ya'akov Meshorer, *The Coinage of Aelia Capitolina* (Jerusalem: Israel Museum, 1989).

FOURTEEN

ROMAN AND LATE ANTIQUE PERIOD SYNAGOGUES IN PALESTINE

THE ORIGINS OF THE SYNAGOGUE

The word *synagogue* comes from Greek words meaning to gather or assemble together. The Hebrew term for synagogue, *beth knesset*, means "house of assembly." A synagogue building is a congregational hall, analogous to a church or mosque. In contrast, ancient temples (including the Jerusalem temple) were not congregational buildings but instead were conceived of literally as the house of the deity – the house in which the god dwelled. Usually only priests entered ancient temples, to service the needs of the deity (to feed, clothe, and bathe the deity). Everyone else remained outside the temple, around an altar where priests offered sacrifices to please or placate the deity and keep his presence among them.

In discussing the origins of the synagogue, it is important to bear in mind that this term (and analogous terms) can denote the congregation or assembly (a gathering of Jews) as well as the building that houses them (just as the term *church* can denote a congregation as well as a building). It is difficult to pinpoint the origins of the synagogue because the earliest gatherings did not take place in purpose-built congregational halls and therefore left no traces in the archaeological record. Even today, synagogue assemblies can take place anywhere, even in church buildings! For this reason, a wide range of theories exists about when and where the institution of the synagogue first developed. The following is a summary of these theories.

1) Synagogues developed during the First Temple period (before 586 B.C.E.), as a result of the centralization of the cult in the Jerusalem temple. Small

286 ଼

sanctuaries (early synagogues) were established around the country to allow for the worship of the God of Israel even outside Jerusalem. This theory, which has few adherents, relies on understanding a couple of vague biblical terms as referring to synagogues.

2) Synagogues developed during the Babylonian exile. The rationale behind this theory is that only by having an institution such as the synagogue would the Judeans have been able to maintain their religious identity while in exile. Although this is a logical argument with many followers, it lacks historical or other support.

3) Synagogues developed in Judea during the time of Ezra and Nehemiah. When Ezra was sent by the Persian king to implement Jewish law as royal law, he assembled the Jews in order to read and explain to them the law (Torah). Because synagogues are assemblies of Jews, typically for the purpose of reading and studying the Torah, it is not incorrect to call the gatherings assembled under Ezra synagogues. The question is whether the gatherings under Ezra were a direct precursor of the institution of the synagogue or a more isolated phenomenon.

4) Synagogues developed in Hellenistic Egypt (third and second centuries B.C.E.). Some scholars argue that synagogues originated among Jews living in the Diaspora, enabling them to maintain their Jewish identity in a Gentile environment. Perhaps the largest and most influential Diaspora community of the Hellenistic and early Roman periods was located in Egypt, especially in Alexandria. It was here that the Torah was first translated into another language (from Hebrew to Greek). A number of inscriptions from Egypt dating to the Hellenistic period refer to Jewish "prayer houses" (Greek *proseuche/ae*). The inscriptions typically are dedicated in honor of the Greek rulers of Egypt. Unfortunately, there are no remains of buildings that can be identified as "prayer houses," only the inscriptions. Therefore, the nature of these "prayer houses" and their possible relationship to synagogues are unclear, although this theory has a substantial following.

5) Synagogues developed during the Hasmonean period. This theory was proposed by a modern scholar who noted that the book of Ecclesiasticus, which was written by a Jewish sage in Jerusalem ca. 180 B.C.E., does not refer to the institution of the synagogue. He concluded that synagogues must not have existed yet, and therefore developed only during the Hasmonean period (in the second half of the second century B.C.E.). This is a weak argument from silence with few adherents.

Despite the lack of consensus, there is no doubt that synagogues existed by the first century B.C.E. and first century C.E., as Josephus refers to them and the New Testament describes Jesus and Paul preaching in synagogues.

SYNAGOGUE BUILDINGS OF THE HERODIAN (EARLY ROMAN) PERIOD (PRE-70 C.E.)

The Theodotus Inscription

By the first century B.C.E. and first century C.E., we begin to find archae-ologically identifiable remains of synagogue buildings. Among these is the "**Theodotus inscription**," which was discovered in 1913 in a cistern to the south of the Temple Mount. The inscription commemorates the dedication of a synagogue building, which presumably stood somewhere nearby. Although no remains survive of the building, the inscription provides valuable information about early synagogues. It reads as follows:

> Theodotus, son of Vettanos, a priest and an **archisynagogos**, grandson of an *archisynagogos*, built the synagogue for the reading of Torah and for teaching the commandments; furthermore, the hostel, and the rooms, and the water installation for lodging needy strangers. Its foundation stone was laid by his ancestors, the elders, and Simonides.

The synagogue's founder has a Greek name (Theodotus), and his father's name – Vettanos – is also foreign (perhaps Latin and possibly indicating Roman citizenship). Some scholars have speculated that the foreign origin of Theodotus' family indicates that this synagogue served a congregation of Diaspora Jews. The use of Greek for the inscription points to Theodotus' elite status. Although Jews in Roman Palestine spoke Aramaic as their everyday language, the upper classes also knew Greek, which was the official language of administration in the Roman East (in contrast, Latin was hardly used in the Roman East, usually limited to Roman officials and soldiers). The personal names, the use of Greek, and the fact that they were priests indicate that this was an elite family. In fact, Theodotus describes himself as an *archisynagogos* and the grandson of an *archisynagogos* – a Greek term meaning "leader of the synagogue." Noticeably absent from this inscription is any reference to rabbis. This is because rabbis did not serve as ordained leaders of synagogue congregations in ancient synagogues, in contrast to modern practice. Instead, in Roman Palestine the term *rabbi* was an informal title of respect used to address a sage with expertise in Jewish law (Torah). *Archisynagogos* is the most common title used in ancient synagogue inscriptions to denote synagogue leaders (there are other terms as well), although it is not clear whether it was a purely honorific title (for example, given to a major donor), or whether it entailed administrative or liturgical responsibilities (such as leading a prayer service or giving a sermon). It is possible that the meaning of this title changed over time and that it was used in different ways by different Jewish congregations.

14.1 The Theodotus inscription. Courtesy of Zev Radovan/BibleLandPictures.com.

After listing the name and lineage of the founder, the inscription describes the purposes for which the synagogue was built. Conspicuously absent is any reference to prayer or liturgy, as formal prayer services were not yet conducted in synagogues. This feature developed after the destruction of the second temple in 70, as synagogues began to assume a more central place in Jewish religious life. Instead, the Theodotus inscription describes the original function of synagogues: a congregation of Jews for the purpose of "the reading of Torah and for teaching the commandments." Synagogues provided a setting where Jews could have the Torah read and explained to them, so they could live their lives according to the laws of the God of Israel (in Roman terms, their ancestral laws). The reading of the law (Torah) is still at the core of every synagogue service today. The book of Acts (13:14–15) describes as follows a visit by Paul and Barnabas to a synagogue at Antioch in Pisidia (Asia Minor):

> And on the sabbath day they went into the synagogue and sat down. After the reading of the law and the prophets, the officials of the synagogue sent them a message saying, "Brothers, if you have any word of exhortation for the people, give it." (NRSV)

The passage in Acts echoes the Theodotus inscription by referring to "the reading of the law" (Torah). It also mentions the reading of the prophets (readings from prophetic books of the Hebrew Bible), apparently referring to the Haftarah that follows the Torah reading in synagogue on the sabbaths and

14.2 Aerial view of the synagogue at Masada. Courtesy of Zev Radovan/BibleLandPictures
.com.

festivals. After these readings, Paul and Barnabas were invited to teach the
congregation about their interpretation of the law.

The synagogue built by Theodotus included a hostel, presumably for Jews
on pilgrimage to the Jerusalem temple. This highlights the fact that attending
synagogue was not intended to be a substitute for participation in the temple
sacrifices. Even if some Jewish groups such as the Essenes or Jesus' movement
criticized or rejected the sacrificial cult in the Jerusalem temple because they
considered it polluted or corrupt, they took for granted the existence of the
temple and sacrifices.

Pre-70 Synagogue Buildings

The synagogue at Masada is perhaps the best-known synagogue in Palestine
dating before 70 C.E. The synagogue was installed in a casemate room of the
Herodian fortification wall on the northwest side of the mountain (see Chapter
10). Originally this room had a small front porch or antechamber and a main
room with five columns supporting the roof. It apparently was a reception
hall during Herod's time, and may have been used as a stable by the Roman

14.3 The Gamla synagogue. Photo by Jim Haberman.

garrison that occupied the mountain after Herod's death. The Jewish rebels who occupied Masada during the First Jewish Revolt converted this room into a synagogue by removing the wall of the antechamber to make one large room (and reconfiguring the columns supporting the roof), and installing rows of benches along the walls. They also added a small chamber at the back of the room.

The synagogue at Masada lacks the distinctive features that we associate with later synagogue buildings, such as a **Torah shrine** (for storing Torah scrolls), and Jewish symbols and iconography. Furthermore, although this side of the mountain is closest to Jerusalem, the room is not oriented toward Jerusalem but lies at an angle. Later synagogues typically are oriented toward Jerusalem, because Jews pray facing the Temple Mount. The lack of these features in the synagogue at Masada reflects its early date, before the development of a standardized prayer service and liturgy. In other words, the room at Masada is a synagogue in the most basic sense of the word: a hall that accommodated gatherings of Jews for the reading of the Torah. The benches indicate that this room was used for assemblies, and the fact that only Jews occupied the mountain at the time of the revolt indicates that it was a *Jewish* hall of assembly. Had this room been found in a non-Jewish context, we could not call it a synagogue, and had it been found at a site with a mixed Jewish and non-Jewish population, we could not identify it with certainty as a synagogue.

In a pit dug into the dirt floor of the back room (which had been added by the rebels), Yigael Yadin found fragments of biblical scrolls belonging to the books of Ezekiel and Deuteronomy. In Judaism, it became customary to bury or deposit in a synagogue sacred writings that are damaged or no longer used, because they cannot be destroyed (although not all synagogues have such deposits). The pit found by Yadin might represent an early example of this type of deposit, which is called a *geniza*.

A handful of other synagogue buildings dating before 70 C.E. have been found at other sites in Palestine. The Jewish rebels who occupied Herodium during the First Revolt converted Herod's triclinium (dining room and reception hall) into a synagogue by adding benches around the walls. A slightly earlier example of a synagogue is found at Gamla, the Jewish town overlooking the Sea of Galilee that was destroyed by the Romans in 67 C.E. (see Chapter 9). It consists of a rectangular assembly hall lined by benches and with columns to support the roof, abutting the fortification wall on the eastern side of the town. The synagogue is constructed of finely cut blocks of basalt and has columns with Doric capitals. The lintel over the main doorway was decorated with an incised rosette flanked by date palms. A *miqveh* was installed in a room adjacent to the hall. The Gamla synagogue antedates those at Masada and Herodium, as it was built before the outbreak of the First Revolt, and differs in having been purpose-built (constructed as a synagogue from the start). However, all these early (pre-70) synagogues are relatively modest structures with benches lining the interior and columns to support the roof (allowing for an expanded hall to accommodate assemblies). Some have additional features such as a *geniza* or *miqveh*, but they lack Torah shrines and are not oriented toward Jerusalem.

In 2009, Israeli archaeologists announced the discovery of a pre-70 synagogue building at Mary Magdalene's home town of Migdal (Magdala/Tarichaea), on the northwest shore of the Sea of Galilee. The Migdal synagogue is a relatively modest rectangular hall lined with benches. However, the floor of the hall is paved with a mosaic, whereas other early synagogues have packed dirt or plastered floors. In the middle of the hall the excavators discovered a unique object: a large rectangular block of stone decorated on all sides (except the bottom) with carved reliefs, including a rosette (on the top) and a menorah flanked by amphoras (on one side). Not only is this a rare depiction of a menorah antedating 70 C.E., but it is the first (earliest) example of this symbol decorating an ancient synagogue. This discovery suggests that even before 70 some Jews related the activities in synagogues to the Jerusalem temple – a phenomenon that became much more pronounced in the centuries after 70. The function of the stone block is not known (perhaps an offering table or a table on which the Torah scroll was laid?), and the synagogue is not yet published, although preliminary reports in the media can be found online.

Synagogue Buildings after 70 C.E.: The Traditional Typology

Historical Background

After 70 C.E., Jerusalem and the Temple Mount lay in ruins, and despite Jewish hopes and expectations, the outcome of the Bar-Kokhba Revolt made it clear that the temple would not be rebuilt soon. Judaism survived these traumas by transforming itself from a religion centered on a temple with a sacrificial cult led by priests into a community-based religion focused on prayer and liturgy in synagogues. In other words, the institution of the synagogue became increasingly important to Jewish religious life in the centuries following the Bar-Kokhba Revolt. This is reflected by the discovery of dozens of synagogue buildings around Palestine dating to this period.

The rabbis played a key role in the transformation of Judaism in the centuries following the temple's destruction. These were not rabbis in the modern sense of the word (ordained leaders of synagogue congregations), but rather scholars or sages who were experts in Jewish law (Torah). The rabbis interpreted the Torah in ways that allowed Jews to worship the God of Israel and observe his laws even without a temple. Their approach to Jewish law is similar to that of the Pharisees before 70, to whom they might be related. Around 200 C.E., generations of rabbinic rulings were collected and edited by Rabbi Judah ha-Nasi ("the Prince") in a series of volumes called the Mishnah. Later rabbinic rulings and elaborations on the Mishnah were collected in volumes called the Talmud, one produced in Palestine (the Jerusalem or Palestinian Talmud, ca. 400 C.E.), and one in Babylonia (the Babylonian Talmud, ca. 500 C.E., which is considered the more authoritative of the two).

Very few Jewish writings aside from rabbinic literature have survived from the period after 70 C.E. This literature gives the impression that the rabbis were the main – and even the only – leaders in Jewish society at this time. The rabbis did not discuss matters that were not of interest to them, and they dismissed or disregarded the opinions of Jews who lay outside their circles (who are often denoted as *minim* or heretics by the rabbis). Although rabbinic literature is a valuable source for the period after 70, it presents only a partial and biased picture of Jewish society and religious practices. For example, the rabbis hardly mention Christianity, despite its rapid spread (and eventual legalization) during this period. In contrast, the writings of the early church fathers are filled with attacks on Jews and Judaism. Recently, scholars have begun to acknowledge the complexity of Jewish society in Palestine after 70 C.E. For example, Jewish sectarianism – or at least some sectarian practices – may have continued for centuries. In addition, it is now clear that the priestly class did not disappear after the destruction of the second temple, but continued to wield considerable influence both within and without rabbinic circles.

In the early twentieth century, the first remains of monumental ancient synagogue buildings dating to the rabbinic period came to light in archaeological excavations. Soon thereafter, Eleazar Sukenik (see Chapter 6) established a typology (sequence of types) of these buildings in chronological order, with each type distinguished by certain characteristics and dated to a different period. Later the typology was expanded upon by another Israeli archaeologist, Michael Avi-Yonah. According to this sequence, the earliest type (Galilean synagogues) dates to the second and third centuries; this is followed by Transitional synagogues of the fourth century, and finally Byzantine synagogues of the fifth and sixth centuries. However, as we shall see, discoveries since Sukenik's time indicate that all three types are roughly contemporary, dating from the fourth to sixth centuries. The following is a review of these types, with descriptions of representative examples of each. It is important to bear in mind that although our discussion focuses on synagogues, these buildings did not stand in isolation but were located in the midst of villages and towns whose congregations they served.

Galilean Synagogues

Capernaum

The synagogue at Capernaum is a classic example of the Galilean type. It is a monumental structure built of well-cut limestone blocks (ashlar masonry), consisting of the synagogue (the hall) and a courtyard on one side (this discussion focuses on the hall alone). The hall is a basilica, with the narrow (shorter) sides oriented north-south. Engaged pilasters (square columns that are part of the wall) decorated the sides and back of the building's exterior. The building was covered with a pitched, tiled roof, which was supported by wooden beams carried on columns inside the building. The main entrances, consisting of one large doorway flanked by two smaller ones, were in the south (Jerusalem-oriented) wall. The interior of the hall was surrounded on three sides (east, west, and north) by columns with Corinthian capitals on raised pedestals. The hall was paved with large flagstones, and stone benches lined the east and west walls. The hall was two stories high, with the columns inside supporting a second-story gallery level that overlooked the central part of the interior (the **nave**). The inner face of the main doorway, which led into the nave, was flanked by two stone platforms for Torah shrines. This means that after entering the hall, worshipers had to turn in a complete circle to face the direction of prayer (the Jerusalem-oriented wall).

14.4 Aerial view of the synagogue at Capernaum. Courtesy of Zev Radovan/BibleLand
Pictures.com.

The building was richly decorated with carved stone reliefs, many of which
were concentrated on the outside of the southern (Jerusalem-oriented) façade,
around the doorways and windows. A large, semicircular window above the
main doorway allowed light to enter the nave. The reliefs consist mostly of
geometric and floral motifs, including examples of the seven species (grapes and

14.5 Corinthian capital from Capernaum with a menorah.

14.6 Relief from Capernaum showing the Ark of the Covenant/Torah shrine.

grapevines). Figured images were also depicted in the reliefs, most of which were later damaged, such as a pair of felines facing each other on the lintel of a doorway. A couple of undamaged reliefs are carved with two eagles facing each other and holding a garland in their beaks, and a horse with a fish tail (a sea-horse!). Whereas Jewish art before 70 C.E. was almost completely **aniconic** (without figured images), synagogues of the period after 70 are filled with figured and even pagan images, as we shall see. Jewish symbols and ritual objects are also represented at Capernaum, such as a menorah flanked by a **shofar** (ram's horn) and incense shovel carved on a Corinthian capital. One relief shows a wheeled structure with engaged pilasters on the sides; a pitched, tiled roof; and a double paneled door at one short end. This structure apparently depicted the Ark of the Covenant, and perhaps also the Torah shrine in ancient synagogues, which may have been modeled after the ark.

Chorazin

Three miles north of Capernaum is the ancient Jewish village of Chorazin. The synagogue in this village is another example of the Galilean type, although it is constructed of the local basalt instead of limestone. It has the same characteristic features as Capernaum: a rectangular hall built of ashlar masonry, oriented so that one short wall faces south toward Jerusalem; there is a central doorway flanked by two smaller ones in the main façade; the hall is paved with flagstones and encircled by pedestaled columns (with Ionic capitals) that divided the

14.7 Relief from Chorazin showing a head of Medusa or Helios.

interior into a **nave** surrounded by three aisles; stone benches lined the walls; a Torah shrine flanked the interior of the doorway; and carved stone reliefs were concentrated especially on the main façade. The reliefs include the head of a Medusa or the sun (Helios), and a series of medallions showing *putti* (cupids)

14.8 Reconstruction of the synagogue at Kfar Baram. Courtesy of Zev Radovan/BibleLand Pictures.com.

14.9 Main doorway of the synagogue at Kfar Baram.

treading grapes, a common motif in Greco-Roman art. There is also a stone seat of Moses (seat for an elder) bearing a dedicatory inscription in Aramaic.

Kfar Baram

Kfar Baram lies at the northern end of upper Galilee, just two miles from Israel's border with Lebanon. The synagogue's main façade (the Jerusalem-oriented wall) is still preserved to its original two-story height (not reconstructed). This building has the characteristic features of the Galilean type described for Capernaum and Chorazin. It also had a porch supported by columns in front of the main façade. A large, semicircular window that is still preserved above the central doorway in the main façade let light into the interior. The lintel of the main doorway was carved in relief with two winged females holding a wreath between them. In a later period the female figures were carefully chipped away, leaving only the wreath intact. These figures depicted Nikae (Victories) — Nike was the Greco-Roman goddess of victory (wreaths were awarded to victors). Eventually this motif was absorbed into early Christian art, which transformed Victories into angels.

14.10 Relief of a Victory from Ephesus.

Transitional Synagogues

Hammath Tiberias

Hammath Tiberias (Hebrew for "the hot springs of Tiberias") is located on the western shore of the Sea of Galilee, just south of the city of Tiberias. The site takes its name from hot sulfur springs that bubble up from underground at this spot. In the 1960s, an Israeli archaeologist, Moshe Dothan, excavated a series of synagogue buildings that were built over the course of several centuries, one above the other, in the midst of the village. The synagogue that is the focus of our interest (and is the most famous in the series) dates to the fourth century. It is a classic example of the Transitional type. In contrast to the Galilean type, the synagogue was built of roughly cut basalt stones (not ashlars) and lacked carved reliefs. Instead, the interior of the building was decorated with mosaics (discussed later).

The building is a **broadhouse**, meaning that the main axis is parallel to the short walls instead of the long walls. Therefore, the southern, Jerusalem-oriented wall and the north wall are the long walls. The main entrance was through a doorway in the long north wall, which led into the nave. This doorway was not in the center of the north wall because an extra row of columns inside the building created an extra aisle on one side, so the nave was not in the center. A stone platform in front of the south wall held the Torah shrine. Unlike the arrangement in Galilean synagogues, at Hammath Tiberias the Torah shrine

14.11 Mosaic floor in the nave of the synagogue at Hammath Tiberias. Courtesy of Zev Radovan/BibleLandPictures.com.

was opposite the main entrance, meaning that worshipers faced the direction of prayer upon entering the building without turning around.

The floors of the aisles and nave of the synagogue at Hammath Tiberias were covered with mosaics, most of which were decorated with geometric and floral motifs, except for the nave, which contained figured images. Just inside the main doorway (north wall) were square panels framing donor inscriptions in Greek, which would have been seen upon entering the synagogue. All of the inscriptions follow the same formula. For example, the inscription in the upper left panel reads, "Maximos [the Greek version of the Hebrew or Aramaic name Gedaliah], having made a vow, fulfilled it, long may he live!" Maximos paid off the pledge he made to the synagogue, and was commemorated in the inscription. The donor inscriptions are flanked by a pair of lions, perhaps representing the ancient symbol of the tribe of Judah.

The central part of the nave contains a square panel framing a circular medallion. In the center of the medallion is a depiction of the Greco-Roman sun god **Helios**, riding in a chariot pulled by four horses across the heavens (the chariot and horses were largely obliterated by a later wall that was sunk through the floor). Helios has one hand raised, and the other hand holds a globe and whip. Rays radiate from his head. Surrounding Helios are depictions of the twelve signs of the zodiac, each with its attributes and labeled in Hebrew with their names. For example, Libra is a young man holding scales in his hand, and Virgo is a young woman represented holding a torch like the goddess Kore/Persephone. Some of the male figures are nude and uncircumcised! In the corners of the square outside the medallion are female personifications of the four seasons with their attributes, each labeled in Hebrew. The meaning or significance of these pagan images and others will be discussed later.

Above Helios and the zodiac cycle is a panel that was in front of the Torah shrine. The center of the panel shows the façade of a structure with a double paneled door and pitched roof, apparently representing the Ark of the Covenant and perhaps the Torah shrine. This structure is flanked by various Jewish ritual objects: menorahs, shofars, incense shovels, and *lulavs* and *ethrogs* (the bundle of branches and citrus fruit used in the celebration of Sukkot, the Feast of Tabernacles).

Byzantine Synagogues

Beth Alpha

During the fifth and sixth centuries, synagogue buildings continued to undergo changes. Synagogues of this period are called Byzantine because the Jews of Palestine were living under Byzantine Christian rule. **Beth Alpha** is a classic example of the Byzantine synagogue type. Similar to Transitional synagogues such as Hammath Tiberias, the building is constructed of field stones with no carved reliefs, and the floors are covered with decorated mosaics. However, the building's plan resembles that of an early church. It consists of a large courtyard (**atrium**) that provided access to a narrow porch (**narthex**) in front of the main

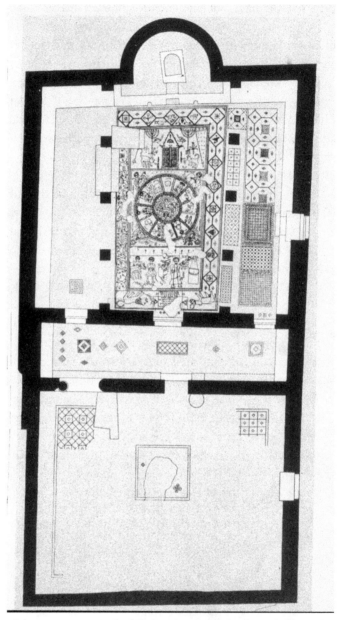

14.12 Plan of the synagogue at Beth Alpha. Courtesy of Zev Radovan/BibleLandPictures.com.

hall (basilica). The main hall has two rows of piers (square pillars) dividing the interior into a nave flanked by aisles. A large semicircular niche (apse) in the southern (Jerusalem-oriented) wall contained the Torah shrine. This modest building did not have a second story or gallery level. Instead, the aisles were only one story high, and the walls on either side of the nave rose to a height of two stories, creating a **clerestory** pierced by windows to let light into the interior.

14.13 The offering of Isaac and dedicatory inscriptions in the mosaic floor of the synagogue at Beth Alpha. Courtesy of Zev Radovan/BibleLandPictures.com.

The floors of the entire structure (including the courtyard and porch) were paved with mosaics with geometric and floral designs. However, the nave was paved with three panels containing figured scenes, surrounded by a decorated border. Just inside the main entrance (on the north side, opposite the Jerusalem-oriented wall), the mosaic contained two inscriptions flanked by a bull and a lion. One inscription, in Greek, states that the mosaic was laid by two local craftsmen named Marianos and his son Hanina, who are known to have worked on other mosaics in this area. The Beth Alpha congregation was a rural (farming) community (in contrast to the urban congregation at Hammath Tiberias), which paid the craftsmen in kind (produce and livestock) instead of in cash. The second inscription, in Aramaic, is important because it is one of the only dated inscriptions associated with an ancient Palestinian synagogue. The inscription mentions that the mosaic was laid during the reign of Justin. Although there were two emperors named Justin (Justin I and Justin II), both ruled during the sixth century, providing a general date for the mosaic (unfortunately, the part of the inscription that specified a precise date is not preserved).

The area inside the decorated border (which contains the inscriptions) is divided into three panels. The first (lowest) panel (closest to the main door in the north wall) is decorated with a biblical scene depicting the binding or offering of Isaac by his father Abraham. The figures are labeled with their names in Hebrew. Isaac is depicted on the right as a small boy with his hands bound behind his back, just as he is about to be tossed onto a flaming altar by Abraham, who holds a large knife in his hand. At this moment, the hand of God appears emerging from the heavens above, accompanied by the command, "do not lay [your hand upon the boy]." To the left of Abraham is a bush to which a ram is tethered, and an inscription that says, "and behold [here is] the ram." To the left of the ram, two of Abraham's servants lead a donkey.

The central panel contains a depiction of Helios, the zodiac cycle, and the four seasons similar to that at Hammath Tiberias, but in a less skillful artistic style. Helios is depicted frontally in his chariot pulled by four horses. The signs of the zodiac are labeled in Hebrew, and the personifications of the four seasons occupy the corners of the panel.

The uppermost panel (in front of the Torah shrine) is decorated with a depiction of the Ark of the Covenant and perhaps Torah shrine (a structure with double paneled doors and a pitched roof) flanked by Jewish ritual objects, including menorahs, *lulavs* and *ethrogs*, and incense shovels. An "eternal lamp" is shown hanging from the top of the ark, and the area around the ark is filled with additional objects and figures including birds and lions (perhaps lions of Judah). On either side of the panel two curtains are depicted as if they have been drawn aside to reveal the ark and surrounding objects, recalling the veil that existed in the Holy of Holies in the Jerusalem temple, as well as the later practice of hanging a curtain in front of the scrolls in a Torah shrine.

Naaran

Just outside of Jericho, by the springs at **Naaran**, is another synagogue of the Byzantine type. Its plan is similar to Beth Alpha: a courtyard, porch, and hall with apse in the Jerusalem-oriented wall. The floors are paved with mosaics decorated with geometric and floral designs, except the nave, which has figured scenes. The mosaics suffered heavy damage from shelling during World War I. Nevertheless, the outline of a Helios and zodiac cycle is still visible, as well as a panel containing a depiction of the Ark of the Covenant surrounded by Jewish ritual objects. A narrow panel between these showed Daniel in the lions' den. Daniel is depicted as a man facing the viewer with his hands raised, flanked by two lions.

Sepphoris

In 1993, a fifth-century synagogue decorated with stunning mosaics was discovered in excavations at Sepphoris. The building has an unusual plan: the nave is flanked by an aisle on only one side (north); there is a rectangular platform instead of an apse at the end of the nave; and the building is oriented northwest-southeast, with the platform for the Torah shrine located against the northwest wall. A handful of other ancient synagogues also are not oriented

14.14 Drawing of the mosaic floor in the nave of the Sepphoris synagogue. From Z. Weiss, *The Sepphoris
Synagogue* (Jerusalem: Israel Exploration Society,
2005), p. 57 Fig. 2. Courtesy of Zeev Weiss, The
Sepphoris Excavations. Drawing by Pnina Arad.

toward Jerusalem, indicating that this direction of prayer was not yet universally observed in Judaism. The hall was entered by turning ninety degrees through a narthex.

The narthex and aisle were paved with mosaics containing geometric and floral patterns, and the nave was decorated with seven successive registers (or "bands" in the excavator's language) of figured scenes and Jewish ritual objects (according to the excavator's numbering, Register 7 was the first one seen upon entering the nave from the narthex, and Register 1 was in front of the platform for the Torah shrine). Register 6 was divided into two panels, and Registers 1, 2, and 4 were divided into three panels each. Register 7, which is very poorly preserved, apparently depicted the visit of the angels to Abraham and Sarah, announcing that Sarah will bear a son. Register 6, also poorly preserved, portrayed the binding or offering of Isaac by Abraham. The largest register (about twice as wide as the other registers) contained a medallion with Helios surrounded by the signs of the zodiac and the four seasons in the corners. The signs of the zodiac were labeled in Hebrew not only with their names (Libra, Virgo, etc.), but also the corresponding month (for example, Kislev and Tishrei). The figure of Helios was depicted not in human form but as a ball of fire with radiating rays in a chariot pulled by four horses across the heavens.

The registers above this (1–4) showed scenes and objects associated with the Tabernacle or Jerusalem temple and the sacrificial cult. The right and central panels of Register 4 depicted the basket of first fruits and the showbread table. The left panel of Register 4 displayed a lamb, a jar of oil, a vessel containing fine flour, and two trumpets – all of which are connected with the daily sacrifice portrayed in Register 3. Register 3 showed Aaron (poorly preserved) next to a large rectangular altar, flanked on one side by a large water basin with animal spouts and on the other side by a lamb and a bull. Register 2 depicted the Ark of the Covenant and perhaps Torah shrine (a gabled structure with two paneled doors) flanked by menorahs, shofars, incense shovels, and *lulavs* and *ethrogs*. Register 1 had a wreath framing a Greek dedicatory inscription flanked by two lions, each holding a bull's head in its front paws.

Was there a central unifying theme behind the images in this mosaic? The excavator, Zeev Weiss, proposes that this was a single composition referring to God's promise to the Jewish people (through the agency of Abraham), and their future redemption with the reestablishment of the Jerusalem temple. Although Weiss might be right, other interpretations have been suggested. It is difficult to make a case for a unified theme in most ancient synagogues because generally only the decoration on the floors has survived, whereas often the walls were decorated too (with paintings and/or inscriptions). The floors were part of a larger decorative program, most of which is gone.

14.15 Mosaic floor in the Jericho synagogue. Courtesy of Zev Radovan/BibleLandPictures
.com.

Late Ancient Synagogues

Jericho

During the seventh and eighth centuries, all three Abrahamic faiths were
affected by the iconoclastic movement, which opposed the depiction of figured images in religious art. It was at this time that some of the figured images
in earlier synagogues, such as the reliefs at Capernaum, were damaged. A synagogue at Jericho, which might date to this period, perhaps reflects the influence
of iconoclasm. The building has the same plan typical of Byzantine synagogues,
and like them, the floors are covered with mosaics. However, the mosaics of
the Jericho synagogue contain no figured images at all. Instead, the nave is
decorated with a highly stylized depiction of the Ark of the Covenant/Torah
shrine. Below it is a medallion containing a menorah flanked by a shofar and
lulav and ethrog, accompanied by the Hebrew phrase *shalom al-Yisrael* ("peace
on Israel").

SYNAGOGUE BUILDINGS AFTER 70 C.E.: AN EVALUATION OF THE TRADITIONAL TYPOLOGY

Sukenik's typology of ancient synagogues, which we have just reviewed, follows a linear progression model. Many archaeologists in Israel and the United States still believe this typology is accurate, at least in its main outlines. However, the ongoing discovery and excavation of ancient synagogue buildings – dozens more than were known in Sukenik's time – have called into question the validity of the typology.

The biggest challenge to the traditional typology comes from Capernaum, where Franciscan archaeologists have been conducting excavations in the synagogue and adjacent courtyard since the late 1960s (the Franciscans have custody of the part of the site that includes the synagogue). As mentioned above, the synagogue at Capernaum is a classic example of the Galilean type (dated to the second to third century, according to Sukenik's typology). The synagogue was first excavated in 1905 by two German archaeologists, Heinrich Kohl and Carl Watzinger. In the early twentieth century, archaeological methods and scientific techniques were much less developed and precise than they are today. Therefore, much of the material that would be used now to date the building was discarded by Kohl and Watzinger. For this reason, the synagogue at Capernaum was dated to the second and third centuries not on the basis of archaeological evidence (such as associated pottery and coins) but on the basis of its architectural style. Specifically, scholars noted similarities between the layout and relief decoration of Capernaum on one hand, and Roman temples in Syria of the second and third centuries on the other. Other Galilean type synagogues were then dated to the same period on the basis of comparisons with Capernaum.

In their excavations at Capernaum, the Franciscans made an astonishing discovery. Below the paving stones of the floor of the synagogue and courtyard, they found more than 25,000 small bronze coins and large quantities of pottery dating to the fourth and fifth centuries. The latest of these finds date to approximately 500 C.E., indicating that the synagogue was built no earlier than the beginning of the sixth century – centuries later than previously thought! Because Capernaum is always cited as the classic example of a Galilean synagogue, this discovery removes the cornerstone of Sukenik's typology. Furthermore, the pottery and coins associated with more recently excavated Galilean synagogues date to the fourth to sixth centuries, indicating that Capernaum is not alone in being a late example of this type.

The discoveries at Capernaum have created an ongoing controversy in the field of ancient synagogue studies. Some scholars have tried to dismiss these findings by arguing that the Capernaum synagogue originally was built in the second or third century, but later was destroyed and rebuilt, which would account for the fourth- and fifth-century pottery and coins under the floor. However, reports published by the Franciscan archaeologists give no indication of an earlier phase or evidence that the synagogue was rebuilt. This argument also fails to account for the dating of other Galilean type synagogues to the fourth to sixth centuries.

The inescapable conclusion is that Sukenik's typology can no longer be considered valid. The limited data available in Sukenik's time supported the typology, but today we have a wealth of additional information, which is much more accurate. The differences between the traditional synagogue types are due not to different dates but to other factors, such as geography and local building materials, the preferences of the congregations or donors, and perhaps different movements or liturgies within Judaism. For example, Galilean type synagogues cluster in the area to the north and northwest of the Sea of Galilee, with a related type characteristic of the Golan. The later dating of Galilean type synagogues means that the earliest monumental synagogues in Palestine were constructed in the fourth century. Synagogues of the second and third centuries, like Jewish public buildings before 70, were relatively simple, unadorned halls lined with benches.

Judaism and Christianity

The appearance of monumental synagogue architecture and art in the fourth century should be understood within the context of the time, especially with regard to the rise of Christianity, which was legalized and adopted by Constantine in 313 C.E. Before that, Christians had been persecuted and forced to worship in secret because Christianity was outlawed in the Roman Empire. Judaism was legal (at least until the partial bans implemented by Hadrian) because the Romans considered it an ancient, ancestral religion, in contrast to Christianity, which was a new religion and therefore illegal. Once Christians could worship openly and without fear of persecution, they began to erect monumental church buildings with elaborate decorative programs. Some of the earliest monumental churches, such as the Church of the Holy Sepulcher in Jerusalem and the Church of the Nativity in Bethlehem, were constructed by Constantine (see Chapters 15 and 16). Christianity laid claim to the Jewish (or more accurately, the ancient Israelite) heritage and temple traditions, with Jesus being the fulfillment of the old law (Old Testament/Hebrew Bible) and the ultimate sacrifice. Jews had been criticized by some Greeks and Romans as "atheists" because of their refusal to worship any god but the God of Israel. Now Judaism found itself under attack by a closely related religion, which shared some of the same scriptures and claimed to supersede it.

Some of the church fathers bitterly attacked Jews and Judaism. For example, in a series of sermons called *Discourses against Judaizing Christians*, delivered in

Antioch (Syria) in the late fourth century, **John Chrysostom** described Judaism as a heresy and Jews as Christ-killers, and denounced Christians who adopted Jewish practices such as sabbath observance or attending synagogue (suggesting that there were close contacts between Jews and Christians). Although rabbinic literature hardly refers to Christianity, there is evidence that some Jews responded to these attacks. For example, a Jewish version of the Gospels called the *Toldot Jeshu*, which probably dates to the fifth century, attempts to show that Jesus could not be the messiah because not only was he not descended from David, but he was also illegitimate. The struggle between Judaism and Christianity was expressed in art and architecture as well. Followers of both religions attempted to bolster their claims to legitimacy and supremacy by citing scripture. Little wonder, then, that many of the same biblical scenes are depicted in Jewish and Christian art. For example, we have seen that the binding or offering of Isaac by Abraham is portrayed in the mosaic floors of the synagogues at Beth Alpha and Sepphoris. For Jews, this episode represents God's eternal promise to his people. The same scene is a common motif in early Christian art, but Christians describe it as the *sacrifice* of Isaac by Abraham because they understand the episode as prefiguring Christ's ultimate sacrifice. Similarly, the story of Daniel in the lion's den, which is depicted in the synagogue at Naaran, is common in early Christian art.

JUDAISM AND THE JERUSALEM TEMPLE

Christianity proclaims that Jesus is the messiah whose sacrifice guarantees salvation to believers. Salvation is offered to participants in the rituals and liturgy conducted inside churches, and is reflected in the images decorating these buildings. Worshipers in early Christian churches were surrounded by depictions of biblical scenes focusing especially on the lives of Jesus and Mary, which were placed strategically in relation to the liturgy conducted inside the building.

Judaism differs from Christianity in lacking a centralized authority with leadership hierarchy. Judaism has no pope, bishops, archbishops, or deacons. Therefore, it is all the more startling to see the same symbols represented in synagogues throughout Palestine and the Diaspora. This suggests that despite the diversity of building types, which might reflect different movements or liturgies (or maybe not), certain symbols were meaningful to a broad swath of the Jewish population. In the centuries after 70 the menorah became the symbol of Jewish identity (and hope for salvation), much as the cross eventually became a symbol for Christians. The menorah and other common Jewish ritual objects, such as the Ark of the Covenant, the *lulav* and *ethrog*, and incense shovels, are associated with the Jerusalem temple (the *lulav* and *ethrog* are used in the Feast of Tabernacles, which was one of the three main pilgrimage holidays to the temple). These symbols are depicted frequently in ancient synagogues as well as in other contexts, such as Jewish tombs. This surely reflects the continued anticipation among Jews that one day the temple would be rebuilt and the sacrificial cult reinstituted. This nearly occurred in the mid-fourth century, when the emperor **Julian** ("the Apostate") rejected Christianity and granted the Jews permission to rebuild the Jerusalem temple. However, Julian died soon thereafter in battle, ending Jewish hopes and plans for the temple's immediate reestablishment.

The temple and sacrifice imagery is especially explicit in the uppermost four registers of the Sepphoris synagogue. But this theme also underlies other scenes decorating synagogues. For example, Abraham's offering of Isaac refers to sacrifice, as tradition places this episode on Mount Moriah, Jerusalem's Temple Mount.

Helios and the Zodiac Cycle

Since the first example came to light nearly a century ago, much attention has focused on Helios and the zodiac cycle, although this motif has been found in only six ancient synagogues (all in Palestine). In addition, a long inscription in the mosaic floor of the synagogue at Ein Gedi includes a list of the signs of the zodiac. Scholars have struggled to understand why some congregations placed a depiction of the Greco-Roman sun god in the center of their synagogue buildings. Many interpretations have been suggested, none of which is universally accepted. It is likely that the motif of Helios and the zodiac cycle had different meanings or could be understood on different levels depending on the viewer, a common phenomenon in Byzantine art.

Before attempting to analyze and interpret these images, it is necessary to distinguish between Helios as the *sun* and Helios as the *sun god*. In the ancient Mediterranean world, the sun was not understood to be a ball of hot gases, but was conceived of as a male figure driving across the dome of heaven in a chariot every day (the heavens were visualized as a dome over the earth). Whereas the Greeks and Romans worshiped the figure of the sun (Helios) as a god, the Jews did not, despite the fact that they would have conceived of the sun in the same way. In other words, the figure of Helios in synagogue mosaics should be understood as a depiction of the sun, but this does not mean that Jews worshiped the sun as a god. By late antiquity it became common to depict rulers and even Jesus in the guise of Helios, as intermediaries interceding on behalf of the people with a supreme heavenly power or deity above. The Helios in synagogues might represent an intermediary figure of this type, a possibility that we shall consider here.

If Helios is the sun, the signs of the zodiac would represent the heavenly constellations surrounding him. The circular medallion containing Helios and the zodiac cycle would then be an allusion to the dome of heaven. Some church buildings had a dome towering over the nave, and in later Byzantine churches, the figure of Christ Pantokrator (the all-powerful Jesus) is represented in the center of the dome. In Roman buildings such as Hadrian's Pantheon or the octagonal room in Nero's Golden House (palace), the dome has a large opening (*oculus*) in the center through which the sun was visible. Ancient Palestinian synagogues did not have domes because they were beyond the means of the congregations. Instead, most synagogues had pitched, tiled roofs carried on trussed wooden beams that spanned the building's interior. The circular medallion with Helios and the zodiac cycle in the middle of the nave floor might then be an allusion to the dome of heaven – an attempt to represent a three-dimensional concept in two dimensions. In this case, we should imagine the figure of Helios as dominating the building from the center of an (imaginary) dome above, surrounded by the heavenly constellations and the four seasons in the corners. Helios and the zodiac would represent God's creation, with the interior of the synagogue literally conceived of as a microcosm of the universe (a similar concept governed the decorative schemes of Byzantine churches).

The prominent depiction of Helios as the sun also suggests a connection with an ancient Jewish solar calendar. The Jewish calendar used today is a lunisolar calendar that synchronizes twelve lunar months with the slightly longer solar year. Although this calendar was adopted by the rabbis, there is evidence that a solar calendar was preferred in some ancient Jewish circles, especially priestly groups such as the Qumran sect. In fact, some scholars believe that the Qumran sect separated from the rest of the population over calendrical disputes, adopting a solar calendar that might have been used previously in the temple. In other words, the prominence of Helios and the signs of the zodiac, which at Sepphoris are labeled also with the names of months, might allude to an ancient solar calendar associated with priestly circles and the Jerusalem temple.

Some synagogue leaders might have been members of the priestly class. In fact, the first century C.E. synagogue leader (*archisynagogos*) Theodotus was a priest. Many scholars believe that priests lost their standing after the destruction of the Jerusalem temple in 70, having been replaced by rabbis as the leaders of Jewish society. However, accumulating evidence now indicates that priests reemerged as a force in Jewish society in the fourth, fifth, and sixth centuries, and perhaps never lost their prominence after 70. In other words, Jewish society after 70 was composed of different and sometimes overlapping groups that vied for power and prestige. The emphasis in synagogue art on the Ark of the Covenant, Jerusalem temple, and sacrificial cult, combined with dedicatory inscriptions mentioning priests, suggest that priests played leadership roles in some congregations and were a significant force in Jewish society in general.

Rabbinic literature tells us nothing about figured images decorating synagogues, which is why the initial discovery of these buildings in the early twentieth century came as such as surprise and shock. A few passages refer to rabbis ruling for or against the use of pagan images in different contexts, but never explicitly in connection with synagogues. It is also doubtful that most rabbis exercised much control over synagogues. Rather than the synagogue, the study house (**beth midrash**) seems to have been the main locus of rabbinic activity.

Another corpus of Jewish literature from this period, called **Hekhalot literature**, might be more helpful in understanding the images in synagogue art. *Hekhalot* literature refers to works describing magical and mystical beliefs and practices that are used to obtain Torah knowledge and direct access to God. *Hekhalot* comes from the Hebrew word *hekhal*, which means temple or sanctuary, because this literature envisioned a series of successive heavenly sanctuaries or temples (usually seven) populated by myriads of angels and other divine beings, with God enthroned in the highest heaven. Typically, a mystic uttered magical words and phrases (including the name of God) or practiced certain rituals to compel one of the divine beings to come to earth and do his bidding, or ascended to the heavenly sanctuaries where God's secrets and knowledge were revealed to him. *Hekhalot* literature has been marginalized in the study of rabbinic period Judaism for several reasons: although there are references to magical and mystical beliefs and practices in rabbinic literature, the rabbis generally seem to have disapproved of such practices (as something they could not control); this literature is very difficult to understand and nearly impossible to date and contextualize with precision, and even the authors' identities and social context are unknown; and our modern biases against magic and mysticism have marginalized this literature. However, there is plenty of evidence that magical and mystical beliefs and practices were an integral and widely accepted part of late antique Judaism (and even Christianity).

Some scholars have proposed interpreting the figured images in ancient synagogues, and especially Helios and the zodiac cycle, in light of magical and mystical beliefs and practices. For example, some prayers invoke Helios, requesting his assistance as an intermediary being from the heavenly sanctuaries. Or perhaps the figure in synagogue mosaics represents another divine being in the guise of Helios, much as Jesus and earthly rulers sometimes were portrayed as Helios in late antiquity. In this case, the figure of Helios might represent **Metatron**, the most powerful divine angel in the heavenly sanctuaries. Metatron originally was a human named **Enoch**, the seventh forefather from Adam. At the end of his life, according to the Hebrew Bible, Enoch did not die – instead, "Enoch walked with God; then he was no more, because God took him" (Genesis 5:24). In the late Second Temple period and later, there was much speculation concerning Enoch's disappearance from earth. A number of works were written about Enoch, some fragments of which are represented

14.16 Christ Pantokrator in the dome of the church at Daphni in Greece, ca. 1100. National Geographic Image ID 415670, by James L. Stanfield/National Geographic Stock.

among the Dead Sea Scrolls but were not included later in the Jewish, Protestant, or Catholic canons of sacred scripture. Enoch was thought to have been taken to heaven by God, where he was transformed into Metratron, a divine super-angel with powers second only to those of God himself. Because, according to the biblical account, Enoch lived for 365 years (a figure that recalls the number of days in a solar calendrical year), Metatron was believed to have knowledge of calendrical secrets and especially the workings of the solar calendar. *Hekhalot* literature describes Metatron commanding the celestial bodies and sharing some of his knowledge with mystics. Therefore, it is possible that Helios should be understood as Metatron, a divine intermediary between the

14.17 The west wall of the Dura Europos synagogue with the Torah shrine niche. Courtesy of Zev Radovan/BibleLandPictures.com.

congregation and God. Similarly, Christ Pantokrator (the all-powerful Christ) often was depicted as an intermediary figure in the domes of later Byzantine churches.

The identification of Helios as Metatron or another divine intermediary is highly speculative. For one thing, the figure of Helios is never labeled in synagogue mosaics, leaving his identity unknown. In addition, *Hekhalot* literature does not refer to synagogues or synagogue art at all. Furthermore, it is unclear whether *Hekhalot* literature is prescriptive or descriptive – that is, we do not know whether the rituals described were practiced or not (this same is true of much of rabbinic literature). However, even if Helios was not identified as an intermediary figure by the synagogue congregations, there is little doubt that these images were intended to be multivalent (have different meanings). The figure of Helios could have been understood in one way by some viewers and in another way by others. The richness of the imagery and new discoveries undoubtedly will continue to fuel scholarly debates and speculation.

14.18 Interior of the Sardis synagogue looking east toward the Torah shrines.

Sidebar: Diaspora Synagogues

Dozens of ancient synagogue buildings have been discovered around the Mediterranean and Near East. One of the first such buildings to be found – and, arguably, the most spectacular – came to light in the 1932 excavations at **Dura Europos**. Dura Europos was a caravan city by the Euphrates River (in modern Syria). Originally founded in the Hellenistic period, the city later came under Parthian control and finally was occupied by the Romans, until it was destroyed by the **Sasanid Persians** in 256 C.E. The synagogue was installed in a house on the western side of the city. During the Sasanid siege, the inhabitants piled an earthen rampart against the inside of the city's fortification wall to buttress it. The synagogue was buried under the rampart, preserving the mud-brick walls and the wall paintings covering them. The paintings were divided into three registers, with each register containing panels with biblical scenes. A Torah shrine niche built into the western (Jerusalem-oriented) wall was also decorated with paintings, including a depiction of the Jerusalem temple and the binding or offering of Isaac. The extensive painted program in the Dura synagogue has been the subject of much scholarly interpretation and debate. Presumably other ancient synagogues had similar painted programs, but unfortunately, their wall paintings have not survived.

The largest ancient synagogue building discovered so far is located at **Sardis**, in central western Asia Minor (Turkey). It came to light in the 1960s during excavations in a Roman civic bath-and-gymnasium complex. The ancient Jewish community acquired a room in the complex and converted it into a synagogue by installing liturgical furniture, including two Torah shrines flanking the main doorway, a marble table on which the Torah scrolls could be opened and read, and benches. The synagogue was decorated lavishly with mosaic floors resembling carpets and colored marble panels covering the walls. Scholars estimate that the hall could have held up to 1,000 congregants!

In the early 1960s, the construction of a road to the Leonardo de Vinci airport brought to light a synagogue in Rome's ancient port city of **Ostia**. Like the synagogues at Sardis and Dura Europos, the Ostia synagogue was installed in a pre-existing building – a house or possibly a collegial hall (a hall belonging to a guild or social club) – that was converted for use by the addition of liturgical furniture, including a Torah shrine. Dozens of other examples of Diaspora synagogue buildings or architectural fragments and inscriptions belonging to synagogues exist at sites around the Roman world.

Sidebar: Women in Ancient Synagogues

For a long time scholars assumed that women played little, if any, role in ancient synagogues. In some archaeological reports, the second-story gallery found in a few synagogue buildings is described as a "women's gallery," on analogy with contemporary Orthodox synagogues. However, rabbinic literature says little about the participation of women in synagogues, and we know even less about the ancient liturgy. We do not know to what extent women participated in synagogue services, and, if they did participate, whether they were segregated from the men. In the 1980s a scholar named Bernadette Brooten published a book called *Women Leaders in the Ancient Synagogue*. She documented about two dozen of ancient inscriptions that refer to women with Jewish leadership titles including *archisynagogos* (leader of the synagogue). Brooten argued that if we assume such titles are not merely honorific but indicate real leadership roles for men, the same must be true for women. Brooten's book created a paradigm shift in the field of synagogue studies, and it is still widely cited as authoritative.

Brooten's work was a product of the feminist movement of the 1960s and 1970s, and the theoretical models that inform it are outdated by today's standards. For example, there is no need to assume that these titles were functional rather than honorific for men or women. The possibility that these titles were honorific – bestowed on wealthy patrons and their families – is suggested by the discovery of a few inscriptions in which young children hold titles such as leader of the synagogue. Furthermore, Brooten considered the body of evidence as a whole, rather than distinguishing between inscriptions from different centuries and different parts of the Mediterranean. Inscriptions naming women with leadership titles generally date to the fourth and fifth centuries, and most of them come from western Asia Minor and the Aegean (with no examples from Palestine). This evidence suggests that the status of women within Jewish communities varied, and that some women might have enjoyed more prominence in the synagogue setting in western Asia Minor. It is important to bear in mind that even so, only a small number of women – all of whom belonged to the upper class – attained any prominence.

Sidebar: Samaritan Synagogues

The diverse populations who made up ancient Palestine's rich tapestry included Samaritans (see Chapters 3 and 4). Like their Jewish neighbors, during the fourth to sixth centuries C.E. the Samaritans worshiped in synagogues. A few of these buildings have been discovered in the district of Samaria, where the Samaritan population was concentrated. Samaritan synagogues resemble Jewish synagogues and Christian churches in being congregational halls with features such as benches to accommodate assemblies, and liturgical elements such as orienting the building toward the direction of prayer. The Samaritans also decorated their synagogues with mosaic floors, which include depictions of many of the same ritual objects shown in Jewish synagogue mosaics, such as the Ark of the Covenant, menorahs, and incense shovels. However, not all the motifs depicted in Samaritan and Jewish art are the same, because of differences between their respective sacred scriptures and liturgies. For example, Samaritan synagogues are oriented toward Mount Gerizim (their sacred mountain) instead of Jerusalem's Temple Mount. In addition, the lack of any figured images in Samaritan synagogues suggests a stricter interpretation of the Second Commandment than that among their Jewish neighbors. There are also differences in details – for example, Samaritan mosaics depict trumpets instead of shofars among the ritual objects.

The emperor Justinian (see Chapter 15) closed Samaritan synagogues and attempted to convert the Samaritans forcibly to Christianity. This sparked the outbreak of a Samaritan revolt in the mid-sixth century, which was suppressed brutally. As a result, the Samaritan population was decimated and subsequently declined. Today there are fewer than 1,000 Samaritans, most of them living near Mount Gerizim and in the Israeli town of Holon.

Recommended Reading

Bernadette Brooten, *Women Leaders in the Ancient Synagogues* (Atlanta: Scholars, 1982).

Moshe Dothan, *Hammath Tiberias* (Jerusalem: Israel Exploration Society, 1983).

Steven Fine, *This Holy Place: On the Sanctity of the Synagogue During the Greco-Roman Period* (South Bend, IN: University of Notre Dame, 1997).

Erwin R. Goodenough, *Jewish Symbols in the Greco-Roman Period, Vols. 1–13* (abridged edition; Princeton, NJ: Princeton University, 1988).

Lee I. Levine, *The Ancient Synagogue: The First Thousand Years* (New Haven, CT: Yale University, 2000).

Lee I. Levine (ed.), *Ancient Synagogues Revealed* (Jerusalem: Israel Exploration Society, 1983).

Anders Runesson, *The Origins of the Synagogue: A Socio-Historical Study* (Stockholm: Almqvist and Wiksell International, 2001).

Zeev Weiss, *The Sepphoris Synagogue: Deciphering an Ancient Message through Its Archaeological and Socio-Historical Contexts* (Jerusalem: Israel Exploration Society, 2005).

Michael J. White, *Building God's House in the Roman World: Architectural Adaptation among Pagans, Jews and Christians* (Baltimore: ASOR/Johns Hopkins University, 1990).

FIFTEEN

THE BYZANTINE (EARLY CHRISTIAN) PERIOD (313–640 C.E.)

JERUSALEM

HISTORICAL BACKGROUND

Trajan and Hadrian were members of the long-lived Antonine dynasty, which came to an end with the death of Commodus in 192 C.E. The next dynasty was established by Septimius Severus, the first emperor of non-Italian descent (he was North African and his wife was Syrian). After the last member of the Severan dynasty died in 235, a prolonged period of civil war broke out. Over the next fifty years there was a rapid succession of claimants to the Roman throne, only one of whom died a natural death (the others were murdered or killed in battle). The instability on the throne affected all aspects of Roman life, resulting in inflation and devaluation of the currency, as well as hostile invasions as barbarians overran the borders of the empire. For the first time in centuries, a new fortification wall was built around the city of Rome.

The crisis of the third century ended when a general named Diocletian became emperor in 284. Diocletian is known as one of the last great perse-cutors of Christians. He instituted wide-ranging reforms that affected nearly every aspect of Roman life, including changing the monetary system and estab-lishing a line of border forts to protect the empire. Diocletian even reformed the system of government. He realized that the empire had grown too large for one man to manage alone, and that the principle of dynastic succession was a source of instability. Therefore, Diocletian split the empire into two halves, east and west, and appointed an emperor (called an Augustus) to rule over each half. He also appointed two co-rulers with the title Caesar to assist the emperors, one each for the east and west. The Caesars were intended to ensure a peaceful and orderly transition to the throne by replacing the Augusti when they retired. Diocletian's system of rule by four men (two Augusti and

15.1 Statue of the Tetrarchs in Venice.

two Caesars) is called the **Tetrarchy**, and each of the four rulers is called a **tetrarch**.

In 305, Diocletian retired to a palace in the town of Split (Spalato), in his native Illyria (modern Croatia). He forced the other Augustus to retire as well, the idea being that the two Caesars would take over. Instead, a civil war erupted between the other co-rulers and their sons. In 312, Constantine (the son of the Caesar of the west) defeated Maxentius (the son of the Augustus of the west) at the battle at the Milvian Bridge. Before this battle, Constantine reportedly had a dream or vision in which he saw two winged Victories (angels) holding a banner bearing the **Chi-Rho** symbol (the Greek monogram of Christ). Constantine vowed to become a Christian if he won the battle, although he was not baptized until he was on his deathbed. After his victory in the battle, Constantine assumed rule of the western half of the Roman Empire. In 313 Constantine and Licinius (the ruler of the eastern half of the empire) issued the **Edict of Milan** legalizing Christianity, which now became the religion of the emperor himself.

In 324, Constantine defeated Licinius in battle and became the sole ruler of the Roman Empire. He established a new imperial capital at **Byzantium**, a city strategically located on the land bridge between the continents of Europe and Asia. Following the precedent set by Alexander the Great centuries earlier, Constantine refounded the city and named it after himself: **Constantinople** (Constantinopolis – "the city of Constantine") (modern **Istanbul** in Turkey). Constantine's new capital city was modeled after Rome, including being built on seven hills and having a palace complex overlooking a hippodrome (like the Palatine Hill overlooking the Circus Maximus in Rome). But unlike Rome, the new capital was filled with Christian churches, not pagan temples. Constantine dedicated the churches to concepts or ideals that were personified and had been worshiped as pagan gods, such as Holy Wisdom (**Hagia Sophia**) and Holy Peace (Hagia Eirene).

After Constantine's death in 337, the Roman Empire (now officially a Christian empire) remained unified until 395, when Theodosius I died. After Theodosius' death the empire split into two halves – east and west – ruled by his sons. With a brief exception, never again was the Roman Empire united under the rule of a single emperor. Soon after the split, barbarian tribes – including the Ostrogoths in Italy, Vandals in North Africa, Franks in France, and Visigoths in Spain – began to overrun and occupy parts of the western half of the empire. The territories they settled eventually were transformed into the states of medieval Europe. The unstable situation in the western half of the empire culminated in 410 with the sack of Rome by Alaric and the Goths.

The eastern half of the Roman Empire became known as the Byzantine Empire, after the capital city (formerly named Byzantium), although the Byzantines always considered themselves Romans. In fact, many scholars refer to the fourth to sixth centuries as the Late Roman period, not the Byzantine period (although most archaeologists working in Palestine call it Byzantine). In contrast to the west, the eastern half of the empire remained unified and secure through the sixth century. Justinian, the Byzantine emperor from 527 to 565, attempted to reunify the empire by conducting a "reconquest" of the western half of the Mediterranean. Justinian was a great builder who reconstructed Constantine's Hagia Sophia (which still stands today in Istanbul) and sponsored the construction of many other churches and monasteries around the empire, including the monastery of St. Catherine at the foot of Mount Sinai. He also established a series of forts to protect the empire's borders from invasions. Justinian is known for having persecuted pagans and Jews, and he closed the last schools of Greek philosophy that were still operating in Athens.

Justinian's reconquest bankrupted the imperial treasury. After his death, the Byzantines lost control of the western half of the Mediterranean and began to suffer invasions of their own borders. In 614, Syria and Palestine were overrun by the Sasanid Persians. The Sasanids were aided by the local Jewish population, who had suffered under Byzantine Christian rule and hoped for permission to rebuild the Jerusalem temple. Jewish hopes were dashed when the Sasanids accommodated with the Christian majority before being ousted by the Byzantines in 628. The Byzantine reconquest of Syria and Palestine was short-lived. Between 634 and 640, Palestine fell to Muslim tribes from Arabia, never to be retaken by the Byzantines. By the seventh and eighth centuries, the territories under Byzantine rule were limited to Asia Minor and Greece, although the Byzantine Empire continued to exist until 1453, when Constantinople fell to the Ottoman Turks.

JERUSALEM

Jerusalem benefited greatly from the legalization of Christianity, becoming one of only five **Patriarchate** cities (the seat of a patriarch) in the entire Roman Empire. Pilgrims poured into the city, bringing with them money that boosted the economy and fueled a building boom. Some churches and monasteries were the beneficiaries of imperial patronage. For example, the empress **Eudocia**, the estranged wife of Theodosius II, settled in Jerusalem in the mid-fifth century and sponsored a number of building projects, including churches, monasteries, and a new city wall.

Because Christianity was outlawed (which meant that Christians could not worship openly) until Constantine issued the Edict of Milan, the earliest churches were built during Constantine's reign. Not surprisingly, Constantine focused much of his attention on the Holy Land – and especially Jerusalem. He erected the **Eleona Church** on the Mount of Olives (Eleona comes from the Greek word for olives), a large complex including a monastery and a circular chapel marking the spot where Jesus is believed to have ascended to heaven (see Luke 24:50–52).

The Madaba map shows Jerusalem at the height of its expansion during the Byzantine period, when the city extended from the line of the current north wall of the Old City to Mount Zion and the City of David on the south. Numerous churches erected along the streets originally laid out by Hadrian are visible on the Madaba map as basilical structures with red-tiled roofs (see Figure 13.3).

The Church of the Holy Sepulcher

On the west side of Jerusalem's main *cardo*, Constantine built the Church of the Holy Sepulcher (originally called the Church of the **Anastasis** [Greek for resurrection]). The Church of the Holy Sepulcher was established on the north side of Hadrian's western forum, where the temple to Aphrodite and basilica were located. Constantine razed the temple after being informed by the local Christian community that it was built over the tomb of Jesus. Under the temple was a rocky area containing rock-cut tombs with loculi dating to the late Second Temple period. Constantine cut back the rock to isolate the loculus that reportedly had contained Jesus' body, which he enshrined in a circular domed structure

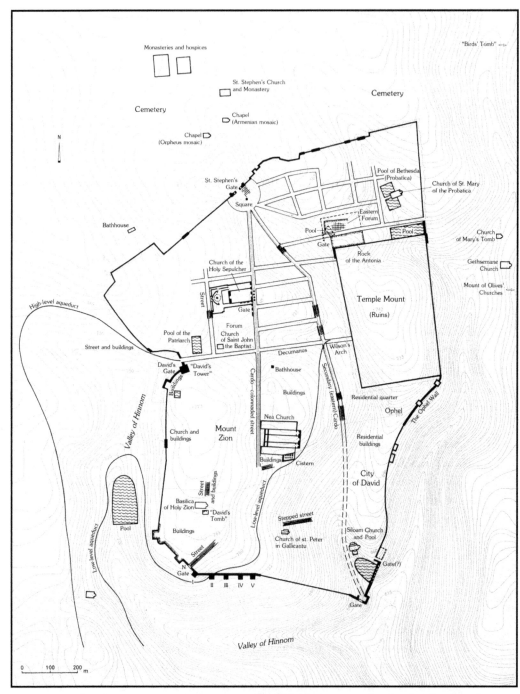

15.2 Plan of Byzantine Jerusalem. From E. Stern (ed.), *The New Encyclopedia of Archaeological Excavations in the Holy Land* (New York: Simon and Schuster, 1993), vol. 2, p. 7769. By permission of Hillel Geva and the Israel Exploration Society.

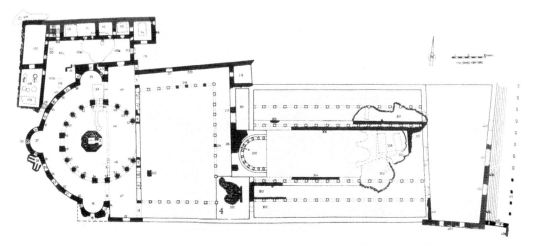

15.3 Plan of the Constantinian Church of the Holy Sepulcher. After V. C. Corbo, *Il Santo Sepolcro de Gerusalemme, Aspetti arceologici dale origini al period crociato* (Jerusalem: Studium Biblicum Franciscanum, 1981), vol. 2, Pl. 3. By permission of the Studium Biblicum Franciscanum.

called the **Rotunda**. A few loculi belonging to this cemetery are still preserved just outside the walls of the Rotunda, which modern Christian tradition identifies as the tombs of Joseph of Arimathea and Nicodemus. The presence of these loculi indicates that this area was a Jewish cemetery in the time of Jesus and therefore lay outside the walls of the city. This is the closest archaeology comes to verifying the authenticity of the Church of the Holy Sepulcher, although it is impossible to prove that Jesus' body was laid to rest in one of these loculi (see Chapter 11).

Because little survives of the Constantinian church, the Madaba map provides valuable evidence of its original layout and appearance. The map prominently depicts the church on the western side of the main *cardo*, from which it was approached by a set of steps. On the map, the basilica is shown as a large, rectangular building with a pitched, red-tiled roof. Immediately behind (to the west of) the basilica a dome is visible on the map, representing the Rotunda. Drawing on information from the map and archaeological remains, we can reconstruct the Constantinian church as follows. The entrance was from the main *cardo* by way of an atrium (courtyard). The church itself consisted of the Hadrianic basilica, which Constantine converted to use as a Christian basilica (hall of worship). A large apse (semicircular niche) at the west end of the hall contained the altar. Whereas in most early Christian churches the apse (which indicates the direction of prayer) was oriented toward the east, in the Constantinian Church of the Holy Sepulcher it was oriented toward the west, to face the tomb of Christ. A chapel on the south side of the church enshrined a rocky outcrop venerated as **Golgotha** or **Calvary**, the hill on which Jesus

15.4 *Aedicule* in the Rotunda of the Church of the Holy Sepulcher. Courtesy of Zev Radovan/BibleLandPictures.com.

was crucified (today a chapel enshrining the rock of Golgotha is located on the south side of the Crusader church, next to the main entrance; discussed later). A courtyard to the west of the church (basilica) provided access to the Rotunda, which enshrined the tomb of Christ.

The surviving remnants of the Constantinian church are concentrated in the Russian Alexander Hospice, which occupies the area between the main *cardo* and the current Church of the Holy Sepulcher. These remains consist of the steps leading up to the entrance to the Hadrianic basilica (which Constantine converted into a Christian hall of worship) and the façade of the building (see Chapter 13). In addition, the apse of the Constantinian basilica is preserved under the current apse (which was built by the Crusaders; discussed later).

The Church of the Holy Sepulcher has suffered much damage throughout the centuries from human agents and natural catastrophes such as earthquakes. The most extensive damage was done in the year 1009, when an Egyptian Fatimid caliph named al-Hakim ordered the church to be razed. Only the Rotunda was left standing. A couple of decades later, the Byzantines were given permission to build a courtyard with chapels abutting the Rotunda, but the church was

15.5 South façade of the Church of the Holy Sepulcher. Courtesy of Zev Radovan/BibleLand Pictures.com.

not rebuilt. Al-Hakim's destruction provided the excuse for the Crusades, the ostensible goal of which was to restore the Church of the Holy Sepulcher. After the Crusaders took Jerusalem in 1099, they immediately rebuilt the church (that is, the basilica or hall of worship). The Crusaders built their basilica abutting the Rotunda, with the apse facing east instead of west. The apse at the eastern end of the Crusader church lies above the apse at the western end of Constantine's basilica; the area that had been occupied by the original basilica (up to the line of the main *cardo*, now the site of the Russian Alexander Hospice) was excluded from the Crusader church.

The current church is largely a product of the Crusader reconstruction. Instead of entering directly from the main *cardo* as in the original church, access is on the south side of the building. The Crusaders built the church in the late Romanesque–early Gothic style that was characteristic of Western Europe in the early twelfth century. The south façade had two large side-by-side doorways framed by clusters of columns and with slightly pointed, decorated arches (archivolts) above. The lintels of the main doorways (which have been removed) were carved with scenes from the life of Jesus. The vaults and dome inside the church are supported on massive piers with clusters of engaged columns, and are articulated with ribs. Three radiating chapels are attached to an ambulatory that encircles the apse.

The Rotunda is the only part of Constantine's church that is still standing. However, over the centuries it, too, has suffered tremendous damage. The floor level has risen, making the piers and columns appear stubby and truncated; the dome has been rebuilt repeatedly; and none of the original interior decoration survives. The tomb is enshrined in a free-standing structure (an *aedicule* or *edicule*), which in its current form was built after a fire in 1808 did extensive damage to the church. Today, different parts of the church are in the custody of different denominations, including Greek Orthodox, Latin Catholics, Armenians, Copts, and Ethiopians.

THE NEA CHURCH

The Madaba map shows Byzantine Jerusalem at its height, around 600 C.E. As we have seen, the Church of the Holy Sepulcher is depicted prominently on the western side of the main *cardo*. A close look at the map reveals the presence of numerous other churches scattered throughout the city, which are represented as basilicas (rectangular buildings) with pitched, tiled roofs. One basilica is visible at the southern end of the western hill (today's Mount Zion), at the site of the present Church of the Dormition. Another basilica is visible on the north side of the Via Dolorosa (north of the Temple Mount, which is not shown in the map; see the Sidebar). Even the area outside the city was filled with churches and monasteries, many of which have come to light in archaeological excavations. For example, a large church and monastery dedicated to St. Stephen was located to the north of the city, at the site of the current École Biblique et Archéologique Française de Jerusalem (the home institution of Roland de Vaux, who excavated Qumran).

On the Madaba map, a large basilica is depicted on the eastern side of the *cardo*, at its southern end. This is the Nea (Greek for new) Church, an abbreviated form of its full name: the New Church of Mary, the Mother of God (Greek **Theotokos**), which was built by the emperor Justinian in the sixth century. The Nea Church is described by Justinian's court biographer, Procopius. However, after the Nea Church was destroyed centuries ago, it was never rebuilt and subsequently was forgotten. Avigad's excavations in the Jewish Quarter in the 1970s brought to light parts of the Nea Church for the first time, in the same location shown on the Madaba map. The church was an enormous basilica – the largest so far discovered in Palestine – measuring more than 300 feet in length! In addition to a large apse at the end of the nave, there were smaller apses at the end of each aisle.

The Nea Church was built on uneven ground that sloped down toward the south. To level the area, Justinian's architects constructed a platform supported on underground arches and vaults (similar to Herod's extension of the Temple Mount, which is supported on Solomon's Stables). The vaulted spaces under the platform of the Nea Church were used as cisterns. Here Avigad made a stunning discovery: the original dedicatory inscription of the church was still embedded

Sidebar: The Temple Mount

Jerusalem's most conspicuous feature – the Temple Mount – is not depicted on the Madaba map. The reason is simple: during the Byzantine period, the Temple Mount was abandoned, without any buildings standing on it. The Second Temple had been destroyed centuries earlier, and many of its architectural fragments had been robbed out for reuse. Hadrian's shrine or temple to Capitoline Jupiter was razed after Christianity was legalized. Ancient sources suggest that during the Byzantine period, the Temple Mount was used as a garbage dump. The Christian population deliberately left the Temple Mount lying in ruins because they considered this proof of Jesus' prediction that the second temple would be destroyed (see, for example, Mark 13:1–4). The despoiled Temple Mount esplanade served for Christians as a witness to the truth of Jesus' prophecy and as a visual symbol of the triumph of Christianity over Judaism.

in the wall of a cistern. The inscription confirms that Justinian built the church, and is dated according to an indiction, which is a fifteen-year cycle used in the Byzantine calendar. The inscription, which is in Greek, reads:

> And this is the work which our most pious Emperor Flavius Justinianus carried out with munificence, under the care and devotion of the most holy Constantinus, Priest and *Hegumen* [leader or head of a monastery], in the thirteenth (year of the) indiction.

The Nea Church is a wonderful example of the confluence of different types of evidence: an ancient literary description, the visual depiction on the ancient Madaba map, and recent archaeological discoveries.

15.6 Inscription from the Nea Church. Courtesy of Zev Radovan/BibleLandPictures.com.

Sidebar: The Garden Tomb (Gordon's Calvary)

Just north of the Damascus Gate lies the **Garden Tomb** or **Gordon's Calvary**, which is venerated by some Protestants as the site of Jesus' crucifixion and burial. The tradition associating this spot with Jesus originated in the nineteenth century, when General Charles Gordon visited Jerusalem. Gordon was a decorated British officer who conducted successful military campaigns in China and the Sudan. In 1882–1883, Gordon spent a year in Jerusalem. An evangelical Christian, he visited the holy sites associated with Jesus but was put off by the rituals of the Catholics and the eastern Orthodox denominations in the Church of the Holy Sepulcher. Gordon also rejected the Church of the Holy Sepulcher as the site of Jesus' crucifixion and burial because it lies within the walls of the Old City (he was unaware that this site was outside the city walls at the time of Jesus).

After searching for a more likely candidate, Gordon decided that a rocky outcrop to the north of the Old City was the site of Jesus' crucifixion and burial. Gordon imagined that the outcrop resembled a skull (Golgotha means "skull hill" in Aramaic), and ancient rock-cut tombs are hewn into it. Since then, the site became popular among Protestants from Western countries. However, recent archaeological investigations have demonstrated that although the tombs cut into the rocky outcrop at the Garden Tomb are ancient, they do not date to the time of Jesus (late Second Temple period). Instead, some of the tombs date to the late Iron Age (late First Temple period; seventh–early sixth centuries B.C.E.) and others date to the Byzantine period (fifth and sixth centuries C.E.). In fact, the area to the north of the Old City is filled with hundreds of Byzantine tombs associated with numerous churches and monasteries, stretching from the W. F. Albright Institute of Archaeological Institute on Salah ed-Din Street to the École Biblique (Church of St. Stephen).

Although the Garden Tomb is a lovely spot for pilgrims seeking a quiet retreat for contemplation and prayer, there is no historical or archaeological evidence supporting its identification as the site of Jesus' crucifixion and burial.

The *Cardo*

Avigad's excavations included the southern end of the main *cardo* (south of its intersection with the main *decumanus*). As we have seen (Chapter 13), his findings indicate that this part of the main *cardo* was established in the sixth century, not in Hadrian's time, as scholars previously thought. Avigad suggested that the northern half of the main *cardo* is Hadrianic, and that it was extended to the south in the sixth century, after settlement had spread to this

Sidebar: The Golden Gate

This is the only gate in the eastern wall of the Temple Mount, and today its two arched passageways are blocked up. Christian tradition identifies this as the Beautiful Gate, which is mentioned in Acts 3:1–6 as the site where Peter healed a lame beggar. Christians also believe that this is where Jesus entered the Temple Mount on Palm Sunday (see John 12:13). These traditions likely have little basis in fact, as the steep slope of the Kidron Valley made access from the east difficult. Instead, in the Herodian period many pilgrims entered the Temple Mount through the Hulda Gates. Furthermore, the Golden Gate's architectural style and decoration point to a Byzantine or Umayyad date of construction, although it might be built over an earlier gate (perhaps the Shushan/Susa Gate of the Second Temple period). Either way, the location suggests that the gate was used for ceremonial purposes only. It is impossible to know which gate in the Herodian Temple Mount should be identified with the "Beautiful Gate" mentioned in Acts, as this name is not attested in any other source. In Arabic the Golden Gate is called the Gate of Mercy, based on a passage from the **Quran** that refers to a gate in a wall that has mercy on the inside and punishment on the outside.

area. In fact, Avigad proposed connecting the extension of the main *cardo* to the south with the construction of the Nea Church. He suggested that the *cardo* was extended to connect the Church of the Holy Sepulcher with the Nea Church, enabling processions of pilgrims to make their way from one church to the

15.7 Reconstruction of Jerusalem's main *cardo*. By Leen Ritmeyer ©.

other. Avigad's theory is attractive and is supported by the fact that the same pottery types were found under the pavement of the southern end of the main *cardo* and under the Nea Church.

Recommended Reading

Nahman Avigad, *Discovering Jerusalem* (Nashville, TN: Thomas Nelson, 1983).

Martin Biddle, *The Tomb of Christ* (Gloucestershire, UK: Sutton Publishing, 1999).

F. E. Peters, *Jerusalem: The Holy City in th Eyes of Chroniclers, Visitors, Pilgrims, and Prophets from the Days of Abraham to the Beginnings of Modern Times* (Princeton, NJ: Princeton University, 1985).

Yoram Tsafrir (ed.), *Ancient Churches Revealed* (Jerusalem: Israel Exploration Society, 1993).

SIXTEEN

THE BYZANTINE (EARLY CHRISTIAN) PERIOD (313–640 C.E.)

PALESTINE UNDER CHRISTIAN RULE

In the eyes of the Romans, Palestine was a remote and relatively uncivilized province inhabited by a troublesome people with a peculiar ancestral religion and strange customs. For Christians, however, this is the Holy Land, the land of the Bible and the prophets. Here Jesus Christ was born, preached, died, and was resurrected. Therefore, Constantine's legalization of Christianity had an immediate and profound impact on Palestine. Almost overnight the country was transformed from an undeveloped backwater to one of the most important provinces in the Roman world. Thousands of pilgrims poured in to visit sites associated with Jesus and the Bible. The money they spent for food, lodging, transportation, guides, and souvenirs propelled the local economy. Beginning in the fourth century, hundreds of churches, monasteries, and hostels were built around the country, some funded by imperial patrons wishing to display their piety. The population increased to levels that remained unmatched until the twentieth century. Existing towns and cities, such as Jerusalem and Caesarea, expanded to their greatest size, and new settlements were established in marginal and previously uninhabited parts of the country, such as the Negev desert. Byzantine period remains are represented at nearly every excavated site in Palestine. In this chapter we survey just a few of the hundreds of Byzantine sites outside Jerusalem.

BETHLEHEM: THE CHURCH OF THE NATIVITY

According to the Gospels of Matthew and Luke, Jesus was born in Bethlehem, which is three miles south of Jerusalem. Prior to the Byzantine period, Bethlehem was a small village, but under Christian rule it became a major pilgrimage center. In fact, the Church of the Nativity is one of only three churches built

16.1 Map of Byzantine Palestine. Ancient World Mapping Center, University of North Carolina at Chapel Hill (www.unc.edu/awmc).

by Constantine in Palestine (the others are the Church of the Eleona and the Church of the Holy Sepulcher in Jerusalem). The Church of the Nativity is similar to the Church of the Holy Sepulcher in that it consists of a basilica (hall of worship) together with a building enshrining a central focal point. Whereas in the Church of the Holy Sepulcher the tomb of Christ was enshrined within the circular, domed Rotunda, Constantine's Church of the Nativity had an octagonal building surrounding a cave or grotto venerated as the spot where Jesus was born.

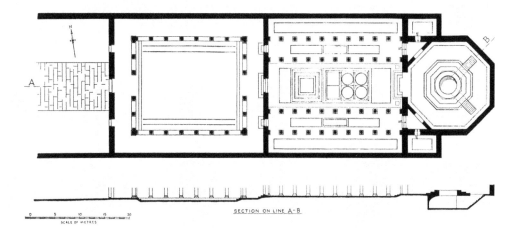

16.2 Plan and section of the Constantinian Church of the Nativity in Bethlehem. From E. T. Richmond, "Basilica of the Nativity, Discovery of the Remains of an Earlier Church," *Quarterly of the Department of Antiquities of Palestine* 5 (1936), p. 66 Fig. 1.

Like the Church of the Holy Sepulcher, the Constantinian Church of the Nativity included a large basilica with four rows of columns dividing the interior into a nave flanked by four aisles (two on each side), which was entered through a courtyard (atrium). Three doorways in the west wall provided access from the courtyard into the basilica, which was paved with geometric mosaics. Like the Church of the Holy Sepulcher, the focal point of the Church of the Nativity (the grotto) was located at the end of the nave – that is, the direction of prayer. However, unlike the Church of the Holy Sepulcher, in the Church of the Nativity the building enshrining the focal point was not separated from the basilica by a courtyard but lay at the end of the nave, replacing an apse.

In the sixth century, Justinian rebuilt the Church of the Nativity, which had been damaged during the Samaritan revolt. Justinian's basilica is longer than Constantine's (which was almost square), and had a narthex (porch) added between the courtyard and the entrance to the basilica. The biggest changes, however, were made to the structure enshrining the grotto. Instead of an octagonal building, the grotto was surrounded by three large apses in the shape of a cloverleaf, one apse on each side (east, north, and south), lying at the eastern end of the nave. Justinian also widened the nave, making the aisles narrower.

Unlike the Church of the Holy Sepulcher, the Church of the Nativity has not been damaged and reconstructed extensively since Justinian's time. Under the Crusaders in the twelfth century, the interior was redecorated with wall paintings and mosaics, only a few patches of which still survive. The wooden roof was replaced in the seventeenth century. However, the building itself (including the columns and capitals in the nave) is a product of Constantine's

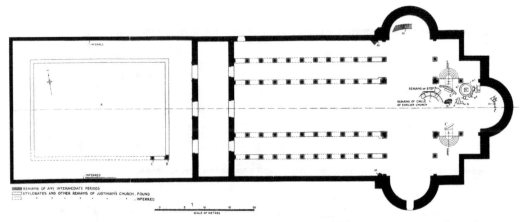

16.3 Plan of the Justinianic Church of the Nativity in Bethlehem. From E. T. Richmond, "Basilica of the Nativity, Discovery of the Remains of an Earlier Church," *Quarterly of the Department of Antiquities of Palestine* 5 (1936), p. 72 Fig. 1.

and Justinian's time. The church provides a good impression of the appearance of an early Christian basilica.

BETH SHEAN

The Decapolis, a league of the most Hellenized cities in Palestine, was formed after Rome's annexation of the Hasmonean kingdom. The Decapolis cities were concentrated in northeastern Palestine, outside the most heavily Judaized

16.4 Interior of the Church of the Nativity in Bethlehem. Courtesy of Zev Radovan/ BibleLandPictures.com.

16.5 Colonnaded street at Beth Shean with the tel in the background.

regions. Beth Shean is only one of two Decapolis cities located inside Israel's pre-1967 borders (the second Decapolis city is **Hippos-Susita**, which is located on the Golan Heights just inside Israel's pre-1967 border with Syria). The other Decapolis cities are in Jordan (see Gerasa, discussed later). Beth Shean was an important city throughout antiquity because of its strategic location at a major crossroads in the Jezreel and Jordan Valleys. Beth Shean is also blessed with an abundance of fresh-water springs (and proximity to the Jordan River), a warm climate, and, fertile agricultural land. Beth Shean was first settled in prehistoric times, and the Bronze and Iron Age tel (artificial mound) still dominates the site. In the Hellenistic period the city was refounded as Scythopolis ("city of the Scythians"), and occupation moved from the tel to the area below. Beth Shean's importance increased in 389 C.E., when it became the capital of one of the administrative provinces of Palestine (the province of Palaestina Secunda, or Second Palestine). The city reached its maximum size in the Byzantine period, when the fortification walls were extended to a length of some three miles. The population is estimated to have reached about 40,000 by the sixth century. Although much of the pagan population converted to Christianity during the Byzantine period, the city included sizeable Jewish and Samaritan communities.

Large-scale Israeli excavations conducted at Beth Shean since 1986 have brought to light the Roman and Byzantine civic center, which lies at the foot of the tel. The civic center was bisected by broad, paved, colonnaded streets lined by shops and surrounded by public monuments, temples, and (later) churches.

16.6 Tyche mosaic from Beth Shean. Courtesy of Zev Radovan/BibleLandPictures.com.

The monuments include a fountain building, a Roman theater (with the banks of seats supported on stone-built vaults as at Caesarea, rather than on the natural slope of a hill), two large public bath houses, an *odeion* (small covered theater) or *bouleterion* (meeting hall for the city council), and a forum with a Roman-style basilica along one side. During the Roman period a temple to Zeus Akraios (the highest Zeus) was built on top of the tel; in the Byzantine period the temple was replaced by a round church and monastery. In 507, a new commercial center called "the Sigma" was added alongside one of the colonnaded streets. It consisted of shops and taverns built around a semicircular space (shaped like the Greek letter *sigma* [Σ]; in this period the Greek sigma is shaped like a C, hence the semicircular shape), with a portico (a row of columns supporting a tiled roof creating a covered porch) in front. A dedicatory inscription informs us that the Sigma was built by the governor of Palaestina Secunda. Many of the shops in the Sigma were paved with mosaic floors, including one depicting the city goddess (**Tyche**). She wears a crown of city walls and holds in one hand a cornucopia (horn of plenty) that overflows with agricultural produce, symbolizing abundance and prosperity.

In the second century C.E., a hippodrome was established to the south of the city (originally outside the city walls). Two hundred years later, the hippodrome was shortened and converted into an amphitheater (an oval arena). By the end of the sixth century the amphitheater had ceased to function. Beth Shean continued to flourish after the Muslim conquest in the seventh century, but declined after devastating damage caused by the earthquake of 749.

Gerasa (Jerash)

Gerasa (modern Jerash in Jordan) is another Decapolis city. Although there are earlier remains, like Beth Shean, Gerasa reached its greatest size and level of prosperity during the Roman and Byzantine periods. The area within the city walls was bisected by broad, colonnaded streets consisting of a main *cardo* and two main *decumani*. The Chrysorhoas River (usually a dry riverbed) runs through the middle of the city from north to south, to the east of the main *cardo*. The area east of the river was the residential quarter (largely covered by the modern town). It was divided into *insulae* (blocks) by a grid of streets that was oriented differently from the *cardo* and *decumani*, and may go back to the Hellenistic period. Bridges spanning the river connected the residential quarter with the rest of the city.

Public monuments and temples were laid out alongside the main *cardo*. A sanctuary of Artemis, the patron deity of Gerasa, was located in the center of the city on the western side of the main *cardo*. The temple sat in the middle of an enormous, raised *temenos* approached by a monumental staircase and series of gates. A temple dedicated to Zeus overlooked a large oval plaza just inside the south gate of the city (see Figure 13.6). The public entertainment arenas included two theaters (both inside the walls, one on the north and one on the south), and a hippodrome to the south of the city (outside the walls). A monumental, triple-arched gate next to the hippodrome was erected to commemorate Hadrian's visit in 130 C.E.

During the fifth and sixth centuries, churches were built around Gerasa, eight of which have been discovered so far. One of the churches, dated by an inscription to 530–531, was constructed over a synagogue. The mosaic floor of the synagogue (which is covered by the church) included a scene depicting animals entering Noah's Ark and an inscription recording the names of three donors surrounding a menorah, *lulav* and *ethrog*, shofar, and incense shovel. Although scholars once believed that Gerasa declined during the early Islamic period, recent excavations have brought to light monumental remains including a large congregational mosque, which was installed in a Roman bath house (that went out of use), at the intersection of the main *cardo* and southern *decumanus*. Like Beth Shean, Gerasa declined in the wake of devastating damage caused by the earthquake of 749.

The Negev Towns

The population boom during the Byzantine period led to the establishment of settlements in previously marginal areas such as the Negev desert. After the Romans annexed the Nabataean kingdom in 106 C.E., they moved the caravan routes to the north, out of Nabataean control. The Nabataeans turned to other sources of livelihood, developing a sophisticated irrigation technology that enabled them to cultivate the desert. In the centuries following the Roman annexation, many of the former Nabataean trading posts became permanent settlements with an agricultural base (see Chapter 5). They included the Negev towns of **Mampsis** (Arabic **Kurnub**; Hebrew **Mamshit**), Elusa (Hebrew Halutza), Subeita (Hebrew Shivta), Oboda (Hebrew Avdat), Nessana (Hebrew Nitzana), and Ruheibeh (Hebrew Rehovot-in-the-Negev). These towns reached the height of their size and prosperity during the fifth to seventh centuries. By this time the Nabataeans had converted to Christianity, and churches were erected in all the towns. The desert around the towns was dotted with farmhouses that included agricultural fields and terraces, livestock pens, and agricultural installations such as wine presses and olive presses. During the Byzantine period, high-quality wine from the Negev was exported throughout the Mediterranean in torpedo-shaped ceramic jars called Gaza amphoras (so called because the wine was exported from the port at Gaza). Seminomadic pastoralists wandered the more marginal areas outside the settlements, herding sheep and goats and finding occasional employment in the towns and farms.

Mampsis, in the central Negev, is a small, compact town that had an economy based on trade rather than agriculture. The inhabitants lived in spacious, two-story-high houses built of ashlar masonry, with rooms surrounding an open, paved courtyard. Because of the shortage of wooden beams in the Negev, the rooms were roofed with stone slabs laid on top of closely spaced stone arches. One house contained a stable with stone troughs (mangers). A room in another house was decorated with colorful wall paintings depicting Greek mythological figures including Leda and the swan, and Eros and Psyche. Nearby a bronze jar containing 10,500 Roman silver coins dating from the first to third centuries was discovered. The excavator speculated that the money belonged to a horse breeder who was hoarding his wealth.

During the fourth or fifth century, a fortification wall was built around Mampsis. Soon afterward, two churches were erected in the town: the Eastern Church and the Western Church. The churches have similar plans: an atrium (courtyard) with peristyle columns that created an open area surrounded by covered porches on all four sides, and a basilical hall with two rows of columns dividing the interior into a nave flanked by aisles. The nave terminated in a large apse, and there were small rooms at the ends of the aisles. The Western Church, which is the smaller of the two churches, was inserted into a pre-existing residential quarter. The aisles were paved with stone but the nave was covered with a colorful mosaic that included octagonal medallions filled with birds and baskets of fruit. In front of the bema (the raised area in the apse), two peacocks (a common Christian motif alluding to Paradise) are depicted flanking an amphora with a vine. A donor named Nilus is commemorated in two inscriptions as having built the church.

16.7 Western Church (church of Nilus) at Mampsis.

The Eastern Church is located on the highest point in the town, and might have included a monastery. The floors of the aisles were paved with stone and the nave had a simple geometric mosaic. **Reliquaries** associated with a cult of saints and martyrs were discovered under the floors of the rooms at the ends of the aisles. In the corner of one of these rooms, a small grave containing a single bone was found, which was covered with a paving stone pierced by a hole through which oil could be poured. Presumably the bone belonged to someone venerated as a saint. Other burials were found below the floors of both side rooms. A chapel to one side of the basilica might have been used by **catechumens**. It opened onto a baptistery with a cruciform baptismal font (a cross-shaped pool) sunk into the floor and a small round basin or tub next to it. The font was surrounded by four small columns decorated with crosses on their capitals, which originally held a canopy. The font, which was accessed by going down steps inside the arms of the cross, was big enough to accommodate adults, a necessity among a population that was in the process of undergoing conversion to Christianity. Infants and small children could have been baptized in the small basin.

We do not know why Byzantine towns had multiple churches. Perhaps the churches had different functions (such as a cathedral versus a monastic church), perhaps they were used on different occasions, or perhaps they served different denominations with distinctive liturgies. Early Christianity was characterized by a diversity of theologies, dogmas, and practices, which were represented by different movements (many of which were condemned as heresies by their opponents). These differences caused deep – and sometimes violent – divisions among the Christian population, who disagreed on matters such as the nature of Christ and his birth (human or divine; one or more persons or natures), the status of the Virgin Mary (mother of God or not), and whether (and to what degree) Christians should observe Jewish practices and law.

In the early Islamic period, passersby inscribed Arabic invocations on the stone walls of the apse of the Eastern Church at Mampsis, which had ceased to be used as a church. Although many churches ceased to function as churches in the decades following the Muslim conquest, many of the Negev towns and farms flourished until the eighth and ninth centuries.

DESERT MONASTERIES

During the Byzantine period, hundreds of monasteries populated by thousands of monks were established in the deserts of Egypt, Syria, and Palestine. Many monastic communities formed when a holy man seeking solitude and an ascetic lifestyle attracted a following. Some monasteries were established in proximity to holy sites, such as the monastery of St. George (or monastery of Choziba) in Wadi Qelt near Jericho, where monks settled around a cave where they believed the prophet Elijah had been fed by ravens. The Jordan Valley and Judean Desert, and especially the area around Jericho, attracted a large number of monks because of the region's proximity to Jerusalem and the concentration of sites with biblical associations. A monastery was even established atop the mountain of Masada. There were also monastic communities in the remote mountains of the southern Sinai desert. An important book on the desert monasteries of Palestine and Egypt, published in 1966 by Derwas Chitty, was aptly titled *The Desert a City* – a reference to the density of monastic settlement.

Monastic communities were organized along different lines. The most basic type of monasticism consisted of an individual (called an **anchorite**) living in complete isolation and solitude, without any community. Another organizational model, called a *laura* (Greek for "lane," probably referring to the paths connecting the monastic cells to the church), was made up of individual hermits who lived in solitude in scattered cells or caves but congregated on weekends for communal prayer and worship. Some monastic communities were organized as a *coenobium* (pronounced coin-OH-bee-yum), which means "communal life" in Greek. A *coenobium* consisted of groups of monks who lived communally in an enclosed complex that included a church and/or chapel, living quarters (cells), a dining room, storerooms and cisterns, service quarters, and gardens or agricultural plots. Members of a *coenobium* worked, prayed, and dined together according to a fixed schedule.

The robust monastic movement and holy sites in the deserts of Palestine attracted many followers from other parts of the Mediterranean, including Asia Minor and Armenia, Cyprus, Greece, and Italy. Some of these immigrants became

16.8 Monastery of Mar Saba.

the leaders of Palestinian desert monasteries. For example, **Sabas**, a native of Cappadocia in Asia Minor, settled in the Judean Desert at the age of 18. He soon attracted a following and founded a *laura* called "the Great *Laura* of Sabas." Sabas eventually initiated or participated in the establishment of nine other monasteries in the Judean Desert. The Great *Laura* (the monastery of Mar Saba), which dramatically overhangs the steep cliffs of the Kidron Valley midway between Jerusalem and the Dead Sea, is one of only a few Byzantine monasteries in the Judean Desert that is still active today (another is the monastery of St. George in Wadi Qelt, mentioned earlier). The conversion of most of the population to Islam, combined with a lack of security, led to the decline and abandonment of most of the desert monasteries in the centuries following the Muslim conquest.

MATERIAL CULTURE

Late Roman Red Ware

By the first century B.C.E. and first century C.E., fine table ware (dining ware) was characterized by a glossy red slip. Eastern Terra Sigillata was produced at centers around the eastern Mediterranean, including Phoenicia and Asia Minor, whereas Western Terra Sigillata was manufactured in Italy and Gaul. For hundreds of years, people around the Roman world continued to set their tables with red-slipped dishes. By the fourth and fifth centuries, the centers of

16.9 Late Roman Red Ware bowls stamped with fish and Christogram motifs, provenance unknown, fourth–fifth centuries C.E. By permission of the Israel Museum, Jerusalem. Photo © The Israel Museum, Jerusalem.

fine ware production had shifted to North Africa (especially modern Tunisia), Cyprus, and Phocaea in Asia Minor. Although still red-slipped, the later dishes (called Late Roman Red Ware) differ from their predecessors in various ways, including the tint or hue of the slip and the clay, and the shapes of the vessels. Sometimes Late Roman Red Ware dishes are stamped with Christian designs or motifs, such as crosses, fish, and lambs. Late Roman Red Ware is common at Byzantine sites around Palestine, although it is found in limited quantities because it was imported.

Fine Byzantine Ware

After Jerusalem's legionary kiln works ceased producing pottery (around 200 C.E.), local potters began manufacturing imitations of the Roman types. These imitations included bowls with an elaborately molded rim, a ring base, and nicked (rouletted) decoration covered by an uneven, drippy red slip (Jerusalem rouletted bowls), and deep and large basins with horizontal, ridged rims

16.10 Byzantine pottery including Fine Byzantine Ware. Courtesy of Zev Radovan/Bible LandPictures.com.

(rilled rim basins) or arched rims (arched rim basins). Arched rim basins continued to be manufactured for centuries, but during the sixth century the other types were replaced by a new repertoire. One of the newly introduced types was **Fine Byzantine Ware** (FBW), which is characterized by hemispherical cups with a ring base made of hard-fired, orange-brown ware. The surface of the vessels was burnished (polished), sometimes in bands. Many of the cups were decorated with an incised wavy line below the rim. Jars, jugs, and juglets with incised nicks on the shoulder were also made of FBW. FBW is common in the Jerusalem area, and may have been intended to replicate gold vessels in a cheaper material. FBW continued to be manufactured through the early Islamic period, although the repertoire of shapes changed (with an expanded range of vessels in open shapes – plates, cups, bowls – but no jars, jugs, or juglets), and sometimes with added painted decoration.

Oil Lamps

Early Roman oil lamps were characterized by a round body with a closed, decorated discus and short, flaring nozzle. During the fourth, fifth, and sixth centuries, oil lamps became pear-shaped (elongated), with no discus and a large filling hole in the center of the body. One type of oil lamp common in Judea in

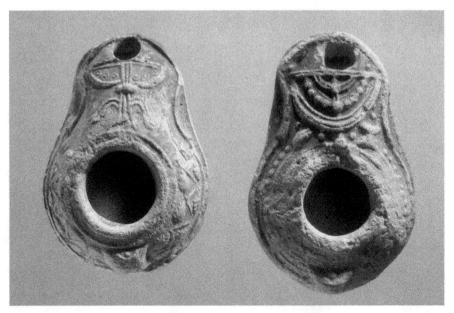

16.11 Beit Nattif oil lamps decorated with menorahs. Courtesy of Zev Radovan/Bible LandPictures.com.

the third to fifth centuries, called Beit Nattif lamps (after the site where evidence of their manufacture was first discovered), are made of soft, light-colored clay covered with a dark red or brown slip. The upper surface of the lamps is decorated with delicate relief designs (made in a mold), including occasional Jewish or Christian symbols such as menorahs or crosses.

The type of lamp characteristic of Jerusalem in the Byzantine period is made of unslipped, hard-fired, light brown ware. Sometimes this type is called "slipper lamps" because of the pear (oval) shape of the body. Raised, radiating lines encircle the filling hole, and a palm branch or tree (or, less likely, a menorah) occupies the space between the filling hole and the nozzle (hence the common name, "candlestick" lamps). On some lamps, a Greek inscription surrounds the filling hole instead of radiating lines. The most common inscription reads "the light of Christ shines for all," whereas other formulas include "good oil lamps" and "of the Mother of God." These lamps apparently were purchased by pilgrims who used them in processions in the Church of the Holy Sepulcher and other churches in Jerusalem. This is suggested by the fact that the phrase "the light of Christ shines for all" seems to have been part of the liturgy recited in the Church of the Holy Sepulcher. The lamps might have been used especially during the evening (Vespers) services and perhaps during the Ceremony of the Holy Fire, which today ushers in the Greek Orthodox Easter. After use, the lamps were kept as sacred talismans or souvenirs called "blessings" (*eulogiae*) in Greek because they were believed to bestow a blessing on the owner.

16.12 "Candlestick" lamp with a cross and Greek inscription. Courtesy of Zev Radovan/ BibleLandPictures.com.

Sidebar: *Martyria*

Constantine's Church of the Holy Sepulcher and Church of the Nativity in Bethlehem consisted of basilicas (congregational halls of worship) attached to a round or octagonal structure. Whereas the basilicas have a long axis with a focal point (the altar) at one end, the round and octagonal structures enshrine a focal point in the center – that is, they are centralized structures. Basilicas were well suited to the purposes of congregational prayer, accommodating large numbers of worshipers who could be segregated from the altar area, and facilitating processions of clergy from the entrance through the nave and to the altar. In contrast, centralized structures facilitated the movement of large numbers of pilgrims by enabling them to circumambulate the focal point.

In early Christian architecture, such centralized buildings are often called ***martyria*** (singular: ***martyrium***) because they were built to enshrine a site associated with a martyr (a witness to the truth of Christianity). Domed, centralized structures had a long history in Roman architecture – for example, the octagonal room in Nero's Domus Aurea (Golden House) or Hadrian's Pantheon in Rome. In the ancient world, the dome was understood as representing or symbolizing the dome of heaven. Early Christian buildings adopted centralized structures as appropriate for enshrining sites associated with martyrs because of the celestial associations of the dome and because they were well suited to accommodating visits by large numbers of pilgrims. The Rotunda of the Church of the Holy Sepulcher and the octagonal structure in Constantine's Church of the Nativity in Bethlehem are examples of *martyria*.

Recommended Reading

Ora Limor and Guy G. Stroumsa (eds.), *Christians and Christianity in the Holy Land: From the Origins to the Latin Kingdom* (Turnhout, Belgium: Brepols, 2006).

S. Thomas Parker, "The Byzantine Period: An Empire's New Holy Land," *Near Eastern Archaeology* 62.3 (September 1999): 134–80.

Robert L. Wilken, *The Land Called Holy: Palestine in Christian History and Thought* (New Haven, CT: Yale University, 1992).

@@ @@ @@ @@

SEVENTEEN

EPILOGUE

EARLY ISLAMIC JERUSALEM (638–750 C.E.)

HISTORICAL BACKGROUND

In the early seventh century, a charismatic, prophetic figure named Muhammed began to attract a following in the Arabian Peninsula. In 622, warned of an assassination plot, Muhammed fled from Mecca to Medina. His flight, called in Arabic the **Hegira** (or **Hejira**), marks the beginning of the Muslim calendar (which dates events after 622 as A.H. or After [the] Hegira). After Muhammed died in 632, four elected caliphs succeeded him as leaders of the new religion of Islam. Almost immediately after Muhammed's death, his followers began to spread Islam beyond the Arabian Peninsula through a series of military campaigns. Beginning in 634, Muslim tribes began to take over parts of Palestine. Jerusalem apparently surrendered peacefully in 638. Caesarea, the last major city in Palestine to fall to the Muslims, capitulated after a seven-month siege, after the Byzantine emperor withdrew support by way of the sea. Palestine was taken by the Muslims during the reign of the caliph **Omar** (634–644). Although for a long time scholars believed that the Muslim conquest of Palestine was accompanied by widespread destructions followed by a rapid decline in prosperity, recent research indicates that Palestine continued to flourish under early Islamic rule.

Islam spread quickly as the Muslims extended their control over most of the Near East (except for Asia Minor, which remained under Byzantine rule), Egypt, North Africa, and eventually Spain. After the death of the fourth caliph, the **Umayyad dynasty** was established, whose members ruled over the vast, newly created empire from 661 to 750. The Umayyads chose Damascus, Syria, as their capital. The Umayyads sponsored many building projects around Palestine, including a series of desert palaces such as **Khirbat al-Mafjar** near Jericho, and a large congregational mosque in Damascus. Jerusalem benefited especially

17.1 The Dome of the Rock.

from Umayyad patronage. The Umayyad dynasty was overthrown in 750 by the **Abbasids**, who moved the capital of the Muslim empire to Baghdad.

JERUSALEM

The Temple Mount: The Dome of the Rock

The most conspicuous monument in Jerusalem today is the Dome of the Rock, a golden-domed structure in the middle of the Temple Mount. In Arabic the Temple Mount is called *al-Haram al-Sharif*, which means "the noble enclosure," and Jerusalem's sacred status in Islam is reflected by its Arabic name, *al-Quds*: the holy [city]. The Dome of the Rock is one of the earliest surviving Muslim monuments anywhere. It was built in the last decade of the seventh century by an Umayyad caliph named **Abd al-Malik** (ruled 685–705). The Dome of the Rock almost certainly occupies the site of the earlier Jewish temples, although it was constructed centuries after the second temple was destroyed. During the Byzantine period there were no buildings on the Temple Mount, which ancient sources suggest was lying in ruins and used as a garbage dump.

Abd al-Malik cleared the debris and enshrined a rocky outcrop in a domed, octagonal building. This rocky outcrop (a natural high point in the center of the Temple Mount) is venerated by Muslims as the place where Abraham offered his son for sacrifice (Muslim tradition identifies the son as Ishmael instead of Isaac). Later Muslim tradition came to identify this as the spot from which

17.2 Interior of the Dome of the Rock. National Geographic Image ID 1002978, by Ira Block/National Geographic Stock.

Muhammed was transported by a magical horselike creature to heaven, where he met with the Old Testament prophets. According to the Quran, Muhammed's night journey took him from "the farthest mosque" (Arabic *al-masjid al-aqsa*) to heaven. Eventually Muslim tradition located the site of the farthest mosque on Jerusalem's Temple Mount.

The rocky outcrop in the center of the Dome of the Rock is encircled by two concentric rows of columns enclosed within octagonal walls (the outer circle of columns follows the octagonal layout of the walls). The inner circle of columns supports a clerestory with a dome above. Although some elements have been replaced since the seventh century (including the dome and the exterior tiles), the structure has survived intact and still retains much of its original interior decoration. The colorful marble columns and Corinthian capitals are *spolia* – reused architectural pieces taken from Byzantine churches in Jerusalem, some of which may have been lying in ruins at the time of the Muslim conquest. The flat surfaces (lower parts of the walls) of the interior are covered with marble revetment (veneer), with the slabs cut to display the patterns of the veins. The curved surfaces (upper parts of the walls, undersides of arches, and the clerestory of the dome) are covered with colored mosaics. There is extensive use of gold leaf in the mosaic cubes, which glitters in the dimly lit interior. Many of the mosaics are geometric and floral patterns, but there are also depictions of jeweled crowns and other pieces of jewelry. Myriam Rosen-Ayalon, an Israeli art historian and archaeologist, has suggested that these represent the Byzantine crown jewels, symbolizing the Muslim victory over the Byzantines.

Although the Temple Mount was desolate when Jerusalem came under Muslim rule, its history and significance were well known. Abd al-Malik clearly chose this site because of its biblical associations. However, when Jerusalem surrendered to the Muslims it was a Christian city. In fact, Jerusalem was a jewel in the crown of the Byzantine Empire, the seat of a Patriarch and the place where Jesus spent his final days. Byzantine Jerusalem was filled with dozens of monumental churches and monasteries, among them the Church of the Holy Sepulcher. The new religion of Islam had to define its relationship to Christianity and compete for converts with the wealthy and firmly established religion. Abd al-Malik chose the most conspicuous spot in Jerusalem to make his statement.

Many years ago a prominent French-born scholar of Islamic art, Oleg Grabar, who spent most of his life in the United States, made an important observation. He noted that the Dome of the Rock and the Rotunda of the Church of the Holy Sepulcher are similar in dimensions and are both centralized buildings (*martyria*). Furthermore, the architectural elements and decoration of the Dome of the Rock, including the marble columns and capitals, marble revetment, and gold and colored mosaics are characteristic of Byzantine churches (and ultimately derive from Roman art and architecture). Grabar speculated that Abd al-Malik modeled the Dome of the Rock after the Rotunda of the Church of the Holy Sepulcher, in an attempt to surpass Christianity's most famous shrine. Indeed, the interior of the Dome of the Rock gives a much better impression of the original appearance of the Rotunda, which has suffered greatly and no longer has its original decoration. The mosaic above the inner face of the outer circle of columns in the Dome of the Rock contains a long inscription from the time of Abd al-Malik, consisting of verses from the Quran (a later caliph replaced Abd al-Malik's name with his own). The passages cited include several dealing with the death and resurrection of Jesus and the nature of the virgin birth – that is, questions of dogma on which Islam had to clarify its position versus Christianity. For example, Jesus is recognized as a prophet but not as the son of God.

The Dome of the Rock is much more complex than simply an Islamic imitation of the Rotunda of the Church of the Holy Sepulcher. Scholars have pointed to different sources of influence, including Sasanid Persia (the jewelry depicted in the mosaics) and Arabia (the circumambulation of a sacred monument such as the Kaaba in Mecca). Nevertheless, Grabar put it best when he said, "The Dome of the Rock appears as a monument constructed in order to make a statement for the whole city of Jerusalem and for its surroundings. . . . It became the visual rival of the Holy Sepulchre and the Nea church. It is seen immediately as one leaves the Holy Sepulchre, signaling the rebirth, under a new Muslim guise, of the old Jewish Temple area" (*The Shape of the Holy*, p. 104).

The Al-Aqsa Mosque

The al-Aqsa mosque apparently was constructed by Abd al-Malik or his son, al-Walid (ruled 705–715). It sits at the southern end of the Temple Mount, in the area of Herod's Royal Stoa. Unlike the Dome of the Rock, the al-Aqsa mosque has been modified through repeated repairs and reconstructions. Much of the current mosque, including the façade, is the result of later modifications. The original building is thought to have been a broad hall consisting of a central nave flanked on each side by seven rows of columns, which created seven aisles (a hypostyle plan typical of early Islamic mosques). A niche called a **qibla** in the south wall at the end of the nave marks the direction of prayer (toward Mecca). The ceiling of the nave immediately in front of the *qibla* had a dome, but the rest of the building was covered with a flat ceiling carried on wooden beams.

The Dome of the Rock is a monument enshrining a central focal point that was designed to facilitate the circumambulation of multitudes of pilgrims. In contrast, the al-Aqsa mosque is a hall for congregational prayer and worship, analogous to synagogues and churches. For example, when Anwar Sadat visited Jerusalem in 1977, he prayed in the al-Aqsa mosque, not in the Dome of the Rock. Although in plan the al-Aqsa mosque is a broad house because of the extra aisles, it is similar to a basilica in having a focal point at the end of the nave.

The Area to the South and West of the Temple Mount

After the Six-Day War in 1967, the Israeli archaeologist Benjamin Mazar conducted large-scale excavations around the southern and western sides of the Temple Mount (the British archaeologist Kathleen Kenyon had carried out limited excavations in this area in the 1960s). Mazar's excavations brought to light

17.3 The al-Aqsa mosque.

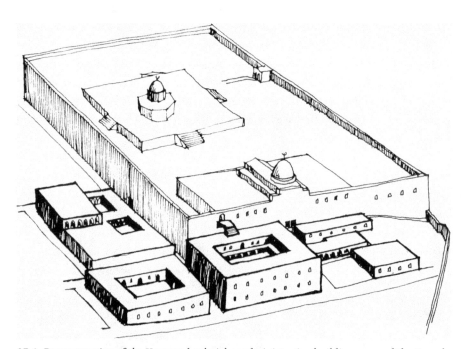

17.4 Reconstruction of the Umayyad palatial or administrative buildings around the Temple Mount. From *The Mountain of the Lord* by Benjamin Mazar, assisted by Gaalyah Cornfield, copyright © 1975 by Hamikra Baolam, Ltd. Used by permission of Doubleday, a division of Random House, Inc.

Sidebar: Where Are the Remains of the First and Second Temples?

Most scholars believe that the Dome of the Rock occupies the spot where the first and second temples once stood. This makes sense because the Dome of the Rock sits on a natural high point in the center of the Temple Mount. However, no identifiable remains survive of the temples, and probably none will ever be found. The reason is simple. The second temple was destroyed some 600 years before the Dome of the Rock was constructed. In the intervening centuries, much of the stone was carried off for reuse, and under the Byzantines the Temple Mount became a garbage dump. When Abd al-Malik built the Dome of the Rock, he presumably cleared away the refuse to expose the rocky outcrop. In other words, the Dome of the Rock was founded on bedrock (which lies at a high level at this spot), rather than having been built on top of the remains of the second temple building. Even if excavations could be conducted under the Dome of the Rock (which is impossible), they probably would reveal little of the second temple aside from cuttings in the bedrock. The fact that the Dome of the Rock sits on bedrock provides a stability that has helped the building survive earthquakes. In contrast, the al-Aqsa mosque has suffered damage because it sits on the southern end of the platform, which is supported by Solomon's Stables (the underground arches built by Herod).

Nearly all archaeological work relating to the Temple Mount generates controversy. In the 1970s, Mazar's excavations were widely condemned because of the misperception that they were being conducted underneath the Temple Mount. In recent years, the Waqf (the Muslim religious authority that has custody of the Temple Mount) has cleared the area under the al-Aqsa mosque (Solomon's Stables) in order to install another mosque. The dirt and debris cleared out of this area was dumped in the Kidron Valley. A group led by Israeli archaeologists has been collecting the dumped material and sifting it for finds. Both the Waqf and the archaeologists have been criticized for these activities.

important remains from various periods, including the late Iron Age, Herodian period, and Byzantine period. Perhaps the most important and surprising remains date to the early Islamic period. Under the Umayyads, a series of huge buildings were erected surrounding the southern and western sides of the Temple Mount. These buildings consisted of two stories of rooms surrounding large open courtyards paved with stone. The rooms were decorated with mosaic floors and colorful wall paintings.

Although scholars debate whether these buildings functioned as royal palaces or administrative centers, there is no doubt they were constructed by the Umayyad caliphs. The building immediately to the south of the al-Aqsa mosque was connected to the Temple Mount by a bridge, providing direct access to the mosque. The size and richness of these buildings reflect a substantial investment by the Umayyads in the development of Jerusalem, and attest to the importance of the holy city for Islam.

Recommended Reading

Meir Ben-Dov, *In the Shadow of the Temple: The Discovery of Ancient Jerusalem* (New York: Harper & Row, 1985).

Oleg Grabar, *The Shape of the Holy: Early Islamic Jerusalem* (Princeton, NJ: Princeton University, 1996).

Oleg Grabar and Benjamin Z. Kedar (eds.), *Where Heaven and Earth Meet: Jerusalem's Sacred Esplanade* (Austin: University of Texas, 2009).

Joshua Prawer and Haggai Ben-Shammai (eds.), *The History of Jerusalem: The Early Muslim Period, 638–1099* (New York: New York University, 1996).

Robert Schick, "Palestine in the Early Islamic Period: Luxuriant Legacy," *Near Eastern Archaeology* 61.2 (June 1998): 74–108.

Alan Walmsley, *Early Islamic Syria: An Archaeological Assessment* (London: Duckworth, 2007).

⊘⊘ ⊘⊘ ⊘⊘ ⊘⊘

GLOSSARY*

*Words are in bold the first time they appear in the text.

Abbasids: the Muslim family who overthrew the Umayyad dynasty in 750 C.E. and moved the capital to Baghdad.

Abd al-Malik (ruled 685–705 C.E.): the Umayyad caliph who built the Dome of the Rock.

Achaemenid: the ancient Persian Empire (ca. 550–330 B.C.E.).

Actium: the site of a naval battle in Greece where Octavian defeated Mark Antony and Cleopatra in 31 B.C.E.

Aelia Capitolina: the name that the Roman emperor Hadrian gave to Jerusalem after he rebuilt it.

agora (= Latin forum [plural: fora]): commercial center of a town or city.

agrarian: agriculturally based.

Ahab (mid-ninth century B.C.E.): the king of Israel who was condemned by the biblical writers for his marriage to Jezebel.

Akko (or Acre): a city on the northern coast of Palestine, refounded as Ptolemais in the Hellenistic period.

Akra: a fortress in Jerusalem built by Antiochus IV Epiphanes and razed by Simon, the brother of Judah Maccabee.

al-Aqsa mosque: an early Islamic mosque (congregational prayer hall) at the southern end of Jerusalem's Temple Mount (*al-Haram al-Sharif*), built by Abd al-Malik or his son al-Walid (705–715 C.E.).

Alexander the Great (ruled 336–323 B.C.E.): the Macedonian king who conquered the Persian Empire.

Alexander Jannaeus (ruled 103–76 B.C.E.): the Hasmonean king who succeeded Aristobulus I.

Alexandrium-Sartaba: a Hasmonean-Herodian fortified desert palace in the Jordan Valley.

al-Haram al-Sharif: the Arabic term for Jerusalem's Temple Mount, meaning "the noble enclosure."

Ammonites: the Iron Age inhabitants of the biblical kingdom of Ammon in northern Transjordan, whose capital city was Rabbath-Ammon.

amphitheater: an oval arena used for animal and gladiator fights, such as the Colosseum (Flavian amphitheater) in Rome.

amphora: a large, two-handled jar with a pointed base used to transport oil, wine, and grain.

amulet: a charm believed to have magical or protective powers.

Amygdalon pool (or Hezekiah's pool or the pool of the towers): a Herodian period pool by Herod's three towers and palace in Jerusalem.

anaerobic: lacking oxygen.

Ananus: the Jewish high priest who had James the Just tried and executed by the Sanhedrin.

anastasis: Greek for resurrection.

Anatolia: see Asia Minor.

anchorite: a monk or hermit who lives in individual isolation.

aniconic: without figured images.

anta (plural: *antae*): the thickened end (jamb) of a porch wall.

Antioch: the capital of the Roman province of Syria.

Antiochus IV Epiphanes (ruled 175–164 B.C.E.): the Seleucid king who rededicated the Jerusalem temple to the Greek god Olympian Zeus, provoking the outbreak of the Maccabean Revolt.

Antipas: an Idumaean who was forcibly converted to Judaism by the Hasmoneans and was the paternal grandfather of Herod the Great.

Antipater: the father of Herod the Great.

Antonia: a fortress erected by Herod the Great at the northwest corner of Jerusalem's Temple Mount and named in honor of Mark Antony.

Antonine dynasty (96–192 C.E.): the dynasty established by Nerva, who was succeeded by Trajan and Hadrian.

Aphrodite (Roman Venus): the Greco-Roman goddess of love.

apocalyptic: an outlook anticipating the imminent end of this world and a coming time of salvation.

Apocrypha (deutero-canonical works): works included in the Catholic canon of sacred scripture but not in the Hebrew or Protestant Bibles.

Apodyterium: the dressing room in a Roman bath house.

apse: a large, semicircular niche in a religious building.

aqueduct: a water channel.

Aramaic (language): a language related to Hebrew that was the common language of the ancient Persian Empire and the everyday language of the Jews of Palestine in the time of Jesus.

Aramaic script: the script that has been used to write the Hebrew language since 586 B.C.E.

Arch of Ecce Homo ("behold the man!"): the remains of a Hadrianic triple-arched gateway in the Church of the Sisters of Zion in Jerusalem, identified in modern Christian tradition as the spot where Pontius Pilate displayed Jesus after crowning him with thorns and clothing him in a purple robe.

archisynagogos: Greek for "leader of a synagogue."

architrave: the lower part of the entablature.

Aretas IV: the Nabatean king around the time of Jesus.

Aristobulus I (104–103 B.C.E.): the successor of John Hyrcanus I, and the first Hasmonean ruler to adopt the title "king."

Aristobulus II: the younger son of Salome Alexandra.

artifact: any portable, human-made object.

ascetic: denying oneself physical or bodily pleasure.

Asclepius: the Greco-Roman god of healing and medicine.

Ashkelon: originally established as one of the cities of the Philistine pentapolis, located on the southern coast of Palestine.

ashlar: a well-cut block of stone.

Asia Minor: the land mass that corresponds roughly with the Asian part of modern Turkey.

Assyria: an ancient empire in northern Mesopotamia.

Athens: a city in Greece.

atrium: an open courtyard, often with a peristyle, outside a church or Byzantine type synagogue.

Attica: the district in which the city of Athens is located.

Augustus Caesar (lived 63 B.C.E.–14 C.E.): the title bestowed on Octavian (Julius Caesar's stepnephew and heir) by the Roman senate in 27 B.C.E.

Avdat: see Oboda.

Baal (or Bel): the national deity of the Canaanites and Phoenicians.

Babatha: a Jewish woman from Nabataea who took refuge in the Cave of Letters, where her personal documents were discovered by archaeologists.

Babylon: the capital city of Babylonia.

Babylonia: an ancient empire in southern Mesopotamia.

Bacchus: see Dionysos.

ballista: a machine that fires round stone projectiles (like cannon shot).

Barclay's Gate: a small gate on the western side of Herod's rebuilt Temple Mount in Jerusalem.

baris: a Greek word for fortress.

Bar Kathros: the name of the priestly family that apparently owned the Burnt House in Jerusalem.

Bar-Kokhba Revolt (the Second Jewish Revolt against the Romans): 132–135 C.E., so called after its messianic leader, Simeon Bar-Kokhba (or Simeon Bar-Kosiba).

basalt: a hard, black volcanic rock characteristic of eastern Galilee and the Golan.

basilica: Roman public building with a rectangular layout and columns inside to support the roof.

baulk (or balk): a vertical bank of earth left standing on the side of an excavated area which is used for recording purposes.

Bedouin(s): nomadic or seminomadic inhabitants of Palestine.

Beersheba: a city in the Negev.

Ben-Hinnom Valley: a deep valley that encompasses Jerusalem's western hill on the west and south and joins with the Kidron and Tyropoeon Valleys.

Beth Alpha: a village in the Jordan Valley with a Byzantine type synagogue building.

Bethar: the last stronghold of the Bar-Kokhba Revolt to fall to the Romans, located near Bethlehem.

Bethesda pools: see Bezetha pools.

Beth Guvrin (or Eleutheropolis): a town near Marisa in southern Judea that flourished in the Late Roman period.

Bethlehem: a village (today a town) southwest of Jerusalem, revered as the birthplace of both King David and Jesus.

Beth midrash: a rabbinic study house.

Beth Shean (Hellenistic Scythopolis): a Decapolis city located in the Jordan Valley.

Beth Shearim: a town in Lower Galilee that was the residence and final resting place of Judah ha-Nasi, and the site of a Jewish necropolis of the third and fourth centuries C.E.

Bezetha pools (or Bethesda pools or Sheep's Pools): Herodian-period pools to the north of Jerusalem's Temple Mount.

Binyanei Ha'uma: modern Jerusalem's convention center and the site of the kiln works of the Tenth Roman Legion.

Birket el-Hamra: a Herodian period pool near the junction of the Kidron, Tyropoeon, and Ben-Hinnom Valleys in Jerusalem.

Birket Isr'il: see pool of Israel.

Birtha of the Ammonites: see Iraq el-Amir.

boss: the protruding central part of a stone with drafted margins.

Broad Wall: name given by the Israeli archaeologist Nahman Avigad to a thick wall built by Hezekiah on the north side of Jerusalem's western hill.

broadhouse: a rectangular building oriented so that the main axis is parallel to the short walls instead of the long walls.

bulla (plural: bullae): a small clay lump used to seal a document or container.

Burnt House: a villa in Jerusalem's Jewish Quarter that was destroyed by the Romans in 70 C.E.

Byzantium: see Constantinople.

Caesarea Maritima: originally a small Palestinian coastal town called Straton's Tower, which Herod the Great refounded as Caesarea Maritima in honor of Augustus.

Caiaphas: the family name of Joseph, the priest who presided over the trial of Jesus according to the Gospel accounts.

caldarium: the hot room or steam room in a Roman bath house.

caliga (plural: *caligae*): the heavy nailed sandal worn by Roman legionaries.

Calvary: see Golgotha.

Canaan: the name given to Palestine in the Hebrew Bible, before the arrival of the Israelites.

Canaanites: the Bronze Age inhabitants of Palestine.

Capernaum: a village on the northwest shore of the Sea of Galilee that was the center of Jesus' Galilean ministry and is the site of a monumental, Galilean type synagogue building.

capital (of a column): the element at the top of a column.

Capitolium: a temple dedicated to the Roman god Capitoline Jupiter.

cardo: a north-south road or thoroughfare in a Roman city.

cardo maximus: the main north-south thoroughfare in a Roman city.

Carthage: a city in modern Tunisia (North Africa) that was founded as a Phoenician colony and later destroyed by Rome.

casemate wall: a type of fortification wall consisting of two parallel walls divided into rooms.

Cassius Dio: a third-century C.E. Roman historian who provided information about the Bar-Kokhba Revolt.

Catechumen: someone being instructed in the principles of Christian faith who has not yet undergone full conversion through baptism.

Cave of Horror: a cave in Nahal Hever which contained remains from the time of the Bar-Kokhba Revolt.

Cave of Jehoshaphat: a rock-cut tomb or burial cave associated with the tomb of Absalom in Jerusalem.

Cave of Letters: a cave in Nahal Hever that contained remains from the time of the Bar-Kokhba Revolt.

Cave of the Pool: a cave in Nahal David used as a hideout by Jewish refugees during the Bar-Kokhba Revolt.

cella: see *naos*.

Chi-Rho: two Greek letters that form the monogram of Jesus Christ.

Chorazin: a Jewish village near Capernaum and the site of a Galilean type synagogue building.

Church of the Holy Sepulcher: a church in Jerusalem enshrining the sites where Jesus was crucified and buried, according to Christian tradition.

Church of the Nativity: a church in Bethlehem enshrining the grotto where Jesus was born, according to Christian tradition.

Church of the Sisters of Zion: a convent on Jerusalem's Via Dolorosa that contains the arch of Ecce Homo, the Lithostratos pavement, and the Struthion pools.

Church of St. Anne: a Crusader period church by the Sheep's Pools.

Cinerarium (plural: *cineraria*): Roman cinerary urn for cremated remains.

circumvallation wall: a Roman siege wall.

circus: see hippodrome.

Citadel: the fortified enclosure next to Jaffa Gate in Jerusalem's Old City.

City of David (or eastern hill or lower city): a small hill to the south of the Temple Mount that is the location of the earliest settlement in Jerusalem.

Cleopatra VII: a Ptolemaic queen known for her affairs with the Roman generals Julius Caesar and Mark Antony.

clerestory: walls rising above the first story level of a nave, which are pierced by windows to let light into the interior.

coenobium: a type of monastery in which monks live a communal lifestyle.

columbarium (plural: columbaria): a cave or structure with rows of small niches in the walls, apparently used as a dovecote.

Community Rule (or Manual of Discipline): a sectarian work found at Qumran.

Constantine (ruled 306–337 C.E.): the Roman emperor who legalized Christianity.

Constantinople (ancient Byzantium/modern Istanbul): literally, "the city of Constantine," refounded by Constantine as the new capital of the Roman Empire.

contubernium (plural: *contubernia*): a group of eight legionaries.

cornucopia (plural: cornucopiae): a horn of plenty.

cryptoporticus: a series of underground arches or vaults.

cuneiform: a script consisting of wedge-shaped symbols, which developed in ancient Mesopotamia.

Cypros: the Nabataean mother of Herod the Great.

Cyrus II: the ancient Persian king who allowed the exiled Judeans to return to Jerusalem and rebuild the temple (539 B.C.E.).

Damascus Document: a sectarian work found among the Dead Sea Scrolls and in the Cairo Geniza.

Daniel: the protagonist and supposed author of an apocalyptic book in the Hebrew Bible.

Darius III: the Persian king defeated by Alexander the Great.

Darom: literally, "south," referring to southern Judea.

David (ca. 1000 B.C.E.): the second king of Israel (after Saul), who made Jerusalem the capital of the United Kingdom after capturing it from the Jebusites.

David's Tower: a Herodian tower in Jerusalem's Citadel.

Dead Sea Scrolls: the remains of more than 900 scrolls representing copies of the Hebrew Bible, other Jewish religious works, and sectarian literature, which were deposited in caves by members of the Jewish sect who lived at the nearby site of Qumran.

Decapolis: a semiautonomous league of Hellenized cities under Roman rule in northern Syria-Palestine.

decumanus (plural: *decumani*): an east-west road or thoroughfare in a Roman city.

decumanus maximus: the main east-west thoroughfare in a Roman city.

Delian League: an alliance of Greek city-states formed under the leadership of Athens after the Persian wars.

dendrochronology: a method of dating by counting tree rings.

Deuteronomy: Greek for "second law," referring to the fifth book of the Pentateuch, supposedly discovered during Josiah's repairs to the Jerusalem temple.

Diaspora: the dispersion of Jews outside of Palestine.

Diaspora Revolt (115–117 C.E.): a revolt that erupted among Diaspora Jewish communities during Trajan's reign.

Diocletian (284–305 C.E.): a Roman general who became emperor and established the Tetrarchy.

Dionysos (Roman Bacchus): the Greco-Roman god of wine and theater performances.

Dioscuri: Castor and Pollux, the sons of Zeus.

discus: the top of an oil lamp.

Dome of the Rock (691 C.E.): an early Islamic monument enshrining a rocky outcrop on Jerusalem's Temple Mount (*al-Haram al-Sharif*).

drafted margin: a flat border along one side of a stone used in construction.

Dura Europos: a caravan city by the Euphrates River in Syria with a richly decorated synagogue building of the third century C.E.

Eastern hill: see City of David.

Eastern Terra Sigillata (or Eastern Sigillata): a type of fine, red-slipped (red-coated) pottery of the Hellenistic and Roman periods that was produced in the eastern Mediterranean.

Eastern Sigillata A (ESA): a type of fine, red-slipped (red-coated) pottery produced in Phoenicia in the Hellenistic and Roman periods.

Edict of Milan (313 C.E.): the edict issued by Constantine and Licinius which legalized Christianity in the Roman Empire.

Edomites: the inhabitants of the biblical kingdom of Moab, on the southeast side of the Dead Sea.

Ein Gedi: an oasis on the western shore of the Dead Sea.

Eleazar ben-Yair: the leader of the Jewish rebels at Masada.

electrum: a natural alloy of gold and silver.

Eleona Church: a church and monastery erected by Constantine on the Mount of Olives.

Elephantine (pronounced el-uh-fan-TEEN-ee; Hebrew Yeb): a late Iron Age and Persian period military colony in upper (southern) Egypt that included Israelite families and was the site of a temple dedicated to the God of Israel.

Eleutheropolis: literally, "city of the free"; see Beth Guvrin.

Elijah: the Israelite prophet who opposed Ahab and Jezebel's promotion of foreign cults.

Ennion: a Phoenician master glassmaker of the first century C.E.

Enoch: in Genesis, the seventh forefather from Adam, who was transformed into Metatron in *Hekhalot* literature.

entablature: the horizontal strip between the top of the porch columns and the roof eaves (the cornice).

epigrapher: an expert in ancient scripts and inscriptions.

Epistle of James: see Letter of James.

Erectheum: a fifth-century B.C.E. temple on the Acropolis in Athens.

Essenes: a Jewish sect of the late Second Temple period, some of whose members lived at Qumran and deposited the Dead Sea Scrolls in the nearby caves.

ethrog: a citron, a type of citrus fruit that resembles a large, bumpy lemon and is used with a lulav in the celebration of the Feast of Tabernacles (Sukkot).

Eudocia: a Byzantine empress who settled in Jerusalem in the mid-fifth century C.E.

extramural: located outside the walls (suburban).

Ezra: a priest and scribe sent by the Persian king to implement Jewish law as the law of Judea (Yahud).

fascia (plural: fasciae): three narrow, horizontal strips in an Ionic architrave.

Feast of Tabernacles: see Sukkot.

Fine Byzantine Ware (FBW): a type of fine ware (table dishes) characteristic of Jerusalem in the Byzantine and early Islamic periods.

flagstones: a pavement made of stones laid with the flat surface up.

Flavian dynasty (69–96 C.E.): the Roman dynasty established by Vespasian.

Flavius Josephus (Joseph ben Mattityahu/Joseph son of Mattathias) (lived ca.37–100 C.E.): the Jewish historian who chronicled the First Jewish Revolt against Rome.

Flavius Silva: the commander of the Roman forces at the siege of Masada.

forum: see agora.

four-room house: a type of house that is characteristic of Israelite settlements during the Iron Age.

fresco: painted decoration on a plastered wall (technically, fresco is painting on wet plaster and secco is painting on dry plaster).

frieze: the upper part of the entablature.

frigidarium: the cold-water bath in a Roman bath house.

Galilee: the northern part of Palestine, bounded on the east by the Sea of Galilee and on the west by the Mediterranean Sea.

Gamla (or Gamala): a Jewish town in the southern Golan overlooking the Sea of Galilee which was destroyed by the Romans in 67 C.E.

Garden Tomb: rock-cut tombs to the north of Jerusalem's Old City that were erroneously identified by the nineteenth century British general Charles Gordon as the site of Jesus' crucifixion and burial.

Gaza: originally established as one of the cities of the Philistine pentapolis, located on the southern coast of Palestine.

Gemaryahu son of Shaphan: a scribe mentioned in the book of Jeremiah whose name has been found on a bulla in the City of David.

Geniza: a repository for damaged Jewish sacred writings.

Gerasa (modern Jerash): one of the Decapolis cities, today in Jordan.

Gihon spring: a perennial fresh-water spring at the eastern foot of Jerusalem's City of David.

Giv'at Ram: the part of Jerusalem in which Binyanei Ha'uma is located.

glacis: a fortification system characteristic of the Bronze Age in the Near East, consisting of a huge plastered earth embankment with a wall at the top.

Golan: the mountainous plateau east of the Sea of Galilee.

Golgotha (Latin Calvary): Aramaic for "skull hill"; the rocky outcrop enshrined in the Church of the Holy Sepulcher that is venerated as the spot where Jesus was crucified.

Gordon's Calvary: see Garden Tomb.

Gospel: an account of the life of Jesus; the four canonical Gospels included in the New Testament are attributed to Mark, Matthew, Luke, and John.

Hadrian (ruled 117–138 C.E.): the Roman emperor whose plans to rebuild Jerusalem as Aelia Capitolina provoked the outbreak of the Second Jewish Revolt against the Romans (the Bar-Kokhba Revolt).

Hagia Sophia (St. Sophia): a church in Constantinople (modern Istanbul), dedicated by Constantine to Holy Wisdom and rebuilt by Justinian.

Hammath Tiberias: literally, "the hot springs of Tiberias," referring to a suburb south of Tiberias that is the site of a Transitional type synagogue building.

Hannibal: the general who led Carthage's forces against Rome during the Second Punic War.

Hanukkah: a Jewish holiday commemorating the Maccabees' victory against Antiochus IV Epiphanes and the rededication of the Jerusalem temple to the God of Israel in 164 B.C.E.

Hapax legomenon: a word that occurs only once in the Hebrew Bible.

hasid: Hebrew meaning "pious one."

Hasmoneans: the family and descendants of Mattathias, the father of Judah Maccabee.

Hazor: a large tel in Galilee.

Hegesippus: a second-century C.E. church historian who describes the martyrdom of James "the Just."

Hegira (or Hejira): Arabic for "flight," referring to the prophet Muhammed's flight from Mecca to Medina in 622 C.E., which marks the beginning of the Muslim calendar.

Hekhalot literature: ancient Jewish magical-mystical writings describing heavenly temples (*hekhalot*) populated by angels and other wondrous beings, with the God of Israel enthroned in the highest heavenly temple.

Heliodorus affair: an episode named after the Seleucid finance minister Heliodorus, which culminated with the refoundation of Jerusalem as a Greek *polis* named Antiochia and the Zadokites' loss of control over the high priesthood in the Jerusalem temple.

Helios: Greek for the sun, and the name of the Greco-Roman sun god.

Hellenistic: literally, "Greek-like," referring to the introduction of Greek culture to the ancient Near East in the wake of Alexander the Great's conquests.

Heracles (=Roman Hercules): a mythological Greek hero usually shown wearing a lionskin cape.

Herod Agrippa I (ruled 37–44 C.E.): the grandson of Herod the Great and Mariamne, who ruled Palestine on behalf of the Romans.

Herod Agrippa II (died ca. 92 C.E.): the son of Herod Agrippa I, who ruled a small vassal kingdom in Lebanon.

Herod Antipas (ruled 4 B.C.E.–39 C.E.): Herod's son and successor, who inherited the districts of Galilee and Peraea.

Herod Archelaus (ruled 4 B.C.E.–6 C.E.): Herod's son and successor, who inherited the districts of Judea, Idumaea, and Samaria.

Herod Philip (ruled 4 B.C.E.–33/34 C.E.): Herod's son and successor, who inherited the northern Palestinian districts of Gaulanitis, Trachonitis, Batanea, and Panias.

Herod the Great (ruled 40–4 B.C.E.): an Idumaean Jew who was appointed client king of Judea by the Romans.

Herodium (or Herodion): one of Herod the Great's fortified desert-palaces and his final resting place, located southeast of Bethlehem.

Herodotus: a fifth-century B.C.E. Greek author and historian.

Hezekiah: the king of Judah who fortified Jerusalem against an Assyrian attack in 701 B.C.E.

Hezekiah's pool: see Amygdalon pool.

Hezekiah's Tunnel: a water system in Jerusalem built by King Hezekiah on the eve of the Assyrian attack in 701 B.C.E.

hieroglyphs: a script that developed in ancient Egypt.

Hippodamian: a type of city planning named after the ancient Greek architect Hippodamus of Miletos.

Hippodamus: see Hippodamian.

hippodrome (= Roman circus): an elongated course or track for horse and chariot races with one curved end and one flat end.

Hippos-Susita: a Decapolis city in the Golan.

Hiram: a king of Tyre who established a commercial alliance with Solomon and supplied him with building materials for the first Jerusalem temple.

Hittites: the inhabitants of a Late Bronze Age kingdom in central Anatolia (Asia Minor).

Holy Grail: the goblet used by Jesus at the Last Supper.

horreum (plural: *horrea*): Latin for warehouse.

House of Ahiel: a four-room house in the City of David, so-called because an ostracon inscribed with the name Ahiel was found in it.

Hulda Gates: a pair of gates in the southern end of Herod's rebuilt Temple Mount that were the main pilgrim thoroughfares.

hypocaust: a Roman heating system used especially in bath houses that worked by creating a double floor carried on small pillars (*suspensura*), heated by hot air from a furnace that circulated between the two floors.

Hyrcania: a Hasmonean-Herodian fortified desert palace west of Qumran.

Hyrcanus (died 175 B.C.E.): a Tobiad who constructed palatial buildings at Iraq el-Amir.

Idumaea: the *medinah* located to the south of Yahud (Judea) under the Persian Empire, which was inhabited by descendants of the Edomites.

Idumaeans: the descendants of the biblical Edomites, who moved into southern Judah after 586 B.C.E. and were forcibly converted to Judaism by the Hasmoneans.

in-antis: between the *antae*.

inhumation: the burial or interment of a whole corpse (as opposed to a cremation).

in situ: in its original position.

insula (plural: *insulae*): a city block.

Iraq el-Amir (ancient Tyros/Birtha of the Ammonites): the Tobiad capital of the district of Ammon in the early Hellenistic period.

Istanbul: see Constantinople.

Ituraeans: the native population of Upper Galilee and the Golan, who were forcibly converted to Judaism by the Hasmoneans.

James the Just: the brother of Jesus (died 62/63 C.E.).

"James ossuary": an ossuary falsely identified as the possible repository of James the Just's remains.

Jamnia (or Yavneh): a town on the southern coast of Palestine that became the seat of the Jewish academy of law after 70 C.E.

Jason's Tomb: a Hasmonean period rock-cut tomb in Jerusalem.

Jebusites: according to the Hebrew Bible, Jerusalem's inhabitants before David's conquest.

Jerash: see Gerasa.

Jericho: a town by an oasis at the northern end of the Dead Sea.

Jewish Antiquities: Josephus' history of the Jewish people.

The Jewish War: Josephus' account of the First Jewish Revolt against the Romans.

Jezebel: Ahab's Tyrian wife, who was condemned by the prophet Elijah for promoting the cult of Baal in Samaria.

John the Baptist (or Baptizer): an itinerant preacher and charismatic leader known for his ascetic lifestyle and for immersing his followers in the Jordan River.

John Chrysostom (ca. 400 C.E.): an archbishop of Constantinople and important early church father.

John Hyrcanus I (ruled 134–104 B.C.E.): a Hasmonean ruler who succeeded Simon.

John Hyrcanus II: the older son of Salome Alexandra.

Jonathan (Hasmonean leader/ruler from 160–142 B.C.E.): the brother and successor of Judah Maccabee.

Joseph of Arimathea: according to the Gospel accounts, a wealthy follower who interred Jesus' body in his own family's rock-cut tomb.

Joseph ben Mattityahu: see Flavius Josephus.

Josephus: see Flavius Josephus.

Josiah: the king of Judah who was responsible for the Deuteronomistic reform and was killed at Megiddo by the Egyptian pharaoh in 609 B.C.E.

Jotapata (Hebrew Yodefat): the last fortified town in Galilee under Josephus' command to fall to the Romans (67 C.E.).

Judah: the southern part of the United Kingdom of Israel.

Judah ha-Nasi (Judah the Patriarch): a rabbi who compiled and edited the Mishnah (ca. 200 C.E.).

Judah Maccabee (died 160 B.C.E.): the leader of the Jewish revolt against Antiochus IV Epiphanes.

Judea: the name of the district of Judah after 586 B.C.E.

Judea Capta: literally, "Judea has been conquered or vanquished," referring to the slogan on a series of coins minted by the Flavian emperors.

Julian "the Apostate" (ruled 361–363 C.E.): a Roman emperor who attempted to reinstate the worship of pagan gods and granted the Jews permission to rebuild the Jerusalem temple.

Julio-Claudian dynasty (27 B.C.E.–68 C.E.): the dynasty established by Augustus, which ended with Nero.

Julius Caesar: the Roman general who ruled Rome as dictator from 48 to 44 B.C.E.

Justinian (ruled 527–565 C.E.): a Byzantine emperor who reunified the Roman Empire.

Kedesh: an important Persian period administrative center in Upper Galilee.

Ketef Hinnom: a late Iron Age cemetery on the northwest side of Jerusalem's Ben-Hinnom Valley.

Kfar Baram: a village in Upper Galilee with a Galilean type synagogue building.

Khazneh ("the Treasury"): the most famous rock-cut tomb at Petra, perhaps belonging to the Nabataean king Aretas IV.

Khirbat al-Mafjar: an Umayyad desert palace outside Jericho.

Kidron Valley: a deep valley on the east side of Jerusalem that separates the Mount of Olives from the City of David.

kore: Greek for "young woman"; sometimes the name given to Demeter, a fertility goddess.

kosher: food conforming to the requirements of biblical Jewish law.

krater: a large, deep bowl used for mixing wine and water.

Kurnub: see Mampsis.

Lachish: an important city in Iron Age Judah that was destroyed by the Assyrians.

laura: a type of monastic community in which the monks live in solitude and gather on weekends for communal prayer and worship.

legate: a high-ranking Roman official who commanded a legion.

Leontopolis: a town in Egypt's Nile Delta that was the site of an Oniad temple from the second century B.C.E. to 73 C.E.

Letter of Aristeas: a pseudepigraphic work of the Hellenistic period that purports to tell the story of the translation of the Pentateuch from Hebrew to Greek.

Letter of James: a work included in the New Testament that is attributed to James, the brother of Jesus.

Linear B: the script used to write the Greek language in the Mycenean kingdoms.

Lion of Wrath: the nickname given to Alexander Jannaeus in sectarian literature from Qumran.

Lithostratos pavement: a Hadrianic stone pavement in the Church of the Sisters of Zion in Jerusalem, which is identified in modern Christian tradition as the spot where Jesus stood when Pontius Pilate sentenced him to death.

loculus (plural: loculi; Hebrew *kokh* [plural: *kokhim*]): a burial niche for a human body (inhumation) in a tomb.

locus (plural: loci): Latin for "spot" or "place"; a term used by archaeologists to designate any excavated feature.

Lower City: see City of David.

lulav: a bundle of date, myrtle, and willow branches used in the celebration of the Feast of Tabernacles (Sukkot).

Macedon(ia): a tribal kingdom in northeast Greece that was Alexander the Great's homeland.

Machaerus: a Herodian fortified desert palace on the eastern side of the Dead Sea.

Madaba map: a mosaic floor of a church in Madaba, Jordan, depicting a map of Palestine ca. 600 C.E.

Magdala: see Migdal.

Mamila pool: a Herodian period pool outside Jaffa Gate in Jerusalem's Old City.

Mampsis (or Mamshit or Kurnub): one of the Nabataean towns of the Negev.

Mamshit: see Mampsis.

mantle (Greek *himation*; Latin *pallium*): a rectangular cloak worn over a tunic.

Manual of Discipline: see Community Rule.

Marcus Agrippa (died 12 B.C.E.): Augustus' son-in-law and designated heir (who predeceased Augustus), and a close friend of Herod the Great.

Maresha: see Marisa.

Mariamne: Herod the Great's Hasmonean wife.

Marisa (or Maresha or Tell Sandahannah): a Hellenistic period town in Idumaea.

Mark Antony: a Roman general who split the rule of Rome with Octavian and is known for his affair with Cleopatra VII.

marl: a soft, chalky rock in the Dead Sea region.

Martyrium (plural: *martyria*): a structure enshrining a site associated with a martyr.

Masada: Herod's desert palace-fortress on the southwest shore of the Dead Sea.

masonry: construction of stone.

Masoretic Text (MT): the standardized text of the Hebrew Bible considered authoritative by Jews today.

Mattathias Antigonus (died 37 B.C.E.): the son of Aristobulus II, and the last Hasmonean to rule as king.

Mausoleum at Halicarnassos (modern Bodrum in Turkey): the monumental tomb of Mausolus, which was one of the seven wonders of the ancient world.

Mausolus (died 353 B.C.E.): a king of Caria in southwest Asia Minor.

Medinah (plural: *medinot*): the smallest administrative unit in the ancient Persian empire.

Megiddo (the Book of Revelation's "Armageddon"): an important tel guarding a major mountain pass into the Jezreel Valley.

menorah: a seven-branched lampstand or candelabrum in the Jerusalem temple.

Mesopotamia: Greek for "the land between the rivers," referring to the territory between the Tigris and Euphrates Rivers and corresponding with the modern country of Iraq.

Metatron: the most powerful angel in the heavenly temples described in *Hekhalot* literature.

metopes (pronounced met-uh-PEES): panels alternating with triglyphs in a Doric frieze.

Migdal: the hometown of Mary Magdalene, on the northwest shore of the Sea of Galilee.

miqveh (plural: *miqva'ot*): a pool used as a Jewish ritual bath.

Mishnah: collections of rabbinic legal rulings (oral law) on the Torah (see also Judah ha-Nasi and Talmud).

Mithras: a Near Eastern deity whose cult became popular among Roman soldiers.

Mithraeum: a shrine to Mithras.

Moabites: the Iron Age inhabitants of the biblical kingdom of Moab on the northeast side of the Dead Sea.

Modiin: the hometown of the Hasmoneans, located midway between Jerusalem and modern Tel Aviv.

monolithic: consisting of a single stone.

mortarium (plural: *mortaria*): a large, heavy, thick-walled bowl used for grinding.

mosaic: a pavement made of pebbles or cut stone cubes (tesserae) laid in a plaster or mortar bedding.

Mount Gerizim: the sacred mountain of the Samaritans.

Mount of Olives: a high mountain ridge on the eastern side of Jerusalem.

Mount Zion: the southern end of Jerusalem's western hill.

Mycenean kingdoms: the city-states of Late Bronze Age Greece, named after the citadel of Mycenae.

Naaran: a village outside Jericho with a Byzantine type synagogue building.

Nabataeans: an Arab people who established a kingdom in southern Jordan, the Negev, and the Sinai which bordered on the Hasmonean kingdom and was annexed by the Romans in 106 C.E.

Nahal David: a riverbed with perennial fresh-water springs at Ein Gedi.

Nahal Hever: a dry riverbed south of Ein Gedi that contains the Cave of Letters and Cave of Horror.

naos (or *cella*): the main room in an ancient Greek temple.

narthex: a porch in front of a basilical church or synagogue.

nasi: literally, "prince"; see Patriarch.

nave: the central part of a basilical hall.

Nea (New) Church: a large church dedicated to the *Theotokos* by Justinian, located at the southern end of Jerusalem's main cardo.

necropolis: literally, "city of the dead," referring to a cemetery.

nefesh: Hebrew for "soul," referring to a monumental marker, often in the form of a pyramid, which was erected over a rock-cut tomb.

Negev: a desert in southern Palestine.

Nehemiah: a Jew sent by the Persian king to govern Yahud.

Nero: a Roman emperor who was the last member of the Julio-Claudian dynasty.

Nicanor's Gate: a gate in Herod's rebuilt temple that was donated by Nicanor, a wealthy Alexandrian Jew.

Nicanor's Tomb: the rock-cut tomb of Nicanor, an Alexandrian Jew who donated a gate to the Jerusalem temple.

Nicolaus of Damascus: Herod the Great's court biographer.

Oboda (or Avdat): a Nabataean town in the central Negev.

Octavian: see Augustus.

oculus: literally, "eye," referring to the circular opening in the center of a dome.

Omar (ruled 634–644 C.E.): the caliph under whom Jerusalem surrendered to Muslim rule.

Oniads: a branch of the Zadokite priestly family, named after one of its members (Onias).

Onias III: the Jewish high priest at the time of the Heliodorus affair.

Ophel: a biblical term that is thought to refer to the area between Jerusalem's Temple Mount and the northern end of the City of David.

Opisthodomos: the back porch of an ancient Greek temple.

Opus reticulatum: literally, "reticulate work"; a Roman construction method characterized by laying the brick facing of a concrete wall in a net pattern.

Opus sectile: colored stone or tile pavement.

Oral Law: the rabbinic interpretation of written law (Torah) (see also Mishnah).

ossuary: a small box used to contain bones gathered in a rock-cut tomb after the flesh decayed.

Ostia: Rome's ancient port city and the site of an ancient synagogue building.

ostracon (plural: ostraca): an inscribed potsherd.

'Otsar (plural: *'otsarot*): a small pool attached to a *miqveh* that may have been used for storing undrawn water.

paleographer: see epigrapher.

Paleo-Hebrew: the biblical Hebrew script used to write the Hebrew language during the Iron Age.

Pantheon (the temple of all gods): a domed temple in Rome that was designed by Hadrian.

parchment: processed animal hide, used for making scrolls in antiquity.

Parthenon: a fifth-century B.C.E. temple dedicated to Athena on the Acropolis in Athens.

Parthians: successors of the ancient Persians.

patera: a handled bowl for pouring liquid offerings (libations).

Patriarch (Jewish): the head of the academy at Jamnia.

Patriarchate (Christian): the seat of a Patriarch.

Pediment: the open triangular space above the porch of a building that has a pitched roof.

Peloponnesian War (431–404 B.C.E.): a war fought between Athens and Sparta and their allies.

Pentateuch: see Torah.

Peraea: a Judaized territory east of the Jordan River and Dead Sea.

peristyle: the columns surrounding a building that support the overhanging roof eaves and create a porch.

Persephone: see Kore.

Persia: the ancient country that corresponds roughly with modern Iran.

pesher (plural: *pesharim*): a type of commentary on prophetic books that was employed by the Qumran sect.

Petra: the capital of the Nabataean kingdom.

Pharisees: a Jewish movement in late Second Temple period Judea characterized by scrupulous observance of ritual purity and the adoption of orally based interpretations of the Torah (Oral Law).

Pharos of Alexandria: the lighthouse of Alexandria, which was one of the seven wonders of the ancient world.

Phasael (died 40 B.C.E.): the older brother of Herod the Great.

Philip II (ruled 359–336 B.C.E.): the father of Alexander the Great.

Philistines: one of the Sea Peoples who settled along the southern coast of Palestine ca. 1200 B.C.E. and established a kingdom with five main cities (pentapolis).

Philo Judaeus (lived ca. 20 B.C.E.–50 C.E.): a Jewish philosopher in Alexandria, Egypt.

Phoenicians: the Iron Age descendants of the Canaanites, who inhabited the northern coast of Syria-Palestine (modern Lebanon).

pier: a square or rectangular pillar built as a support for a ceiling or roof.

pilum (plural: *pila*): the long javelin that was the main piece of offensive equipment of a Roman legionary.

Pliny the Elder (lived 23–79 C.E.): a Roman author and naturalist who died in the eruption of Mount Vesuvius.

polis (plural: *poleis*): a Greek city or a city with a Greek style of government and institutions.

Pollio: Gaius Asinius Pollio, a prominent Roman politician, orator, and writer who served as consul in 40 B.C.E.

Pompey: a Roman general who annexed the Hasmonean kingdom to Rome in 63 B.C.E.

Pontius Pilate: the Roman prefect of Judea from 26 to 36 C.E., who sentenced Jesus to death according to the Gospel accounts.

Pool of Israel (or Birket Isr'il): a Herodian period pool to the northeast of Jerusalem's Temple Mount.

Pool of Siloam: originally the pool at the end of the Siloam Channel in Jerusalem, which later was replaced by the pool at the outlet of Hezekiah's Tunnel.

Pool of the Towers: see Amygdalon pool.

praetorium: a palace or living quarters of the Roman governor.

prefect/procurator: a low-ranking Roman governor.

principia: the headquarters in a Roman military camp.

pronaos: the front porch of an ancient Greek temple.

proseuche (plural: *proseuchae*): Jewish "prayer houses" in Hellenistic Egypt, which some scholars identify as early synagogues.

proto-Canaanite (or proto-Sinaitic): a script that was developed by the Canaanites which improved upon the Egyptian system of writing by reducing the number of symbols.

provenance (or provenience): the point of origin of an artifact.

pseudepigrapha (adjective: pseudepigraphic): a type of literary work that bears a false name (is falsely attributed by the author to someone else).

pseudo-Nabataean: a term sometimes used to describe Jerusalem painted bowls of the first century C.E.

Ptolemies: Ptolemy and his successors.

Ptolemy (ruled 323–283 B.C.E.): one of Alexander's generals, who established a kingdom based in Egypt.

Punic Wars: a series of wars fought between Rome and Carthage during the third and second centuries B.C.E., which ended with Carthage's destruction in 146 B.C.E.

Qasr el-Abd: a monumental building at Iraq el-Amir identified with the *baris* at Tyros described by Josephus.

Qibla: the direction of prayer in Islam (toward Mecca), usually marked in a mosque by a niche.

Qos: the national deity of the Edomites and Idumaeans.

Qumran: an Essene settlement by the northwest shore of the Dead Sea that is ringed by caves in which the Dead Sea Scrolls were found.

Quran: the central religious text of Islam.

Rabbath-Ammon (Hellenistic Philadelphia; modern Amman in Jordan): the capital of the biblical kingdom of Ammon.

Rabbi: "master" or "teacher"; an informal, honorific title originally given to men who were considered experts in the interpretation of Jewish law.

Rabbinic: the type of Judaism associated with the rabbis of the period after the destruction of the second temple in 70 C.E.

radiocarbon (C14) dating: a method of dating that measures the amount of carbon 14 in organic materials.

rampart: see glacis.

rehydroxylation: a new and experimental laboratory-based technique for dating pottery based on measuring hydroxyl groups.

reliquary: a container for sacred or holy relics.

Robinson's Arch: a bridge that provided from the Tyropoeon Valley to the southern end of Herod's rebuilt Temple Mount.

rosette: a common decorative motif in ancient Jewish art consisting of a stylized circular flower.

Rotunda: the circular domed structure enshrining the tomb of Christ in the Church of the Holy Sepulcher.

Royal Basilica: see Royal Stoa.

Royal Stoa: a monumental, all-purpose public building at the southern end of Herod's rebuilt Temple Mount.

Russian Alexander Hospice: a building belonging to the White Russian Church that contains remains of Hadrian's western forum in Jerusalem, including part of the Hadrianic basilica that was converted by Constantine into the Church of the Holy Sepulcher.

Sabas: a Byzantine monk who founded numerous monasteries in the Judean Desert.

Sadducees: a branch of the Zadokite family that became the Jerusalem elite in the first century B.C.E. and first century C.E.

Salome Alexandra (ruled 76–67 B.C.E.): a Hasmonean queen who was married to Aristobulus I and then Alexander Jannaeus, and ruled on her own after their deaths.

Samaria (or Samaria-Sebaste): originally the capital of the northern kingdom of Israel, the city eventually gave its name to the surrounding district and the inhabitants of that district (Samarians or Samaritans).

Samaritans (or Samarians): the Yahwistic population of the district of Samaria, who the Judeans considered schismatics.

Sanballat (I and III): governors of Samaria under the Persians.

Sanhedria tombs: rock-cut tombs in the modern neighborhood of Sanhedria in Jerusalem.

Sanhedrin: the ancient Jewish law court.

sarcophagus: coffin.

Sardis: an ancient city in western central Asia Minor with the largest ancient synagogue building ever discovered.

Sasanid Persians: the successors of the Parthians.

Satrap: the governor of a satrapy.

satrapy: the largest administrative unit in the ancient Persian empire.

scriptorium: a writing room.

Scythopolis: see Beth Shean.

Sea of Galilee: a brackish-water lake in eastern Galilee.

Sea Peoples: groups of peoples, apparently of Aegean origin, who settled along the coast of Palestine ca. 1200 B.C.E.

Sebastos: Greek for Augustus.

Seleucids: Seleucus and his successors.

Seleucus (ruled 305–281 B.C.E.): one of Alexander the Great's generals, who established a kingdom based in Syria and Asia Minor.

Semitic languages: a language family that includes Phoenician, Hebrew, Aramaic, and Arabic.

Sennacherib: the Assyrian king who besieged Jerusalem during Hezekiah's reign.

Sepphoris: one of the major towns or cities of Roman-Byzantine period Galilee.

Septuagint (LXX): the ancient Greek translation of the Pentateuch.

seven species: the seven agricultural products which in the Hebrew Bible (Deuteronomy 8:8) symbolize the fertility of the Land of Israel: wheat, barley, grapes, figs, pomegranates, olives, and dates.

Sheep's Pools: see Bezetha pools.

Shofar: the ram's horn blown during the celebration of the Jewish High Holidays (Rosh Hashanah [the New Year] and Yom Kippur [the Day of Atonement]), commemorating the ram offered for sacrifice by Abraham instead of his son Isaac.

Sicarii: literally, "dagger men," referring to an urban terrorist group active in Judea in the first century C.E.

Sidon: one of the Phoenician cities.

Siloam Channel: a Bronze Age water system in the City of David.

Simeon Bar Kosiba: the real name of the leader of the Bar-Kokhba Revolt.

Simon (ruled 142–134 B.C.E.): the youngest brother of Judah Maccabee and the successor of Jonathan.

Siq: the narrow, winding canyon leading into Petra that terminates at the Khazneh.

Siwa: an oasis in Egypt with an oracular shrine dedicated to Zeus Ammon that was visited by Alexander the Great.

Solomon: ruled the United Israelite Kingdom after King David's death and built the first Jerusalem temple (ca. 960 B.C.E.).

Solomon's pools: Herodian period water collection pools south of Bethlehem.

Solomon's Stables: a popular name designating the cryptoportius built by Herod the Great under the southern end of Jerusalem's Temple Mount.

Soreg: a low stone fence with inscriptions in Greek and Latin prohibiting Gentiles from entering the Jerusalem temple.

Sparta: a city in Greece.

spina: literally, "spine," referring to the wall running down the center of a hippodrome.

spolia: reused or recycled architectural pieces.

stela (plural: stelae): a standing stone that represented a deity or was an object of worship.

stoa: originally in the Greek world, a porch-like structure alongside a public space.

stratigraphy: the sequence of occupation layers (strata) at an archaeological site.

stratum (plural: strata): an occupation layer or level at an archaeological site.

Straton's Tower: see Caesarea Maritima.

Struthion Pools: originally a moat outside Herod's Antonia fortress, later covered by the Hadrianic pavement identified as the Lithostratos.

stucco: molded plaster used as interior decoration.

stylobate: the stepped platform of a Greek temple.

Suetonius: a Roman author who wrote biographies of the emperors.

Sukkot (Feast of Tabernacles): originally an agricultural festival and one of the three pilgrimage holidays to the Jerusalem temple; the name refers to the huts in which the Israelites dwelled during their forty years of wandering in the desert.

Sultan's Pool: a Herodian period pool in Jerusalem's Ben-Hinnom Valley.

suspensura: little pillars used to support the upper floor of a hypocaust system, through which the hot air circulated.

Talmud: the Mishnah with additional rabbinic interpretations and rulings called the Gemara (literally, "completion") (Mishnah + Gemara = Talmud).

Talpiyot Tomb: a rock-cut tomb in Jerusalem's modern Talpiyot neighborhood, falsely identified, according to a recent claim, as the tomb of Jesus and his family.

Targums: ancient Aramaic translations of the Hebrew Bible.

Tarichaea: see Migdal.

Teacher of Righteousness: the nickname of the founder or refounder of the Qumran sect.

tel (or tell): an artificial mound consisting of accumulated layers of occupation, formed as the result of a glacis or rampart.

Tel Dor: a Phoenician city on the coast of Palestine.

Tell Jemmeh: a Persian period site in the northwest Negev.

Tell Sandahannah: see Marisa.

temenos: Greek for sacred precinct.

Temple Mount (Hebrew *har ha-bayit*; Arabic *al-haram al-sharif*): the enormous esplanade or open plaza in the southeast corner of Jerusalem's Old City, on which Solomon's temple and the second Jewish temple stood, now the site of the Dome of the Rock and the al-Aqsa mosque.

Temple Scroll: a literary work represented among the Dead Sea Scrolls that describes an ideal future city of Jerusalem featuring an enormous temple.

tepidarium: the warm room of a Roman bath house.

terminus ante quem: Latin for "date before which."

terminus post quem: Latin for "date after which."

Terra Sigillata: literally, "stamped clay," a type of fine red-slipped (red-coated) pottery of the Hellenistic and Roman periods.

tessera (plural: tesserae): a small cut stone cube in a mosaic.

Tetrarch: one of the four rulers of the tetrarchy.

Tetrarchy: the rule of the Roman Empire by four men (see Diocletian).

Theodotus inscription: a dedicatory inscription belonging to a pre-70 C.E. synagogue in Jerusalem.

theophoric: a personal name that is based on or incorporates the name of a deity.

Theotokos: the Greek term referring to Mary, the mother of God.

tholos: a Greek word denoting any circular structure.

Thucydides (pronounced thoo-SIH-deh-dees): a Greek historian of the fifth century B.C.E. who chronicled the Peloponnesian War.

Tiberias: one of the major towns or cities of Roman Galilee, founded by Herod Antipas in honor of the emperor Tiberius.

Tiberius (ruled 14–37 C.E.): the Roman emperor who succeeded Augustus.

Titus (ruled 79–81 C.E.): Vespasian's older son and his successor as emperor.

Tobiads: a Judean family descended from Tobiah which governed the district of Ammon during the Persian and Hellenistic periods.

Tobiah: a Jew who was the governor of Ammon under the Persians.

toga: a Roman mantle with a curved hem.

Tomb of Absalom: a free-standing monument containing burial chambers in Jerusalem's Kidron Valley.

Tomb of Bene Hezir: a rock-cut tomb in Jerusalem's Kidron Valley belonging to the priestly family of Hezir.

Tomb of Queen Helena of Adiabene (or the Tombs of the Kings): a monumental rock-cut tomb in Jerusalem belonging to Queen Helena, ruler of the kingdom of Adiabene in Syria, who converted to Judaism in the mid-first century C.E.

Tomb of Zachariah: a free-standing, solid rock monument in Jerusalem's Kidron Valley that served as the *nefesh* of the tomb of Bene Hezir.

Tombs of the Kings: see tomb of Queen Helena of Adiabene.

Torah (or Pentateuch): the Five Books of Moses (Genesis, Exodus, Leviticus, Numbers, and Deuteronomy), considered by Jews to be the written law of the God of Israel.

Torah shrine: a cabinet or installation to house or store Torah scrolls.

Trajan (ruled 98–117 C.E.): the Roman emperor during whose reign the Diaspora Revolt occurred.

Transverse Valley: a shallow ravine that defines Jerusalem's western hill on the north, terminating on the east at the Tyropoeon Valley and Temple Mount.

tribunal: a podium.

triclinium: a dining room; from Greek words for "three couches," referring to the arrangement of dining couches lining three sides of a room.

triglyph: a triple-grooved vertical element in a Doric frieze.

tripartite: having three parts or rooms.

Trojan War: according to Greek tradition, a war fought ca. 1200 B.C.E. between the kings of Mycenean Greece and the inhabitants of the city of Troy in northwest Asia Minor.

trompe l'oeil: a painting that creates the appearance of three dimensions through false perspectives.

tuleilat el-enab: an Arabic word referring to piles of stones on hillsides which were collected in connection with desert agriculture.

tunic: a dress that was the basic article of clothing for men and women in the Roman world.

Tyche (Roman Fortuna): the Greco-Roman goddess of good fortune and prosperity.

Tyre: one of the Phoenician cities.

Tyropoeon Valley ("the Valley of the Cheesemakers" or Central Valley): a valley that originates in the area of the modern Damascus Gate on the north side of Jerusalem's Old City and runs along the western side of the Temple Mount and the western side of the City of David, joining the Kidron Valley at the south.

Tyros: see Iraq el-Amir.

Umayyad dynasty (661–750 C.E.): the first Muslim dynasty, whose capital city was Damascus.

United Kingdom (or United Monarchy): the kingdom ruled by David and Solomon, consisting of the territory of the twelve tribes of Israel.

Upper City: see western hill.

Venus: see Aphrodite.

Vespasian (ruled 69–79 C.E.): the Roman general who subdued the First Jewish Revolt and became Roman emperor.

Via Dolorosa: Italian for "the way of sorrow," referring to a road in Jerusalem venerated by modern Christian tradition as the route traversed by Jesus from the point where he was sentenced to death by Pontius Pilate and ending with the site of his crucifixion and burial.

Villa of Dionysos: a mansion on Sepphoris' acropolis that is so called because the triclinium is paved with a mosaic showing the mythological drinking contest between Dionysos and Heracles.

wadi (Hebrew *nahal*): Arabic for riverbed.

Wadi ed-Daliyeh: a riverbed containing a cave that was used as a hideout by Samaritan rebels fleeing from Alexander the Great's troops.

Wadi Qelt: a riverbed containing several freshwater springs that originates in Jerusalem and flows down to Jericho.

War Scroll: a sectarian work found among the Dead Sea Scrolls that describes a forty-year-long apocalyptic war.

Warren's Shaft: a Bronze Age water system in the City of David that is named after the nineteenth-century British explorer Captain Charles Warren.

Western Hill: the hill in Jerusalem defined by the Tyropoeon Valley on the east, the Ben-Hinnom Valley on the west and south, and the Transverse Valley on the north.

Western Terra Sigillata (or Western Sigillata): a type of fine, red-slipped (red-coated) pottery produced in the Roman period in the western Mediterranean.

Wicked Priest: nickname given to the opponent of the Teacher of Righteousness.

Wilson's Arch: a bridge spanning Jerusalem's Tyropoeon Valley that provided access to Herod's rebuilt Temple Mount.

window wall: a wall in ancient Galilean village houses that was pierced with a row of windows to allow light into the interior.

yahad: Hebrew for "unity," a term used by the Qumran sect to refer to their community.

Yahud: the medinah of Judea under the Persian Empire.

Yavneh: see Jamnia.

Yeb: see Elephantine.

Yodefat: see Jotapata.

Yohanan ben Zakkai: a rabbi who established an academy of Jewish law at Jamnia after 70 C.E. and became its first Patriarch.

Zadok: the first high priest appointed by Solomon to officiate in the Jerusalem temple.

Zadokites: the high priestly family whose members claimed descent from Zadok.

Zealots: a sect or faction in first century C.E. Judea.

Zenon: a Ptolemaic finance officer who visited Syria-Palestine in 260–258 B.C.E.

Zeus Ammon: the deity worshiped at the oracular shrine at Siwa in Egypt.

꩜ ꩜ ꩜ ꩜

TIMELINE

B.C.E.

ca. 3000: beginning of the Bronze Age/Canaanite period.

ca. 1200: beginning of the Iron Age; the Israelite tribes enter Canaan and settle the hill country, and the Philistines establish a kingdom on the southern coastal plain.

ca. 1000: the death of Saul and establishment of the kingdom of David.

ca. 960: Solomon builds the first temple on Jerusalem's Temple Mount.

ca. 930: after Solomon's death, the United Kingdom splits into Israel (north) and Judah (south).

722: the kingdom of Israel falls to Assyria.

701: the Assyrians invades Judah, destroy Lachish and besiege Jerusalem (under King Hezekiah).

586: end of the Iron Age; the Babylonians destroy Jerusalem and Solomon's temple and disperse the Judahite (Judean) elite.

539: King Cyrus II of Persia issues an edict allowing the exiled Judeans to return to their homeland and rebuild the temple.

516: the second temple is consecrated.

490–480: Persian invasions of Greece.

ca. 450: Ezra and Nehemiah in Jerusalem.

336: Alexander the Great becomes king of Macedon.

334: Alexander invades the Persian Empire.

332: Alexander conquers Palestine.

323: Alexander dies in Babylon.

301: the final division of Alexander's empire; Seleucus takes Asia Minor and Syria and Ptolemy takes Egypt and Palestine.

198: Palestine comes under Seleucid rule.

167: Antiochus IV Epiphanes outlaws Judaism and dedicates Jerusalem temple to Olympian Zeus, provoking the outbreak of the Maccabean Revolt

164: Antiochus IV rescinds his edict outlawing Judaism, and the Jerusalem temple is rededicated to the God of Israel, but the Maccabean Revolt continues.

ca. 150–140: the Maccabees establish an independent Jewish kingdom ruled by their descendants (the Hasmoneans). In the decades that follow, the Hasmoneans increase the size of their kingdom through territorial expansion.

ca. 100: a sectarian community settles at Qumran (the site associated with the Dead Sea Scrolls).

63: the Roman general Pompey annexes the Hasmonean kingdom.

40: the Parthians invade Syria-Palestine; Herod flees to Rome and is appointed king of Judea.

37: Herod defeats Mattathias Antigonus.

31: Octavian defeats Mark Antony and Cleopatra at the battle of Actium; afterward, he reconfirms Herod as king of Judea and increases the size of Herod's kingdom.

4: Herod dies and his kingdom is divided among three of his sons; Jesus is born around this time.

C.E.

6: Herod's son Archelaus is deposed and replaced by the Romans with prefects or procurators, who establish their base of administration at Caesarea Maritima.

26–36: Pontius Pilate is Roman prefect and executes Jesus.

37–44: rule of Herod Agrippa I, the grandson of Herod the Great and his Hasmonean wife Mariamne.

44–66: all of Palestine is under the administration of procurators.

62/63: James the Just (brother of Jesus) is executed by the Jewish Sanhedrin in Jerusalem and Paul is executed in Rome.

66: the First Jewish Revolt against Rome begins.

67: Galilee is subdued by the Romans and Josephus surrenders to Vespasian.

68: the sectarian settlement at Qumran is destroyed and the community flees, depositing the Dead Sea Scrolls in the nearby caves.

69: Vespasian becomes Roman emperor, leaves his son Titus in charge of subduing the revolt.

70: Jerusalem falls to the Romans and the second temple is destroyed.

73/74: Masada falls after a siege.

115–117: the Diaspora Revolt (during the reign of Trajan).

132–135: Second Jewish Revolt against the Romans (Bar-Kokhba Revolt) (during the reign of Hadrian).

Second-third centuries: period of rabbinic Judaism.

313: Constantine and Licinius issue the Edict of Milan, legalizing Christianity.

324: Constantine establishes Constantinople (formerly Byzantium) as the new capital of the Roman Empire.

395: the Roman Empire splits into West and East (East = the Byzantine Empire)

527–565: the reign of the Byzantine emperor Justinian.

614: the Sasanid Persian conquest of Palestine.

634–640: the Muslim conquest of Palestine (Jerusalem surrenders in 638).

661–750: the Umayyad dynasty rules Palestine from their capital in Damascus.

750: the Abbasid dynasty overthrows the Umayyads, and moves the capital to Baghdad

1914–18: World War I and the collapse of the Ottoman Empire. Palestine comes under the British Mandate.

1948: the British Mandate ends, Palestine is partitioned, and the State of Israel is established.

INDEX

CPSIA information can be obtained
at www.ICGtesting.com
Printed in the USA
LVHW101521070920
665253LV00019B/1317